Frommer's

4th
Edition

FRUGAL TRAVELER'S GUIDES

London
FROM $60 A DAY

by Marilyn Wood

Macmillan • USA

ABOUT THE AUTHORS

Marilyn Wood came to the United States from England to study journalism at Columbia University. The former editorial director of Prentice Hall Travel, she has also worked as a reporter, ranch hand, press officer, and book reviewer. In addition, Marilyn is the author of *Marilyn Wood's Wonderful Weekends from New York City* and *Frommer's Toronto* and the co-author of *Frommer's Canada*.

MACMILLAN TRAVEL

A Simon & Schuster Macmillan Company
1633 Broadway
New York, NY 10019

Find us online at **http://www.mgr.com/travel** or
on America Online at **Keyword: Frommer's**

ISBN: 0-02-861245-0

ISSN: 1055-5331

Editor: Douglas Stallings
Production Editors: Denise Hawkins, Lori Cates
Design by Michele Laseau
Digital Cartography by Ortelius Design and Roberta Stockwell
Maps Copyright © 1997 by Simon & Schuster, Inc.

SPECIAL SALES

Bulk purchases (10+ copies) of Frommer's and selected Macmillan travel guides are available to corporations, organizations, mail-order catalogs, institutions, and charities at special discounts, and can be customized to suit individual needs. For more information write to: Special Sales, Macmillan General Reference, 1633 Broadway, New York, NY 10019.

Manufactured in the United States of America

Contents

List of Maps

An Invitation to the Reader

In researching this book, we discovered many wonderful places—hotels, restaurants, shops, and more. We're sure you'll find others. Please tell us about them, so we can share the information with your fellow travelers in upcoming editions. If you were disappointed with a recommendation, we'd love to know that, too. Please write to:

Marilyn Wood
Frommer's London from $60 a Day, 4th Edition
Macmillan Travel
1633 Broadway
New York, NY 10019

An Additional Note

Please be advised that travel information is subject to change at any time—this is especially true of prices. We therefore suggest that you write or call ahead for confirmation when making your travel plans. The authors, editors, and publisher cannot be held responsible for the experiences of readers while traveling. Your safety is important to us, however, so we encourage you to stay alert and be aware of your surroundings. Keep a close eye on cameras, purses, and wallets, all favorite targets of thieves and pickpockets.

What the Symbols Mean

✪ Frommer's Favorites

Hotels, restaurants, attractions, and entertainment you should not miss.

The following abbreviations are used for credit cards:

AE	American Express	EU	Eurocard
CB	Carte Blanche	JCB	Japan Credit Bank
DC	Diners Club	MC	MasterCard
DISC	Discover	V	Visa
ER	enRoute		

The Best of London for the Frugal Traveler

Contradictory, expert, disputatious, bawdy, humorous, proud, whining, amateur, stoic—these are just a few of the adjectives that come to my mind when I think of London and Londoners. In this book, I've tried to guide you to places that will reveal some of these vivid characteristics, and the examples I've outlined above are just a few of the suggestions that you will find later on to experience London. So enjoy. During your stay, you'll discover your own particular London, but it would take several lifetimes to discover the whole of this sprawling, 600-square-mile conurbation.

1 Frommer's Favorite London Experiences

- **A Visit to the East End:** Home to London's famous Cockneys and gateway for most of the city's immigrants, the East End is best visited on a Sunday, when a lively outdoor market takes over Petticoat Lane.
- **Observing a Parliamentary Debate:** You wouldn't expect lawmakers to make catcalls and boo, but that's exactly what they do in the House of Commons. Debates here can be exciting, not sleep-inducing as they are Stateside.
- **An Evening at the Royal National Theatre:** There's a definite thrill attending the complex on the South Bank. People gather in the foyer to listen to whatever musical group is playing, to browse the bookstore, and to dine in the Mezzanine. You can spend a memorable evening indeed and cap it off with a stroll along the river terrace.
- **Afternoon Tea at Brown's:** It's not cheap, but it's not exorbitant either. For a short while you can be treated like royalty and in winter loll in front of the log fire for as long as you like. Make reservations as far in advance as possible.
- **A Pub Crawl in Soho:** Perfect for pubbing, Soho's crowded pub scene means you can experience a variety of atmospheres—and not have to stumble too far to reach the next one.
- **Attending Evensong at One of London's Classic Churches:** Go to St. Martin-in-the-Fields, for example, or listen to the uplifting music in the stirring atmosphere of the Brompton Oratory.

- **Visiting the Courts of the Old Bailey:** Watch the bewigged judges and barristers argue a criminal case or similarly peruked barristers do the same for civil cases at the Royal Courts of Justice.
- **A Lazy Afternoon at Lord's Cricket Ground:** Even though the game has changed, becoming faster and more commercial, Lord's is still the place to see this ultra-British game played.
- **A Ride atop the Number 188 Bus from Euston to Greenwich:** With the whole of London practically at your feet, this is the best—and cheapest—tour in town.
- **An Afternoon in Hyde Park or St. James's Park:** Meander along the Serpentine, stopping to admire Epstein's statue of Pan; admire the pelicans and other birds in St. James's Park.
- **Going to a Promenade Concert at the Royal Albert Hall:** Preferably on the last night when jingoism still erupts as the crowd roars out the anthem "Land of Hope and Glory."
- **Cruising up the River Thames to Hampton Court:** Just imagine that you're being conveyed along the river on a barge to the accompaniment of Handel's "Water Music" or Royal Fireworks.
- **A Trip to Greenwich:** This is one of the great architectural complexes in London, if not in Britain.
- **Jazz Brunch at the Victoria and Albert Museum:** What better way to spend a Sunday; afterward you can see some of the most exquisite decorative arts collections in the world.
- **An Early Morning at the Portobello Market:** Also check out the many antique stores along Westbourne Grove—still a treasure trove of beautifully crafted, if expensive, antiques.
- **A Visit to One of the City's Historic or Riverside Pubs:** Try the Dove in Hammersmith, the George Inn near Waterloo, or the Spaniards on the edge of Hampstead Heath.
- **A Day Trip to the English Countryside:** Whether you go to Stratford-upon-Avon, Oxford, Cambridge, or Windsor, a day in England's rolling hills and open countryside will make you wish you never had to leave. My choice, though, would be Cambridge.

2 The City Today

London positively resonates with history. Walk down any London street, and you will encounter homes of famous writers, artists, or scientists; views that you might recognize from paintings by Canaletto, Turner, Monet, Pissarro, and Whistler; squares that have seen riot and mayhem; and streets that have witnessed great pageants.

Most first-time visitors arrive in London with preconceived notions—about bowler-hatted businessmen clutching their black umbrellas as they briskly walk down the street; about politicians cheering, shouting, and insulting each other in the Commons; about scandals, royal and otherwise (Remember Profumo, Christine Keeler, and more recently, Sir Anthony Blunt?); about afternoon tea, bangers and mash, and lager and lime; about Rugby, cricket, tennis, and fair play; about the Beatles, punk, and Sir Michael Tippett; about palaces, pageantry, and peers. Before we leave home our heads are already filled with a seemingly endless panoply of images, characters, sounds, and stories that have been passed along to us from literature, film, music, the media, photography, and more. These preconceived notions can make it difficult for an outsider to penetrate the often befuddling customs of the country. Under the immediate surface of pageantry and politesse, London is hard to characterize because

Impressions

An American in London . . . cannot but be impressed and charmed by the city. The monumentality of Washington, the thriving business of New York, the antique intimacy of Boston, plus a certain spacious and open feeling reminiscent of Denver and San Francisco—all these he finds combined for his pleasure.
                    —John Updike, "London Life," in *Picked Up Pieces* (1976)

it's so complicated and contradictory. The levels of conversation may be many; rather like the dialogue of a Eugene O'Neill play, consisting of text, subtext, and subsubtext. On the surface, London conveys stability, confidence, solidity, masculinity, and love of tradition, but underneath it's clear there are conflicting signs of unrest.

Some things about Londoners you'll observe right away: their need for privacy—note how many pubs have enclosed booths, and how much you have to strain to overhear their conversations. Their passion for nature and gardening is seen in the number and quality of the parks, the Green Belt surrounding the city, and the plants that grace the humblest abode. Their love of liberty as practiced in the Mother of Parliaments can be read about in the papers and witnessed in the House of Commons. Their seemingly contradictory love of social order, which leads to exclusivity and snobbery, can be observed in their obsessive concern with class.

Other conflicts are also obvious: between tradition and modernity; between Britain and the Continent; between urban and rural; between practical laissez-faire and formal planning. These conflicts actually contribute to the city's stimulating allure. In many ways, they are indications of how this once-powerful city that ruled an empire and claimed half the world is adjusting to its smaller-world roles. London is fast-paced, internationally-minded, clogged with traffic, and filled with people from all over the globe. London is also an architectural juxtaposition of the old and elegant against the ugly and modern.

Still, in the face of demands from the communities of new Londoners, especially women and minorities, the bastions of prejudice and the Establishment are breaking down. As they do, the problems that afflict London—homelessness, poverty, drugs, and violence—have become clearer, especially in the last decade.

You will find homeless people on the streets and in the stations; crime is more common than it was; and if you visit the outer boroughs, especially the East End, you'll stumble on unrepaired sidewalks and see graffiti-splattered walls. You won't be able to go inside an attractive, historic church, because the doors will be bolted against you on account of vandalism.

At the heart of London, though, everything is more sanguine. Shoppers crowd the stores even though the prices are astronomical. The city still pulsates. People hang out in the wine bars and pubs at lunch and after work. Somehow, Londoners seem to be even more in love with technology than their American counterparts, and the number of cellular phones that one encounters on the streets is astonishing. Among the latest gathering spots is the Cyberia Cafe, where you can reserve a computer terminal and sign on to the Internet.

Although Covent Garden, Soho, and Camden are still the major hangouts, other areas have been gentrified, especially south of the river and in the Docklands area. Ever since Margaret Thatcher took over the reins of power and abolished the London County Council, urban stresses have begun to show. The local councils compete with each other for funds and power, and the city is showing distinct signs of decay, especially the dirty, traffic-clogged streets.

If you talk to people or read the newspapers, you'll discover that the country's institutions are in decline. The state (public) educational system has deteriorated to the point where many parents now choose to send their children to private schools if they can afford it. The monarchy has been under assault from the press, and scandals have so reduced respect for the royal family that there is serious discussion about replacing the crown. It's no longer a wild idea of the Left.

The church is also in retreat. With fewer people attending services, many churches have closed and congregations have been combined. However, while the Church of England and the Roman Catholic Church are in decline, there are signs of life among other faiths. The impressive Hindu temple in Neasden is testament to that. And more and more Londoners are turning to New Age philosophies and pop psychology à la Princess Diana. The city has a network of spiritualist churches at which mediums appear regularly, and aromatherapy shops seem to be on every street corner.

The times they are a-changin' in London. Thatcher's long reign broke the rule of the Old Establishment, ushering in the reign of the self-made man and inadvertently opening up society in a much more democratic way. It has both coarsened the culture and invigorated it at the same time.

3   A Look at the Past

Dateline

- **43** Londinium settled by Roman invaders.
- **50** London Bridge built across the Thames.
- **61** Boudicca sacks London.
- **190–220** City walls built.
- **350** Saxons invade.
- **410** Romans retreat.
- **457** Londoners take refuge behind city walls.
- **604** First St. Paul's built. Mellitus appointed Bishop of London.
- **886** Alfred the Great takes London from the Danes.
- **1066** William of Normandy (the Conqueror) crowned king.
- **1078** Construction of White Tower begun.
- **1097** William Rufus builds Westminster Hall.
- **1123** St. Bartholomew's Hospital founded.
- **1176–1209** London Bridge built of stone.
- **1192** Henry FitzAilwin elected first mayor of London.

continues

London is full of history—yet many visitors, faced with the traffic-clogged streets and the many ugly, modern buildings wonder where exactly history can be found, and if it only exists in the blue plaques that are attached to so many buildings in celebration of some remarkable personage or event. But it is there, in living color, in the pageantry of the monarchy, in the pubs, the gentlemen's clubs, in the Houses of Parliament, in the Inns of Court, and in the people's very bones, it seems. Although London has always been a commercial city and the mercantile spirit has always placed commerce and development ahead of urban planning (which has meant that much of the past was destroyed), still a great heritage remains. History is to be found everywhere, tucked away secretly down tiny alleyways or more openly at St. Paul's or Westminster. Here in London you will see history at work in the daily life of the city.

The City of London proper is contained in one square mile, which today is the financial district. The story of London is how that one square mile grew to be what it is today, a 600-mile conurbation in which 6.4 million people live. Early in its history, villages grew up outside the walled city—Kensington, Clerkenwell, Knightsbridge, Hampstead, Highgate, and many more. Today, of course, they've all been joined together into one large unit. Each village, however, has a history and flavor of its own, so take some time to explore particular London neighborhoods that interest you. The section that follows tells the story of how the fabric of contemporary London was woven over the last 2,000 years.

EARLY ROMAN, SAXON & DARK AGE LONDON

By any measure, London is a very old city. Archaeological excavations have proved that there were early settlements here as far back as 2500 B.C. Although scholars debate the origin of London's name, most people think it's derived from the Celtic words *Llyn Din,* meaning "lake-side fortress."

Origins notwithstanding, most historians agree that the British Isles began to fall under Roman control in A.D. 43. Julius Caesar visited twice and camped on the very ground where Heathrow stands today. The Romans built a bridge across the Thames to their Kentish Highway, which ran from Canterbury via London to Chester. Some Roman roads are still in use—Oxford Street, Bayswater Road, and Edgeware Road, for example. It's believed that the London stone set into the wall at 111 Cannon Street was the milestone used to fix all distances in Roman Britain. First a military base, London was transformed by the Romans into an important trading center. They constructed buildings with tiled roofs, mosaic floors, and public baths. To protect the city against the "barbarians," they built a wall around it (between A.D. 190 and 220). Fragments of this can be seen in the Museum of London. When the empire started to crumble around A.D. 410, the Romans withdrew, leaving Londoners and the Britons to resist the Anglo-Saxon invasions.

Confusion followed the Romans' departure. From the 7th to the early 9th centuries, the tribal kingdoms of Kent, Mercia, Northumbria, and the West Saxons fought each other for control of Britain. The Roman settlement was abandoned. Saxonstown, as it was known, grew up around Covent Garden, the Strand, and Charing Cross. Later this area became known as Lundenwic, the suffix *wic* meaning trading town.

The Anglo-Saxons were followed by the Vikings, who finally occupied the city in 871–72. Alfred the Great fought back and, in 886, was able to make peace with the Danes. The Londoners resettled the area within the old Roman walls and abandoned their Saxon settlement farther west. The population of the city at this time was about 12,000, and the town was large enough to be divided into 20 wards, each with aldermen who in turn reported to the town reeve. Few traces of this period remain.

- 1214 King John grants city a charter.
- 1215 Magna Carta signed.
- 1348–49 Black Death sweeps London.
- 1381 Peasants' Revolt.
- 1397 Richard Whittington, a wealthy merchant, elected lord mayor.
- 1401 Water piped in from Tyburn.
- 1455 Wars of the Roses begin.
- 1461 Edward of York crowned king.
- 1483 Richard, Duke of Gloucester, imprisons (and possibly murders) crown prince Edward V and his brother; crowns himself Richard III.
- 1485 Henry Tudor defeats Richard at Bosworth. Henry VII launches Tudor dynasty.
- 1509 Henry VIII succeeds to the throne. Marries first of six wives.
- 1513 Henry VIII builds navy and opens dockyards at Deptford and Woolwich.
- 1536–40 Dissolution of the monasteries. Church of England established, with king at head.
- 1553 Mary Tudor made queen. Lady Jane Grey, the "Nine Days' Queen," is executed.
- 1558 Elizabeth I (1558–1603) succeeds throne.
- 1588 Spanish armada defeated.
- 1599 Globe Theatre built.
- 1600 London expands to areas south of the Thames.
- 1605 Guy Fawkes and his Gun-powder Plot to blow up King James I and Parliament is foiled.
- 1631 Inigo Jones builds Covent Garden.
- 1637 Hyde Park opened to public.

continues

- 1642–58 Oliver Cromwell leads Parliamentary forces during Civil War and later Protectorate.
- 1649 King Charles I beheaded before the Banqueting House in Whitehall.
- 1660 Monarchy restored under Charles II.
- 1665 Great Plague strikes 110,000 Londoners.
- 1666 Great Fire destroys 80% of the medieval city.
- 1675–1710 Wren rebuilds 51 churches, including St. Paul's.
- 1688 Bloodless Revolution: James II banished; William and Mary invited to throne.
- 1694 Bank of England established.
- 1725 Mayfair developed.
- 1739–53 Mansion House built.
- 1759 British Museum founded.
- 1780 In Gordon Riots, mobs protest against Papists.
- 1801 First census. Population: 959,000.
- 1802 West Indian Dock opens.
- 1826 University College established.
- 1829 Metro Police established.
- 1832 First Reform Bill enfranchises some property owners.
- 1837 Victoria, 18, succeeds her uncle, William IV.
- 1840s Influx of Irish immigrants, who come to flee famine and political repression.
- 1847 British Museum opens.
- 1851 Hyde Park hosts the Great Exhibition, which finances development of South Kensington.
- 1858 The Great Stink. Royal Opera House opens.

continues

In the late 10th century, the Vikings began raiding again. London resisted, but finally accepted first Sweni in 1013, and later his son Canute. After Canute's death, Edward, the son of Ethelred the Unready, became king. Ruling from 1042 to 1066, the pious Edward devoted one-tenth of his income to rebuilding the abbey of St. Peter at Westminster. He also built a palace on the site of today's Westminster Hall and transferred the court to Westminster, which was outside the city walls. Edward died on January 6, 1066, and was buried in his new church at Westminster. Today at the abbey, you can see the tomb of Edward the Confessor, the king who in large measure created Westminster. Edward's mother was Norman, and after his death a battle for the throne raged between Saxon and Norman. The merchants and barons in the city supported the Saxon king, Harold, primarily because they had extracted a guarantee of rights and privileges from him, but Harold was defeated at the Battle of Hastings and William the Conqueror marched on London, burned Southwark, and forced the city to surrender.

MEDIEVAL LONDON   William had himself crowned in Westminster. He was smart enough to understand the power vested in the city, and he maintained the rights he had previously granted it, including the right to elect its own leaders, as it had done for centuries and as it still does today. Favored barons were granted tracts of land on which they built huge, fortified stone houses, known as *burhs*. None of these mansions survive, but street names such as Bucklersbury and Lothbury tell us where they once stood.

During the 11th century, the old Saxon London of wood and thatch was converted into Norman stone. William began the massive, impregnable White Tower in 1078, not only as a fortification against invaders, but also to intimidate Londoners.

The 12th, 13th, and 14th centuries were dominated by the Crusades, the Hundred Years' War with France, and the Wars of the Roses—the struggle between the House of Lancaster and the House of York for the English throne. Despite all this strife, London continued to grow and thrive. It's hard to imagine, but there was only one bridge—London Bridge—over the River Thames until 1749. The original bridge was built of wood and replaced many times, but in 1176 a stone bridge was begun. It took 33 years to complete and cost 200 lives. It was 940 feet long with 20 arches and had upon it a chapel dedicated to Thomas à Becket. Timbered houses lined the cobbled roadway that was only 12 feet wide and the only way southeast out of the city. Across this bridge the medieval kings of England set out to Crécy, Potliers, and Agincourt. At the southern end of the bridge, heads of traitors were impaled on the turrets of the gate (one foreign visitor in the 16th century noted 30 heads on display).

The River Thames was the city's main highway, and you could travel from London to Westminster in 1372 for only two pence. It was lined with wharves, each assigned a particular type of cargo—hay, fish, and wool. A contingent of Hanseatic merchants were located downriver at the Steelyard. Road travel was difficult. Some roads were wide enough for 16 knights to ride abreast (these were dubbed royal roads), but most were narrow, made of dirt, and poorly maintained. In the late 14th century, it took $4^1/2$ days to ride from London to York, traveling about 44 miles a day. Wagons took even longer.

The wealth of the city was built on trade—on wool in particular. Indeed, sheep outnumbered people 300 to 1. But only a handful of merchants controlled this trade, which by the 1480s was exporting via London a million yards of cloth to Europe. Other trades flourished, too. In 1422, the clerk of the Brewers Company recorded 111 trades being carried on in the city—drapers, soapmakers, cord wainers, goldsmiths, haberdashers, vintners, and many more. Guilds set standards, trademarks, and prices, and they arranged pensions for their members. As the guilds grew prosperous, they built impressive halls, many of which survive today like Drapers' Hall, Fishmongers' Hall, and Goldsmiths' Hall.

Daily life was hard for most. Londoners lived in constant fear of plague and fire. In 1348–49, the Great Plague carried off 30% to 40% of the population. At the height of the epidemic, 200 dead were buried each day in one London cemetery. Drink was the common relief from the hardships and terrors of daily life. In 1309, the city had 1,334 taverns, each brewing its own individual ale. Religion also provided solace. In 1371, London had 106 churches and numerous monasteries. Holy Days, royal celebrations, and fairs, like the famous St. Bartholomew fair, provided relief. For example, on the occasion of the visit of Henry VI in 1432, young

- **1863** The first Underground connects Paddington to the City.
- **1877** First Wimbledon Tennis Championship.
- **1882** Law Courts built in the Strand.
- **1888** London County Council established.
- **1889** Great Dock Strike.
- **1894** Tower Bridge opens.
- **1901** Queen Victoria dies. Edward VII ascends throne.
- **1907** Central Criminal Court (the Old Bailey) constructed.
- **1910** King Edward VII dies and is succeeded by George V.
- **1914–18** World War I. London bombed from planes and airships.
- **1922** BBC begins broadcasting.
- **1936** King George V dies. Prince of Wales succeeds throne as Edward VIII, but abdicates to marry Wallis Simpson.
- **1937** Edward's younger brother crowned King George VI.
- **1939–45** World War II. Air raids and rocket attacks destroy much of the city: 30,000 killed, 50,000 injured.
- **1947–48** New Commonwealth influx.
- **1948** London hosts Summer Olympics.
- **1951** Royal Festival Hall opens.
- **1952** King George VI dies.
- **1953** Queen Elizabeth II crowned in first nationally televised coronation ceremony.
- **1955** Heathrow Airport opens.
- **1956** Clean Air Act.
- **1960s** Swinging London—Mary Quant, the Beatles, et al. The controversial Centre Point Tower and Barbican Centre constructed.

continues

- **1965** Churchill (b. 1874) dies. Greater London Council formed.
- **1973** Britain joins European Community.
- **1974** Covent Garden Market moves out to Nine Elms.
- **1976** Royal National Theatre opens.
- **1979** Margaret Thatcher becomes Britain's first woman prime minister, heading a Conservative government.
- **1981** Charles, prince of Wales, marries Lady Diana Spencer in St. Paul's Cathedral. Docklands Development Corporation established.
- **1982** The Thames Flood Barrier is completed downstream at Woolwich. Barbican Arts Centre opens.
- **1988** Musem of the Moving Image opens.
- **1989** Design Musem opens.
- **1990** Thatcher steps down as prime minister. Conservative John Major replaces her.
- **1992** Royal family rocked by scandals. Queen agrees to pay income tax.
- **1993** IRA bomb explodes in London.
- **1994** Channel Tunnel officially opens.

women representing Mercy, Grace, and Pity dispensed the wine of joy and pleasure at the Great Conduit water pump in Cheapside; at every coronation the conduits flowed with wine, and celebrations lasted for days.

The Court had its own pleasures. Jousting tournaments were held in Smithfield and Cheapside. The king went hunting for deer, boar, and hare. Among the wealthy classes, chess was so popular that *The Rules of Chess* was the second book Caxton chose to print.

Westminster, linked to London by Whitehall and the Strand (and primarily via the Thames), was the center for the court and the government. From the early 14th century on, the king summoned his nobles to council at Westminster. The treasury and the courts were in Westminster Hall; here, too, the exchequer functioned, using tally sticks to keep the accounts. The sum of money owed was marked in notches along the stick, which was then split in half, one half being retained by the exchequer and the other by the debtor. It was the later burning of these old sticks in 1854 that destroyed the buildings at Westminster.

By the early 14th century the population had reached 50,000. City living conditions were awful: Pigs and poultry roamed the streets along with packhorses and dogs; the streets were open sewers; there was no clean water supply since water was drawn directly from the Thames at the Great Conduit in Cheapside; and fires were frequent. In the Plantagenet era there's a record of one street being piled so high with garbage that passage was impossible. Many individuals scraped by as rakers and gong farmers (that is, by digging through the garbage and excrement).

TUDOR AND ELIZABETHAN LONDON   The modern history of London begins with the Tudors, who ascended the throne at the end of the 15th century. The first Tudor, Henry VII, laid the solid administrative foundations on which the later Tudors built a great nation under a strong monarchy.

Between 1500 and 1600, the population of London rose from 50,000 to 200,000. The wealth of the city grew, much of it acquired by the English Company of Merchant Adventurers, who traded in Antwerp. These merchants traded wool to the Dutch and shipped back to England in the mid-16th century such items as tennis balls, licorice, Bruges silks, warming pans, thimbles, and dye for cloth. The richest men in England were the 800 or so wholesale traders who carried on this trade, and it was they who founded, in 1571, the first financial institution in the city, the Royal Exchange, which functioned until 1939.

Under the Tudors, England grew in economic and political power. Henry VII's son, Henry VIII, was a powerful Renaissance prince who competed with archrival Francis I of France and also dared to challenge the pope. Henry VIII laid down the foundations of both the British Army and Navy when he incorporated the Fraternity of Artillery in 1537, established dockyards at Deptford and Woolwich, and commissioned ships like the *Great Harry*.

Patronage of the arts and architecture was an important way to display power, and Henry invited great painters like Holbein to his court, built Nonsuch Palace (long gone), and embellished Whitehall and St. James. He also enclosed Hyde Park, St. James's Park, and Green Park for his own hunting and other pleasures.

He is, of course, best known for separating the English church from Rome and for dissolving the monasteries and confiscating church wealth and lands, including Wolsey's Whitehall Palace (he'd already taken over Hampton Court, Wolsey's country place, in 1529). Frustrated in his desire for a male heir, he married six times, executing two of his wives. Anne Boleyn passed under the water gate at the Tower in 1536 on the way to her execution, performed by a headsman from Calais, who used a sword instead of an ax. It is said that the severance was so swift that her lips were still moving in prayer when her head was on the ground. Catherine Howard was also beheaded, but she tested the block first and died proclaiming her love for Culpepper, who had already been executed for his dalliance with her.

Henry VIII's appetite was prodigious, and his reputation for extravagance well earned. His kitchen at Hampton Court Palace was 100 feet long, 38 feet wide, and had ceilings 40 feet high. Every year £300,000 was spent on food and £50,000 on drink. At each of the two main meals of the day the Great Master of the Household was allotted 10 gallons (80 pints) of ale and 6 quarts (12 pints) of wine; the Lord Chamberlain, however, was only entitled to 4 gallons of ale and a quart and a half of wine at each meal, while a female member of the court was allowed 3 gallons of ale and a pitcher of wine every day, in addition to what she could drink at table. Little wonder that people died of apoplexy brought on by overeating, as did Queen Anne much later.

In 1558, Elizabeth ascended the throne, ushering in a period marked by colonial expansion, economic growth, and the flowering of the arts. A popular queen and a master politician, she secured the country 30 years of peace as she advanced England's interests against those of Catholic France and Spain; in 1588 her navy defeated a large Spanish armada that had set out to attack England. For this victory, Elizabeth gave thanks in St. Paul's.

During the Elizabethan period, literature and the arts flourished. Edmund Spenser published his epic poem, *The Faerie Queene*, dedicating it to Elizabeth, while the statesman and philosopher Francis Bacon, the soldier, explorer, and poet Sir Walter Raleigh, and others of equal versatility wrote books on history, science, and philosophy. At the same time, the English theater came into its own. In 1576, the first playhouse, called "The Theatre," was built by James Burbage in Shoreditch, followed by the Rose on Bankside in 1587, the Swan in 1595, and the Hope in 1614. Playgoing became central to London life, with as many as 40 plays a year being presented at the Rose, including works by Christopher Marlowe, John Webster, Ben Jonson, Thomas Middleton, and of course, William Shakespeare, who had joined Burbage's company in 1599.

STUART LONDON Political instability followed the death of Elizabeth, as an increasingly assertive, and largely Puritan, Parliament sought to promote its prerogatives and limit those of the monarch. The initial struggle between king and Parliament was played out in London. During James I's reign the conflict simmered, but under Charles I, the conflict exploded. The king was forced to dissolve several parliaments. In response, Parliament brought the king's ministers to trial, including Thomas Wentworth, Earl of Strafford, who was charged with 28 crimes and defended himself for 18 days in Westminster Hall. Charles fled to York and raised his standard at Nottingham in 1642. London prepared for a Royalist attack. Trained bands were called out, armed boats patrolled the Thames, and 100,000 men were pressed into digging 18 miles of trenches linking 24 bastions. The attack never came. Instead, the battle between Royalist and Parliamentary troops was fought around the country—at Edgehill, Oxford, Marston Moor, Naseby, and Preston. The king was defeated and in 1649, stood trial in Westminster Hall, and was condemned to death. On January 30, 1649, Charles I took his last walk through St. James's Park, flanked by guards and a troop of halberdiers in front and behind with colors flying and drums pounding. The procession crossed a gallery at what is now Horse Guards Parade and entered the Banqueting House of Whitehall Palace. Four hours later, Charles I stepped via a window onto the wooden scaffold. After saying his prayers, he pulled off his doublet, lay down his head, and was dispatched with an ax. Legend has it that his last words were: "To your power I must submit, but your authority I deny." Today, an equestrian statue stands at the head of Whitehall looking down to the spot where he died; at the other end of Whitehall outside Westminster Hall stands a statue of Oliver Cromwell, the Puritan general who as Lord Protector, ruled England from 1649 to 1658 following Charles's execution.

Charles I had been a great patron of the arts and invited Rubens and Van Dyck to his court. In 1621, Rubens painted the ceilings of the Banqueting House in Whitehall for £3,000 and a gold chain. Under Cromwell the arts died. Theaters were closed and the city fell under a pall until Cromwell's funeral in 1658, described by the diarist John Evelyn as the "joyfullest funeral that ever I saw." The heads of Cromwell and his generals Ireton and Bradshaw were impaled and placed above the roof of Westminster Hall. It's said that his head remained there for 25 years until it was blown down and stolen by a sentry.

The Restoration of the Merry Monarch, Charles II, restored the city to life. The theaters reopened. The king kept a lavish court at Whitehall Palace. Political and social climbers flocked there to curry favor either directly with the king or with one of his many mistresses. Courtiers came to chat with Charles while his wig was being combed and his cravat tied. One courtier might be awarded a frigate, another a company or a favorable judgment.

All the merrymaking was interrupted by two major catastrophes—the Great Plague (1665) and the Great Fire (1666). The first victim of the plague died on April 12, 1665; by December of that year, 110,000 had died. The king and his court left for Hampton Court, and other members of the upper class dismissed their servants and fled. In the city, the unemployed roamed the city looting and pillaging. Day and night, grave diggers dug mass graves but were unable to keep up with the corpses that piled up in mounds. The stench of death was horrid. When a person was diagnosed with the plague, everyone in that household was locked up for 40 days, which only increased the number of sick. Eventually, the plague ran its course, and in February 1666 the king deemed it safe enough to return to London. We all probably know the nursery rhyme "ring a ring o' roses," which refers to the first sign of the disease— a rash.

The king had hardly been in the city a few months when the Great Fire broke out in the early morning of September 2, 1666, at the bakery of Robert Farriner in Pudding Lane. Fanned by strong easterly winds, it quickly spread throughout the city. Samuel Pepys described flames leaping 300 feet into the air, warehouses blazing, and people jamming the river and roads in vain attempts to flee. The lord mayor, Sir Thomas Bludworth, had been awakened with the news but returned to bed with a dismissive, "a woman might piss it out." By mid-morning when the fire had

Dr. Johnson—The Man Who Invented the English Language

A most extraordinary Londoner and a wonderful character, Samuel Johnson's writings captured the life of London in the 18th century. Born in Lichfield, Johnson (1709–84) was the son of a bookseller. He went to Oxford but was forced to leave as he couldn't pay the tuition. In 1737, he arrived in London and began a journalism career, writing essays and articles for *The Rambler*. In 1755, after nine years of labor in his Gough Street quarters, he produced his famous *Dictionary of the English Language*, which set down the spellings and meanings of English words for the very first time. In that respect, Johnson could be said to have created the English language in a standard form. Before this time, there was no comprehensive source an English speaker could turn to for the accepted spellings and meanings of words. The dictionary is still considered an important authority on the language today.

Johnson met the Scottish diarist James Boswell in 1763, and it's Boswell who documented the lexicographer's habits and attitudes in the *Journal of the Tour to the Hebrides* (1785) and *The Life of Samuel Johnson* (1791). Intensely human, generous, and compassionate, Johnson was a cat lover and would buy oysters for his cat Hodge himself, just so that his servants did not "take against the poor creature," if he ordered them to do so.

Unfashionable, he usually wore a drab brown suit. (Unlike most of his contemporaries, Johnson possessed "no relish for clean linen.") Still, he once shocked the audience at a performance of his *Mahomet and Irene* by appearing in his box at Drury Lane in a brilliant scarlet waistcoat embroidered with gold lace.

A gregarious man, Johnson frequented many taverns and coffeehouses. He had a regular seat at the Turk's Head in Gerrard Street, where he formed the Literary Club with Joshua Reynolds. Regular members were David Garrick, Oliver Goldsmith, Edmund Burke, and Boswell. Among his companions, he indulged his passion for conversation and aphorism. Many of the latter are still fresh. I like his definition of *angling*—a stick and a string with a worm on one end and a fool on the other.

consumed 300 houses, Pepys described the mayor running hither and thither wailing, "Lord, what can I do? I am spent. People will not obey me. I have been pulling down houses but the fire overtakes us faster than we can do it." The Duke of York (later James II) was put in charge of fire fighting, and the king himself also helped. The fire burned for four days, ranging over 400 acres within the city walls and 60 more acres outside, totally destroying 87 churches, 44 livery halls, and 13,000 half-timbered houses. Ten thousand were left homeless. The fire wiped out medieval London. From then on, it was decreed that all buildings be constructed of stone and brick.

Although the king saw an opportunity to create an elegantly planned city and invited architects—Sir Christopher Wren among them—to submit plans, London needed immediate rebuilding. The medieval plan was retained, and to this day London's streets follow the same routes they did in the Middle Ages. Streets were widened, though, and pavements were laid for the first time.

Six commissioners were appointed to rebuild the city. Wren was one of them. He rebuilt 51 churches (23 survive today along with the towers of six) and designed the 202-foot-high monument commemorating the fire. His greatest achievement was the rebuilding of St. Paul's.

Mayhem & Riot

London has had a long tradition of riots. One of the early uprisings, the Peasants' Revolt (1381) was brought on by the introduction of the poll tax. Wat Tyler and John Ball led a peasant army to London, assembling at Black Heath and Mile End beyond Aldgate, to demand an end to serfdom and feudalism. Such was the commotion that young King Richard II, who had decided to meet with the rebels, was unable to land his barge at Greenwich. Frustrated, Tyler and his men went to Southwark where they freed the prisoners of Marshalsea. Then they burned the Chancery at Lambeth Palace and marched down Fleet Street, sacking Savoy Palace, the home of the corrupt and hated politician John of Gaunt. They tossed Gaunt's furnishings, jewelry, and silver into the Thames. Whomever they disliked and who happened to cross their path—especially lawyers—they killed. The rebels took the Tower of London and beheaded both Sudbury, the Archbishop of Canterbury, and Hales, the royal treasurer.

Again, the king tried to appease the mob and met with them at Smithfield, but Tyler arrogantly increased his demands. The lord mayor, William Walworth, who had accompanied the king, stabbed and killed Tyler. Richard made concessions to the mob, and eventually they dispersed, but once they did, the king's promises were revoked.

In 1517, the Evil May Day riots occurred when a preacher at St. Paul's Cross stirred up a crowd against foreigners. Troops were called out to control the disturbance. Guns were fired from the tower, and 400 were taken as prisoners. The ringleaders were hanged, then drawn and quartered, and finally gibbeted.

In 1688, England experienced the "Bloodless Revolution," when James II, who had tried to reintroduce Catholicism, was driven from the throne. The Dutch prince William and his wife, James's sister Mary, were invited to take the throne.

From 1660 to 1690, London underwent a property boom, especially in Piccadilly, the Strand, and Soho. In 1656, Covent Garden Market opened as a temporary market in the garden of the Earl (later the Duke) of Bedford. In fleeing from the Great Fire and the Great Plague, many of the gentry had discovered the advantages of living outside London in the villages north and west of the city, such as Bloomsbury, Kensington, Hackney, Islington, and Hampstead. During this period, London began to take on the appearance that it has today as the aristocracy developed their estates, building houses for rent and laying out squares like Bloomsbury (1666) and St. James (1665), which were the first of many squares that were developed in the late 17th and early 18th centuries.

18TH-CENTURY LONDON   During the 18th century the city of London experienced explosive growth, the population jumping from 490,000 in 1700 to 950,000 in 1800. In the process the city was transformed. Mayfair and the West End were developed. Squares were laid out as the focal points of private and corporate estates. Each was associated with a particular oligarchy—Hanover Square with the Whig aristocracy and the Earl of Scarborough; Cavendish with the Tories under the Earl of Oxford; and Lincoln's Inn, New Square, and Bedford Square with lawyers. Wealth flowed back from overseas colonies in America and also from colonies established by the East India Company, the Royal Africa Company, and the Hudson's Bay Company—all of which had been formed in the 17th century. The Port of London flourished. Between 1720 and 1780 port trade tripled. Eighteen hundred vessels were

In the 17th century, mobs were an ever-present chorus on the political stage. Foreign visitors were surprised to observe how passionate and voluble the normally taciturn, complacent Englishman became on political issues. Religious conflicts were often at the heart of many of the ugly riots that broke out, like the torchlit pope-burning processions of 1673 to 1680. To stop disturbances, the Riot Act was passed in 1715, but not to much avail. In 1736, the Irish living in London were targeted. In 1743, the Gin Act provoked riots. Nearly every election was a cause for riot.

Even ministers of Parliament have incited riots. In 1778, a mob led by Lord George Gordon, MP, marched to Westminster agitating against the repeal of anti-Catholic laws in the Catholic Relief Act. More than 50,000 Gordon rioters ran amok, pillaging and burning the homes and private chapels of Roman Catholics. Storming Newgate, they freed prisoners. Breaking into Langan's distillery in Holborn, they consumed and burned 120,000 gallons of gin. In Bloomsbury, they burned down the home of Lord Chief Justice Mansfield. Moving on to the city, they attacked the Bank of England, where they were met with a volley of gunfire. Three hundred people were killed, 450 jailed, 160 tried, and 25 hung. MP Gordon was aquitted on treason charges.

In the 1880s, the early trade unionists rallied in Trafalgar Square and then went on a binge terrorizing the West End. London's tradition of rioting has continued in the 20th century, with the latest probably being the demonstrations in Trafalgar Square to protest and overturn Thatcher's poll tax.

---

jammed into the Upper Pool of the Thames in a space for 500, while larger ships lay downriver at Woolwich, offloading their cargoes onto 3,500 lighters, or barges. Because of the congestion, it sometimes took three or four weeks to unload one vessel. The River Thames was the city's supreme highway and the source of its great wealth. As the century progressed, the role of the Thames was systematically reduced as other forms of transportation were developed and additional bridges were built, such as the one at Westminster in 1749. The stagecoach was introduced in the second half of the 16th century, the hackney coach in 1625, the sedan chair in 1634, and much later, in 1829, Shillibeer's horsedrawn omnibus. Other social developments also helped change the face of the city. Increased wealth and an incipient concern for the poor led to the establishment of major public institutions like the Foundling Hospital (1742), Chelsea Hospital (1692), and Greenwich Hospital (1705); the British Museum (1755); and the Royal Academy of Arts (1768). A rudimentary fire department was begun. Charity schools, including august institutions that still operate today—such as St. Paul's, Westminster, and Christ's Hospital—already accommodated 3,000 pupils by 1710.

The major social institution, other than the church, was the coffeehouse, where men gathered to exchange views and gossip about politics and society. Literary groups formed. Addison, Steele, and Swift all frequented Burtons in Russell Street; Samuel Johnson could be found in the Turks Head at no. 142 the Strand; East India Company merchants frequented the Jerusalem Coffeehouse in Cornhill; and indeed, the first stock exchange was informally started at Jonathan's Coffeehouse in 1722. London's first newspaper, the *Daily Courant,* was launched in 1702 and was reaching 800 readers by 1704. Later in the century the *Guardian, Spectator,* and *Rambler* were all being published regularly, and for a fee Grub Street hacks would produce anonymously any kind of libel or satire—a tradition that continues to this day.

The politics of the age, which can best be summed up in one word, corruption, were captured by Hogarth most acidly in his series entitled *The Election*. Votes were bought and sold. Politicians stole from the public purse. Walpole, for example, was reckoned to have remodeled his house from proceeds he gained while he was prime minister. Riots were common; during the worst, the Gordon Riots in 1780, several prisons were burned and the Bank of England and Downing Street were attacked.

In the 18th century, social life was gruesome for many. In Spitalfields, the center of silk-weaving, masters hired out looms, employing female and child labor. Workhouses and prison workshops were common too. To see the seamier side of London life just look closely at Hogarth's *Gin Lane* or *The Rake's Progress*.

Those who could afford it took their leisure at Vauxhall Gardens (1660) or at Ranelagh Pleasure Gardens (1742). Horse racing, archery, cricket, bowling, and skittles, along with less salubrious pastimes like bullbaiting and prizefighting, were favored pursuits. Freak shows were also popular and could be found at Don Saltero's Coffee House in Chelsea. Mrs. Salmon's waxworks in Fleet was another popular venue.

Theater continued to thrive under actor-managers like David Garrick and Richard Brinsley Sheridan, both at Drury Lane. Musicians and composers were welcomed at the courts of the Hanoverian kings. Johann Christian Bach, Franz Joseph Haydn, and Mozart were all invited to perform at the court. The composer most identified with the London of this period is, of course, Handel, and it was during the reign of George III that the annual performance of that composer's *Messiah* was inaugurated. Outside of the court and the church, the city's musical traditions were launched by one Thomas Britton, who from 1678 to 1714 arranged weekly concerts in a loft above his Clerkenwell coal house.

Under the Georges, a great many artists and literary figures rose to prominence: among them, the painters Sir Joshua Reynolds (who became head of the Royal Academy of Arts, founded by George III in 1768), Thomas Gainsborough, William Turner, and William Hogarth; the great lexicographer and wit Samuel Johnson; his biographer, James Boswell; the poet Alexander Pope; the novelists Samuel Richardson and Henry Fielding; and the historian Edward Gibbon. Gibbon's multivolume *History of the Decline and Fall of the Roman Empire,* one of the great achievements of English literature, caused George III to remark, "Always scribble, scribble, scribble. Eh, Mr. Gibbon?"

19TH-CENTURY LONDON   In the 19th century, London became the wonder of the world—a wonder that was based on imperial wealth and power. In 1811, at the age of 58, the Prince of Wales, son of George III, was made regent for his father, who had become totally insane. He set up an alternate court at Carlton House and also at his extravagant palace in Brighton. At both, he lavishly and openly entertained his mistresses including the famous Mrs. Fitzherbert (whom he had married illegally), but treated his wife Caroline abominably, to the point of banning her from his coronation, which took place in 1820 at an extraordinary cost of £238,238. Largely condemned by the populace for his extravagance and dissolute behavior, he did, however, contribute to the city's architectural growth and harmony, working with architect John Nash to bring some urban planning to the city. Together they laid out Regents Street, a grand highway leading from Carlton House to Piccadilly.

Plump as a partridge, Victoria ascended the throne in 1837. As the century progressed, London was further transformed into a modern industrial society, the center of an empire that ruled half the world. Victorian London was shaped by the growing power of the bourgeoisie and the queen's moral stance. The racy London of the preceding three centuries seemed to disappear, but in actuality it just went underground.

Extremes of wealth and poverty marked life in Victorian London. Thirty percent of the population lived below the poverty level. Children worked long hours in factories and sweatshops or as chimney sweeps and shoeblacks. Immigrants—Irish and European—poured into the overcrowded and foul slums. People lived in appalling conditions. Gin consumption was prodigiously high in the 1820s. In an effort to reduce this, a tax on beer was abolished, and many beer houses opened as a result. The River Thames was the city's main sewer and the source of its drinking water. In 1858, the Great Stink caused by the hot summer drew sensational attention to this fact.

As the century progressed, both political and social reforms were slowly applied. In 1832, the First Reform bill was passed. Social reformers worked to improve living conditions. Lord Shaftesbury strove for improvements in labor and education, Elizabeth Fry in prisons, and Florence Nightingale in hospitals. In 1870 the Education Act made elementary education compulsory.

Transportation was revolutionized. The first underground railway ran from Paddington to Farringdon in 1863, carrying 12,000 passengers in its first year. In 1890, the first electric tube ran on the Northern Line. Railway networks spread out across the country, and all entered central London at impressive gateways like Victoria, Charing Cross, St. Pancras, and Euston stations.

In 1851, the iron-and-glass Crystal Palace was built in Hyde Park to house the Great Exhibition, which showcased the industrial and technological wonders of the age. More than six million people flocked to see the display. With the encouragement of Prince Albert, science and technology advanced. Beginning in 1880, electric lighting illuminated London interiors.

The middle class enjoyed theater, music halls, and sports. By 1850, London had more than 50 theaters, which produced everything from popular blood-and-thunder melodramas to pageants at Christmas and Easter. Toward the end of the century, the works of Oscar Wilde, Arthur Wing Pinero, James Barrie, and George Bernard Shaw improved the repertory. Actor-manager Henry Irving and actress Ellen Terry made the Lyceum in the Strand the most exciting theater anywhere in the world. The music hall was even more popular than the theater. By 1870, the city had more than 400 music halls, compared with 57 theaters. People flocked to the Hackney Empire and the London Coliseum to hear Marie Lloyd, Dan Leno, and other stars belt out Cockney tunes and other ribald folk songs. Spectator sports were also popular—football, rugby, and cricket in particular. Tennis became so when the All England Croquet Club, desperate to revive its sinking fortunes, added tennis to its rostrum in 1874. So successful was the ploy that the first Wimbledon Championship was held in 1877. The manufacture of the safety bicycle in 1885 launched a biking craze that started women on the way to liberation. The "New Woman" of the 1890s took to the road on a bike without a chaperone. Shopping, too, was becoming a pastime, and already department stores were opening to satisfy the need—Whiteleys (1863, now converted into one of London's best shopping malls), Harrods (the 1860s), Liberty (1875), and Selfridge (1909).

Here in this energetic capital, Victoria celebrated her golden jubilee before ushering in the 20th century.

THE EARLY 20TH CENTURY The opening years of the century during the reign of Edward VII (1901–10) were filled with confidence. Britain was at the height of its power and Londoners looked forward to a radiant future. Some historians, though, have pinpointed the economic decline of Britain as early as the turn of this century, arguing that the country was already losing markets and trade to the United States.

At home, social revolution marched on. The trade union movement gained recruits. Women campaigned vigorously for the vote, chaining themselves to railings and protesting at the Houses of Parliament. In November 1911, 223 women were arrested when, angered by the government's failure to introduce a suffrage bill, they went on a window-smashing spree. Between 1905 and 1914, 1,000 suffragettes were imprisoned at Holloway. Ultimately, World War I and the social changes it wrought would help women gain the franchise.

Rivalry between Britain and Germany had been building for many years, and war broke out in 1914. British men marched off expecting the victory to be sure and fast. Instead, the war bogged down in the trenches, and terrible slaughter was committed. Back home, 900 bombs were dropped on London, killing 670 people and injuring almost 2,000. The Great War shattered the illusion of the liberal middle class that peace, prosperity, and social progress would continue indefinitely in a strong and beneficent British Empire.

The peace imposed on the Germans at Versailles led inexorably to economic dislocation and ultimately to the Crash of 1929 and the Great Depression that followed in the 1930s. The country's stability was further threatened by a grave constitutional crisis in 1936, when the new and immensely popular king, Edward VIII, abdicated after refusing to renounce his love for Wallis Simpson, an American divorcée. His brother succeeded him as George VI.

Meanwhile, fascism was rising in Germany and threatening the peace with its expansionist ambitions. British and French attempts at appeasement failed and, in 1939, World War II began when Hitler marched into Poland. In 1940–41 and again in 1944–45 London lived through the Blitz. More than 20,000 people were killed and vast areas of the city were destroyed. Even the House of Commons, that redoubtable symbol of British democracy, was hit. But the spirit of the Londoners proved indomitable. They dug trenches in public parks to resist an invasion, and night after night, as waves of German planes approached, they ran for their shelters. One hundred and fifty thousand slept in the Underground; others stayed home; and still others continued partying defiantly.

The indomitable spirit of those war years (1940–45)—personified by Prime Minister Winston Churchill and by the royal family itself, which chose to remain in London despite the dangers—still evokes proud memories among Londoners. But for many, these memories are bittersweet: Britain had won the war but lost the peace. Unlike Germany and Japan, which received help under the Marshall Plan and infusions of American capital, Britain was impoverished, her industrial plant antiquated and obsolete. Dissolution of the empire followed swiftly and the nation's morale plummeted.

POSTWAR AND CONTEMPORARY LONDON.   Postwar London was a glum place. Rationing continued until 1953. Only the coronation of Queen Elizabeth II in June 1953, watched by 20 million on their TV screens, seemed to lift London's spirits. Heathrow was formally opened in 1955, and in that same year Mary Quant opened her boutique on the King's Road. The coffee bar, the comprehensive school, rock and roll, and antinuclear protests all arrived in the 1950s, setting the stage for the Swinging London of the 1960s. Wowing young people around the world were the Beatles, the Kinks, the Rolling Stones, The Who, Eric Clapton's Yardbirds, and the Animals. Sixties' London was suddenly the fashion and arts capital of the world.

The Blitz

Hilter launched his blitz of London on September 7, 1940. Bombs fell on the Woolwich Arsenal, the Victoria and Albert Museum, and the East India and Commercial Docks. In the second week of the assault, more than 1,400 incendiary canisters were dropped on the Docklands. The philospher Bertrand Russell predicted that pandemonium would sweep the city. The government prepared for the worst, anticipating as many as 18,750 casualties if bombing was continued for a week. Three lines of defense were prepared to be manned by the army and the Home Guard. A last stand was even planned in Whitehall, where machine guns were mounted on key buildings.

The government issued 2.25 million Anderson shelters, intended to be buried in the backyard—the only trouble was that most Londoners didn't have backyards. Children were evacuated to the country.

Abandoning plans to invade England, Hitler continued to bomb London. More than 3,000 incendiary bombs were dropped on December 8, 1940. Twenty-one days later, the heart of London was destroyed, but St. Paul's stood out surrounded by flames—a symbol of London's endurance.

In May 1941, the city experienced its worst bombing, when 1,436 people were killed. The House of Commons, Westminster Abbey, and the Tower of London were all hit. Thousands were left homeless, and local authorities struggled in vain to rehouse them. From September 1940 to May 1941, 20,000 tons of bombs rained down on London—20,000 died and 25,000 were injured. Hilter's attempt to demoralize the nation failed. Spirits remained high and, although people complained about the ineptitude of the authorities, daily life continued. Londoners were told to "dig for victory." Dig they did, planting their allotments. Londoners kept chickens and rabbits, and the swimming pool at the Ladies Carlton Club in Pall Mall was used as a pigsty.

The attack was renewed in 1944, but this time it was doodle bugs, or missiles. These were devastating, more destructive than anything launched before. On November 25, 1944, a crowded Woolworths at New Cross was hit and 160 people were killed.

In total, the blitz destroyed or damaged 3.5 million homes, close to half of London's housing. It wiped out whole communities like Stepney and Bermondsey. Yet, it couldn't conquer the spirit of the Londoners.

The pace dropped in the 1970s when the Beatles disbanded, but the trendy movement continued with the establishment of Terence Conran's Habitat chain, Anita Roddicks's Body Shop, and Saatchi and Saatchi, the world's largest advertising empire. In 1976, the city finally got its Royal National Theatre, first conceived of in 1848. The Barbican Arts Centre opened in 1982 and the Museum of the Moving Image in 1988.

Other less heart-warming developments also occurred during the postwar years. When the United States closed its doors to immigration from the West Indies in 1952, the annual number of West Indians heading for Britain rose from 1,000 to 20,000. They settled in particular areas—the Jamaicans in Brixton and Stockwell, Trinidadians and Barbadians in Notting Hill. The presence of these new immigrants brought calls to stop immigration from such right-wing politicians as Conservative Enoch Powell. In summer 1958, London experienced its first race riots in Notting

Hill. Parliament responded by limiting immigration but prohibiting discrimination in housing and employment. More race riots followed in 1981 and 1985, and the situation continues to fester as second- and third-generation black youths find themselves treated as second-class citizens in what they regard as home. Immigrants also arrived from India and Pakistan in the 1950s and 1960s; the Punjabi Sikhs gathered in Southall and the Bengali Muslims around Brick Lane in Tower Hamlets. Their communities have also been under attack; at first they turned the other cheek, but today the Asians, who have become extremely successful entrepreneurs and businesspeople, are fighting back and demanding justice.

Economically, the postwar years were hard. The economic decline of the country, though, was initially masked by the nation's continued reliance on preferential Commonwealth trade. In 1950 most Commonwealth exports flowed through London, making the port one of the busiest in the world. But in the 1960s many Commonwealth countries gained their independence and began to create their own industries and to diversify their markets. Germany, Japan, and the United States were competing, too, and London was hit hard. The death blow came for the Dockyards when they fought against containerism. The East India dock closed in 1967, followed by St. Katharine's in 1968, and the Royals in 1981. Only Tilbury, which had containerised, survived. At the same time, manufacturing jobs were lost as major companies like Thorne-EMI and Hoover relocated to other areas. Unemployment in the poorer boroughs of London like Tower Hamlets and Southwark rose from 10,000 in the 1960s to 80,000 in the 1980s. Although some of the economic slack has been taken up by financial services and tourism, the city is still declining in population and wealth, as is evident on London streets today.

Promising to revitalize the economy, Margaret Thatcher and the Conservatives came to power in 1979, intent on reversing what observers saw as Britain's decline. Thatcher's reforms included the privatization of major industries—from insurance companies to British Airways—which had been nationalized by the Labour government after World War II. She reduced the power of the trade unions, traditional supporters of the Labour Party, and dismantled parts of the welfare state. At the height of her power in the early 1980s, she stood her ground defending the Falkland Islanders against the invading Argentinians. For a brief moment, gunship diplomacy returned, resuscitating English pride. Later, fiercely protective of British sovereignty, Thatcher refused to agree to a German-backed monetary union within the European Community and opposed other moves toward the creation of a federal entity. In doing so, however, she angered many backbenchers in her own party. In 1990, after the longest tenure of any modern British prime minister, Thatcher was forced out of office and replaced by her chancellor of the exchequer, John Major. His popularity has plummeted both in the nation and in his own party, and it looks as though he will be replaced in the very near future.

In the 1990s, the House of Windsor became the subject of unusually intense tabloid coverage. It was announced that the heir to the throne, Prince Charles, and his consort, the popular Princess Diana, were separating. The prince's romantic involvement with Camilla Parker Bowles, a married woman, was implicated. Prince Andrew, the Duke of York and second in line to the throne, let it be known that he and his wife, Sarah Ferguson, who had been photographed in an intimate setting with another man, were divorcing.

For the first time in a long time, the British are seriously questioning the wisdom of supporting a royal family in imperial style; perhaps a more modest, Europeanlike monarchy would do. As a gesture, the queen agreed to pay taxes on her income and to open Buckingham Palace to the public to help finance the repairs to Windsor Castle after a fire there.

The scandals that have generated world headlines, however, are small compared to other problems that face the city. During her ministry, Thatcher systematically whittled away the powers of the Greater London Council (a Labour stronghold), and in 1986 the GLC was abolished, leaving London as the only major city in the western world without a single, overall authority to govern itself. As a consequence, the various boroughs stagger along with few resources to deal with the economic and social problems that afflict any major city today—homelessness, racism, drugs, despair, and alienation. As the boroughs quarrel among themselves, London deteriorates.

4   Famous Londoners

Francis Bacon (1909–92)   Born in Dublin, he came to London at age 14 and taught himself to paint. This Expressionist painter first caused a furor with his *Three Studies for Figures at the Base of a Crucifixion* displayed at the Tate in 1944. His work—such as his famous series of carcasses—explores grotesque and satirical themes.

Aubrey Vincent Beardsley (1872–98)   The most famous Victorian illustrator and a master of art nouveau. He illustrated editions of both Alexander Pope's *Rape of the Lock* and Oscar Wilde's *Salome.* He died at age 26 of tuberculosis.

Annie Besant (1847–1933)   An atheist and Fabian in her youth, she discovered theosophy in 1889 and became a disciple of the spiritualist Helena Blavatsky. She went to India and established the Indian Home Rule League and later introduced her protégé Krishnamurti to the West.

William Blake (1757–1827)   This Romantic poet is known for visionary, symbolic poems such as his *Songs of Innocence* (1789) and *Songs of Experience* (1794). He also received critical acclaim for his illustrations of *The Book of Job,* Dante's *Divine Comedy,* and Milton's *Paradise Lost.*

William Booth (1829–1912)   Minister and social worker, he founded the Salvation Army in 1878.

James Boswell (1740–95)   He wrote the classic English biography *The Life of Samuel Johnson* (1791), and his *London Journal* established him as a colorful portrayer of 18th-century London.

Thomas Carlyle (1795–1881)   A Scottish historian, he moved to London in 1834 to gain access to reference works for his manuscript on the French Revolution, which took more than three years to write. He developed a great friendship with Emerson and became an influential social critic.

Thomas Chippendale (1718–79)   The most famous furniture designer in English history, he set up a workshop in St. Martin's Lane.

Sir Noel Coward (1899–1973)   This wit and gossip wrote and produced plays, such as *Private Lives,* that still delight audiences. He also wrote the screenplay for *Brief Encounters,* several novels, and many songs, including "Mad Dogs and Englishmen," which he performed himself.

Charles Dickens (1812–70)   This master of English literature portrayed the social ills of Victorian London, from his first book *Sketches by Boz* to his last, *The Mystery of Edwin Drood.* While residing at 48 Doughty Street in WC1 for only two years (1837 to 1839), he produced the *Pickwick Papers, Nicholas Nickleby,* and *Oliver Twist.*

Sir Arthur Conan Doyle (1859–1930)   Creator of Sherlock Holmes, fiction's most famous sleuth, Conan Doyle resided at 12 Tennison Rd. in SE 25. Besides his popular mysteries, he wrote serious historical novels. A professed spiritualist, he was knighted in 1902.

Margaret Drabble (b. 1939)   In her early novels, such as *The Millstone* and *The Middle Ground,* Drabble explored the conflict between tradition and modernity. Her later works have focused largely on the role of women in English society.

Henry Fielding (1707–54)   His early career as a writer of comedy, farce, and burlesque ended when the Licensing Act was passed in 1737—the law partly inspired by his own attacks on Walpole. Fielding then turned to the novel and helped make it the most popular form of literature in England. He produced the classics *Joseph Andrews* (1742) and *Tom Jones* (1749). He also served as a magistrate in London and established an early type of police force.

Elizabeth Fry (1780–1845)   This Quaker philanthropist worked to improve the conditions of women at Newgate prison. Fry also set up soup kitchens.

David Garrick (1717–79)   A great Shakespearean actor, theatrical producer, and playwright. He is buried in Poets' Corner in Westminster Abbey.

William Hogarth (1697–1764)   A painter and engraver, Hogarth revived the medieval art form of morality pictures. His *Harlot's Progress, The Rake's Progress,* and *Marriage à la Mode* are a series of satirical engravings.

Jack the Ripper (???)   Although his identity has never been confirmed, there has been much speculation that he might have been a member of the royal family. He murdered six prostitutes, all found in the East End in 1888.

Glenda Jackson (b. 1936)   She first won acclaim in the 1960s for her stage performances with the Royal Shakespeare Company. Then she garnered two Academy Awards for her roles in *Women in Love* and *A Touch of Class.* In 1992, she gave up acting to take her seat in Parliament as Labour MP for Hampstead.

Samuel Johnson (1709–84)   Most famous for his *Dictionary of the English Language* and his complete edition of Shakespeare, Johnson left Oxford without a degree. He came to London at age 28. While residing at 17 Gough Square, he frequented London's coffeehouses and founded what is still the most famous London eating club. Original members of the "Club" included playwright Oliver Goldsmith, political philosopher Edmund Burke, and painter Joshua Reynolds. Johnson was a master of aphorism, as evidenced by his definition of fishing: "A stick and string with a worm on one end and a fool on the other."

John Keats (1795–1821)   Born in London, Keats gave up a career in surgery to become a poet. When *Endymion* was published in 1818, he was called "a Cockney poet." Shelley argued that these vicious attacks caused the breakdown of his health. He contracted tuberculosis, sailed for Italy in 1820, and died in Rome in 1821.

Lillie Langtry (1852–1929)   The greatest English beauty of her era, she achieved fame as the publicly acknowledged mistress of the Prince of Wales, the son of Queen Victoria (later Edward VII). She became a stage actress and reigned as an arbiter of taste from her town house near Cadogan Square.

Karl Marx (1818–83)   After being expelled from Paris, Marx moved to London in 1849. Extremely poor, he lived with his family in two small rooms at 28 Dean Street in Soho, often subsisting on potatoes and bread. His studies in the British Museum Reading Room were his primary occupation, and it was here that he wrote his most famous work, *Das Kapital.* In September 1864, he took part in the first meeting of the International Working Men's Association, held at St. Martin's Hall in London. He is buried in Highgate Cemetery.

George Orwell (1903–50)   Born in India as Eric Arthur Blair, he attended Eton and moved to Burma before returning to live penuriously in Europe—an experience he described in *Down and Out in Paris and London* (1933). He is most famous for *Animal Farm* (1946) and *1984* (1949).

Samuel Pepys (1633–1703)   In his celebrated *Diaries* (1660–69), Pepys meticulously and vividly recorded the events of his day. He founded the civil administration of the Royal Navy, converting it from an occasional service to a permanent and efficient military force. He resided at what is now 12–14 Buckingham St.

Alexander Pope (1688–1744)   Born in London to Catholic parents, he contracted Pott's disease early in life. This caused a curvature of the spine and stopped him from growing taller than 4 feet 6 inches. Barred from education because of his religion, he taught himself. His poem "The Rape of the Lock" (1714) mocked the fashionable society of the day. His translations of the *Iliad* and the *Odyssey* brought him great wealth. In *The Dunciad (1728),* he scolded literary hacks and other enemies; his *Essay on Man* (1734) was his most ambitious work.

Henry Purcell (1659–95)   The major figure of English baroque music, Purcell was an organist at Westminster Abbey. Composer of the opera *Dido and Aeneas,* he also wrote many odes, the most famous of which is *Sound the Trumpets,* composed for James II's birthday.

George Bernard Shaw (1856–1950)   Born in Ireland, Shaw came to London in 1876 and worked as a journalist and music critic. He revolutionized the theater with his issue-oriented plays that satirized the institutions and philosophies of the period. *Pygmalion,* which mocked the class system, has become his most famous play. *Saint Joan* and *Heartbreak House* are two other major works that still find an audience.

Sir Arthur Seymour Sullivan (1842–1900)   This composer was the musical half of the enormously popular duo Gilbert and Sullivan—famous for such operettas as *The Mikado, The Yeoman of the Guard,* and *H.M.S Pinafore.* Sullivan also composed one of the most famous Anglican hymns, "Onward Christian Soldiers."

William Makepeace Thackeray (1811–63)   Born in Calcutta, India, he studied at Cambridge and law at the Middle Temple. His novels appeared in serial form in magazines. *Vanity Fair* (1848) is a brilliant satire of early 19th-century upper-middle-class life; it was followed by *Pendennis, Henry Esmond,* and *The Newcomes.*

Joseph Mallord William Turner (1775–1851)   Son of a London barber, J. M. W. Turner became Britain's greatest landscape painter. At 14, he entered the Royal Academy and went on to paint landscapes in watercolors and seascapes in the Dutch tradition. His interest with the violent moods of nature has been attributed to the effect his mother's madness had on him. He lived at 23 Queen Anne St.

Evelyn Arthur St. John Waugh (1903–66)   This London-born author satirized the madcap frivolity of the English aristocracy in such works as *Vile Bodies, The Loved One,* and, most famous of all, *Brideshead Revisited.*

Oscar Wilde (1854–1900)   Born in Dublin, he is most famous for his witty, sophisticated plays *The Importance of Being Ernest, Lady Windermere's Fan,* and *An Ideal Husband.* He also wrote two collections of fairy tales and a novel, *The Picture of Dorian Gray.* In 1891, the Marquess of Queensberry accused him of having homosexual relations with the Marquess's son, Lord Alfred Douglas. In response, Wilde brought a libel action against him. In turn, Wilde was charged with homosexual offenses and served two years in jail where he wrote his most famous poem, *The Ballad of Reading Gaol.* Released in 1897, he went to live in Paris and died in poverty.

Virginia Woolf (1882–1941)   In her writing, such as the essay *Street Haunting* or in her novel *Mrs. Dalloway,* Woolf's excitement about her city appears in almost every line. From about 1906, Woolf was identified with a brilliant circle of writers and artists who called themselves the Bloomsbury Group. She lived at 29 Fitzroy Square.

Sir Christopher Wren (1632–1723)   Mathematician and astronomer, Wren became a celebrated architect responsible for rebuilding much of London after the Great Fire of 1666. He designed 51 churches, including St. Paul's Cathedral, St. Bride's in Fleet Street, and St. Mary Le Bow in The City. He was also responsible for the Royal Hospital in Chelsea and the Royal Naval College in Greenwich. Knighted for his service, Wren is buried in St. Paul's Cathedral.

5   Architecture

Little remains, at least aboveground, of Roman or Saxon London, although at the Museum of London visitors can view substantial Roman archaeological finds unearthed during building developments. The story of London's buildings really begins with the Normans and with the finest extant example of Norman military architecture, the White Tower at the Tower of London. It has massive walls that are 20 feet wide at their base while the four stories rise to a height of 90 feet. Inside, the chapel of St. John is a classic early Romanesque design complete with a line of cubiform capitals supporting the nave.

The Gothic style that followed was practiced in England from 1170 to 1560, longer than in Continental Europe, largely because the break with Rome effectively cut off England from the full influence of the Renaissance. There are three periods of English Gothic—Early, Decorated, and Perpendicular, the last reigning from 1375. The greatest masterpiece of Perpendicular design in London is the Henry VII chapel at Westminster Abbey, with its ornate fan vaulting. Other examples of Perpendicular Gothic are St. George's Chapel in Windsor and King's College in Cambridge. Other great Tudor-Gothic buildings include Westminster Hall (1395) with its incredible hammer-beam roof and the great hall at Hampton Court Palace (1535). To get a good sense of what Tudor London looked like, visit Staple Inn, a wonderful gabled-timber building in Holborn. It was Inigo Jones (1573–1652) who brought the Renaissance style to England. Jones had traveled to France and Italy and directly experienced those countries' Renaissance buildings. Appointed surveyor to the royal family, he designed the Queen's House at Greenwich and the Banqueting Hall (1619–22) in Whitehall, which both display pure Roman classicism. For the most part, though, English architects did not excel at classicism.

Christopher Wren (1632–1723) dominated the second half of the 17th century. A founding member of the Royal Society, Wren was initially interested in science and astronomy; he was 30 years old before he began his architectural career. After the Great Fire of London in 1666, Wren presented an urban plan for a new London. Rejecting his plan—the costs were deemed too high—London lost the opportunity to rebuild on a grand open scale. The city was rebuilt according to its original medieval plan of narrow streets lined with tall buildings, which contributes mightily to the problems of congestion today. Still, Wren did build 53 churches in addition to

St. Paul's. The most outstanding examples of his work are St. Bride's (1680–1701); St. Mary Le Bow (1671–80); St. Stephen Walbrook (1675–87); St. Lawrence Jewry (1670–86); Christ Church, Newgate Street (1704); and St. Magnus Martyr, London Bridge (1670–1705).

Among Wren's team of artisans were wood-carver Grinling Gibbons, ironworker Jean Tijou, and painter Sir James Thornhill. Wren also expanded Hampton Court Palace, and he designed Kensington Palace and the Royal Hospital at Greenwich. The early 18th century ushered in a more traditional baroque form of architecture, practiced by a famous trio, John Vanbrugh, Nicholas Hawksmoor, and Thomas Archer. Vanbrugh is best known for Castle Howard in Yorkshire and Blenheim Palace in Oxfordshire. Famous for his bold steeples, Hawksmoor built St. Mary Woolnoth in London. Archer is responsible for St. John, Smith Square.

In the 1720s, baroque faded and was replaced with Palladianism, a classical style based on the works of Andrea Palladio, which dominated from 1720 to 1760. Its major practitioners were Colen Campbell and William Kent, both of whom concentrated on country houses. These estates were usually landscaped by England's famous Capability Brown.

One architect who favored neither baroque nor Palladianism was James Gibbs (1682–1754) who designed St. Martin-in-the-Fields (1722) and St. Mary-le-Strand (1714–17), two churches that were copied throughout New England and the colonies.

During the second half of the 18th century, a revival in classicism occurred. Sir William Chambers (1723–96), the surveyor-general, created the Thames-side Somerset House in grand Palladian style. For his designs of domestic homes, the more innovative Robert Adam (1728–92) drew his inspiration from Greek temples and Roman villas. Adam's decorative team embellished them with stucco, metalwork, and murals.

The most familiar architectural "look" recognized by visitors to London—the symmetrically designed terrace set around a square—was also developed in the 18th century. It had first been used in Bath by John Wood and his son. In London a series of squares was laid out: Grosvenor, Hanover, Berkeley, Cavendish, Bedford, and Portman. Sadly, one of the greatest examples of the style—the Adelphi, a riverfront terrace designed by Robert Adam—was destroyed in 1937. John Nash (1752–1835) was one of the greatest exponents of the style. He designed Regent's Park and the terraces around it, along with Regent Street, which he laid out for the Prince Regent.

One of Britain's most individual architects was Sir John Soane (1753–1837), and anyone who is interested in architecture ought to visit his home in Lincoln's Inn Fields. Among his more famous works besides the house are Dulwich Picture Gallery and the Bank of England.

After 1840, England was swept by a Gothic Revival and, later, a series of revivals of Renaissance and Baroque. The best example of the Gothic Revival in London is the Palace of Westminster, designed by Sir Charles Barry (1795–1860) and decorated in a marvelous manner by Pugin (1855–85). Other exponents of the style were Edmund Street (1824–81), who designed the Law Courts in the Strand; Alfred Waterhouse (1830–1905), who built the richly decorated Romanesque Natural History Museum; and Sir George Gilbert Scott (1811–78), who designed the impressive St. Pancras Station and Midland Hotel, as well as the Albert Memorial. Other late Victorian architects include Thomas Collcutt, whose work can be seen in the Palace Theatre (1890) on Cambridge Circus, the Savoy Hotel (1889–91), and the

Wigmore Hall (1890). Another amazing building of this period is the Byzantine Westminster Cathedral (1895–1903), designed by J. F. Bentley.

In the last two decades of the 19th century, architects abandoned the ornate heaviness of Gothic Victorian and returned to greater simplicity. The Queen Anne style that evolved was most used by Norman Shaw; his work can be seen at New Scotland Yard, which incorporates some baroque elements. Shaw also designed a great number of brilliant London houses.

Throughout the 19th century, as science and manufacturing progressed, architects experimented with new building materials like glass and iron. At the Palm House at Kew, visitors can see one of the early experiments with glass, but the most dramatic example of this experimentation was the Crystal Palace built for the Great Exhibition of 1851. It was 1,851 feet long and 450 feet wide and contained 900,000 feet of glass that was supported on 3,300 iron columns with 2,224 girders. Sadly, this magnificent example of engineering was destroyed in 1936.

The 20th century opened with a return to traditionalism and a revival of baroque, considered an appropriate style for such a great imperial capital. The buildings that most exemplify this are: the Old Bailey, the War Office in Whitehall, and both Victoria and Waterloo Stations.

A revival of French Renaissance followed. Designed by Arthur J. Davis, the Ritz Hotel (1903–6) is a true Beaux Arts building, with mansard roof and a rhythmical sequence of spaces, ending with the restaurant that overlooks Green Park. Between the wars Sir Edward Lutyens dominated the architectural scene. Beginning as an Arts and Crafts sympathizer, he later advocated free-style classicism. Among his London buildings are Britannic House (1920–26), the Reuter's Building in Fleet Street, and the Cenotaph in Whitehall.

The only pioneering work was done at the turn of the century by William Morris and Philip Webb, who founded the Arts and Craft movement as an alternative to historicism. They argued that buildings should relate to their sites and that local materials and elements of style should be employed (something that Frank Lloyd Wright was to do in the United States). Morris and Webb rejected mass production and called for a revival of individual craftsmanship in the decorative arts. They were largely ignored, and as a consequence, English architecture stagnated, dominated by neoclassical and other historical forms that expressed the grandiosity of empire. In fact, there was no real modern architecture in London until after 1945. The only major Arts and Crafts buildings of note were created by C. F. A. Voysey and Harrison Townsend—most of their work is out in the suburbs, but Townsend's Horniman Museum is on London Road, Forest Hill in South London.

The Festival Hall designed by R. H. Matthew and J. L. Martin for the Festival of Britain in 1951 went a long way to converting the public to acceptance of modern architecture and has stood up well. It consists of a series of flowing interior spaces and was the first building in London to apply acoustical science. The Royal National Theatre (1967–77) by Denys Lasdun is another well-designed and highly functional building that blends in well with its riverside location. In contrast, the Barbican (begun in 1955) looks brutish and ugly and is impossible to navigate unless you're carrying a map of the complex. Designed by Chamberlin, Powell, and Bon, the Barbican incorporates an arts center, a school, and housing for 6,000.

Two of the more famous modern architects are Sir Basil Spence (1907–76) and Sir Hugh Casson (b. 1910) both of whom were influenced by the International School. Most of the former's major buildings are outside London, but the brutish approach can be seen at his Knightsbridge Barracks (1967–69) in Kensington. Sir Hugh Casson designed the Elephant House at the zoo. Architects Philip Powell

(b. 1921) and John Hidalgo Moya (b. 1920) built the Museum of London. Other influential architects include Peter and Alison Smithson, who designed the Economist Buildings, in St. James's Street, and James Stirling, most of whose buildings are outside of London.

Perhaps the most infamous building in London, designed by R. Seifert in the 1960s, is the Centre Point (1962–66) office block, which looms over Tottenham Court Road. For many years it stood vacant and was the focus of a protest by the homeless. Today it has become a landmark of sorts, but it stands, as do most of Seifert's skyscrapers, as an example of what Pevsner has called the ruination of the London skyline.

6   On London Clubs

ARE YOU CLUBBABLE?

Perhaps it has to do with the weather, but whatever the reason, a lot of English life seems to take place behind closed doors. The English love the notion of the club and they're adept at forming them. Whatever the activity, there's a club for it—political, social, professional, or sporting. They love to associate with people of like mind and spirit. It seems gentlemen like to have a place to escape from their wives—particularly in London, where a number of gentlemen's clubs still steadfastly refuse to allow women. The women-at-clubs issue has become a hot controversy, with some members resigning to protest what they consider benighted policies.

Unless you're invited by a member, you'll not be allowed to enter the hallowed portals of most clubs. To give you an edge if you find yourself engaged in conversation with a high-born English gent, I'll name a few.

Boodle's is the quintessential St. James club to which country gentlemen repair when they visit London. Founded in 1762 by Edward Boodle, it has counted among its members the historian Edward Gibbon, the Duke of Wellington, slave abolitionist William Wilberforce, and both the elder and younger Pitts of English politics.

The **Carlton Club,** also in St. James, is the Conservative club par excellence founded in 1832 by the Tories after they had taken a severe beating in the election. Club rules require that members share the views and principles of the Conservative party. Among its early members were Disraeli and, oddly enough, Gladstone—until 1860, when he resigned after being insulted for his more liberal views. Important decisions made here include the election of Bonar Law as leader and the withdrawal from Lloyd George's coalition in 1922.

The **Reform Club** in Pall Mall is the counterpart for radicals. It was founded in 1836. Fans of the movie *Around the World in 80 Days* might remember that Phineas Fogg accepted the bet in this club's smoking room. Today, the Reform is more social than political. It's been open to women since 1981.

On Garrick Street, the **Garrick** is a club for actors, painters, and writers. Thackeray, Dickens, and Irving were all members. Today, its membership is drawn primarily from publishing, TV, and film. It's been a hotbed of controversy for its stern refusal to admit women.

The **Travellers** was indeed started for travelers by Lord Castlereagh in 1819. Particularly for diplomats, this was a place to share stories and findings. Today, this social club is not restricted to "travelers."

The most aristocratic of them all is **White's** in St. James. Its membership rolls have included several kings—George IV, William IV, and Edward VII. Admirals and prime ministers have all gathered here, too. Originally White's Chocolate House, it was founded in 1693. The essayist Richard Steele, the poet and satirist Alexander

Pope, and poet and dramatist John Gay all frequented it. Pope wrote in his *Dunciad* (1728) that this was "a place to teach oaths to youngsters and to nobles wit." Jonathan Swift thought ill of White's and is reckoned to have shook his fist at the building every time he passed by. Members dined here or went on drinking binges or gambled all night. Bets were placed on anything—births, marriages, and deaths. Lord Arlington placed a bet on which of two raindrops would reach the bottom of a window first. White's has remained largely a social club, except for a spree of partisan politics in the 1790s when supporters of William Pitt the younger gathered here.

A list of all of London's clubs would get very long—especially if one includes the many livery companies (professional societies), which maintain grand halls and traditions that are centuries old. Clubs are part of the English landscape, and pubs in their own way operate as such. Then, there are the sports clubs, which also excite the great passions of Londoners.

7   Recommended Books & Films

GENERAL HISTORY   For a very personal portrait of London, John Russell's *London* is filled with entertaining anecdotes and fascinating observations; it's enhanced by large color photographs and illustrations. For a drier but nevertheless interesting discussion of all of the social institutions of England, Anthony Sampson's *Anatomy of Britain* and his later *Changing Anatomy of Britain* can't be beaten. If you're a lover of fascinating minutiae, then you'll love *The London Encyclopedia* (Macmillan, 1983), edited by Ben Weinreb and Christopher Hibbert. Hibbert's *London: The Biography of a City* (Penguin, 1969) is also another treasure from this great and very accessible historian. *London: A Social History* (Hamish Hamilton, 1994) by Roy Porter brings the history of this great city to life. For children, *The Wonderful Story of London* (Odhams, 1956) will capture the imagination; it may only be available in secondhand bookstores. Other favorites of mine include novelist and literary critic V. S. Pritchett's *London Perceived* (Hogarth, 1986) and Virginia Woolf's *London Scene: Five Essays* (Random House, 1986), which depicts the city in the 1930s and is a literary gem.

For 17th-century history, nothing compares to Pepys and Evelyn. For the flavor of the 18th century, read Daniel Defoe's *Tour Through London About the Year 1725*. For insight into 19th-century England from an outsider's point of view, pick up Taine's fascinating *Journey Through England*. A magnificent, not-to-be missed work of modern history is E. P. Thompson's *The Making of the English Working Class*. For a turn-of-the-century portrait of London's East End, see Jack London's portrait.

Other great historical works worth reading are *London Life in the Eighteenth Century* by M. Dorothy George, an enlightened and readable study of life in the Georgian period; *The Making of Modern London,* by Gavin Weightman and Steve Humphries, on the Victorian development of London; and *The Long Weekend,* by Robert Graves and Alan Hodge, a fascinating and straightforward account of Britain between the wars. Specialty books include *Americans in London* (William Morrow, 1986) by Brian N. Morton, a street-by-street guide to the clubs, homes, and favorite pubs of more than 250 famous Americans. Many literary guides are available, too. *The Writer's Britain,* by Margaret Drabble, is an illustrated favorite, although not strictly about London.

ARCHITECTURE   For an easy and succinct overview, read the sections on England in Doreen Yarwood's excellent *The Architecture of Europe* (Batsford, 1974). For exclusive coverage of England, there's *A History of English Architecture* (Penguin, 1979) by Peter Kidson, Peter Murray, and Paul Thompson. Among the many books on London, the giant of them all is Pevsner's *London* (Penguin, 1957) a two-volume survey. This labor of love recently has been revised (1993) by Bridget Cherry; it's only available in England. The *Architects of London* (Architectural Press, 1979) by Alistair Service bring those master builders to life. Nairn's *London* (Penguin, 1988) is another very personal book about London, its history, and buildings. Donald Olsen's *The City as a Work of Art: London, Paris and Vienna* (Yale University Press, 1986) is a well-illustrated text tracing the development of these great cities. The poet John Betjeman has always concerned himself with the preservation of England's history and heritage, especially its buildings; his *Victorian and Edwardian London* (Batsford, 1969) expresses his love for that era in particular.

FICTION   It's hard to know where to begin because of all the arts, but England is probably richest in literature. Chronologically, start with Chaucer, who delivers a wonderful portrait of medieval London in his *Canterbury Tales*. Follow with Shakespeare and Ben Jonson. Then the essayists Addison and Steele, whose *De Coverley Papers* portray 17th-century society and its concerns in graphic detail. Pepys and Evelyn, of course, are wonderful friends with which to explore the London of this period. For the 18th-century, Fielding is a great companion and Swift and Defoe, too. Boswell's *London Journal* and his other books also make wonderful reading. Anything by Dickens or Thackeray will provide insight into Victorian London. The period from the turn of the century to the 1920s and 1930s is best captured in the works of Virginia Woolf, Henry Green, Evelyn Waugh, P. G. Wodehouse, and Elizabeth Bowen. Contemporary authors that provide insight into London society are Margaret Drabble, Martin Amis, Angela Carter, and a legion of others.

BIOGRAPHY   As for biographies, again there are so many to choose from. Among the great ones are Jackson Bate's portrait of Samuel Johnson and the many royal portraits that have been written by Antonia Fraser, as well as her book on Oliver Cromwell. Other marvelous political biographies include Blake's *Disraeli*. For a portrait of Disraeli's opponent Gladstone, see those written by Richard Shannon or H. C. Matthews. When it comes to Winston Churchill, you can read his autobiography written in brilliant English, or turn to Martin Gilbert's *Churchill: A Life* (St. Martin's, 1991). Richard Ellman's life of *Oscar Wilde* (Knopf, 1988) captures turn-of-the-century society. As for the royals who have been so much in the tabloids, two books dredge up all the lurid details—Anthony Holden's *The Tarnished Crown* (Random House, 1993) and A. N. Wilson's *The Rise and Fall of the House of Windsor* (W. W. Norton & Company, 1993).

2 Planning a Trip to London

Your trip will be much more enjoyable—and certainly a lot smoother—if you plan it properly. This chapter is designed to help you do so, step-by-step.

1 Saving Money in London

THE $60-A-DAY PREMISE

London is expensive, more expensive than any American city, including New York, but this doesn't mean that you can't enjoy a marvelous, affordable vacation here—that's the raison d'être for this guidebook.

Our premise is that two people traveling together can have a fine vacation for $35 a day per person. That $70 is meant to cover the price of a double room and two meals a day. The budget breaks down as follows: $35 for the room (half of $70), $9 for lunch, and $16 for dinner. (The budget takes into account that you'll be served a full breakfast at your hotel.) This sum will provide you with more than adequate accommodations (sometimes even with an in-room bath), a decent lunch at a pub or similar venue, and a fine repast at an ethnic restaurant in the evening. Sticking to this budget, you won't feel at all deprived. If you want to, you can do it for less, believe me. Naturally, you can also do it for more. I've included some recommendations for taking either the higher or lower route in this book, too.

Having an affordable vacation doesn't mean that you'll have to stay in grubby, faded accommodations, eat lousy fast food, and generally have a less than fun vacation. Twenty years ago, you might have had to do just that, but today you don't. Because London has changed.

There are still bed and breakfasts that provide comfy lounges; crisp, clean rooms; and full, hearty breakfasts. True, they're harder to find, and the average price is higher than a comparable room in, say, Paris; but they do exist, and this book will help you find them. I have scoured the neighborhoods of London to find the best. In Bloomsbury, for example, you'll find typically English hotels for modest travelers. If you don't mind staying out in Hampstead, you can enjoy a great value there at La Gaffe. If you're on a very strict budget, then consider staying at a youth hostel or at any one of several fine university accommodations like London School of Economics Holborn Residence—they're here too.

The biggest revolution for frugal travelers, though, has occurred in the food industry. Gone are fast-food abominations like Joe Lyons, shops selling inedible ice cream, and chains claiming to serve burgers. World cuisine has arrived: the French with croissants and chains of bistros, the Indians, Chinese, Italians, Greeks, and many other ethnic groups bringing good-quality budget food to Londoners long starved for such. The pubs are offering better fare, too, and have become much more family-friendly. Even authentic English cuisine has been rediscovered and promoted by such food writers as Jane Grigson. The selections contained in this book will guide you to the best, low-cost options available, the places frequented by the locals who don't have huge discretionary incomes.

As for sightseeing, while some of the stock-in-trade sights are overpriced (like Buckingham Palace and the Tower of London), many other top attractions and pageants are free: many of London's major museums, the city's lovely parks, most churches, and of course, the city streets, which are lined with buildings resonating with literary and historical associations.

FORTY-FIVE MONEY-SAVING TIPS

Now, to further overcome any skepticism you might have and to generate your own money-saving ideas, here are 45 ways to save money in what was once called the Big Smoke.

PRETRIP PLANNING AND TRANSPORTATION SAVINGS

1. Information pays; forewarned is forearmed. These adages apply to travel today—so read as much as you can about London before you go, talk to people who have been there recently, and get as much free information from the tourist office as you possibly can.
2. Reserve and pay in advance. You can often save money on airfare, car rentals, and local transportation if you book weeks or months in advance and pay Stateside. For example, from the British Tourist Office, you can obtain a Visitor Card for discounted transportation on the bus and tube; this card can only be purchased outside England. Rental cars are always cheaper if they are booked and paid for in U.S. dollars ahead of departure.
3. Travel off-season. London is great in the winter. Cultural life is at full throttle. Rooms are easier to find and are also cheaper. Dining and sightseeing are less frenetic. You don't have to go in darkest February—in April or October you'll still benefit financially.
4. Shop around for your airfare. Often the most expensive part of a trip is the cost of the airfare, so scour your newspaper for the latest information on airfares and call all the airlines. Air carriers are motivated to fill every seat on each flight, so they adjust pricing frequently and offer special promotions. Investigate legitimate charter flights that use scheduled airlines but offer low fares.
5. Fly during the week. It's cheaper than flying Friday, Saturday, or Sunday.
6. If you have plenty of time and schedules are not of any great consequence, then consider going as a courier.
7. Pack light. You won't need a porter and you're less likely to succumb to the desire for a taxi. *Note:* Luggage carts are free in London's airports.
8. Take public transportation from the airport to the city. The Piccadilly Line of the Underground runs directly from Heathrow to downtown. This costs about $50 less than a cab—that's close to a day's whole budget.
9. Consider taking a package tour. Sometimes you can secure a week or more in London for a very low price that includes airfare, transfers, accommodations, and some

sightseeing discounts. You needn't join the group activities, and you can enjoy the price tag.

ACCOMMODATIONS & DINING

10. When you're seeking out potential hotels, look in a university area, such as Bloomsbury. Check out the more remote areas of the city, like Hampstead, where you're likely to find better values.

11. Think about what you really want in a hotel room. If a TV, telephone, and private bathroom are not crucial to you, then you can enjoy some low-priced budget hotels that have appealing rooms.

12. Negotiate the price of your hotel room. Ask the management if they'll give you a discount if you stay three nights or more; suggest trade-offs—a lower price for a smaller room or a room minus TV and so on. If you're a student or senior, ask for special discounts. If you're on a hotel-lined street like Sussex Gardens or Ebury Street near Victoria, keep checking out accommodations until you find one for your price.

13. Depending on your particular peccadilloes, consider staying at a youth hostel or at any one of several fine university accommodations like Imperial College.

14. Stay at a hotel that provides a full breakfast, not a continental one.

15. Bring a knife, fork, plate, and corkscrew so that you can enjoy the wares from the city's charcuteries and other food halls (including Harrods).

16. If picnicking in a park or eating in your hotel room is not your style, then opt for one of the many low-cost dining establishments. Pubs offer good fare at lunch, as do wine bars. Sandwich and light fare and other eat-on-the-run shops abound. At dinner, the options range from some of the best Indian in the world to Chinese, Malaysian, Greek, Italian, Middle Eastern, and Japanese. You name it, the cuisine can be found in London. There are also chains—like the Stockpot, which has been keeping Londoners happy for years—and they offer good value.

17. At many a London restaurant, you'll find the English equivalent of the French prix fixe: the table d'hôte or the two-course or three-course set menu. It's a good option that usually features the freshest ingredients.

18. At most restaurants, service is included—don't make the mistake of tipping twice.

SIGHTSEEING & ENTERTAINMENT

19. Walk—it's the best way to explore a city and meet its citizens. Use public transportation, too. Take advantage of whatever discounts are available, like the TravelCard.

20. Make creative sightseeing choices. Some of the best things in life are free. In London, a walk down any street will likely turn up a number of buildings that are marked with blue plaques, indicating that someone famous lived there or some historic event took place there.

21. If you're interested in antiques, window-shop along New Bond Street or Westbourne Grove around Portobello. Check out Fulham Road if you want to see the latest in British interior design.

22. Students can present their student ID to get discounted admissions, wherever granted. Men and women age 60 and older can receive senior citizen discounts at some attractions.

23. Hang out at the outdoor markets. There's a variety to choose from—Camden Town on the weekends for a youth-oriented avant-garde experience akin to Canal Street in New York City; Bermondsey and Portobello for antiques; and Billingsgate and New Covent Garden for produce.

24. Most churches are free to the public. Take time to contemplate the brilliant interiors of Wren's churches or the many memorials that every church seems to have.

25. Take advantage of the many free exhibits at museums, such as the main galleries of the British Museum and the National Gallery and the permanent collection of the Tate Museum.

26. Enjoy the free entertainment that's invariably given at Covent Garden—be it a jazz trio or a couple of young music students delivering Mozart arias with much more than amateur aplomb.

27. Tour the historic monuments and attend the pageantry events—the Changing of the Guard at Whitehall, the Lord Mayor's Show.

28. Enjoy the architecture of London. Westminster Abbey is free (though you must pay a hefty price to see the crypts of famous people and the Poets' Corner), as are the many buildings that line the streets from the Tudor Staple Inn to the modern Lloyd's building. Don't overlook the squares and terraces in every neighborhood from Trafalgar to Bloomsbury.

29. Explore the parks. Don't sit on a deck chair though—there's a charge. Opt for the classic park bench.

30. Visit the Old Bailey and the Royal Courts of Justice in the Strand and, of course, the Houses of Parliament. They're all free and will provide an introduction to the institutions and social philosophies of contemporary London.

31. Visit the cemeteries. Not just Highgate—there are several that contain the remains of many other worthies who chose London as their home. Check out Brompton Cemetery on Old Brompton Road, the Dog's Cemetery in Kensington Gardens, Hampstead Cemetery on Fortune Green Road.

32. For London's cheapest tour, ride the no. 188 bus from Euston to Greenwich, or any of the other routes, for that matter.

33. Nightlife. Go to venues early or very late and you'll receive a discount.

34. Go to the kiosk in Leicester Square for half-price theater tickets.

35. Attend matinees instead of evening performances.

36. On Monday nights when all tickets are only £4, go to the Royal Court Theatre, one of the city's most exhilarating.

37. Attend free lunchtime concerts in the churches or at the Royal Festival Hall.

38. At many a jazz or other music club, sitting at the bar instead of at a table can save you money.

39. Come to London to shop in January during the sales; there really aren't any great bargains otherwise.

40. Check out Marks & Spencer and other discount stores.

41. Window-shop along some of the city's most famous retail streets—New and Old Bond Streets, Jermyn Street.

42. Just for fun, drop into one or more of the auction houses to preview the objects—Sotheby's, Phillip's, or Christies.

43. For antique browsing, go to one of the great centers like Westbourne Grove around Portobello.

44. Get your VAT refund—a whopping 17.5%. Fill out the appropriate forms in the shop; get the form and your receipt stamped at customs; and mail them back to the retailer.

45. Don't call home from a hotel phone unless you know that you can access USA Direct or a similar company. Check to see if there's a charge for the connection to USA Direct.

2   Visitor Information & Entry Requirements

VISITOR INFORMATION

Information about travel in London and elsewhere in Great Britain can be obtained from the **British Tourist Authority (BTA).** The BTA has two offices in the United States. The main office is at 551 Fifth Ave., 7th Floor, New York, NY 10176-0799 (☎ **800/462-2748** or 212/986-2200; phone lines are open Mon–Fri from 9:30am to 7pm). The visitor office is open Mon-Fri from 9am to 7pm. A second office is located at 625 N. Michigan Ave., Suite 1510, Chicago, IL 60611 (**no phone**). Office hours are weekdays only 9am to 5pm.

You can also purchase a **London for Less™** card through the BTA, which gives you discounts on major attractions, restaurants, hotels, tours, concerts, and theater performances—it also allows you to make commission-free currency exchanges at Travelex branches. The card costs £12.95 ($20.07) and can save you considerably more. The card is valid for either a 4- or 8-day period, and comes with a nice fold-out map and guidebook. You can also purchase it at Tourist Information Centres in London.

The BTA also maintains offices in **Australia,** at 210 Clarence St., Sydney, NSW 2000 (☎ **02/261-607**); in **Canada,** at 111 Avenue Rd., Suite 450, Toronto, ON M5R 3J8 (☎ **416/925-6326**); and in **New Zealand,** at Suite 305/3rd Floor, Dilworth Building, CNR Customs and Queens Sts., Auckland 1 (☎ **9/303-1446**).

In London, visit the main British Tourist Authority office in the British Travel Centre, 4–12 Lower Regent St., London SW1 (**no phone**). In addition to information on all of Britain, this center has a British Rail ticket office, a travel agency, a theater ticket agency, a hotel-booking service, a bookstore, and a souvenir shop. Hours are 9am to 6:30pm Monday through Friday and 10am to 4pm Saturday and Sunday. Weekend hours are extended from June through September.

ENTRY REQUIREMENTS

DOCUMENTS

Citizens of the United States, Canada, Australia, and New Zealand need only a valid passport to enter Great Britain.

CUSTOMS

Overseas visitors are allowed to import 400 cigarettes and one quart of liquor duty-free. Film, toiletries, and other items can be imported free of tax, provided they are for your personal use. Live animals, plants, and produce are forbidden. When returning to the United States, citizens are allowed to bring back $400 worth of merchandise duty-free. After that amount, you will be charged a flat 10% tax on the next $1,000 worth of goods. If you do shop in London, make sure you retain your receipts to show Customs officials.

3   Money

CURRENCY

POUNDS & PENCE   The English **pound (£),** a small, thick, round coin, is divided into 100 **pence.** Pence (abbreviated "p") come in 1p, 2p, 5p, 10p, and 50p coins. You may still see some 1- and 2-shilling coins; these are equivalent to 5p and 10p, respectively. Notes are issued in £5, £10, £20, and £50 denominations.

The British Pound & the U.S. Dollar

At this writing, $1 = approximately 65p (or $1.55 = £1), and this was the exchange rate used to calculate the dollar values in this book (rounded to the nearest nickel).

£	U.S. $	£	U.S. $
.05	.08	6	9.30
.10	.16	7	10.85
.25	.39	8	12.40
.50	.78	9	13.95
.75	1.16	10	15.50
1	1.55	15	23.25
2	3.10	20	31.00
3	4.65	25	38.75
4	6.20	30	46.50
5	7.75	35	54.25

At press time, it costs $1.55 to buy one English pound ($1.55 = £1). To make budgeting easier, prices quoted in this book are accompanied by their equivalents in U.S. dollars. Exchange rates are volatile, so remember that these conversions are to be used as a guide only.

TRAVELER'S CHECKS

Traveler's checks in foreign currencies are easily exchanged in London. Banks and companies like American Express and Thomas Cook offer the best rates. *Beware:* Chequepoint and other private currency exchange businesses which stay open late charge high commissions.

Traveler's checks issued in British pounds are accepted at most shops, restaurants, hotels, theaters, and attractions. For the foreign traveler, however, there are two drawbacks to carrying them. First, you'll have to exchange your money into pounds at home, a transaction that usually proves more costly than in London. Second, you'll have to re-exchange your unused pounds after your trip, thus incurring a second transaction fee.

CREDIT CARDS/ATMS

American Express, Diners Club, MasterCard, and Visa are widely accepted. In England, MasterCard is called Access and Visa is known as Barclaycard. Using plastic can be economical as well as convenient. Credit cards eliminate commissions for currency exchange and allow for later billing. Later billing can work out to your advantage or disadvantage, depending on whether the dollar goes up or down with time.

Similarly, today you'll save money if you secure currency from an ATM rather than changing it at the old-fashioned traditional currency exchange offices. The fees are lower and also the rate of exchange used is the "wholesale" rate, which is also better. Check with your bank before you leave regarding the fees charged and anything else you may need to know. For the name of banks overseas that belong to the **CIRRUS** network, call **800/424-7787;** for **PLUS** banks, call **800/491-1145.**

What Things Cost in London	U.S. $
Taxi from Heathrow Airport to London	62.00
Underground from Heathrow Airport to central London	5.90
Local telephone call	.15
Double room at Tophams Ebury Court (splurge)	155.00
Double room at Oakley Hotel (budget)	65.10
Lunch for one, Bahn Thai (moderate)	12.40–26.35
Lunch for one at most pubs (budget)	7.00–9.00
Dinner for one, without wine, at English House (splurge)	32 .15
Dinner for one, without wine, at Chester (moderate)	30.00
Dinner for one, without wine, at Khan's (budget)	6.20–10.85
Pint of beer	2.30–3.10
Coca-Cola in a restaurant	1.55
Cup of coffee	1.18
Roll of ASA 100 film, 24 exposures	7.70
Admission to the British Museum	Free
Movie ticket	7.70–9.30
Cheapest West End theater ticket	11.90

4 When to Go

Spring and fall are the best seasons to go to avoid the crowds that descend on the major sights in summer. In winter, the weather in London can be very dreary, but the cultural calendar is rich and the attractions are less crowded.

THE CLIMATE

London's infamous thick fog was never fog at all. It was smog from coal-burning residential chimneys and power plants. Today, rigidly enforced air pollution controls make it an offense to use a fireplace for its intended purpose, so "fog" is no longer in the forecast. However, rain, drizzle, and showers are. A typical weather forecast any time of year predicts "scattered clouds with sunny periods and showers, possibly heavy at times." Temperatures are temperate, and rarely go below freezing in winter, or above 70° Fahrenheit in summer—although recently there have been some major heat waves.

London's Average Daytime Temperature (°F) & Rainfall (inches)

	Jan	Feb	Mar	Apr	May	June	July	Aug	Sept	Oct	Nov	Dec
Temp.	40	40	44	49	55	61	64	64	59	52	46	42
Rainfall	2.1	1.6	1.5	1.5	1.8	1.8	2.2	2.3	1.9	2.2	2.5	1.9

HOLIDAYS

Most businesses are closed for Christmas on December 25 and for Boxing Day the day after; on New Year's Day, January 1; on Good Friday as well as Easter Monday; and on May 1, which is generally regarded as Labor Day in Europe. In addition, many stores close on bank holidays, which are scattered throughout the year. There's no uniform policy for museums, restaurants, and attractions with regard to closing for holidays.

LONDON CALENDAR OF EVENTS

January
- **Charles I Commemoration.** Banqueting House, Whitehall. Hundreds of men march through central London dressed as cavaliers to mark the anniversary of the 1649 execution of King Charles I. Last Sunday in January.

February
- **Chinese New Year Parade.** Chinatown, at Gerrard and Lisle Streets. Festive crowds line the decorated streets of Soho to watch the famous Lion Dancers. Late January or early February (based on the lunar calendar).

March
- **The Easter Parade.** Battersea Park. London's largest parade features brightly colored floats and marching bands, kicking off a full day of activities. Easter morning.

April
- **The Oxford vs. Cambridge Boat Race.** The dark blues and light blues compete over a Thames course from Putney to Mortlake. The race has been held since 1829, and crowds line the towpaths along the banks of the river and fill the riverside pubs to cheer the teams on. First Saturday in April.

May
- ✪ **Chelsea Flower Show.** This international spectacular features the best of British gardening, with displays of plants and flowers for all seasons. The location, on the beautiful grounds of the Chelsea Royal Hospital, helps make this exposition a world-class affair.

   Where: Chelsea Royal Hospital, Chelsea. **When:** Late May. **How:** For ticket information, write Shows Department, Royal Horticultural Society, Vincent Square, London SW1P 2PE. ☎ **0171/630-7422;** fax 0171/630-6060 or call (for tickets only) 0171/344-4343.

June
- **The Derby.** The highlight of the flat racing season at Epsom Racecourse in Surrey. The Coronation Cup and Oak Stakes are run at the same meet. Usually the first weekend in June.
- **Royal Ascot.** A four-day midweek event held at Ascot Racecourse in Berkshire. The glamorous event of the racing season, as renowned for its fashion extravaganzas as for its high racing standards. The royal family attends. Remember the scene in *My Fair Lady*? Usually the third week of June.
- ✪ **Trooping the Colour.** The official birthday of the queen. Seated in a carriage (no longer on horseback), the royal monarch inspects her regiments and receives their salute as they parade their colors before her. A quintessential British event religiously watched by the populace on TV. The pageantry and pomp are exquisite. Depending on the weather, the young men under the bearskins have been known to faint from the heat.

   Where: Horse Guards Parade, Whitehall. **When:** A day designated in June (not the queen's actual birthday). **How:** Tickets are free and are allocated by ballot. Apply in writing between January and the end of February enclosing an International Reply Coupon to: The Ticket Office, HQ Household Division,

Chelsea Barracks, London SW1H 8RF. Canadians should apply to Royal Events Secretary, Canada House, Trafalgar Square, London SW1Y 5BJ.

❍ **Wimbledon Lawn Tennis Championships.** Ever since the players in flannels and bonnets took to the grass courts at Wimbledon in 1877, this tournament has drawn a socially prominent crowd. Although the courts are now crowded with all kinds of tennis fans, there's still an excited hush and certain thrill at Centre Court. Savor the strawberries and cream that are part of the experience.
    Where: Wimbledon, SW London. **When:** Late June early July. **How:** Advance booking required for Centre and Number One Courts. Write in October for an application form for inclusion in ticket ballot for following year. Outside court tickets available daily at the gates—be prepared for a line. For more information call ☎ **0181/946-2244.** Fax 0181/947-8752.

• **Henley Royal Regatta.** A major social event at which international crew teams compete. Held at Henley-on-Thames, Oxfordshire, it's rowed on an upstream course, against the current, from Temple Island to Henley Bridge—more than a mile. Tickets are obtainable from the Secretary ☎ **01491/572153.** Late June or early July.

July

• **Royal Tournament.** Earl's Court Exhibition Centre in SW5. The British military put on dazzling displays of athletic and military skills. A mixture of pomp, show-biz, and outright jingoism in aid of service charities. For information write to the Royal Tournament Box Office, Earl's Court Exhibition Centre, Warwick Road, London SW5 9TA. ☎ **0171/373-8141.**

• **Henry Wood Promenade Concerts,** Royal Albert Hall, SW 7. A summer musical event that's been running since 1895. The concerts, from jazz to the classics, are given from late July to mid-September and are famous for their Last Nights. The audience stands in the rotunda of the hall and the orchestra ends with a rousing interpretation of Elgar's "Pomp and Circumstance." Tickets go on sale in May. From late July to mid-September.

• **Doggett's Coat & Badge Race.** Instituted in 1715 by Thomas Doggett, comedian and manager of Drury Lane Theatre, to celebrate the accession of King George. The race is rowed in single sculls from London Bridge to Cadogan Bridge, Chelsea, more than a 4^1/$_2$-mile course. The winner is awarded a scarlet uniform and silver badge. Mid- to late July.

August

❍ **The Notting Hill Carnival,** Ladbroke Grove. One of the largest annual street festivals in Europe, this African-Caribbean fair attracts more than half a million people to its two-day celebration. Live reggae, steel bands, and soul music combine with great Caribbean food, camaraderie, and a charged atmosphere. Free.
    Where: Notting Hill, London. **When:** Late August. **How:** Just show up.

September

• **Horse of the Year Show,** Wembley Arena, Wembley. A six-day indoor event that attracts the world's top showjumpers. Usually the last week in September.

November

• **State Opening of Parliament.** Whitehall and Parliament Square. Although the ceremony itself is not open to the public, crowds pack the parade route to see the royal procession. Late October or early November.

❍ **Fireworks Night.** Commemorates the anniversary of the "Gun-powder Plot," a Roman Catholic conspiracy to blow up King James I and his parliament. Huge organized bonfires are lit throughout the city. Guy Fawkes, the plot's most famous conspirator, is burned in effigy. Free.

Where: Hyde Park, Battersea Park, and other public areas in London. **When:** November 5. **How:** Follow the crowds and the smoke.

- **London to Brighton Veteran Car Run.** More than 300 veteran car owners from all over the world compete in this 57-mile run from London's Hyde Park to Brighton. Usually the first Sunday in November; starts at 7am.

- **The Lord Mayor's Procession and Show,** The City. An elaborate parade celebrating the inauguration of the new lord mayor, who travels in a magnificent gilded coach from Guildhall to the Royal Courts of Justice. Usually second Saturday in November.

5 Health, Insurance & Other Concerns

MEDICAL REQUIREMENTS

Unless you are arriving from an area known to be suffering from an epidemic, no inoculations or vaccinations are required to enter Britain. If you are currently on medication, carry a doctor's prescription along with any controlled substances you possess.

INSURANCE
HEALTH INSURANCE

Citizens of Australia and New Zealand are entitled to free medical treatment and subsidized dental care while in Britain. Americans and other nationals will usually have to pay up-front for services rendered. Doctors and hospitals can be expensive, so although it is not required of travelers, health insurance is highly recommended. Most American travelers are covered by their hometown policies in the event of an accident or sudden illness while away on vacation. Also, some credit card companies offer free, automatic travel-accident insurance, up to $100,000, when you purchase travel tickets on their cards. Before you purchase additional protection, check to see if you are already covered in foreign countries by your health maintenance organization (HMO) or insurance carrier.

OTHER TRAVEL-RELATED INSURANCE

You can also protect your travel investment by insuring against lost or damaged baggage, and trip cancellation or interruption costs. These coverages are often combined into a single comprehensive plan, and sold through travel agents and credit card companies. Contact the following companies for more information: **Access America,** 6600 W. Broad St., Richmond, VA 23230 (☎ **800/284-8300**); **Tele-Trip Company,** Mutual of Omaha, Mutual of Omaha Plaza, Omaha, NE 68175 (☎ **800/228-9792**), **Travel Guard International,** 1145 Clark St., Stevens Point WI 54481 (☎ **800/826-1300,** in Wisconsin 800/634-0644), and **Wallach & Co.,** 1078 W. Federal St., P.O. Box 480, Middleburg VA 22117 (☎ **703/687-3166,** or 800/237-6615).

6 Tips for Travelers with Special Needs

FOR TRAVELERS WITH DISABILITIES

Most of London's major museums and tourist attractions are now fitted with wheelchair ramps to accommodate physically challenged visitors. It's common in London for theaters, nightclubs, and attractions to offer discounts, called "concessions," to people with disabilities. Ask for these before paying full price.

For information on traveling in Britain, call **Holiday Care Services (☎ 129/ 377-4535)** during regular office hours.

Artsline (☎ 071/388-2227) offers free information on accessibility to theaters, galleries, and events around the city. The phone line is open Monday to Friday from 9:30am to 5:30pm.

FOR GAY & LESBIAN TRAVELERS

Capital Gay is the city's premier alternative paper. Written by and for gay men and women, this free weekly features news, reviews, and events. *The Pink Paper* is nationally distributed and is also free. Both of these publications are available at gay bars, bookstores, and cafés. At least two monthlies are regularly available at newsstands around town: *Gay Times* is oriented toward men and is known for both news and features; *HIM* has high-quality reporting with glossy beefcake photos. The city's popular listings magazine, *Time Out,* also provides excellent coverage. **The Lesbian and Gay Switchboard (☎ 0171/837-7324)** offers information, advice, and counseling, as well as a free accommodations agency. The line is open 24 hours and is almost always busy. **The Lesbian Line (☎ 0171/251-6911)** offers similar services to women only. It's open Monday through Thursday 6 to 10pm, Friday 2 to 10pm.

FOR SENIORS

In Britain, "senior citizen" usually means a woman at least 60 years old and a man at least 65. Seniors often receive the same discounts as students. Some discounts are restricted to British citizens only.

London's youth hostels welcome older guests. These are some of the cheapest accommodations in the city, and are listed under a special heading in Chapter 4, "Where to Stay."

In addition to organizing tours, the **American Association of Retired Persons (AARP) Travel Service,** 100 N. Sepulveda Blvd., Suite 1020, El Segundo, CA 90024, provides a list of travel suppliers who offer discounts to members.

FOR STUDENTS

Time Out: London Student Guide is published at the beginning of each school year; it's available from most large newsagents and costs £2.50 ($3.85). The **University of London Student Union (ULU),** Malet Street, WC1 (☎ **0171/580-9551**), caters to more than 55,000 students and may be the largest of its kind in the world. In addition to a gym and fitness center, the Malet Street building houses several shops, two restaurants, two banks, a ticket booking agency, and an STA travel office. Concerts and dances are also regularly scheduled here. Stop by or phone for information on university activities. The student union building is open Monday through Saturday from 8:30am to 11pm; Sunday from 9:30am to noon and 12:30 to 10pm. Take the tube to Goodge Street.

The **International Student Identity Card (ISIC)** is the most readily accepted proof of student status. In the United States, it's available from Council Travel Offices nationwide, as well as from the **Council on International Educational Exchange,** 205 E. 42nd St., New York, NY 10017 (☎ **212/822-2600**). The card entitles its holders to an array of travel benefits, including reduced student airfares (offered through Council Travel), discounts on public transportation, museum and cultural event admissions, and other tourist services. When purchased in the United States, the card comes with emergency medical and accident insurance coverage. To be eligible for the ISIC, you must be enrolled in a high school or college degree program. Your application must include proof of student status; such proof may be provided by an official letter from the school registrar or high school principal stating that you are enrolled for the following academic year. Enclose the letter with a $16 registration fee and a single passport-size photo.

London's youth hostels are not only some of the cheapest places to stay, they are also great spots to meet other student travelers. You have to be a member of **Hostelling International (International Youth Hostel Federation)** to lodge at official youth hostels, but joining is easy as membership cards are issued at every hostel in London. To apply for membership in the United States, contact Hostelling International, P.O. Box 37613, Washington, DC 20013-7613 (☎ 202/783-6161). Membership costs $25 a year for people 18 to 54; those 17 and younger pay just $10 and those 55 and older pay $15.

FOR WOMEN

Silver Moon Women's Bookshop, 64–68 Charing Cross Rd., WC2 (☎ 0171/836-7906), is Soho's only dedicated feminist bookseller featuring a huge selection of fiction and nonfiction titles by and for women. Europe's largest women's bookshop, it is open Monday through Saturday from 10am to 6:30pm (until 8pm on Thursday). Tube: Leicester Square.

Women-only dance events occur a couple of nights a week in London at clubs all around the city. These clubs are designed for lesbians and straight women who are not looking to attract the attention of men. Call **London Friend** (☎ 071/837-3337) from 7:30–10pm, or check the listings magazines for upcoming events.

The **London Rape Crisis Centre** (☎ 0171/837-1600) offers immediate help, advice, and counseling to victims.

7 Organized Tours & Packages

Tours and packages are offered by tour operators, airlines, hotels, and transportation companies. A tour usually includes transportation, sightseeing, meals, and accommodations; the entire group travels together and all share the same preplanned activities. A package, on the other hand, may include any or all of the above components, but travelers are usually unescorted and make their own itinerary.

Even if you are an independent traveler, don't shy away from a package; it can be a very good value because packagers buy in bulk and share the discount with the consumer. Check the ads in the travel section of your newspaper. Most of the airlines listed in Section 9, "Getting There," offer both escorted tours and on-your-own packages. Other top London tour operators include **Globus Gateway Cosmos** (☎ 800/556-5454), **Trafalgar Tours** (☎ 800/854-0103), and **Frames-Rickards** (☎ 800/527-2473).

8 Finding an Affordable Place to Stay

When you select a hotel, one obvious rule is to look in those areas where you're most likely to find affordable hotels, like Bloomsbury which is the heart of London's student community. Don't call or head for Mayfair or Belgravia. Chapter 4, "Where to Stay," will guide you to the best budget hotels, hostels, and B&Bs. You may, however, want to consider some additional options for securing low-cost accommodations.

HOMESTAYS Homestays can provide a much deeper insight into the host culture than staying at a typical hotel. The following organizations make this experience possible. **Servas** (from the Esperanto word meaning "to serve") seeks to promote friendship and goodwill through homestays of at least two nights. Contact the **U.S. Servas Committee,** 11 John St., Suite 407, New York, NY 10038 (☎ **212/ 267-0252**). Yearly membership is $55.

Several London-based homestay agencies can also set you up with a local family. Prices range from £14.50 to £55 ($22.47 to $85.25) per night for a double room, most of which are located away from the city's tourist center. **Host and Guest Service,** Harwood House, 27 Effie Rd., London SW6 1EN (☎ **0171/731-5340**); and **London Homestead Services,** 3 Coombe Wood Rd., Kingston-upon-Thames, Surrey KT2 7J4 (☎ **0181/949-4455**) make all the arrangements and require a 25% deposit. Doubles range from £14 to £30 ($21.70 to $46.50).

HOME EXCHANGES   The **Vacation Exchange Club,** P.O. Box 650, Key West, FL 33041 (☎ **305/294-1448** or 800/638-3841), can help you set up a home swap—your house or apartment for a residence in London, in England, or in any other country. The cost of a listing in the directory is the price of membership, which is $70. If you prefer not to be listed but would like a copy of the listings, it still costs $70.

EDUCATIONAL TRAVEL   The **American Institute for Foreign Study,** 102 Greenwich Ave., Greenwich, CT 06830 (☎ **203/863-6087** or 800/727-2437), offers 3- to 12-week study/travel programs starting at about $3,499, including round-trip airfare from New York, all meals, and housing. Add-ons from other U.S. cities are available.

The **Institute for International Education,** 809 United Nations Plaza, New York, NY 10017 (☎ **212/883-8200**), also administers students' applications for study abroad programs in England and other European countries. Write for their free booklet, "Basic Facts on Study Abroad."

The **Council on International Educational Exchange,** 205 E. 42nd St., New York, NY 10017 (☎ 212/661-1414—ask for the Information and Student Services Department), publishes a free magazine entitled *Student Travels.* The council also runs a "Work in Britain" program for U.S. college and university students.

Those 60 and older, along with their spouses of any age (or a "significant other" 50 or older), can take advantage of an educational program sponsored by **Elderhostel,** 75 Federal St., Boston, MA 02110 (☎ **617/426-7788**). This organization sends almost 16,000 people to school abroad every year. Courses last two to four weeks. Fees start at $1,700 and include airfare, meals, lodging, daily classroom instruction, and admission fees.

It's also possible to enroll yourself in summer courses at Cambridge or Oxford University. Request the free brochure "Tours and Special Interest Holidays" from the British Tourist Authority, 551 Fifth Ave., New York, NY 10176-0799 (☎ **212/ 986-2200** or 800/462-2748).

9 Getting There

BY PLANE

Close to 90 scheduled airlines serve London, including almost every major American and international carrier.

THE MAJOR AIRLINES

The major American carriers offering regularly scheduled London flights include: **American Airlines** (☎ 800/433-7300), **Continental** (☎ 800/231-0856), **Delta Airlines** (☎ 800/241-4141); **Northwest Airlines** (☎ 800/447-4747), **TWA** (☎ 800/892-4141), and **United Airlines** (☎ 800/538-2929). **British Airways**

Frommer's Smart Traveler: Airfares

1. Shop all the airlines that fly to your destination.

2. Always ask for the lowest fare, not "discount," "APEX," or "excursion."

3. Keep calling the airlines—availability of cheap seats changes daily.

4. Seek out budget alternatives. Phone "bucket shops," charter companies, and discount travel agents.

5. Plan to travel midweek, when rates are usually lower.

6. If you have the option, fly into Heathrow instead of Gatwick; you'll save about $12 in transportation costs.

(☎ 800/247-9297), the largest British airline, offers a good standard of service from about a dozen cities. **Virgin Atlantic Airways** (☎ 800/862-8621) flies from New York and Newark, New Jersey, as well as from Boston, Los Angeles, San Francisco, Orlando, and Miami.

FINDING THE BEST AIRFARE

London's popularity and the number of airlines flying there mean that the airlines compete heavily for customers. Always check newspapers for special promotions and always shop around to secure the least expensive fare.

The lowest-priced standard economy-class fare usually carries some restrictions like advance-purchase or minimum stay as well as penalties for altering dates and itineraries. You may be able to secure a cheaper fare by staying an extra day, flying during the middle of the week, or by purchasing your ticket a certain number of days in advance—most airlines won't volunteer this information. At the time of this writing, the lowest round-trip summer fare from New York was $619, but this was on British Airways and required a 90-day advance purchase.

BEST-FOR-THE-BUDGET ALTERNATIVES

Alternatives to the traditional travel agent ticket have their advantages (usually price) and their drawbacks (usually freedom). Here's the lowdown:

Bucket Shops   By negotiating directly with airlines, consolidators, or "bucket shops," can sell tickets on major scheduled carriers at deeply discounted rates. The resulting fares are now the least expensive means of traveling to Europe, lower in most instances than charter fares. For example, during the winter from New York, you can buy bucket-shop tickets to London on well-known international airlines for as little as $300 round-trip; figure about $500 in summer. The savings can be anywhere from $200 to $400, depending on whether or not there's a fare war going on between the airlines, in which case the discounts are smaller. There are drawbacks, however. The tickets are restrictive, valid only for a particular date or flight, nontransferable, and nonrefundable except directly from the bucket shop. In addition, they may not always earn frequent flier miles. Bucket-shop tickets are rarely restricted by advance-purchase requirements; if space is available, you can buy your ticket just days before departure. Always pay with a credit card, though, to protect yourself in case the consolidator goes bankrupt.

The lowest-priced bucket shops are usually local operations with low profiles and overheads. Look for their tiny ads consisting of a list of cities and prices in the travel or classified section of your local newspaper.

Nationally advertised consolidators are usually not as competitive as the smaller, back-room operations, but they have toll-free telephone numbers and may be more reliable. The following are just a few of those operating:

TFI Tours International, 34 W. 32nd St., 12th floor, New York, NY 10001 (☎ **212/736-1140** in New York State or 800/745 8000 elsewhere in the United States); **TMI (Travel Management International),** 39 JFK St. (Harvard Square), 3rd floor, Cambridge, MA 02138 (☎ **800/245-3672**); and **UniTravel,** 1177 N. Warson Rd., St. Louis, MO 63132 (☎ **800/325-2222**).

Charters   The second-cheapest way to cross the Atlantic is on a charter flight. Most charter operators advertise and sell their seats through travel agents, making them your best source of information for available flights. Two well-known operators that sell tickets directly to passengers include **Travac,** 989 Sixth Ave., New York, NY 10018 (☎ **800/872-8800** or 212/563-3303), and **Council Charters,** 205 E. 42nd St., New York, NY 10017 (☎ **800/223-7402** or 212/661-0311).

Standbys   Standbys provide another inexpensive means of crossing the Atlantic. In order to fill seats that would otherwise go unsold, many of the airlines offer discounted fares to last-minute travelers. Standby service is usually offered from April to November only on a week-by-week basis.

Going as a Courier   Companies transporting time-sensitive materials, such as film, blood, or documents for banks and insurance firms, regularly hire air couriers. All you have to do to be a courier is give up your checked-baggage allowance to the courier company and make do with a carry-on. The courier company handles the check-in and pickup of packages at each airport. Another drawback, besides restricted baggage, is that you have to travel alone. If two of you are traveling, you may be able to arrange departures on two consecutive days.

Two popular courier services are **Now Voyager, Inc.,** 74 Varick St., Suite 307, New York, NY 10013 (☎ **212/431-1616**, 11:30am to 6pm) and **Halbart Express,** 147–05 176th St., Jamaica, NY 11434 (☎ **718/656-8189**, 10am to 3pm).

Most flights depart from New York, so you may have to tack on the additional cost to get to the gateway city. Prices change all the time, from low to very low. If a company needs emergency courier service and you can fly immediately, you could travel free or for next to nothing—say, $50 round-trip.

LONDON AIRPORTS

London is served by two major airports: Heathrow and Gatwick. Both have good public transport links to central London.

The cheapest route from **Heathrow Airport** to London is by Underground ("the tube"). The 15-mile journey takes approximately 45 minutes and costs £3.80 ($5.90) to any downtown station. Service is convenient, as the Underground platforms are directly below the airport's four terminals. Most transatlantic flights arrive (and depart) from Terminals 1 and 2. Terminal 3 is home to most intra-European flights, while Terminal 4 is the long-haul hub for British Airways exclusively. Heathrow is big, so even those with light luggage would be well advised to use one of the free baggage carts for the long walk to the Underground. Trains depart every 4 to 10 minutes from 6am to midnight. The Airbus, which takes between 1 and 1 1/2 hours, costs £10 ($15.50) round-trip; it travels to Victoria, King's Cross, and central London hotels. A cab will cost £40 ($62).

There are two ways of making the 25-mile trek from **Gatwick Airport** to the city center. The first, and more popular, is by express train, which takes 30–45 minutes to reach Victoria Station. Unfortunately, it costs a hefty £8.90 ($13.80) each way.

The station is just below the airport, and trains depart every 15 minutes from 6am to 10pm (hourly, on the hour, at other times). You can also take the Flightline no. 777 bus operated by **Green Line** (☎ 0181/668-7261). The 70-minute journey costs £7.50 ($11.60) one way, or £11 ($17.05) round-trip. Buses destined for Victoria Coach Station depart from Gatwick's North Terminal hourly, at different times throughout the day.

If you are flying to London on a smaller European commuter plane, you may land at **London City Airport,** located about six miles east of the City of London. Shuttle buses operate every 20 minutes to Liverpool Street Station (a 25-minute journey) where you can pick up the Underground. Another shuttle connects to Canary Wharf where you can take the Docklands Light Railway into town.

BY TRAIN

Most trains originating in Paris arrive at Victoria Station. Trains from Amsterdam arrive at Liverpool Street Station; those from Edinburgh pull into King's Cross Station. All three stations are well connected to the city's extensive bus and Underground network and contain London Transport Information Centres, luggage lockers, telephones, and restaurants.

Eurostar service through the Channel Tunnel from either Paris or Brussels arrives at Waterloo Station

BY BUS

Buses usually meet European ferries and Hovercrafts arriving in Dover and other British ports. Whether you're coming from the Continent or from another part of England, London-bound buses almost always go to (and leave from) **Victoria Coach Station,** Buckingham Palace Road, located one block from Victoria Railway Station.

BY CAR

If you're arriving from the Continent, you can quickly connect with a motorway into London. London is encircled by two inner roads, the A406 and the A205, and the M25 farther out. The M25 connects with the M1 to Birmingham, the M40 to Oxford, the M4 to Bristol, the M3 to Southampton, the M20 to Dover, and the M11 to Cambridge. Once in the city, I would suggest you dispense with the car, because parking is difficult and expensive and the city is a maze of one-way streets.

BY SHIP

Only one cruise ship still crosses the Atlantic with regularity—the *Queen Elizabeth 2.* It's not cheap but the passage is memorable. Prices start at about $2,395 (plus $175 port tax) for the five-day crossing, including return airfare during peak season. For more information, contact **Cunard,** 555 Fifth Ave., New York, NY 10017 (☎ 212/880-7500 or 800/221-4770).

If you have a very flexible schedule, you might consider freighter travel. Most freighters carry no more than 12 passengers and charge less than cruise lines—though more than airlines. You may also find yourself at the mercy of erratic sailing schedules. By freighter tradition, passengers pay for a fixed number of days; if the trip comes in early, they receive a refund; if it takes longer, and it often does, they get the extra days free. Tipping is expected, as it is on cruise ships. On a freighter, you pay about half the daily cost of a passenger liner, or about $100 a day. For more information on freighter travel write for **Fords Freighter Travel Guide,** 19448 Londelius St., Northridge CA 91324 (☎ 818/701-7414).

3 Getting to Know London

London is a huge city that spreads out over 600-plus square miles. It sounds intimidating, but it really isn't. London grew up around The City, which occupies one square mile near Tower Bridge and the palace of Westminster to its west. Around these two areas, villages grew up—Bloomsbury, Hackney, Holborn, Highgate, and Hampstead, for instance. Over the centuries, these villages were absorbed into the city proper. Today, it's easy to get around from one area to another via the Underground or the bus network.

This chapter will help you get your bearings. It provides a brief orientation and a preview of the city's most important neighborhoods. It answers questions about getting around London by public transportation and also contains a Fast Facts section covering everything from bookstores to shoe repairs.

1 Orientation

VISITOR INFORMATION

The **London Tourist Board (LTB)** operates several information offices. On arrival, stop into the one at Heathrow; it's open daily from 8:30am to 6pm. Those arriving via Gatwick, or by train from Paris, can visit the office in Victoria Station's forecourt. The Victoria office is open daily from 8am to 7pm from Easter to October; the rest of the year, it's open Monday through Saturday from 9am to 6pm, and on Sunday from 9am to 5pm. Other LTB Information Centres are located at Liverpool Street Station (open Mon 8:15am to 7pm, Tues to Sat 8:15am to 6pm, and Sun 8:30am to 4:45pm); and in Selfridges department store, open year-round during store hours.

The **British Travel Centre,** 12 Lower Regent St., SW1 (**no phone**), near Piccadilly Circus, provides information on all of Britain. It's open from 9am to 6:30pm Monday through Friday and 10am to 4pm Saturday and Sunday. Hours are usually slightly reduced in winter.

For information about travel by bus, tube, or British Rail, visit a **London Transport Information Centre** in any of the major train stations, or call the **London Regional Transport Travel Information Service** (☎ 0171/222-1234), open 24 hours daily.

CITY LAYOUT
MAIN DISTRICTS, ARTERIES & STREETS

Most visitors won't need to explore the vast area that is Greater London. Instead, they'll concentrate on an area stretching from the Thames Embankment north to Camden Town, west to Kensington, and East to Tower Bridge. Within this area are located all of the major tourist sights and facilities. The logical—although not geographical—center of this area is **Trafalgar Square.** On the north side of the square is the National Gallery, England's most important repository of fine art, and beyond lies cinema-laden **Leicester Square,** restaurant-packed **Soho,** and London's **theater district.** The city's literary and intellectual center, **Bloomsbury,** is farther north still. This district is anchored by the massive British Museum and dotted with a good number of moderately priced hotels.

The Strand branches east from Trafalgar Square, and connects the **West End** with **The City.** A stroll down this street will reveal an eclectic mix of hotels, restaurants, shops, and office buildings. **Covent Garden Market,** a landmark for tourists and shoppers alike, is located just a few blocks north of the Strand.

South of Trafalgar Square is **Whitehall,** the address of many of Great Britain's most important government buildings. No. 10 Downing Street, the official residence of the prime minister, is just off Whitehall, and Big Ben, Westminster Abbey, and Parliament Square are all located at the bottom of the street along the riverbank.

The Mall is a long road that runs west from Trafalgar Square to Buckingham Palace. **Knightsbridge, Kensington,** and **Hyde Park** lie farther west still.

FINDING AN ADDRESS

You will get lost in London. To the chagrin of tourists and postal workers alike, the city's tangle of streets follows no discernible pattern whatsoever. Furthermore, there seems to be little logic to street naming or house numbering. Be warned that Park Walk is not necessarily near Park Crescent, to say nothing of a similarly named street, road, mews, and close. Sometimes odd-numbered houses are on one side of a street, while even-numbered homes are on the other. Other times, numbers will run straight up one side of a street, then down the other.

STREET MAPS

A London street map is essential, even if you are staying on the beaten track. If you need a more detailed map than the one bound into the back of this guide, you'll find that bookstores, food markets, souvenir shops, and most sidewalk newsagents sell local maps. Expect to pay £1.50–£4.50 ($2.35–$7). The London Tourist Board Book and Gift Shop in the Victoria Station information center stocks many maps and guidebooks too.

If you're planning to stay a while in London, you're advised to purchase an **A to Z London Guide,** available at newsstands and bookstores.

Impressions

It is my belief, Watson . . . that the lowest and vilest alleys of London do not present a more dreadful record of sin than does the smiling and beautiful countryside.
——Sir Arthur Conan Doyle, *The Adventures of Sherlock Holmes*

London at a Glance

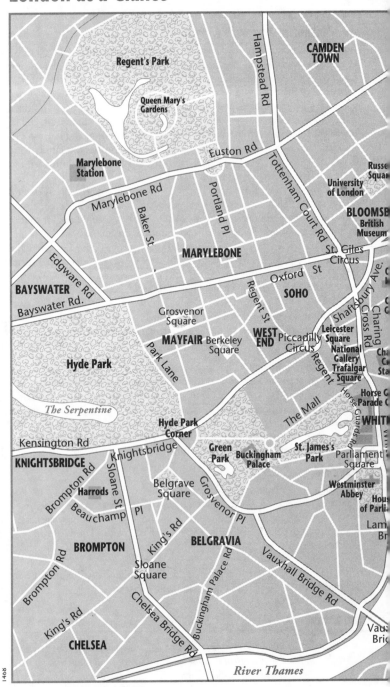

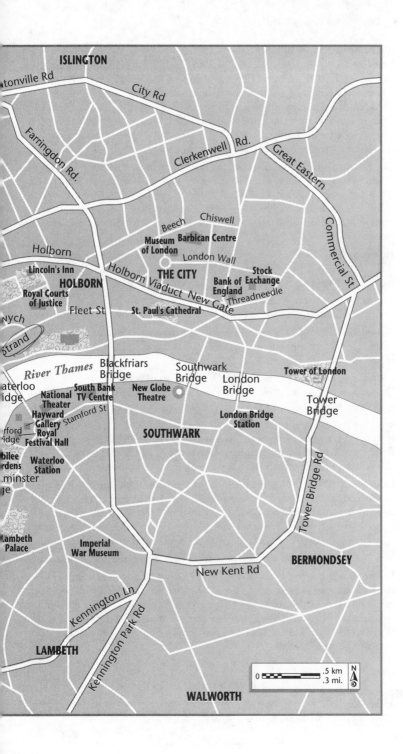

ISLINGTON

tonville Rd

City Rd

Farringdon Rd.

Clerkenwell Rd.

Great Eastern

Beech Chiswell

Holborn

Museum
of London

Barbican Centre

London Wall

Commercial St

Lincoln's Inn

HOLBORN

Holborn Viaduct New Gate

THE CITY

Bank of
England

Stock
Exchange

Threadneedle

Royal Courts
of Justice

Fleet St

St. Paul's Cathedral

nych

trand

River Thames

Blackfriars
Bridge

Southwark
Bridge

London
Bridge

Tower of London

aterloo
idge

National
Theater

South Bank
TV Centre

New Globe
Theatre

Tower
Bridge

Hayward
Gallery

Stamford St

London Bridge
Station

rford
idge

Royal
Festival Hall

SOUTHWARK

bilee
rdens

Waterloo
Station

Tower Bridge Rd

minster
e

Lambeth
Palace

Imperial
War Museum

BERMONDSEY

New Kent Rd

Kennington Ln

Kennington Park Rd

LAMBETH

0   .5 km
     .3 mi.

N

WALWORTH

47

NEIGHBORHOODS IN BRIEF

The City   One square mile, The City is the original walled city, still ruled by the lord mayor. It stretches from Temple and Holborn Bars on the west to Aldgate and Tower Hill on the east and from the Thames to Smithfield and Moorfields in the north. Today, The City is London's financial center, bustling during the day but deserted at night. Here you'll find Guildhall, the Old Bailey, the Bank of England, the Stock Exchange, Lloyd's, St. Paul's, the Barbican, the Museum of London, and at its eastern riverside perimeter, the Tower of London.

The Strand (WC2)   In early London, this thoroughfare connected The City to Westminster and was lined with the palaces of bishops and aristocrats. Today, along this broad street, you'll find the Royal Courts of Justice, King's College, Somerset House (the Courtauld Institute), the Savoy Hotel, and the Inner Temple, as well as shops, hotels, theaters, and restaurants. From Trafalgar Square, it runs east into Fleet Street.

Holborn (WC2, EC1)   North of the Strand, this area has long been associated with the legal profession. Both Gray and Lincoln's Inn are located here.

Westminster/Whitehall (SW1)   The heart of governmental London. Home of the Houses of Parliament, Westminster Abbey, 10 Downing Street, Scotland Yard, and government ministries and offices.

Covent Garden (WC2)   Since the market moved out in 1974, this has become a tourist mecca for shopping, dining, and entertainment. Site of the Royal Opera House and also of the Actors' Church, St. Paul's.

Piccadilly Circus, Leicester and **Trafalgar Squares (W1, WC2)**   The heart of London's theater district is filled with fast-food restaurants and other services.

Soho (W1)   Between Piccadilly and Oxford Street, this fascinating neighborhood of narrow crooked streets was originally London's foreign quarter. Today, it contains some of the city's finest restaurants, both budget and luxury. Chinatown is just across Shaftesbury Avenue, along Gerrard and Lisle Streets. The sex trade is also part of the Soho scene, but it's been substantially cleaned up.

Bloomsbury (WC1)   A genteel neighborhood anchored by the British Museum and Library and the University of London. You'll find streets and squares lined with terraced houses, antiquarian bookstores, and plenty of academic life. Also home to the Percival David Foundation of Chinese Art.

Regent's Park (NW1)   The focal point of this residential area, marked by many John Nash terraces, is the 487-acre park, which also shelters the London Zoo.

Paddington/Bayswater (W2, W9, W10)   This north London residential area has experienced its ups and downs. In the 1950s, it became identified with poor housing and poverty, but today it's enjoying a revival. Bayswater occupies the southern boundaries of Paddington. It's a residential area with a shopping area stretching along Westbourne Grove. Here, you'll find a number of budget hotels and budget restaurants along Sussex Gardens.

Impressions

Hell is a city much like London—a populous and smoky city.
                                    —Percy Bysshe Shelley, *Peter Bell the Third*

London Street Names

The street names of London tell its story from Roman and Norman times and much later. The *bury* in Bucklersbury and Lothbury comes from *burhs,* which were stone mansions of Norman barons. Ludgate, Aldgate, and Cripplegate were the original gates of the walled city. The Barbican is called so because it stands on the site of a watchtower. In the Middle Ages, *cheaps* were markets: hence modern street names like Eastcheap and Cheapside. As the city grew and more crafts were practiced, artisans and merchants had their workshops on certain streets, and so today there's Milk Street, Bread Street, and Friday Street (where fish was sold). Clink Street was the site of a prison, hence the expression "in the clink." Cock Lane in the 14th century was the only street licensed for prostitution.

Notting Hill (W11)   North of Kensington, this area has become a Caribbean enclave. It's famous for the carnival held on August Bank Holiday. The Portobello Market is also here.

Hampstead (NW3)   Originally a village to which Londoners retreated for the waters, Hampstead retains a villagelike ambience. Home to the wealthy and the famous, it encompasses the glorious 800-acre heath. Several homes of famous writers and artists are open to the public.

Camden Town (NW1)   An area of small manufacturers in the late 19th and early 20th centuries, it was home to Greek and Irish communities. Today it's undergoing gentrification. On weekends, it's home to the youth-oriented Camden Market. The canal adds charm to the area.

Highgate (N6, N19)   Another west London village that retains a separate identity. Home to the famous and also to Highgate Cemetery.

Mayfair (W1)   Bounded by Piccadilly, Hyde Park, and Oxford and Regent Streets, this area is considered London's most elegant. It's home to the American Embassy, Savile Row, and the Royal Academy. New Bond Street is lined with galleries and auction houses and other top-quality stores.

St. James (SW1)   The Court of St. James says it all. The Mall leads from Buckingham Palace right along the southeastern boundary of St. James. Home to St. James's Palace, Christie's auctioneers, and such streets as Jermyn, which is lined with stores selling bespoke items for gentlemen.

Belgravia (SW1)   Southeast of Knightsbridge, this aristocratic residential quarter rivals Mayfair in prestige and money. It backs onto Buckingham Palace Gardens.

Knightsbridge (SW1)   A premier residential and shopping area, just south of Hyde Park. It's famous for Harrods.

Kensington/South Kensington (W8, W10, W11, W14, SW5, SW7 SW10)   Both lie south of Kensington Gardens. South Kensington is known for being the home of the Victoria and Albert, the Science, and the Natural History Museums.

Chelsea (SW3, SW10)   A stylish district stretching along the Thames, southwest of Belgravia. Many artists and writers have lived in the stately terraced homes that line its quiet streets and mews: Thomas Carlyle, for one. The King's Road is its major artery.

Earl's Court (SW5)   This residential area, clustered around the station and exhibition building of the same name, is referred to as both Kangaroo Valley (because of its Australian community) and Bedsit Jungle (because of its largely transient population).

South Bank/Southwark (SE1)   The National Theatre, Royal Festival Hall, Queen Elizabeth Hall, and the Hayward Gallery can all be found here, just across Waterloo Bridge.

The East End (E1, E2, E3)   One of London's poorest areas and the home of the true Cockney. Most of the immigrants that came to England—the Jews and Huguenots, for example—settled here. In earlier centuries, this area was undesirable, as the prevailing winds and the west-to-east flow of the River Thames carried stench and pestilence from the city to the East End.

2 Getting Around

BY PUBLIC TRANSPORTATION

Getting around London is easy, thanks to the extensive Underground and bus networks. The system is organized by zone. Most visitors need only concern themselves with zone 1, or Central London. This zone extends from the Tower in the east and Notting Hill on the west, from Waterloo in the south to Baker Street, Euston, and King's Cross on the north. A one-way fare within this area is £1 ($1.55); a round-trip is £2 ($3.10). The fare for buses within zone 1 is the same. If you intend to use public transportation several times in a day, then it's cheaper to buy one of the many passes that are available for use on the Underground, buses, and the Docklands Light Railway. A one-day travelcard for zones 1 and 2 costs £3 ($4.65) adult, £1.60 (2.48) children 5–15. It allows you to travel as often as you like in those zones after 9:30am Monday to Friday and all day Saturday, Sunday, and holidays. If you want to travel for a day before 9:30am, the LT card is available for zones 1 and 2 for £4 ($6.20) adult, £2 ($3.10) children 5–15. A weekly travelcard for zone 1 will cost £12 ($18.60) adult, £4.50 ($7) child; it allows unrestricted travel in that zone. Weekly, monthly, and annual cards are also available at Underground stations, Travel Information Centres, and certain tobacconists and newsagents who display a pass agent sign.

London Regional Transport Travel Information Centres are located in most of the major Underground stations, including Heathrow Central, King's Cross, Oxford Circus, Piccadilly Circus, and Victoria. Off-hour times vary, but all provide service weekdays from 9am to 5pm. LRT also maintains a 24-hour telephone information service (☎ **0171/222-1234**).

A SPECIAL NOTE

If you plan to use public transit extensively, then you should purchase a **Visitor Travelcard** which allows unlimited travel throughout the bus and Underground system, including the link to Heathrow Airport. The pass must be purchased overseas and is available for three, four, or seven days and includes some tourist discount vouchers. Contact the local BTA.

THE UNDERGROUND

Except for Christmas Day when the tube is closed, subway trains run every few minutes beginning at about 5:30am Monday through Saturday and 7am or so on Sunday. Closing times vary with each station, but the last trains always leave between 11:30pm and 1am. Last train times are posted at the entrance of each station.

Tickets can be purchased at the station ticket window or from an adjacent coin-operated machine. An alphabetized fare chart is posted next to most ticket machines. Hold onto your ticket throughout your ride; you'll need it to exit. Pick up a handy tube map, distributed free at station ticket windows. Pick out your destination and note the color of the line that stops there (Bakerloo is brown, Central is red, and so on). Then follow the line back to where you are, noting where you'll have to change to reach your destination. *Note:* The Docklands Light Railway operates from The City to the Docklands area. It only runs during the week. On weekends, it's replaced by buses D9 and D8.

BUSES

The bus network is as extensive as the subway. Red buses operate within London; the green buses travel outside the London area. The red double-deckers were going to be phased out gradually, but tourists protested so vehemently that they have been saved. Note that there are two kinds of bus stops—the compulsory stop (which has a white background) and the request stop (red background). At the first, the bus will stop without being hailed, but at the second you'll need to put your arm out to signal the bus to stop. On a double-decker, the conductor will come to your seat to take your fare. On the buses that have no conductors, you pay as you enter. Fares range from 60p to £2, and weekly passes are available. You can secure a bus map from any London Transport Information Centre. For schedule and fare information, call **0171/222-1234.**

Regular bus service stops after midnight. Night buses have different routes and different numbers than their daytime counterparts. Night service is not as frequent; most routes are serviced only once per hour. Unlike weekly and monthly travelcards, one-day passes are not valid on night buses. The central London night-bus terminus is Trafalgar Square.

BY CAR

Rentals It's a nuisance to keep a car in London, but for excursions, a rental car can come in handy. Making a reservation in the United States is, of course, cheaper. **Avis** (☎ **800/331-1084**) will guarantee a dollar rate at the time of payment, which must be two weeks in advance of the rental. In summer 1996, Avis was offering a compact car for $188 per week, exclusive of a $17^{1}/_{2}$% VAT and CDW (which is about $14.75 a day). The lowest summer rate at **Hertz** (☎ **800/654-3001**), guaranteed in U.S. dollars, was $235, plus tax and CDW. Some of the best rates can be found through **AutoEurope,** P.O. Box 7006, Portland, ME 04112 (☎ **207/828-2525**), which was offering an economy car with stick shift for only $137 per week (exclusive of VAT and CDW). **Kemwel** (☎ **800/678-0678**) was offering a tiny Peugeot 106 for $119 per week.

Gasoline One of the few city gas stations open 24 hours, **Dorset House Service Station,** 170 Marylebone Rd. (☎ **0171/486-6389**), accepts all major credit cards.

Parking Parking is difficult. Most parking meters are enforced from 6am to 6:30pm. Blue signs point the way to **National Car Parks (NCP),** which are located throughout the city. To find the closest, call NCP (☎ **0171/499-7050**). Fines for illegal parking can be stiff. Even worse are the wheel clamps that immobilize violators until the ticket is paid. If you find your car clamped, take the ticket and attached penalty notice to the nearest car pound (the address is on the ticket) to pay your fine.

Central London Bus Routes

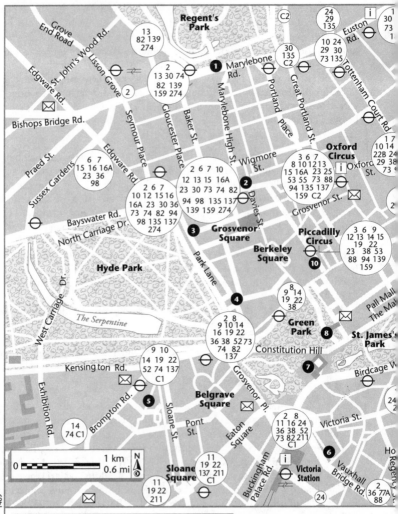

Using the Map

London bus route numbers are shown in circles at places where routes cross. Locate where you are going and then follow the route circles back toward your starting point. This will show if and where you need to change buses and the bus route number or numbers for your trip.

Tube Station ⊖
British Rail Station ⇌

MAJOR ATTRACTIONS

Admiralty Arch **9**
Barbican Centre **25**
British Library and British Museum
Buckingham Palace **7**
Downing Street **16**
Harrods **5**
Horse Guards **15**
Houses of Parliament **18**
Imperial War Museum **20**

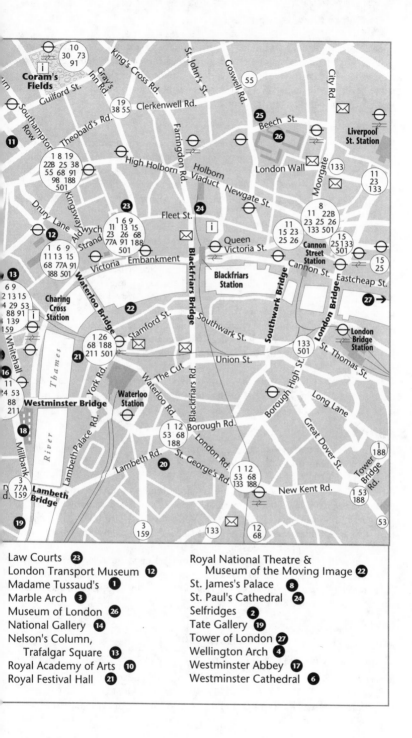

Law Courts **23**
London Transport Museum **12**
Madame Tussaud's **1**
Marble Arch **3**
Museum of London **26**
National Gallery **14**
Nelson's Column,
    Trafalgar Square **13**
Royal Academy of Arts **10**
Royal Festival Hall **21**

Royal National Theatre &
    Museum of the Moving Image **22**
St. James's Palace **8**
St. Paul's Cathedral **24**
Selfridges **2**
Tate Gallery **19**
Tower of London **27**
Wellington Arch **4**
Westminster Abbey **17**
Westminster Cathedral **6**

Special Driving Rules   In Britain, wearing a seat belt is the law. You may not turn right on a red light, and automobiles must stop whenever a pedestrian steps into a crosswalk. Many crosswalks are located in the middle of the block, not at the corner. They're usually marked by white stripes on the pavement (zebra striping) and flashing orange lights on either sidewalk.

BY TAXI

For three or four people traveling a short distance, cabs can make economic sense. A taxi is available when the yellow sign on its roof is illuminated. Hail a cab by raising your arm. The driver will lower the window when he pulls to the curb, so you can state your destination before climbing in. You can also order a cab (☎ **0171/ 253-5000** or 071/286-0286), but the rates will be higher.

The meter begins at £1.20 ($1.85) for the first 564 yards, and then it's 20p for each additional 282 yards or 57 seconds. An extra person is 30p (45¢) and luggage 10p (15¢) per bag. On evenings, weekends, and holidays, there's a 40p (60¢) surcharge.

Minicabs are meterless cars that are driven by any entrepreneur with a license. Technically, these taxis are not allowed to cruise for fares, but must operate from sidewalk offices—many of which are centered around Leicester Square. Minicabs are handy after the tube shuts down for the night and when black cabs are unavailable. They are available 24 hours, are cheaper than black cabs, and can be ordered in advance (☎ **0171/602-1234**). Always negotiate the fare with the office beforehand. If you're approached by a driver (away from the sidewalk offices), hard bargaining is in order.

If you need a taxi from your hotel early in the morning, it is advisable to make a reservation the night before. Try **Computer-cab** (☎ **0171/286-0286**) or **Radio Taxicabs** (☎ **0171/272-0272**).

BY BICYCLE

Bike lanes are unheard of and cars are unyielding—still, some people do ride. For a rental, try **On Your Bike,** 52–54 Tooley St., SE1 (☎ **0171/378-6669**). A 10-speed goes for £8 to £10 ($12.40–$15.50) per day and £25 ($38.75) per week, plus a £50 ($77.50) deposit. The shop is open Monday through Friday from 9am to 6pm, Saturday from 9:30am to 5:30pm, and Sunday 11am–3pm. More centrally located is **Bikepark,** 14 Stukeley St., Covent Garden, WC2 (☎ **0171/430-0083**). This place rents a variety of bikes charging £10–£15 ($15.50–$23.25) a day, but they require a £150 ($232.50) deposit. Open daily in summer; Monday to Saturday in winter.

Serious cyclists should check out the **London Cycling Campaign,** Tress House, 3 Stamford St., SE1 9NT (☎ **0171/928-7220**), for information and advice on biking in the city. Pick up their booklet *On Your Bike*, which shows bike paths and quiet streets for cyclists and costs £5.70 ($8.85).

FAST FACTS: London

Airport   See "Getting There" in Chapter 2.

American Express   American Express has almost a dozen city offices, including 6 Haymarket, SW1 (☎ **0171/930-4411**). Most are open Monday to Friday 9am to 5:30pm, Saturday 9am to noon. To report lost or stolen cards call **0127/ 369-6933**, 24 hours.

Area Code The area code is 0171 in central London, 0181 in outer London. Area codes are necessary when dialing from outside the code. From the United States dial 171 and 181, respectively.

Bookstores Dillons the Bookstore, 82 Gower St., WC1 (☎ **0171/636-1577**), is one of the biggest and best chain bookshops in town. Open Monday and Wednesday to Friday 9am to 7pm, Tuesday 9:30am to 7pm, Saturday 9:30am to 6pm. See Chapter 8, "Shopping A to Z," for more bookstore information.

Business Hours Most banks are open Monday to Friday 9:30am to 3:30pm. Some are also open Saturday 9:30am to noon. Offices are generally open Monday to Friday from 8:30 or 9am until 5 or 5:30pm. By law, pubs can open Monday to Saturday 11am to 11pm, and Sunday 11am to 3pm and 6 to 11pm. Note, however, that some pubs begin serving later than others, and many keep Sunday hours throughout the week. Restaurants usually open for lunch at 11am, and stay open until 11pm or midnight. A very few stay open later (see Chapter 5, "Where to Eat"). Stores are usually open Monday to Saturday 10am to 6pm, but most stay open at least one extra hour one night during the week. The major stores now also stay open Sunday. Some shops around touristy Covent Garden stay open until 7 or 8pm nightly.

Cameras See "Photographic Needs," below.

Climate See "When to Go," in Chapter 2.

Currency See "Money" in Chapter 2.

Currency Exchange As a rule, you will get a better rate for traveler's checks than you will for cash. Banks generally offer the best exchange rates, but American Express and Thomas Cook are competitive and do not charge a commission for cashing traveler's checks, no matter what the brand. Also, don't hesitate to use your credit cards at ATMs. Although you gamble on the rates not swinging too much, the charge for the service for now at least is minimal. *American Express* maintains several offices throughout the city (see above). A conveniently located *Thomas Cook* office is at 1 Woburn Pl., Russell Square WC1 (☎ **0171/837-5275**); open Monday to Friday 8:30am to 5pm, Saturday 9am to noon. The office at King's Cross and the one in front of the British Museum stay open from 8am to 8pm on Saturday. Beware of *Chequepoint* and other high-commission bureaux de change.

Customs See "Customs" in Chapter 2.

Doctors and Dentists If you need a physician or dentist and your condition is not life-threatening, call the operator (☎ **100**) and ask for the local police. They will put you in touch with a specialist. You can also visit *Medical Express*, Chapel Place, W1 (☎ **0171/499-1991**). This private walk-in clinic is open Monday to Friday 9am to 6pm, Saturday 9am to 2pm. Consultations begin at £70 ($108.50). Citizens of Australia and New Zealand are entitled to free medical treatment and subsidized dental care while in Britain.

Driving Rules See "Getting Around," earlier in this chapter.

Drugstores *Bliss Chemist,* 5 Marble Arch, W1 (☎ **0171/723-6116**), is open daily 9am to midnight year-round. Call the operator (☎ **100**) and ask for the police for the opening hours and addresses of other late-night "chemists."

Electricity English appliances operate on 220 volts, and plug into three-pronged outlets that differ from those in America and on the Continent. Hair dryers, irons, shavers, and other American appliances require an adapter and transformer. Do not attempt to plug an American appliance into a European electrical outlet without a transformer; you will ruin your appliance and possibly start a fire.

Embassies/Consulates　The *U.S. Embassy,* 24 Grosvenor Sq., W1 (☎ 0171/ 499-9000), does not accept visitors—all inquiries must be made by mail or phone. The *Canadian High Commission,* Macdonald House, 1 Grosvenor Sq., W1 (☎ 0171/258-6600), is open Monday to Friday 8am to 11am. The *Australian High Commission* is in Australia House on the Strand, WC2 (☎ 0171/379-4334), and is open Monday to Friday 9am to 1pm. The *New Zealand High Commission* is in New Zealand House, Haymarket, SW1 (☎ 0171/930-8422), open Monday to Friday 9am to 5pm.

Emergencies　Dial **999** for police, fire, and ambulance from any phone. No money is required.

Eyeglasses　Several spectacle shops line Oxford Street, King's Road, and other major shopping streets. The department stores Harrods and Selfridges (see Chapter 8, "Shopping") also have opticians on duty and a good selection of frames. The *Contact Lens Centre,* 32 Camden High St., NW1 (☎ 0171/383-3838), is one of the cheapest shops for contacts as well as glasses. Even if you don't have your prescription with you, you can get an exam and new glasses in the same day. It's open Monday to Friday 9:30am to 6:30pm, Saturday 9am to 5pm.

Hairdressers and Barbers　The *Hair Beauty,* 5th floor, Harrods department store, Knightsbridge, SW1 (☎ 0171/584-8881), is a specialty department within the store's hair and beauty salon. Cuts cost £40 to £55 ($62 to $85.25) and up. Open Monday, Tuesday, and Saturday 10am to 6pm; Wednesday to Friday 10am to 7pm.

Holidays　See "When to Go," in Chapter 2.

Hospitals　In an emergency, dial **999** from any phone; no money is needed. *University College Hospital,* Grafton Way, WC1 (☎ 0171/387-9300), is one of the most centrally located. A dozen other city hospitals also offer 24-hour walk-in emergency care. Dial **100** and ask the operator to connect you with the police. They'll tell you which hospital is closest.

Hotlines　The *Restaurant Switchboard* (☎ 0181/888-8080) makes restaurant recommendations and reservations free of charge. It's open Monday to Friday 9am to 8pm; and at *Capital Helpline* (☎ 0171/388-7575), a live human being will answer any legitimate question about London, the universe, or anything. The helpline is open Monday to Friday 10am to 10pm and Saturday to Sunday 8am to 8 pm.

Information　See "Visitor Information," earlier in this chapter.

Laundry/Dry Cleaning　Most laundries open every day. Near Russell Square, try *Red and White Laundries,* 78 Marchmont St.(☎ 0171/387-3667), open daily 6:30am to 8:30pm; a wash costs £1–£3 ($1.55–$4.65), and dryers and soap are £1 ($1.55). Bring plenty of 20p pieces.

Dry cleaning is expensive in London. Expect to pay about £2 ($3.10) per shirt, and £4.99 ($7.75) for a pair of pants. With more than 40 branches, *Sketchley,* 49 Maddox St., W1 (☎ 0171/629-1292), is one of the city's largest cleaning chains. Check the telephone directory for other locations. Alternatively, try *Sinclair Mobile Dry Cleaning* (☎ 0171/739-5614), which offers free pickup and delivery; it charges only £2.20 ($3.25) for pants, and £1.80 ($2.80) for shirts.

Libraries　The British Library, Great Russell Street, WC1 (☎ 0171/636-1544), is one of the largest in the world, holding at least one copy of every book published in Britain. The library is not open to the casual reader, so you'll need a special pass to gain entry, obtainable if you're a bona fide scholar or author. Use the city's many smaller and more accessible local or specialized libraries. *Westminster Central Reference Library,* St. Martin's Street, WC2 (☎ **0171/798-2034**), has the city's best collection of reference materials and periodicals. It's open to the public Monday to Friday 10am to 7pm, Saturday 10am to 5pm.

Liquor Laws   Under British law, no one under 18 years of age may legally purchase or consume alcohol. Beer and wine are sold by supermarkets, liquor stores (called "bottle shops"), and food shops advertising "off-license" sales. Some supermarkets also sell stronger spirits, at excellent prices. Admission-charging nightclubs are allowed to serve alcohol to patrons until 3am or so. By law, hotel bars may serve drinks after 11pm to registered guests only. See "Business Hours," above, for pub hours.

Lost Property   If you lose something on the bus or tube, wait two days before contacting London Regional Transport, 200 Baker St., NW1 (☎ **0171/486-2496**), open Monday to Friday 9:30am to 2pm. The *Taxi Lost Property Office,* 15 Penton St., N1 (☎ **0171/833-0996**), is open Monday to Friday 9am to 4pm. Lost-property offices are also located in all the major British Rail stations.

   To report a loss or theft, call the operator (☎ **100**) and ask for the police.

Luggage Storage/Lockers   The *Gatwick Airport Left Luggage Office* (☎ **0181/763-2020**) never closes, and charges £3 ($4.65) per item for 24 hours, £15 ($23.25) per week. The *Heathrow Airport Left Luggage Offices* (☎ **0181/759-4321**), at Terminals 1, 3, and 4, are open daily from about 6am to 10:30pm. They charge £3 ($4.65) per item for 24 hours. Luggage lockers are also available at *Victoria* (☎ **0171/928-5151, ext. 27514**), *King's Cross* (☎ **0171/922-9081**), and other major British Rail stations. Lockers cost £3.50 to £5 ($5.42 to $7.75) per day, depending on size.

Mail   Post offices are normally open Monday to Friday 9am to 5pm, Saturday 9am to noon. The *Main Post Office,* St. Martin's Place, Trafalgar Square, WC2 (☎ **0171/930-9580**), is open Monday to Saturday 8am to 8pm. Mailboxes, which are usually round red pillars, are well distributed throughout the city. Airmail letters weighing up to 10 grams cost 41p (65¢), and postcards require a 35p (55¢) stamp to all destinations outside Europe. If you ask for special-issue stamps, you'll probably get something pretty. Budget travelers can get more post for the pound by purchasing aerograms for 36p (55¢) each. The deal is even sweeter at £1.99 ($3.10) per half dozen. For information you can also call **0171/2502888**.

   You can receive mail in London, marked "Poste Restante," and addressed to you, care of the London Chief Post Office, King Edward Street, London EC1A 1AA, England. The office is located near St. Paul's Cathedral and is open Monday to Friday 8:30am to 6:30pm. You will need to show identification to collect your mail. If you have an American Express card, or are carrying traveler's checks issued by that company, you can receive mail care of American Express, 6 Haymarket, London SW1, England.

Maps   See "City Layout," earlier in this chapter.

Money   See "Money" in Chapter 2.

Newspapers/Magazines   The extraordinarily large number of local newspapers in London is generally divided into two categories—broadsheets and tabloids. In general, tabloids like the *Sun* and the *Daily Mirror* sensationalize news more than the larger-format papers. The *Times* is the granddaddy of London's opinionated papers, and features a particularly hefty Sunday edition. The *Guardian* is the city's largest left-of-center paper, with in-depth investigative stories and good reporting. The *Daily Telegraph,* known in some circles as the "Torygraph," leans right politically, and is particularly strong in foreign coverage. The *Independent* offers solid middle-of-the-road reporting; this paper features Britain's best arts section every Sunday.

The weekly listings magazine *Time Out* is indispensable for comprehensive coverage of what's happening in the city.

Photographic Needs   Photo processing in London is more expensive than similar services Stateside. *Dixons,* 88 Oxford St., W1 (☎ **0171/636-8511**), with more than 80 branches in London, is the best source for most photographic needs.

Police   Dial **999** in an emergency from any phone; no money is needed. At other times, dial the operator (☎ **100**) and ask to be connected with the police.

Radio   Recent deregulation is improving London radio, and more and more stations are appearing on the radio dial, but variety is still limited. The dozen or so sanctioned stations—heavy on current pop music, talk, and news—are supplemented by a handful of adventurous "pirate" broadcasters. The legal FM stations include: BBC1 (98.8), featuring a Top 40 format; BBC2 (89.1), a middle-of-the-road music station; BBC3 (between 91.3), Britain's best classical; BBC4 (93.5), talk, humor, and call-in shows; BBC Greater London Radio (94.9), album-oriented rock and talk; Capital FM (95.8) American-format pop rock; Choice (96.9) soul; LBC Crown FM (97.3), news, call-in shows, and updates on city arts happenings; Kiss (100) dance sounds; Classic (100.9) classical ; Jazz FM (102.2), Blues, R&B, big band, and the like; Melody (105.8) middle of the road; Virgin (105.8) and Heart (106.2), both album-oriented rock stations.

Religious Services   It sometimes seems like churches in London are almost as ubiquitous as pubs. Protestant houses of worship are on almost every street in the city, and you are welcome to attend Sunday services in any one of them. The London Tourist Board can provide you with a complete list. For a special treat, think about spending Sunday morning in St. Paul's Cathedral (☎ **0171/248-2705**) or Westminster Abbey (☎ **0171/222-5152**). Services are held at the abbey at 8am, 10am, 11:15am, 3pm, and 6:30pm. Times vary at St. Paul's; call for information.

Westminster Cathedral, Ashley Place, SW1 (☎ **0171/798-9055**), is England's Roman Catholic headquarters, and a worthy sight. Services are held Sunday at 7am, 8am, 9am, 10:30am, noon, 5:30pm, and 7pm.

The *Liberal Jewish Synagogue,* 28 St. John's Wood Rd., NW8 (☎ **0171/286-5181**), holds services Friday at 6:45pm and Saturday at 11am.

The *Buddhist Society,* 58 Eccleston Sq., SW1 (☎ **0171/834-5858**), holds regular lectures and meditations. Call Monday to Friday 2 to 6pm for information.

Restrooms   Even if you don't drink, you'll find London's many pubs handy for their facilities. The most lavish restrooms, however, are found in the lobbies of the major hotels. Lately, automatic toilets—which are automatically sterilized from top to bottom after each use—have appeared on sidewalks throughout the city. They are well lit, have piped-in music, and cost just 20p (30¢).

Safety   Take particular caution when exploring the East End, Brixton, and Notting Hill.

Shoe Repair   Most of the major tube stations have "heel bars" that can make quick repairs. More extensive work can be performed in any of the major department stores (see Chapter 8, "Shopping") or at *Jeeves Snob Shop,* 10 Pont St., SW1 (☎ **0171/ 235-1101**); it's open Monday to Friday 8:30am to 5:30pm, Saturday 8:30am to 5pm.

Taxes   A 17.5% Value-Added Tax (VAT) is usually already figured into the price of most items. For example, hotels and restaurants usually include the VAT in their quoted prices. Occasionally they don't, so note the policy, which is usually on the menu/tariff. Tax has been included in all hotel rates quoted in this book. Foreign tourists can reclaim the VAT for major purchases.

Taxis   See "By Taxi," above in this chapter.

Telephone and Fax   See also "Area Code," above in this section. London has two kinds of pay phones. One accepts coins and the other uses a Phonecard, available from newsagents and green BT phonecard machines in £2, £5, £10, and £20 denominations. The minimum cost of a local call is 10p (15¢) for the first two minutes (during peak hours). You can deposit up to four coins at a time, but telephones don't make change, so unless you are calling long distance, use 10p coins exclusively. Phonecard telephones automatically deduct the price of your call from the card. Cards are especially handy for making long-distance and international calls. Some large hotels and tourist areas have credit-card telephones that accept major credit cards. Lift the handle and follow the instructions on the screen.

To reach the *local operator,* dial **100.** The *international operator* is **155.** *London phone information* (called "directory inquiries") can be reached by dialing **142** and is free of charge.

If you need to communicate by fax and your hotel is not equipped, contact *Chesham Executive Centre,* 150 Regent St., W1 (☎ **0171/439-6288**). They charge £5 ($7.75) per page plus VAT to fax the United States; the center is open Monday to Friday 9am to 6pm, Saturday 10am to noon.

Television   London has only four local TV stations: three BBC channels and one independent commercial channel. Many hotels now offer stations from the European Cable Network. These include Eurosport, a sports channel; Sky News, a 24-hour news channel; and MTV, a clone of the American version.

Time Zone   London's clocks are set on Greenwich Mean Time, five hours ahead of U.S. Eastern Standard Time. Daylight saving time is used in England, though the semiannual changeover occurs on a slightly different schedule from the U.S. To find out the exact time by phone, dial *Timeline* (☎ **123**).

Tipping   Most *restaurants* automatically add a service charge. The restaurant's policy will be written on the menu. When a service charge is not included, a 10% to 15% tip is customary. *Taxi drivers* expect 10% to 15% of the fare. Note that tipping is rare in both pubs and theaters.

Transit Info   The *London Regional Transport (LRT) Travel Information Service* (☎ **0171/222-1234**) offers schedule and fare information for bus, Underground, and British Rail service within Greater London. Open 24 hours.

Water   The water is safe to drink. Designer waters like Perrier are popular at restaurants; specify tap water if that's what you want.

4 Where to Stay

Two things seem constant on the London hotel scene: Hoteliers are still famous for their good-humored hospitality, and the "bed and breakfast" remains one of England's staunchest traditions. Of course, morning menus differ from place to place, but most hotels serve up a full breakfast that usually includes cold cereal, eggs, bacon or sausage, toast, and all the coffee or tea you can drink. It's hearty and just might last you through the day. On the downside, London's budget hotels, in general, are not as nice or as cheap as those on the Continent. Rooms are often, but not always, small and worn. They can be furnished in an old-fashioned, practical manner.

Summer is a seller's market. Hordes of tourists competing for coveted hotel rooms keep rates high and fairly rigid. But there are ebbs in the tide, and if you sense that rooms are going unoccupied, ask for a lower rate. In the off-season, prices fall—sometimes by as much as 30%. Further negotiation could get you even lower rates. Remember that unoccupied hotel rooms don't bring in any money to their owners.

A Note to Americans: Upon hearing an American accent, hoteliers will usually offer their best room at their highest rate. Make it clear that you are a budget traveler and not automatically seeking the highest-priced accommodation. Always ask if they have anything cheaper, and note that many hotels will offer a discount for a stay of five nights or more.

Everyone, especially single travelers, should ask to see their room before renting it. Hoteliers are more likely to offer their nicest rooms to travelers who look before they buy. Single travelers may even get a larger room—say a double, if one is available—this way.

Note: Rates quoted below include Value-Added Tax, and are accurate for the summer of 1996. Expect reductions before and after the season.

ABOUT RESERVATIONS

The demand for budget hotels is so great that most of these hotels, which are often small, have high occupancy rates. In summer, you're well advised to book several months in advance. During the off-season, don't worry about booking in advance unless you're set on one particular hotel, or are arriving very late in the day.

Except where noted, the hotels listed in this chapter accept advance reservations. Rooms are typically held with a nonrefundable deposit (preferably in pounds) equaling the cost of one night's stay. When sending a deposit, ask for a confirmation. You may also wish to follow up your reservation request with a telephone call to the hotel. *And if you call from the United States, remember to drop the initial zero from the London area code: dial 171, not 0171.*

If you arrive in London without a reservation, check availability by phone before setting out to the individual hotels. Most hotels will hold a room for you for an hour or so.

HOTEL-BOOKING SERVICES

If you're having difficulty securing a room, you can always consult one of the city's many hotel-booking agencies.

Victoria Station Hotel Reservation Service (☎ 0171/828-4646) books B&Bs and hotels in all price categories. The company works with many budget-priced properties, but their best rates are for London's fancier rooms. By negotiating with some of the city's best hotels, this service can offer cut-price rooms to same-day arrivals—saving up to 50% during the off-season. There is a £5 ($7.75) booking fee. The reservation service window is open daily from 7am to 11pm, and is located across from the ticket office, by the entrance to platform 9. A second office is located in King's Cross Rail Station (☎ 0171/837-5682), next to the Pullman Lounge, at the head of platform 8.

London Tourist Board Information Centre Hotel-Booking Service (☎ 0171/824-8844) offers similar services at their many city offices. A small booking fee of £5 ($7.75) must be paid, along with a deposit that is applied to the price of the room. Offices and hours: Victoria Station Forecourt, open from Easter through October daily from 8am to 7pm, and the rest of the year Monday through Saturday 9am to 6pm, Sunday 9am to 5pm; Heathrow Airport, open daily 8:30am to 6pm; Liverpool Street Station, open Monday 8:15am to 6pm, Tuesday to Saturday 8:15am to 6pm, and Sun 8:30am to 4:45pm; and Selfridges department store, open Monday through Wednesday and Friday and Saturday 9am to 6pm, Thursday 9am to 8pm.

BED & BREAKFAST ORGANIZATIONS

Uptown Reservations, 50 Christchurch St., Chelsea, London SW3 4AR (☎ 0171/351-3445, fax 0171/351-9383) operates a B&B reservation service. All of the rooms are in private homes and have bath or shower. Many are in elegant residences in such areas as Knightsbridge, Chelsea, and Kensington. The prices range from £55 single and £70 double including continental breakfast.

1 Best Bets for the Frugal Traveler

The **Thanet** (8 Bedford Pl.; ☎ 0171/323-6676), in the heart of Bloomsbury, has to be one of the city's very best values because the rooms are spacious and pleasantly turned out with all-modern facilities.

Right around the corner from the British Museum, the **Morgan** (24 Bloomsbury St.; ☎ 0171/636-3735) is located in a typical terrace house and offers nicely furnished rooms.

St. Margaret's (26 Bedford Pl.; ☎ 0171/636-4277) is another Bloomsbury establishment that has a very English air. Among its most appealing features are the comfortably furnished spacious lounges.

Windermere (142–44 Warwick Way; ☎ 0171/834-5163) offers good, modern rooms in a period building.

Fielding (4 Broad Court, Bow St.; ☎ **0171/836-8305**) is a great base for opera lovers since it's right around the corner from the Royal Opera House, tucked away in a quiet alley. The exterior has great charm with its diamond-pane windows. Inside, rooms are small but furnished with some idiosyncrasy at least.

A little remote, **La Gaffe** (107–11 Heath St.; ☎ **0171/435-4941**) is a characterful establishment in this most appealing of London's villages.

At **Aston's Studios** (39 Rosemary Gardens; ☎ **0171/370-0737**), £41–£58 is great for a long-term stay, and each unit has a compact but complete kitchenette, fully equipped with refrigerator, sink, electric stove, and cooking utensils.

Vicarage Private Hotel (10 Vicarage Gardens; ☎ **0171/229-4030**) has a real Victorian style to it. Large, spacious rooms, soaring ceilings, and a quiet location on a small cul-de-sac make this a perfect London retreat.

Abbey House (11 Vicarage Gate; ☎ **0171/727-2594**) is an elegant porticoed Victorian with gracious original architectural elements that give it a certain style, even though the decor is unremarkable.

The supermodern **High Holborn Residence** (178 High Holborn; ☎ **0171/397-5589**) is in a great location near Covent Garden, where accommodations are in apartments housing four or five persons in single rooms. Each apartment has a kitchen, dining room, and bathroom. Other conveniences include a launderette, TV lounge, and bar.

Rosebery Hall (90 Rosebery Ave.; ☎ **0171/278-3251**) is one of the fanciest university accommodations. It has well-furnished modern single rooms, a nice breakfast room, and a bar.

Among the best features of the **Elizabeth Hotel** (37 Eccleston Sq.; ☎ **0171/828-6812**) is its location on this most elegant square. It's well-run, clean, and serves a fine English breakfast.

Hotel La Place (17 Nottingham Pl.; ☎ **0171/486-2323**) benefits from having a mother/son professional hotel management team. The decor is stylish; meals are available; and the small bar is a pleasant haven.

2   Doubles for Less Than £55 ($85.25)

BAYSWATER/PADDINGTON

Centre Français
61–69 Chepstow Place, London, W2 4TR. ☎ **0171/221-8134.** 200 beds (none with bath). £25 ($38.75) single; £42 ($65.10) twin; £11.70 ($18.13) in dormitory. All rates include continental breakfast. MC, V. Tube: Notting Hill Gate.

Welcoming visitors with a particular interest in French culture, Centre Français is an exceptionally friendly place with the look and feel of a college dormitory. Ample-sized rooms are equipped with a desk and chair. In the corridors, you're just as likely to hear French spoken as English. The center is predominantly occupied by students from ages 16 to 35, but the warden is quick to point out that older visitors are also welcomed—especially teachers. Book rooms at least three weeks in advance. A three-course dinner is available in the hotel restaurant for £6 ($9.30).

From the Notting Hill Gate station, cross the street to Pembridge Gardens. Turn right on Pembridge Square, then left onto Chepstow Place. It's a five-minute walk in all.

Dylan Hotel
14 Devonshire Terrace, London, W2 3DW. ☎ **0171/723-3280.** Fax 0171/402-2443. 18 rms (11 with bath). TV. £30–£38 ($46.50–$58.90) single without bath; £43–£48 ($66.65–$74.40)

double bath, £50–£52 ($77.50–$80.60) double with shower only, £54–£59 ($83.70–$91.45) double with bath. All rates include English breakfast. AE, DC, MC, V. Tube: Paddington.

The proprietors want travelers to think of the Dylan as a "home away from home," and you probably will. Mr. and Mrs. Felfeli live here themselves, and their little touches give budget-oriented guests the comforts of home. Bedrooms have tea- and coffee-making facilities. In the breakfast room, a cup-and-saucer collection is displayed. Soft drinks are available in the guest lounge.

From Paddington Station, follow Craven Road six blocks; Devonshire Terrace is on your right.

Elysee Hotel

25–26 Craven Terrace, London W2 3EL. ☎ **0171/402-7633.** Fax 0171/4024193. 50 rms (all with bath) TV TEL. £32 ($49.60) single; £42 double ($65.10). MC, V. Tube: Lancaster Gate.

The Elysee Hotel is a good value located right on the edge of Hyde Park. It's located in a building with an elevator. Rooms are adequately furnished with typical modern furnishings. All have tea- and coffee-making facilities. There's also a bar where guests can relax and socialize.

Hyde Park House

48 St. Petersburgh Place, London, W2 4LD. ☎ **0171/229-1687.** 15 rms (one with bath). TV. £27 ($41.85) single without bath; £40 ($62) twin without bath. All rates include continental breakfast. No credit cards. Tube: Bayswater.

This family-run B&B offers good, clean, quiet accommodations. In the middle of a block of row houses, it's announced by a small awning. There's a quilt on every bed and a refrigerator in every room. Prices include free use of the kitchen, and you'll receive unlimited attention from the family's friendly small dogs.

From Bayswater Underground, turn left onto Moscow Road and left again at the church.

Lords Hotel

20–22 Leinster Sq., London, W2 4PR. ☎ **0171/229-8877.** Fax 0171/229-8377. 68 rms (52 with shower). A/C TEL. £27 ($41.85) single without shower or toilet, £31 ($48.05) single with shower only, £42 ($65.10) single with shower and toilet; £36 ($55.80) double without shower or toilet, £40 ($62) double with shower only, £56 ($86.80) double with shower and toilet; £50 ($77.50) triple without shower or toilet, £54 ($83.70) triple with shower only, £67 ($103.85) triple with shower and toilet. All rates include continental breakfast. AE, DC, MC, V. Tube: Bayswater or Queensway.

Lords is a well-run budget establishment, offering basic rooms that are both clean and neat. A few rooms have balconies—no extra charge. Most are equipped with televisions. The hotel caters to people of all ages, but the basement bar, which stays open late, attracts a young and lively crowd.

From the Bayswater Underground, turn left onto Moscow Road, then right at the Russian Orthodox Church (Ilchester Gardens); Lords is two blocks up on your left.

St. Charles Hotel

66 Queensborough Terrace, London, W2 3SH. ☎ **0171/221-0022.** 17 rms (all with shower; 4 with shower and toilet). £30 ($46.50) single, £44 ($68.20) double with shower only; £47 ($72.85) double with shower and toilet; £2 ($3.10) surcharge for one-night stays. All rates include English breakfast. No credit cards. Tube: Queensway.

Mr. and Mrs. Wildridge are the St. Charles's caring proprietors, and the interior is beautifully kept. Opulent wood paneling and carefully restored ceilings and moldings suggest a high tariff, but a few of the shower-only rooms are within our budget.

Hotels: Notting Hill Gate to Marylebone

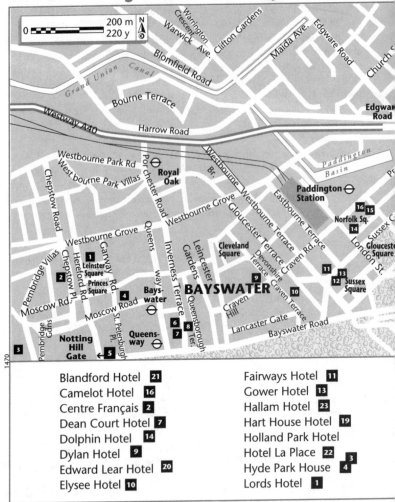

Blandford Hotel **21**
Camelot Hotel **16**
Centre Français **2**
Dean Court Hotel **7**
Dolphin Hotel **14**
Dylan Hotel **9**
Edward Lear Hotel **20**
Elysee Hotel **10**

Fairways Hotel **11**
Gower Hotel **13**
Hallam Hotel **23**
Hart House Hotel **19**
Holland Park Hotel
Hotel La Place **22**
Hyde Park House **4**
Lords Hotel **1**

From the Queensway Underground, turn left onto Bayswater Road and after two blocks take another left onto Queensborough Terrace. The Airbus stop at Queensway is only two blocks from the hotel.

SUSSEX GARDENS

Despite its quiet-sounding name, Sussex Gardens is one of Bayswater's busiest thoroughfares. It starts at the traffic circle south of Paddington Station and runs straight up to Edgware Road. Along both sides of Sussex Gardens, you'll see hardly a house that doesn't announce itself as a hotel. Accommodations are uniformly nondescript, but rates are good. The fierce competition in the off-season means everything's negotiable.

Gower Hotel

129 Sussex Gardens, London, W2 2RX. ☎ **0171/262-2262.** 22 rms (20 with bath). TV TEL. £27 ($41.85) basic single, £35 ($54.25) single with bath; £38 ($58.90) basic double, £53 ($82.15) double with bath. All rates include English breakfast. MC, V. Tube: Paddington.

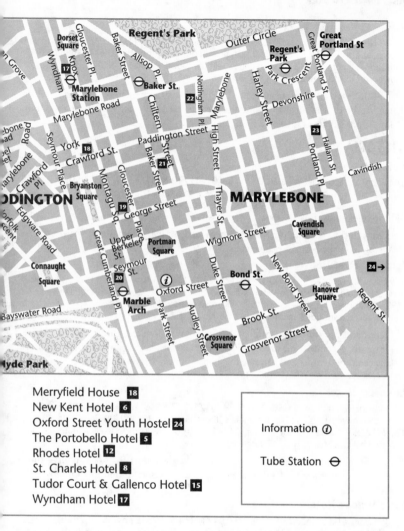

Merryfield House **18**
New Kent Hotel **6**
Oxford Street Youth Hostel **24**
The Portobello Hotel **5**
Rhodes Hotel **12**
St. Charles Hotel **8**
Tudor Court & Gallenco Hotel **15**
Wyndham Hotel **17**

Information ⓘ

Tube Station ⊖

The Gower has only two rooms without bath—both are on the top floor. Although a slant in the roof makes these two small, they're good, clean, and worth the climb. Other rooms have the amenities above plus tea/coffeemakers.

NORFOLK SQUARE

Horseshoe-shaped, Norfolk Square rings a small park just steps south of Paddington Station. It's packed with too many hotels with too few distinguishing marks to mention, but here are two of the best.

Dolphin Hotel

34 Norfolk Sq., London, W2 1RP. ☎ **0171/402-4943.** 30 rms (10 with bath). TV. £33 ($51.15) single without bath; £43 ($66.65) double without bath, £55 ($85.25) double with bath; £53 ($82.15) triple without bath, £63 ($97.65) triple with bath. All rates include buffet breakfast. AE, DC, MC, V. Tube: Paddington.

Refrigerators, coffeemakers, and telephones in some rooms help the Dolphin stand out from its neighboring hotels. Recently redecorated rooms are a good bet.

Tudor Court & Gallenco Hotel

10–12 Norfolk Sq., London, W21RS. ☎ **0171/723-6553.** Fax 0171/723-0727. 33 rms (4 with shower and toilet). TV. £30 ($46.50) single without shower or toilet; £44 ($68.20) single with shower and toilet; £42 ($65.10) double without shower or toilet; £49 ($75.95) double with shower and toilet. All rates include English breakfast. AE, DC, MC, V. Tube: Paddington.

This B&B is owned and managed by outgoing Dave Gupta. Unlike the singles, which tend to be on the small side, doubles are fair-sized. All rooms are neat and clean. Public phones are available on each floor.

VICTORIA

Collin House

104 Ebury St., London, SW1W 9QD. ☎/fax **0171/730-8031.** 13 rms (8 with shower). £38 ($58.90) single without shower; £40 ($62) single with shower and toilet; £54 ($83.70) double without shower; £64 ($99.20) double with shower and toilet. All rates include English breakfast. No credit cards. Tube: Victoria.

Clean, decent accommodations are provided by the Thomases at their terraced Victorian in the heart of Belgravia.

James Cartref House

129 Ebury St., London, SW1W 9DU. ☎ **0171/730-6176.** Fax 0171/730-7338. 11 rms (8 with shower) TV. £40 ($62) single without shower; £54 ($83.70) double without shower; £64 ($99.20) double with shower; £64 ($99.20) triple without shower; £74 ($114.70) triple with shower. All rates include English breakfast. AE, MC, V. Tube: Victoria.

Derek and Sharon James offer warm hospitality to their guests. All rooms are pleasantly decorated and have sinks and teamakers. The proprietors also offer similar accommodations and rates at the James House at 108 Ebury Street, London SW1W 9QD (☎ 0171/730-7338).

Leicester Hotel

18/24 Belgrave Rd., London, SW1V 1QF. ☎ **0171/233-6636.** Fax 0171/932-0538. 60 rms (42 with shower). TV. £26 ($40.30) single without shower; £32 ($49.60) single with shower; £37 ($57.35) double without shower; £42 ($65.10) double with shower. All rates include English breakfast. MC, V. Tube: Victoria.

An excellent value. Decently kept and furnished, the rooms boast bathrooms—tiny, it's true—with showers. Coffeemakers and hair dryers are found in all rooms with showers.

Luna Simone Hotel

47–49 Belgrave Rd., London SW1V 2BB. ☎ **0171/834-5897.** 35 rms (30 with bath). TV TEL. £22 ($34.10) basic single; £36 ($55.80) basic twin; £52 ($80.60) twin with bath. All rates include English breakfast. MC, V. Tube: Victoria.

This family-run hotel is recognizable by the bright orange lettering on the columns out front. A hearty breakfast is served in twin dining rooms, separated into smoking and nonsmoking sections.

The Oak House

29 Hugh St., London, SW1V 1QJ. ☎ **0171/834-7151.** 6 rms (none with bath). TV. £30.50 ($47.30) double/twin; £42 ($65.10) triple. No credit cards. Tube: Victoria.

Between Eccleston and Elizabeth Bridges, this is one of the closest hotels to Victoria Station. From their delightful accents, visitors quickly detect that the proprietors, Mr. and Mrs. Symington, who reside here, are Scottish. Tartan carpeting covers the floors throughout the hotel. There are only six rooms here—all somewhat small—but they're fitted with orthopedic mattresses. No advance reservations are accepted, so when you get to the station, just cross your fingers. Features include built-in hair

Hotels: Westminster & Victoria

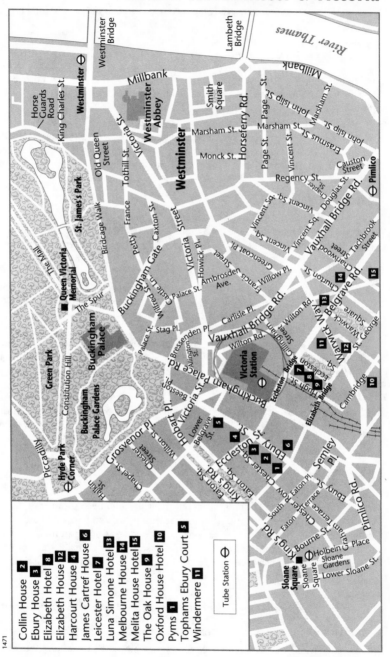

Collin House **2**
Ebury House **3**
Elizabeth Hotel **8**
Elizabeth House **12**
Harcourt House **4**
James Cartref House **6**
Leicester Hotel **7**
Luna Simone Hotel **13**
Melbourne House **14**
Melita House Hotel **15**
The Oak House **9**
Oxford House Hotel **10**
Pyms **1**
Tophams Ebury Court **5**
Windermere **11**

Tube Station ⊖

67

dryers, electric-shaver outlets, tea/coffeemakers, a cutting board, a knife, and even a bottle opener.

Oxford House Hotel

92–94 Cambridge St., London, SW1V 4QG. ☎ **0171/834-6467.** Fax 0171/834-0225. 17 rms (none with bath). £32–£34 ($49.60–$52.70) single; £40–£42 ($62–$65.10) double; £52–£54 ($80.60–$83.70) triple; £70–£74 ($108.50–$114.70) quad. Prices increase by £2 ($3.10) if you stay only one night. All rates include English breakfast. MC, V. Add 5% if you pay by credit card. Tube: Victoria.

Oxford House is owned by interior designer Yanus Kader and his wife, Terri, and their two sons. Done in a floral motif, rooms are pretty and comfortable. The beautiful dining area, with its open kitchen, may remind travelers of home. In the backyard, visit their two friendly rabbits and two cats. South of Belgrave Road near Gloucester Street.

WARWICK WAY

Warwick Way is another hotel-lined street, for the most part, as undesirable as Belgrave Road. Out of dozens of hotels on this thoroughfare, only one is recommendable, and it should be taken only when your other options in the area have been exhausted.

Elizabeth House

118 Warwick Way, London, SW1V ISD. ☎ **0171/630-0741.** 30 rms (9 with bath). £22 ($34.10) single without bath, £26 ($40.30) single with bath; £44 ($66) twin without bath, £47 ($72.85) twin with bath; £10.50–£16 ($16.25–$24.80) per person in multishare room. All rates include continental breakfast. MC, V. Tube: Victoria.

This is a YWCA guest house that accommodates men as well as women. The atmosphere is friendly, the house is clean, and the sparsely furnished rooms will please minimalists. Guests can use two television lounges. Laundry facilities available.

❧ BLOOMSBURY

Bloomsbury's proximity to the West End (and to Soho in particular) has long made it a desirable area for tourists. The University of London and the British Museum are also located here. Although a heavy demand for rooms often brings high prices, some good bargains are still to be found.

GOWER STREET

Some of London's most popular budget hotels are found on Gower Street. These B&Bs are so similar to one another that only their street numbers distinguish them. Stairs are steep, rooms are basic (almost none with bath), and prices are fairly uniform. Special touches and extra-friendly management do set a few apart from the rest. I've listed the ones farthest away from Russell Square first. Incidentally, the best way to reach the Gower Street hotels is from the Goodge Street Underground. Cross into Chenies Street and turn left onto Gower.

Arosfa Hotel

83 Gower St., at Torrington Place, London, WC1E 6HJ. ☎ **0171/636-2115.** 15 rms (2 with bath). TV. £29 ($44.95) basic single; £42 ($65.10) basic double; £54 ($83.70) double with bath; £56 ($86.80) basic triple. All rates include breakfast. No credit cards. Tube: Goodge Street.

This 1950s-style hotel is the least expensive on the block; the rooms are clean and neat—a good value. This was once the home of John Everett Millais, painter and founder of the Pre-Raphaelite Brotherhood. Although the rooms lack amenities, guests have use of a TV lounge with a tea/coffeemaker. Prices here include a breakfast of eggs, toast, and coffee or tea.

Hotels: Bloomsbury to the Strand

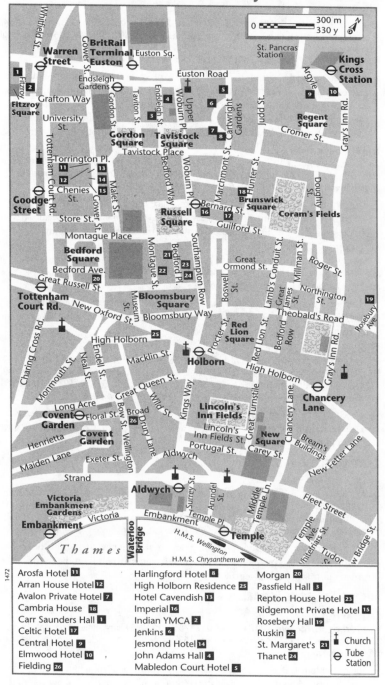

Arosfa Hotel **11**	Harlingford Hotel **8**	Morgan **20**
Arran House Hotel **12**	High Holborn Residence **25**	Passfield Hall **3**
Avalon Private Hotel **7**	Hotel Cavendish **13**	Repton House Hotel **23**
Cambria House **18**	Imperial **16**	Ridgemont Private Hotel **15**
Carr Saunders Hall **1**	Indian YMCA **2**	Rosebery Hall **19**
Celtic Hotel **17**	Jenkins **6**	Ruskin **22**
Central Hotel **9**	Jesmond Hotel **14**	St. Margaret's **21**
Elmwood Hotel **10**	John Adams Hall **4**	Thanet **24**
Fielding **26**	Mabledon Court Hotel **5**	✝ Church ■ Tube Station ⊖

Arran House Hotel

77 Gower St., London, WC1E 6HJ. ☎ **0171/636-2186.** Fax 0171/436-5328. 28 rms (9 with shower and toilet, 4 with shower only). £33 ($51.15) basic single; £42 ($65.10) single with shower and toilet; £47 ($72.85) basic double, £62 ($96.10) with shower and toilet. All rates include English breakfast. MC, V. Tube: Goodge Street.

Arran House stands out on the block because of its exceptionally kind resident proprietor, Maj. W. J. Richards. He has ensured that even guests in the front rooms get a quiet night's sleep by soundproofing all the windows, a modification that I can assure you really works! In addition to laundry and tea- and coffee-making facilities, the hotel offers light meals, prepared by the owner's son, a professional caterer.

Hotel Cavendish

75 Gower St., London, WC1E 6HJ. ☎ **0171/636-9079.** Fax 0171/580-3609. 20 rms (none with bath). £27–£31 ($41.85–$48.05) single; £36–£44 ($55.80–$68.20) twin. All rates include English breakfast. AE, MC, V. Tube: Goodge Street or Russell Square.

This is a nicely furnished, clean, and cozy place run by Mrs. Phillips. Breakfast is served in a pleasant dining room. Guests also have use of a TV lounge and, best of all, the garden in the summer. Rooms have electric kettles for tea-making.

Jesmond Hotel

63 Gower St., London, WC1 6HJ. ☎ **0171/636-3199.** 15 rms (none with bath). TV. £29 ($44.95) single; £40 ($62) double/twin; £18 per person ($27.90) in triple or quad. MC V. All rates include English breakfast. Tube: Goodge Street.

The hotel's proprietors, Mr. and Mrs. Beynon, have been to the United States many times and are acutely aware of American habits and desires. All rooms have tea- and coffee-making facilities.

Ridgemont Private Hotel

65–67 Gower St., London, WC1E 6HJ. ☎ **0171/636-1141.** 34 rms (4 with bath). TV. £29 ($44.95) single without bath; £39 ($60.45) single with bath; £41 ($63.55) double without bath, £52 ($80.60) double with bath; £55 ($82.50) triple without bath, £63.50 ($98.40) triple with bath. All rates include English breakfast. No credit cards. Tube: Goodge Street.

Its friendly atmosphere and warmhearted Welsh proprietors, Royden and Gwen Rees, make the Ridgemont another good choice along Gower Street. Complimentary coffee and tea in the lounge.

Cartwright Gardens

Avalon Private Hotel

46–47 Cartwright Gardens (at Burton Place). London, WC1H 9EL. ☎ **0171/387-2366.** Fax 0171/387-5810. 24 rms (4 with shower). TV. £36 ($55.80) single with shower only, £50 ($77.50) single with shower and toilet; £50 ($77.50) double without shower, £65 ($100.75) double with shower and toilet. AE, JCB, MC, V. Tube: Russell Sq., Euston, or King's Cross.

Rooms have okay 1950s-style furnishings and pink satin coverlets on the beds. The best thing about this place is its location. Guests can play tennis on the courts in the garden out front. Tea/coffeemakers.

Argyle Street & Square

Central Hotel

16–18 Argyle St., London, WC18 HEJ. ☎ **0171/837-9008.** 31 rms (none with bath). TV. £23 ($35.65) single; £33 ($51.15) double; £40 ($62) triple. All rates include English breakfast. MC, V. Tube: King's Cross.

One of the four Caruana brothers, the hotel's proprietors, will happily show you to a simple, reasonably-sized room. If the Central is full, the staff will show you to the Fairway, their other hotel across the street. That one's not quite as nice, so if you can, be choosy.

Elmwood Hotel

19 Argyle Sq., London, WC1H 8AS. ☎ **0171/837-9361.** 11 rms (none with bath). TV. £22 ($34.10) single; £30 ($46.50) double. All rates include English breakfast. No credit cards. Tube: King's Cross.

This nice B&B has been owned by the same resident proprietors for more than 15 years. It's of a higher standard than most in the area. An orange-and-yellow sign out front announces it.

Myrtle Hotel

20 Argyle Sq., King's Cross, London, WC1. ☎ **0171/837-5759.** 14 rms (none with bath). TV. £26 ($40.30) single; £32 ($49.60) double. All rates include English breakfast. No credit cards. Tube: King's Cross.

Accommodations are sparse but clean. Bathless rooms have sinks. With regard to comfort, services, and price, the Myrtle is typical of the area.

HUNTER STREET

On Hunter Street, equidistant from the Russell Square and King's Cross tube stations, I've got one budget choice.

Cambria House

37 Hunter St., London, WC1N 1BJ. ☎ **0171/837-1654.** 37 rms (4 with bath). £25 ($38.75) single without bath; £39 ($60.45) double/twin without bath, £48 ($74.40) double with shower and toilet. Weekly discounts available. All rates include English breakfast. MC, V. Tube: Russell Square.

Located at the corner of Tavistock Place, south of Cartwright Gardens, Cambria House is a Salvation Army establishment in a large, redbrick building. Simple rooms and fairly strict rules come with low rates. No alcohol or smoking is allowed here, and the doors are locked at 11pm; to get around this, obtain a late-night key for a £5 ($3.10) refundable deposit and visit the pub around the corner.

GUILFORD STREET

Celtic Hotel

61–63 Guilford St., London, WC1N 1DD. ☎ **0171/837-6737.** 40 rms (none with bath). £34.50 ($53.50) single, £46.50 ($72.10) double. No credit cards. Tube: Russell Square

This clean and well maintained hotel is run by Mr. and Mrs. Gerra, who make sure that everything is operating smoothly. The rooms are on the small side and contain sinks only. There's a large lounge with TV for guests' use.

CHELSEA/KENSINGTON & S. KENSINGTON

Magnolia Hotel

104–105 Oakley St., London, SW3 5NT. ☎ **0171/352-0187.** 25 rms (9 with shower only, 4 with shower and toilet). TV. £34 ($52.70) single without shower or toilet; £46 ($71.30) double without shower or toilet; £49($75.95) double/twin with shower only, £57 ($88.35) double/twin with shower and toilet; All rates include continental breakfast with boiled eggs. MC, V. Tube: Sloane Square.

Located just off King's Road in Chelsea, this is an extraordinarily well-kept bed-and-breakfast with contemporary decor. The smart, clean rooms have recently been recarpeted and painted by the Magnolia's new Yugoslavian owners.

From the Sloane Square Underground station, take a long walk or any bus going down the King's Road, like nos. 11, 19, or 22.

More House

53 Cromwell Rd., London, SW7. ☎ **0171/584-2040.** 55 rms (none with bath). £24 ($37.20) single; £40 ($62) double; £45 ($69.75) triple. 10% discount for stays of one week or more. All rates include English breakfast. No credit cards. Open July–Aug only. Tube: Gloucester Road.

Hotels: Kensington to Belgravia

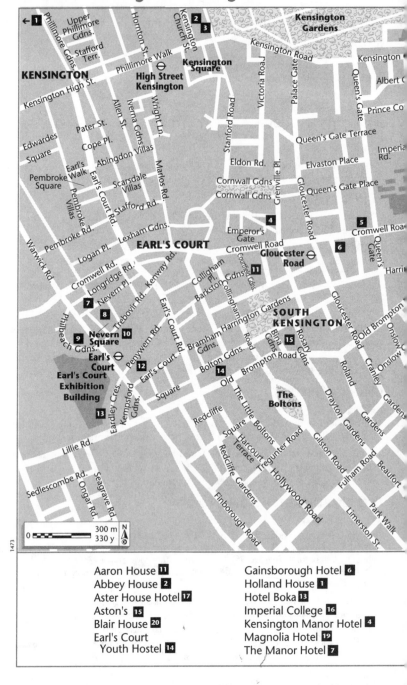

Aaron House **11**
Abbey House **2**
Aster House Hotel **17**
Aston's **15**
Blair House **20**
Earl's Court
  Youth Hostel **14**

Gainsborough Hotel **6**
Holland House **1**
Hotel Boka **13**
Imperial College **16**
Kensington Manor Hotel **4**
Magnolia Hotel **19**
The Manor Hotel **7**

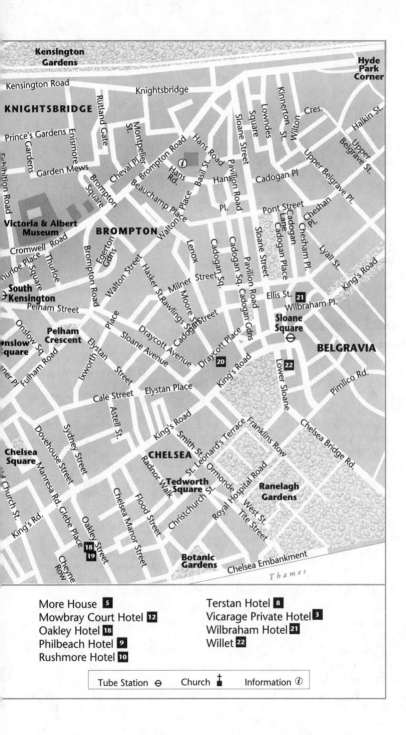

More House **5**
Mowbray Court Hotel **12**
Oakley Hotel **18**
Philbeach Hotel **9**
Rushmore Hotel **10**

Terstan Hotel **8**
Vicarage Private Hotel **3**
Wilbraham Hotel **21**
Willet **22**

Tube Station ⊖   Church ✝   Information ⓘ

This Catholic-run dormitory with an institutional feel is home to foreign students during the school year, but singles and twins are rented to visitors of all faiths from July to August. Well located, the house is across from the Science Museum, and it offers several amenities. There is a refrigerator on every floor, microwave ovens for guests' use, and laundry facilities. Turn right from Gloucester Road Underground and walk five short blocks along Cromwell Road.

Oakley Hotel

73 Oakley St., London, SW3 5HF. ☎ **0171/352-5599.** Fax 0171/727-1190. 13 rms (2 with shower). £30 ($46.50) single; £42 ($65.10) double; £52 ($80.60) double with shower; £56 ($86.80) triple; £15 ($23.25) per person in multishare rooms. All rates include English breakfast. MC, V. Tube: Sloane Square.

Basic rooms and a fun, friendly atmosphere make this economical hotel a welcome oasis in tab-happy Chelsea. The local council of this chic neighborhood forbids a "hotel" sign; a knock on the green door will be answered by a friendly Australian, Brian Millen, the owner and manager. All prices include a full English breakfast and free use of the kitchen.

From the Sloane Square Underground, take a long walk, or the no. 11 or 22 bus down King's Road to Oakley Street. A cab from Victoria will cost about £4; from South Kensington, about £3.

EARL'S COURT

Aaron House

17 Courtfield Gardens, London, SW5 0PD. ☎ **0171/370-3991.** Fax 0171/373-2303. 23 rms (15 with bath). TV. £31 ($48.05) single without bath, £38 ($58.90) single with shower and toilet; £42 ($65.10) double without shower or toilet, £50 ($77.50) double with shower and toilet; £62 ($96.10) triple with shower and toilet. All rates include continental breakfast. MC, V. Tube: Earl's Court.

Announced only by a small, gold sign to the left of the hotel's front door, Aaron House is perhaps the nicest budget hotel in Earl's Court. Beveled glass and beautiful moldings and cornices add a touch of style to this understated B&B. The front rooms, all with baths, are particularly large and overlook a peaceful Victorian square. All rooms have coffee- and tea-making facilities and are pleasantly furnished. Their features might include a carved mantel, a gilded mirror, or hardwood floors.

The hotel is about three blocks east of Earl's Court Underground, on the west side of Courtfield Gardens.

Hotel Boka

33–35 Eardley Crescent, London, SW5 9JT. ☎ **0171/370-1388.** 52 rms (10 with shower). £24 ($37.20) single without shower, £29 ($44.95) single with shower; £33 ($51.15) double without shower, £41 ($63.55) double with shower; £14 ($21.70) per person in multibed room. All rates include continental breakfast. AE, MC, V. Tube: Earl's Court.

Boka's bright, blue-tiled columns stand out in the middle of a pretty Victorian crescent. Inside, you'll find unusually high ceilings and attractive antique bureaus and dressers, some with wood inlay. The staff is friendly.

From Earl's Court Underground, take the Warwick Road exit, cross the street, and turn left to Eardley Crescent.

The Manor Hotel

23 Nevern Place, London, SW5 9NR. ☎ **0171/370-6018.** Fax 0171/244-6610. 27 rms (11 with bath). TV. £25–£30 ($38.75–$46.50) single without bath, £35–£40 ($54.25–$62) single with bath; £35–£40 ($54.25–$62) double without bath, £50–£55 ($77.50–$85.25) double with bath; £42 ($65.10) triple without bath, £46 ($74.40) triple with bath. Discount for stays of one week or more. All rates include continental breakfast. MC, V. Tube: Earl's Court.

Happily devoid of the dark Dickensian feeling that plagues most of the area's hotels, the Manor is light and airy. The carpeting coordinates with the wallpaper. Rooms have hair dryers. The hotel is located two blocks north of the Underground station, at the corner of Templeton Place.

Mowbray Court Hotel

28–32 Penywern Road, Earl's Court, London, SW5 9SU. ☎ **0171/373-8285.** Fax 0171/370-5693. 82 rms (64 with bath). TV TEL. £42 ($65.10) single without bath, £47 ($72.85) single with bath; £52 ($80.60) double without bath, £58 ($89.90) double with shower and toilet; £68 ($105.40) triple with bath. All rates include continental breakfast. AE, DC, MC, V. Tube: Earl's Court.

Hotel managers Tony and Peter make this extra-friendly establishment a particularly good choice for this area. Located a few minutes' walk from Earl's Court Station on a reasonably quiet side street, the hotel offers comfortable rooms. Each has a direct-dial telephone, a safe, and even a trouser press. Same-day laundry/dry cleaning available.

Philbeach Hotel

30 Philbeach Gardens, London, SW5. ☎ **0171/373-1244.** 40 rms (15 with bath). £42 ($65.10) single without bath, £47 ($72.85) single with bath; £52 ($80.60) twin without bath, £62 ($96.10) twin with bath. All rates include continental breakfast. AE, DC, MC, V. Tube: Earl's Court.

Europe's largest and friendliest gay hotel is located in the heart of Earl's Court. Well run and well located, it's the most recommendable budget accommodation of its kind. Behind a typical Victorian town house façade is a clean, cordial establishment. It offers basic rooms, 24-hour reception, and an international clientele. A small, French-style garden restaurant is on the premises.

ELSEWHERE AROUND TOWN

Wyndham Hotel

30 Wyndham St., London, W1H 1DD. ☎ **0171/723-7204.** Fax 0171/723-7204. 11 rms (all with shower). TV. £32 ($49.60) single; £42 ($65.10) twin; £52 ($80.60) triple. All rates include continental breakfast. No credit cards. Tube: Baker Street.

Tucked away on a quiet Marylebone street, this hotel stands apart from others for its value and appearance. All 11 rooms have a shower, TV, and tea/coffeemakers.

From the Baker Street Underground, cross Marylebone Road and turn right. Wyndham Street is the fifth on your left.

3 Doubles for Less Than £65 ($100.75)

BAYSWATER & PADDINGTON

The area usually referred to as Bayswater runs along the northern edge of Hyde Park. Encompassed within its boundaries is Paddington Station, one of the city's major gateways to the north. Bayswater is a densely packed residential district with Indian, Pakistani, and Arab communities. It's also jammed with budget hotels. The area's proximity to the park, good inexpensive restaurants (especially along Queensway and Westbourne Grove), and transportation links to the West End, make Bayswater a desirable location for budget travelers. The Central and District Underground lines run to Bayswater and Paddington Stations, while bus nos. 12, 88, and 289 travel the length of Bayswater Road.

Fairways Hotel

186 Sussex Gardens, London, W2 1TU. ☎ **0171/723-4871.** Fax 0171/723-4871. 17 rms (12 with bath). TV. £40 ($60) single without bath; £56 ($86.80) double without bath, £63 ($97.65) double with bath. All rates include English breakfast. MC, V. Tube: Paddington.

Fairways occupies a John Nash–style Georgian. Done in English florals, rooms have a certain flair and comfortable armchairs good for relaxing. Sinks and tea- and coffee-making facilities. Guest parking available.

Rhodes Hotel

195 Sussex Gardens, London, W2 2RJ. ☎ **0171/262-0537.** Fax 0171/723-4054. 18 rms (16 with bath). TV TEL. £35–£40 ($54.25–$62) single without bath, £45–£55 ($69.75–$85.25) single with bath; £47–£50 ($72.85–$77.50) double without bath, £58.75–£70.50 ($91.10–$109.30) double with bath. Special rates for families of up to five people. All rates include continental breakfast. MC, V. Tube: Paddington.

Most of the rooms here are equipped with private bath, but a few basic singles and doubles are within our budget. Nice additional in-room amenities include fridge, tea- and coffee-making facilities, and hair dryer. If Rhodes Hotel is full, owner Chris Crias will direct you to Argos House, his other hotel around the corner.

VICTORIA

The main—if not the only—reason for staying in this area is the proximity to Victoria Station, as well as pricey Belgravia to the northwest and the more accessible Pimlico to the southeast. As with most areas adjacent to major stations, hundreds of hotels proliferate, but many are not up to standard.

Ebury House

102 Ebury St., London, SW1W 9QD. ☎ **0171/730-1350.** Fax 0171/259-0400. 12 rms (none with bath). £42 ($65.10) single; £57 ($88.35) double. MC, V. Tube: Victoria.

A pleasant bed and breakfast operated by Peter Evans, who offers clean, decent rooms at reasonable prices.

Harcourt House

50 Ebury St., London, SW1W 0LU. ☎ **0171/730-2722.** Fax 0171/730-3998. 10 rms (6 with shower). TV. £45 ($69.75) single without shower, £55 ($77.50) single with shower and toilet; £57 ($88.35) double without shower, £65 ($100.75) double with shower and toilet. All rates include English breakfast. MC, V. Tube: Victoria

Although the rooms have a somewhat drab decor, Harcourt House is a good value. Rooms have sinks, and bathrooms have hair dryers. Breakfast is served from 7:45–8:30am.

Melbourne House

79 Belgrave Rd., London, SW1V 2BG. ☎ **0171/828-3516.** Fax 0171/828-7120. 15 rms (13 with shower). TV TEL. £25–£30 ($38.75–$46.50) single without shower or toilet, £40–£45 ($60–$69.75) single with shower and toilet; £55–£65 ($85.25–$100.75) double with shower and toilet; £70–£80 ($108.50–$124) triple with shower and toilet. All rates include English breakfast. No credit cards. Tube: Victoria.

Melbourne House is far and away the best B&B on Belgrave Road and the only one to earn a listing here. Friendly proprietors John and Manwella completely renovated the hotel in 1992. It offers spacious rooms with television and tea- and coffee-making facilities.

Pyms

118 Ebury St., London, SW1W 9QQ. ☎ **0171/730-4986.** Fax 0171/730-2357. 10 rms (3 with shower). TV. £45–£47 ($69.75–$72.85) single without shower, £60 ($93) single with shower; £60 ($93) double without shower, £75 ($116.25) double with shower. All rates include English breakfast. MC, V. Tube: Victoria.

A hotel in a terraced Victorian. The rooms are clean and furnished with pieces covered in white veneer. TVs are small. Shower facilities are decent. There's also an apartment with sitting area and kitchen available for stays of five days or longer.

🕐 Family-Friendly Hotels

Camelot Hotel *(see p. 85)*   Near Paddington Station, the Camelot is the best choice for families amid the "splurge" hotels. Rooms are on the smallish side, but in London, that's par for the course. Breakfast is all-you-can-eat.

Carr Saunders Hall *(see p. 82)*   Open to travelers only during summer months, the apartments in this student dormitory are one of London's best values. Near the West End, each has a private bath and kitchen. Write for reservations as far in advance as possible.

Oakley Hotel *(see p. 74)*   Families will appreciate the Oakley's friendly atmosphere. A good pick in an otherwise pricey area.

Oxford House Hotel *(see p. 68)*   In addition to comfortable and pretty rooms, rates include breakfast in the beautiful, open kitchen. Children will love Hannibal, a large and friendly rabbit in the backyard.

✪ Windermere
142–44 Warwick Way, at the corner of Alderney Street, London, SW1V 4JE. ☎ **0171/ 834-5163.** Fax 0171/630-8831. 23 rms (19 with bath). TV TEL. £48 ($74.44) single without bath, £59–£76 ($91.45–$117.80) single with bath; £56 ($86.80) double without bath, £73–£83 ($113.15–$128.65) double with bath; £89 triple ($137.95). All rates include English breakfast. AE, MC, V. Tube: Victoria.

An attractive, small hotel with clean and pretty rooms, decked out in pinks and grays and white-painted furniture. Beds have padded headboards. Bathrooms are tiled and also feature hair dryers. The higher-priced, superior rooms are large and accommodate king-size beds. There's a cozy lounge with leatherette furnishings for guests. In the spacious dining room, Windsor-style chairs are set at tables covered with rose-colored cloths. Here breakfast, snacks, and modestly priced evening meals are served.

BLOOMSBURY

A superb area for budget hotels, especially around the British Museum and Russell Square. At Bloomsbury's northern boundary (opposite King's Cross and St. Pancras Stations) are several hotel-packed streets—Birkenhead, Crestfield, Argyle, and Argyle Square; this area is somewhat shabby, though.

Imperial
Russell Square, London, WC1B 5BB. ☎ **0171/278-7871.** Fax 0171/837-4653. 450 rms (all with bath). TV TEL. £65 ($100.75) single; £84 ($130.20) double. MC, V. Tube: Russell Square.

This full-facility hotel is used by lots of group tours. The rooms here are sparkling clean and feature all the modern amenities—plus a kettle for tea-making, pants press, and hair dryer. Occasionally you might find a piece of slashed or torn furniture—not surprising, given the traffic at this hotel. The Atrium Lounge serves afternoon tea and snacks; the Grill is open till 2am.

Jenkins
45 Cartwright Gardens, London, WC1H 9EH. ☎ **0171/387-2067.** Fax 0171/383-3139. 15 rms (6 with bath). TV TEL. £38 ($58.90) single without bath, £50 ($77.50) single with bath; £50 ($77.50) double without bath, £60 ($93) double with bath; £79 ($122.45) triple with shower and toilet. MC, V. Tube: Euston or King's Cross.

Rooms are fairly spacious by London standards and contain comfortable furnishings. Although attractive brass bedside lamps and handsome antique reproductions grace rooms, there's the occasional scratched-up piece, too. Overall this hotel offers superb value; the furnishings, at least in style, are superior to most other budget places. Fridges, coffee/teamakers, and hair dryers are in all rooms. The Jenkins was featured in the PBS Mystery series *Poirot.*

Mabledon Court Hotel

10–11 Mabledon Place, London, WC1H 9BA. ☎ **0171/388-3866.** Fax 0171/387 5686. 32 rms (all with bath). TV TEL. £58 ($89.90) single; £68 ($105.40) double. All rates include English breakfast. AE, MC, V. Tube: Euston or St. Pancras.

A good value. Rooms are modern. Guests have use of a comfortable lounge. Breakfast is served in a pretty dining room. Hair dryers and tea/coffeemakers.

Repton House Hotel

31 Bedford Place, London, WC1B 5JH2. ☎ **0171/436-4922.** Fax 0171/636-7045. 31 rms (all with bath). £49 ($75.95) single; £62 ($96.10) double; £15 ($23.25) per person in a multibed room. All rates include continental breakfast. MC, V. Tube: Russell Square.

The Repton is definitely worth a stay. Clean rather than fancy—that's the owner's philosophy—the sparse rooms are spotless. Tube to Russell Square, turn left, and walk to the square's south side.

Ruskin

23–24 Montague St., Russell Square, London, WC1B 5BH. ☎ **0171/636-7388.** Fax 0171/323-1662. 33 rms (6 with shower). TV TEL. £38 ($58.90) single with shower only; £54 ($83.70) double with shower only, £67 ($103.85) double with shower and toilet. All rates include English breakfast. AE, MC, V. Tube: Russell Square or Tottenham Court Road.

Right across from the British Museum, this hotel has modern accommodations and is exceptionally clean. Sink areas are tiled. Tea kettles and hair dryers are added amenities. The window boxes out front add a welcome touch.

✪ St. Margaret's

26 Bedford Place, London, WC1B 5JL. ☎ **0171/636-4277.** Fax 0171/323-3066. 65 rms (10 with shower). TV TEL. £42.50 ($65.90) single without shower; £53.50 ($82.90) double without shower, £62 ($96.10) double with shower only, £67 ($100.75) double with shower and toilet. All rates include English breakfast. No credit cards. Tube: Russell Square or Holborn.

The rooms are clean and pleasant at this fine hotel. Several comfortable lounges are open to guests. In the attractive breakfast room, the tables are set with fine linens.

✪ Thanet

8 Bedford Place, Russell Square, London, WC1B 5JA. ☎ **0171/636-2869.** Fax 0171/323-6676. 14 rms (8 with bath). TV TEL. £44 ($68.20) single without bath, £55 ($85.25) single with bath; £58 ($89.90) double without bath, £70 ($108.50) double with bath; £83 ($128.65) triple with bath. All rates include English breakfast. AE, JCB, MC, V. Tube: Russell Square.

Ideally situated close to the British Museum, between Russell and Bloomsbury Squares, this is a lovely small hotel in a terraced row of Georgians. The spacious rooms are immaculately kept. The high ceilings give an additional sense of space, and the tall windows open. Bathrooms are tiled. Floral fabrics and wall-to-wall carpeting create a comfortable English atmosphere. Tea/coffeemakers and hair dryers. Breakfast is served in a pretty, dusty rose room; tables are set with rose-colored cloths and have a bud vase of fresh flowers.

CHELSEA & SOUTH KENSINGTON

The expensive residential areas of Chelsea and South Kensington offer few accommodations for budget travelers. With some notable exceptions, the cost of lodging here reflects the location rather than the quality. Chelsea gained fame in the 19th century as London's bohemia, a place for writers and artists. Thomas Carlyle, George Eliot, Oscar Wilde, Henry James—the list of famous former residents is seemingly endless. A room in adjacent South Kensington is only steps away from more than half a dozen top museums and the smart boutiques of Knightsbridge.

In addition to the establishments recommended below, a couple more Chelsea and South Kensington hotels appear in the next price category.

✪ Abbey House

11 Vicarage Gate, London, W8 4AG. ☎ **0171/727-2594**. TV. £38 ($58.90) single; £61($94.55) double. All rates include English breakfast. No credit cards. Tube: High Street Kensington.

Abbey House occupies a lovely, white 1860 Victorian on a quiet garden square. The entryway makes an impression with its black-and-white flooring, potted ferns, and statuary at the top of the staircase landing. The neat and clean rooms are spacious and individually decorated. The hallway bathrooms are decorated in Laura Ashley. The staff is extremely helpful.

✪ Aston's Budget Studios and Aston's Designer Studios and Suites

39 Rosary Gardens, London, SW7 4NQ. ☎ **0171/370-0737**. Fax 0171/835-1419. 60 studios and apartments (38 with bath). A/C TV TEL. Budget studios £41 ($63.55) single; £58 ($89.99) double. Designer studios £100–£110 ($155–$170.50) single or double. AE, MC, V. Tube: Gloucester Rd.

This establishment offers an assortment of studios and suites, which are rented for stays longer than one night. Each unit has a compact but complete kitchenette, concealed behind doors. It's fully equipped with refrigerator, sink, electric stove, and cooking utensils. The budget studio units share bathrooms. The more lavish designer studios and suites boast rich fabrics, marble bathrooms, and lots of electronic equipment, including a telephone answering machine. Laundry and secretarial services available.

✪ Vicarage Private Hotel

10 Vicarage Gardens, London, W8 4AG. ☎ **0171/229-4030**. 18 rms (none with bath). £38 ($58.90) single; £61 ($94.55) double; £73 ($113.15) triple; £84 ($130.20) family room. All rates include English breakfast. Tube: High Street Kensington.

On a quiet residential garden square just off Kensington Church Street, this Victorian house retains many of its original features. A gracious staircase leads to the individually decorated rooms. With typical English floral wallpapers and fabrics, they're a mixture of modern and older pieces. Guests can use the comfortable lounge with a TV. Some rooms have TVs, too.

EARL'S COURT

Although it's located just west of exclusive Chelsea and Knightsbridge, Earl's Court has never achieved the classy status of its neighbors. This convenient neighborhood has dozens of hotels. Many of these accommodations are like hostels, and the quality is often suspect. On Earl's Court Road and Old Brompton Road, the main thoroughfares of the district, are inexpensive restaurants and pubs. Earl's Court Road also has the world's greatest concentration of "bucket shops" (see "Getting There," in Chapter 2, for bucket shop information).

Terstan Hotel

30 Nevern Square, London, SW5 9PE. ☎ **0171/835-1900**. Fax 0171/373-9268. 48 rms (36 with bath). TV TEL. £31 ($48.05) single without bath, £45 ($69.75) single with bath; £56–£60 ($86.80–$93) double with bath; £70 ($108.50) triple. All rates include English breakfast. AE, MC V. Tube: Earl's Court.

On a pleasant square in a modernized Victorian terrace house. The half-paneled rooms here are far from stylish, but they're so well priced they're worth considering. They have desks and coffee-making facilities. Bathrooms are tiled. A lounge, a licensed bar, and a game room are also on the premises. The Terstan is not for non-smokers; the rooms I saw definitely had a smoky odor.

MARYLEBONE

Edward Lear Hotel

28–30 Seymour St., London, W1H 5WD. ☎ **0171/402-5401.** Fax 0171/706-3766. 31 rms (12 with bath), 4 suites. TV TEL. £40.50 ($62.75) single without bath, £76.50 ($118.60) single with bath; £57.50 ($89.15) double without bath, £87.50 ($135.65) double with bath; £77.50 ($120.15) triple without bath, £97.50 ($151.15) triple with bath. All rates include English breakfast. DC, MC, V. Tube: Marble Arch.

A block from Marble Arch, this establishment occupies a pair of brick Georgian houses. In the one on the left once lived Edward Lear, famous for his limericks and illustrations. Rooms are small but comfortable and well kept. They have tea- and coffee-making facilities. The public areas are decorated with floral arrangements.

Merryfield House

42 York St., London, W1H 1FN. ☎ **0171/935-8326.** 7 rms (all with bath). TV. £40 ($62) single; £56 ($86.80) double; £78 ($120.90) triple. Subtract £2 ($3.10) per room per night for stays of more than four nights. All rates include English breakfast. No credit cards. Tube: Baker Street.

Owner Anthony Tyler-Smith and his cat, Mimi, live on the premises; if you're lucky enough to get a room, you'll enjoy their warm hospitality. A hot breakfast is served in your room. Seven compact doubles have private bathrooms, color TVs, hair dryers, and a clock radio. The hotel is two blocks south of Marylebone Road, just off Baker Street; it's three blocks from the Baker Street tube station.

ELSEWHERE AROUND TOWN

Holland Park Hotel

6 Ladbroke Terrace, London, W11 3PG. ☎ **0171/727-5815.** Fax 0171/727-8166. 23 rms (18 with bath). TV TEL. £41 ($63.55) single, £56 ($86.80) single with bath or shower; £56 ($86.80) double without shower, £74 ($114.70) double with bath or shower. All rates include continental breakfast. AE, DC, MC, V. Tube: Notting Hill Gate.

On Ladbroke Square, this hotel offers comfortable and modern rooms that feature wall-to-wall carpeting, pine hutches, armchairs, and coffeemakers. Bathrooms are larger than usual and have faux marble floors. Guests can enjoy the sitting room and, best of all, the garden.

4 Super-Budget Choices

PRIVATE HOSTELS

Many hotels offer dormitory accommodations (often called "multishares") where visitors share a room with other travelers. If you are traveling with a backpack and arrive at one of London's major railroad stations, you may be handed advertisements for these "unofficial" hostels. These are usually legitimate, but investigate the location before you commit. In addition to Hotel Boka in Earl's Court, the Oakley Hotel in Chelsea, and the Repton House Hotel in Bloomsbury, the following hotels offer multishare accommodations and private rooms.

Dean Court Hotel

57 Inverness Terrace, London, W2. ☎ **0171/229-2961.** 16 rms (17 multishare beds; none with bath). £37–£40 ($57.35–$62) double/twin; £52 ($80.60) triple; £17 ($26.35) per person per night, £72 ($111.60) per week in multishare. All rates include continental breakfast. MC, V. Tube: Bayswater or Queensway.

This hotel overlooks a quiet Bayswater street, just 50 yards from bustling Queensway. Recently renovated rooms, a large breakfast, and capable management are all hallmarks of this top budget hotel. There are rarely, if ever, more than four people staying in a multishare; if you require more privacy, ask for one of the well-furnished twins.

New Kent Hotel
55 Inverness Terrace, London, W2. ☎ **0171/229-9982.** Fax 0171/727-1190. 16 rms (19 multishare beds; none with bath). £39–£40 ($60.45–$62) double/twin; £52 ($80.60) triple; £17 ($26.35) per person per night, £75 ($116.25) per week in multishare. All rates include English breakfast. MC, V. Tube: Bayswater or Queensway.

Having the same owner as the adjacent Dean Court (see above), this hotel is just as clean and friendly. It has been recently redecorated.

From Bayswater Underground, cross Queensway onto Inverness Place. Inverness Terrace is just one block away.

YMCA & YWCA HOTELS

Several YMCA and YWCA hotels offer reliable accommodations at great prices, and most include dinner daily. Because they offer low weekly rates, most Ys are filled with longtimers throughout the year. More than a dozen Ys are found in London, but they're not all well located. In a pinch, phone the **National Council of YMCAs** (☎ **0181/520-5599**) for those with available rooms.

Barbican YMCA
2 Fann St., London, EC2Y 8BR. ☎ **0171/628-0697.** Fax 0171/638-2420. 196 rms (none with bath). £24 ($37.20) per person per day without dinner, £135 ($209.25) per person per week with dinner. Reserve at least two months ahead. All rates include English breakfast. MC, V. Tube: Barbican.

This well-located hotel can accommodate almost 250 people, but unfortunately, it usually does. Make reservations as early as possible. Note, too, that it has a fitness center available.

Indian YMCA
41 Fitzroy Sq., London, W1P 6AQ. ☎ **0171/387-0411.** Fax 0171/383-7651. 100 rms (4 with bath). £30 ($46.50) single without bath; £40 ($62) double without bath, £48 ($74.40) double with bath. Discount for stays of one week or more. An additional membership fee of £1 and a reservation fee of 50p will also be charged. All rates include continental breakfast and Indian dinner. No credit cards. Tube: Warren Street.

As its name implies, this hotel caters to Indian citizens. It also prefers long-term stays. Nevertheless, it does maintain a few beds for visitors of other nationalities and shorter stays. There are a TV lounge, reading room, and laundry.

London City YMCA
8 Errol St., London, EC1Y 8SE. ☎ **0171/628-8832.** Fax 0171/628-4080. 110 rms (four with shower). TV. £27 ($41.85) per person per night, £136 ($210.80) per week. All rates include English breakfast and dinner. MC, V. Tube: Barbican or Moorgate.

Located near the Barbican Y, this hotel offers a similar standard of accommodation. All the rooms are singles. This place is generally booked with students during the school term, but you'll probably get a spot here during the summer.

YOUTH HOSTELS

The International Youth Hostel Federation (IYHF) has four establishments in central London, all of which are very crowded during the summer. These are clean but sterile in atmosphere. Breakfast is an additional fee. You can save around £2 by bringing and using your own sheets. MasterCard and Visa are accepted at all London hostels.

You must obtain a membership card to stay at one of IYHF's hostels. Cards are available for £9.30 ($14.40) at the **YHA Shop,** 14 Southampton St., WC2 (☎ **0171/836-8541**). Open hours are Monday, Wednesday, Friday, and Saturday from 9:30am to 6pm; Tuesday 10am to 6pm; Thursday 9:30am to 7pm. MC, V.

Carter Lane Youth Hostel

36 Carter Lane, London, EC4. ☎ **0171/236-4965.** 199 beds. £15 ($23.25) in a dormitory with 15 people; £23 ($35.65) single or twin per person per night for travelers over 21 years (bring your own sheets). MC, V. Tube: St. Paul's.

After more than a year's worth of renovations, Carter Lane reopened in the summer of 1991 with new walls, beds, and appliances. The hostel is situated smack-dab in the heart of the City of London on a small back street near St. Paul's Cathedral. This location is good for sightseeing but poor for restaurants and nightlife, as everything in The City closes when the bankers go home.

From St. Paul's Underground, turn right and make your way toward the front steps of the cathedral; follow Dean's Court, a small street, to the corner of Carter Lane.

Earl's Court Youth Hostel

38 Bolton Gardens, London, SW5. ☎ **0171/373-7083.** Fax 0171/835-2034. 154 beds. £18.10 ($28.05) per person per night for travelers over 18 years, sheets and breakfast included. £16.85 ($26.10). Add £1.55 (2.40) membership fee. MC, V. Tube: Earl's Court.

Located near Holland House, in well-positioned but slightly seedy Earl's Court. It's lively, and stores in the area tend to stay open late.

Exit Earl's Court Underground and turn right. Bolton Gardens is the fifth road on your left.

Holland House

Holland Walk, Holland Park, London, W8 7QU. ☎ **0171/937-0748.** 200 beds. £18 ($27.90) per person per night for travelers over 21. All rates include continental breakfast. MC, V. Tube: Holland Park.

This hostel enjoys the most beautiful setting of all London's IYHF hostels. It's located right in the middle of Kensington's green Holland Park. Kitchen, TV room, quiet room, and laundry facilities.

Oxford Street Youth Hostel

14–18 Noel St., London, W1. ☎ **0171/734-1618.** 87 beds. £18.70 ($29) per person per night including sheets. MC, V. Tube: Oxford Circus.

London's newest "official" hostel is also the smallest and most centrally located. Not surprisingly, it costs more than the others, but if you can get a reservation, it's well worth it.

UNIVERSITY ACCOMMODATIONS

From early July to late September (and sometimes during Christmas and Easter), dozens of centrally located dormitories open their doors to visitors. Almost always, bedrooms are uniformly sparse. Some residence halls only offer singles, and these are relatively inexpensive. Try to reserve months in advance as bookings are often packed solid. Even if you don't have reservations, though, it can't hurt to call and see if they have a cancellation or a "no-show."

Carr Saunders Hall

18–24 Fitzroy St., London, W1P 5AE. ☎ **0171/323-9712.** Fax 0171/580-4718. 148 rms (3 with bath; 78 self-contained apts). £23 ($35.65) per person single or twin; £26 ($40.30) per person with bath. All rates include English breakfast. MC, V. Open early July–late Sept. Tube: Warren Street.

The best thing about this hall is its location, near inexpensive restaurants and the West End. The rooms, mainly singles, are all small and basic. On the plus side, there's a communal kitchen and laundry facilities.

○ High Holborn Residence

178 High Holborn, London, WC1 ☎ **0171/379-5589.** Fax 0171/379-5640. 427 rooms (20 with bath). £26 ($40.30) single; £44–£48 ($68.20–$74.40) double. Open late June to mid-September. Tube: Holborn or Tottenham Court Road.

This very modern residence occupies a great location right across from the Shaftesbury Theatre, close to Covent Garden. Accommodations are predominantly in apartments housing four or five persons in single rooms. Each room has a washbasin, while the apartment has kitchen, dining room, and bathroom. Other facilities include a launderette, TV lounge, and bar.

Imperial College

Room 170, Sherfield Building, Exhibition Road, London, SW7. ☎ **0171/589-5111.** 400 rms (none with bath). £26 ($40.30) single; £42 ($65.10) double. Discounts for stays of more than a week. All rates include continental breakfast. MC, V. Open early July–late Sept. Tube: South Kensington.

This South Kensington dormitory offers luxurious accommodations close to Hyde Park and Royal Albert Hall. The minimum stay in a multishare is one week; if you're going to be in town that long, you won't mind locating here for the duration. Singles are more expensive, though still reasonable by London standards. When phoning, note that the reception is open from 10am to 1pm and again from 2 to 5pm.

John Adams Hall

15–23 Endsleigh St., London, WC1H 0DP. ☎ **0171/387-4086.** Fax 0171/383-0164. 146 rms (none with bath). July–Sept 3, £22.40 ($34.72) single; £39 ($60.45) twin. Mar 10–Apr 25, £22.40 ($34.70) single; £38 ($58.90) twin. All rates include English breakfast. MC, V. Open early July–late Sept, and Easter holiday. Tube: Euston Square.

With high ceilings and large windows, these simple accommodations are typically Georgian.

Passfield Hall

1–7 Endsleigh Place, London, WC1H 0PW. ☎ **0171/387-3584.** Fax 0171/387-0419. 195 beds. Easter, £19.50 ($30.20) per person per night; summer, £20 ($31) single; £36 ($55.80) twin. All rates include English breakfast. MC, V. Open early July–late Sept and Easter. Tube: Euston Square.

A London School of Economics residence, it's somewhat cheaper and much more basic than the nearby John Adams Hall. Passfield occupies ten late-Georgian buildings. The rooms have sinks and central heating. Bed linens and towels are provided. Two TV lounges, launderette, a game room, and free tea and coffee.

○ Rosebery Hall

90 Rosebery Ave., London, EC1R 4TY. ☎ **0171/278-3251.** Fax 0171/278-2086. 298 rms (17 with bath). £21 ($32.55) single; £32–£36 ($49.60–$55.80) double. All rates include English breakfast. No credit cards. Open early July–late Sept and for 5 weeks around Easter. Tube: Angel.

Of the lot of university accommodations, this may be the fanciest. Owned by the London School of Economics, the hall has well-furnished modern single rooms, a nice breakfast room, and a bar. Evening meals are also served but not all the time. It's well located near the Camden Passage antiques market.

CAMPING

Tent City—Hackney

Millfields Road, London, E5 0AR. ☎ **0181/985-7656.** Fax 0181/749-9074. 200 sites. £5 ($7.75) per person. No credit cards. Open June 1 to late Aug. From Victoria Station take bus no. 38 to Clapton Pond, then walk down Millfields Road to Mandeville Street and over the bridge to the site.

Four miles from central London in an East End park, this large, traditional site is set beside a canal. The campground offers toilets, showers, laundry, baggage storage, and a shop.

Tent City
Old Oak Common Lane, London W3 7DP. ☎ **0181/743-5708.** Fax 0181/749-9074. 270 beds, 130 sites. £6.50 ($10.10) per person under the field tent or per space when you bring your own roof. No credit cards. Open June–early Sept. Tube: East Acton. It's a 10-minute walk from East Acton Underground on the Central Line.

A party atmosphere prevails when hundreds of visitors camp here in the summer. Under about a dozen large field tents are dormitory-style accommodations. The main building has showers and toilets. Cooking facilities, low-cost evening meals, laundry facilities.

RVS

The London Tourist Board can supply you with a free brochure listing the many RV sites in and around London that offer full hookup facilities.

5 Long-Term Stays

When staying for a month or more, it's economical to rent an apartment (called a "flat") or a bed-sitting room ("bed-sit"). The latter is usually a room in a house and cooking facilities are provided. Landlords usually require a security deposit, equal to one month's rent. It's returned when you vacate the place in good condition. The magazines *Loot,* the *London Weekly Advertiser,* and *Daltons Weekly* contain good listings; these three publications hit the newsstands on Thursdays. The free, alternative weekly *Capital Gay* also has listings.

Another good place to look for apartments and flat shares is on bulletin boards posted around London. The largest and most famous of these is at 214 Earl's Court Rd., next to the Earl's Court Underground.

Finally, there are a number of accommodation agencies that will do the footwork for you. One is the **Jenny Jones Agency,** 40 S. Molton St., London W1 (☎ 0171/493-4801), which specializes in low-cost rentals of six months or more, and charges no fees to renters. The office is open Monday through Friday from 9:30am to 5:15pm (closing for lunch from 2 to 2:30pm). Contact the London Tourist Board for a list of all of London's rental agencies.

6 Worth a Splurge

Hundreds of hotels fall just slightly beyond our budget, but the following have been selected for their particularly good value.

Aster House Hotel
3 Sumner Place, London, SW7 3EE. ☎ **0171/581-5888.** Fax 0171/584-4925. 12 rms (all with bath). TV TEL. £60 ($93) single; £91–£100 ($141.05–$155) double. All rates include breakfast. AE, MC, V. Tube: South Kensington.

Of a number of small B&Bs on this quiet South Kensington street, Aster House is the most beautiful. The pride with which owners Rachel and Peter Carapiet run this hotel is evident the moment you step into the plushly marbled interior. All rooms have private bath and feature amenities usually found in more expensive hotels—fridge, mini-safe, and ceiling fans. Take special note of the award-winning garden in the rear; it's where the fresh flowers found in each room come from. The enormous breakfast buffet includes the usual eggs and sausages, as well as fresh fruits, cold meats, cheeses, yogurt, and muesli. The morning repast is served in L'Orangerie, the beautiful glass-covered pièce de résistance of this special hotel.

From the South Kensington Station, walk one block down Old Brompton Road to Sumner Place on your left.

Blair House

34 Draycott Pl., London, SW3 2SA. ☎ **0171/581-2323.** Fax 0171/823-7752. 17 rms (all with bath). TV TEL. £73 ($113.15) single; £95 ($147.25) double. Extra bed £19 ($29.45). All rates include continental breakfast; English breakfast £6 ($9.30). AE, DC, MC, V. Tube: Sloane Square.

Although the rooms are pleasant enough here, the prices reflect the Chelsea location; you can secure better values in Bloomsbury. Still, the rooms feature high ceilings and elegant moldings. They're furnished in a modern style with floral fabrics and, occasionally, antique reproductions. All doubles have a coffeemaker, hair dryer, cable TV, and pants press.

Blandford Hotel

80 Chiltern St., London, W1M 1PS. ☎ **0171/486-3103.** Fax 0171/487-2786. 33 rms (all with bath). TV TEL. £64 ($99.20) single; £80 ($124) double; £97 ($150.35) triple. All rates include English breakfast. AE, DC, MC, V. Tube: Baker Street.

Located only a minute or two from the tube, this hotel offers excellent value. Five rooms rented as triples are suitable for families. Coffeemakers and hair dryers are among the amenities.

Camelot Hotel

45 Norfolk Sq., London, W2 1RX. ☎ **0171/262-1980.** Fax 0171/402-3412. 44 rms (30 with bath, 10 with shower only). TV TEL. £40 ($62) single without bath, £48 ($74.40) single with shower only, £56 ($86.80) single with shower and toilet; £76 ($117.80) double with bath; £92 ($142.60) triple with bath; £120 ($186) quad with bath; £150 ($232.50) five-person suite with bath. All rates include English breakfast. DC, MC, V. Tube: Paddington.

Any way you look at it, this artfully decorated hotel is one of the best-value splurges in London. The Camelot combines the look and services of a top hotel with the charm and prices of something more modest. The ultramodern interior is painted in tasteful pastels. The English breakfast has unlimited helpings. In-house movies, tea/coffeemaker. Norfolk Square is in Bayswater, one block south of Paddington Station off London Street.

○ Elizabeth Hotel

37 Eccleston Square, London, SW1V 1PB. ☎ **0171/828-6812.** 38 rms (33 with bath or shower only). £40 ($62) single without bath, £60 ($93) single with bath; £65 ($100.75) double without bath, £75–£85 ($116.25–$131.75) double with bath; £100 ($155) triple. All rates include English breakfast. No credit cards. Tube: Victoria.

On a beautiful quiet square, the Elizabeth is immaculately kept. The well-decorated rooms have pine desks, candlewick-covered beds, and handsome drapes on the floor-to-ceiling windows. The bathrooms are tiled. A comfortable lounge has a TV for guests to use. Winston Churchill lived in a house a few doors down from 1909–13. Guests may also use the gardens and tennis court at the center of the square.

○ Fielding

4 Broad Court, Bow Street, London, WC2B 5QZ. ☎ **0171/836-8305.** Fax 0171/497-0064. 26 rms (all with bath). TV TEL. £65 ($100.75) single; £82 ($127.10) double. Breakfast not included. MC, V. Tube: Covent Garden.

This small hotel is ideal for opera lovers as it's right around the corner from the Royal Opera House. It's tucked away on a pedestrian lane between Bow Street and Long Acre. A vine-covered trellis at the entryway and the mullioned windows give it a country air. Inside, it offers small but clean rooms. They're pleasantly done in English florals. The licensed bar is open to residents only.

Gainsborough Hotel

7–11 Queensberry Place, London SW7 2DL ☎ **0171/957-0000.** Fax 0171/957-0001. 55 rms (all with bath). TV TEL. £55 ($85.25) single; £90 ($139.50) double; from £130 ($201.50) junior suites. All rates include buffet English breakfast. AE, MC, V. Tube: South Kensington.

Each of the rooms here has recently been individually decorated in a very English style with plenty of floral fabrics and handsome reproduction furniture. Nice extra touches include fresh flowers in the rooms as well as a well-lit desk in each room. There's also a restaurant, wine bar, and club on the premises.

Hallam Hotel

12 Hallam St., Portland Place, London, W1N 5LJ. ☎ **0171/580-1166.** Fax 0171/323-4537. 25 rms (all with bath). MINIBAR TV TEL. £67.50 ($104.65) single; £84.50 ($131) double. AE, DC, MC, V. Tube: Oxford Circus.

In a stone-and-brick Victorian, this comfortable and nicely maintained hotel is run by the Baker family. The breakfast room overlooks a pleasant patio. Guests have use of the hotel bar. Tea/coffeemaker, hair dryers.

Harlingford Hotel

61–63 Cartwright Gardens, London, WC1H 9EL. ☎ **0171/387-1551.** Fax 071/387-4616. 44 rms (all with bath). TV TEL. £56 ($86.80) single; £71 ($110.05) double; £79 ($122.45) triple; £87 ($134.85) quad. All rates include English breakfast. MC, V. Tube: Russell Square. Three blocks north of the Russell Square Underground.

The Harlingford is the nicest hotel on this Georgian crescent in Bloomsbury, a convenient location. A hearty breakfast is served in a particularly pleasing, bright dining room on the ground floor. Let the cozy and well-furnished communal lounge entice you away from the TV in your room. Tea/coffeemakers, ice dispenser.

Hart House Hotel

51 Gloucester Place, Portman Square, London, W1H 3PE. ☎ **0171/935-2288.** Fax 0171/9358516. 16 rms (11 with bath). TV TEL. £48 ($74.40) single without bath, £62 ($96.10) single with bath; £72 ($111.60) double without bath, £86 ($133.30) double with bath. All rates include English breakfast. AE, MC, V. Tube: Marble Arch or Baker Street.

Owned and operated by the Bowden family, this hotel is in a historic Georgian row house. Rooms are clean, modern, and comfortable, and equipped with tea/coffeemakers. Breakfast is served in an attractive room furnished with polished wood tables and Windsor chairs. A very convenient location.

✪ Hotel La Place

17 Nottingham Place, London, W1M 3FF. ☎ **0171/486-2323.** Fax 0171/486-4335. 24 rms, 4 suites (all with bath). MINIBAR TV TEL. From £74 ($114.70) single; from £84 ($130.20) double; from £115 ($178.25) family suite. All rates include English breakfast. DC, MC, V. Parking £8. Tube: Baker Street.

In a redbrick Victorian, this hotel offers clean and traditionally furnished rooms. The proprietors are fully qualified hotel professionals. On the premises are a wine bar, which is open 24 hours, and a restaurant. It's popular, so book well in advance. Porter service, elevator, tea/coffeemakers, hair dryers, pants press.

Kensington Manor Hotel

8 Emperor's Gate, London, SW7 4HH. ☎ **0171/370-7516.** Fax 0171/373-3163. 15 rms, 1 suite (all with bath). MINIBAR TV TEL. £61 ($94.55) single; £82 ($127.10) double. All rates include English breakfast. AE, DC, MC, V. Tube: Gloucester Road.

Located in a quiet cul-de-sac, the Kensington Manor offers laundry/valet and room service, unusual for a hotel of its size. The rooms are individually decorated and named after counties of England. Breakfast is buffet-style. Hair dryer, tea/coffeemaker.

✪ La Gaffe

107–111 Heath St., Hampstead, London, NW3 6SS. ☎ **0171/435-4941.** Fax 0171/794-7592. 31 rms (all with bath). TV TEL. £47 ($72.85) single; £75 ($116.25) double. All rates include continental breakfast. AE, MC, V. Tube: Hampstead.

Dating from 1734, this comfortable, informal inn was a shepherd's cottage. The rooms, all nonsmoking, are attractively decorated with pretty furnishings. Each also has a hair dryer and tea- and coffee-making facilities. Several rooms have four-posters and one even has a Jacuzzi, but these are out of our price range at £100 ($155). Windows are double-glazed. On the ground floor, there's a res-taurant and wine bar. A great value only minutes from the Hampstead tube station.

✪ Morgan

24 Bloomsbury St., London, WC1B 3QJ. ☎ **0171/636-3735.** 15 rms (all with bath). TV TEL. £48 ($74.40) single; £72 ($111.60) double. All rates include English breakfast. No credit cards. Tube: Tottenham Court Road.

An excellent value. The beds are covered with pretty floral spreads; the walls are edged with decorative borders. In an oak-paneled room, breakfast is served at comfortable wooden booths. Glass-door showers, hair dryers.

The Portobello Hotel

22 Stanley Gardens, London, W11 2NG. ☎ **0171/727-2777.** Fax 0171-792-9641. 22 rms (all with bath). TV TEL. £85 ($131.75) cabin; £95 ($147.25) single; from £135 ($209) double. AE, DC, MC, V. All rates include continental breakfast. Tube: Notting Hill Gate.

An extraordinarily elegant Victorian, conveniently located near the Portobello Market. The rooms vary from compact cabins to luxurious suites with ornately carved four-posters and antiques. Adding to the beauty and atmosphere is a garden out back. Guests have access to a nearby health club with a pool and Nautilus equipment. Laundry/valet, 24-hour restaurant, and bar.

Rushmore Hotel

11 Trebovir Rd., London, SW5 9LS. ☎ **0171/370-3839.** Fax 0171/370-0274. 22 rms (all with bath). TV TEL. £70 ($108.50) single; £80 ($124) double; £90 ($139.50) triple. All rates include continental breakfast. MC, V. Tube: Earl's Court.

In a Victorian terrace house with eclectic furnishings, the individually decorated rooms have the lofty proportions of the period. You'll find a brass bed in one, modern beds with fabric headboards in another, and country pine in a third. Tea/coffeemakers.

Tophams Ebury Court

28 Ebury St., London, SW1W 0LU. ☎ **0171/730-8147.** Fax 0171/823-5966. 42 rms (23 with bath). TV TEL. £75–£80 ($116.25–$124) single, £105 ($162.75) single with bath; £100 ($155) double, £120 ($186) double with bath. All rates include English breakfast. AE, DC, MC, V. Tube: Victoria.

A quintessential English hotel that's very traditional in tone. All the rooms are individually decorated with fine fabrics and comfortable furnishings. Some have four-poster canopy beds. Room 9 is very private; it's tucked away in the back and has pretty pink walls and a dramatic fabric treatment above the bed. The lounges are extremely comfortable and are furnished with chintz and English antiques. Guests are given honorary membership in Tophams Club, where they can enjoy drinks in the bar. The restaurant specializes in traditional English food. Laundry/valet, babysitting, 24-hour porter.

Wilbraham Hotel

1–5 Wilbraham Place, off Sloane St., London, SW1 9AE. ☎ **0171/730-8296.** Fax 0171/730-6815. 53 rms (40 with bath), 5 suites. TEL. £41 ($63.55) single without bath, £56 ($86.80) single with bath; £68 ($105.40) double with bath; £74–£80 ($114.70–$124) twins with bath. No credit cards. Parking £19 ($29.45). Tube: Sloane Square.

A very British hotel. Rooms are traditionally decorated. On the premises, an old-fashioned bar and buttery has 24-hour room service. Televisions are available on request.

Willett

32 Sloane Gardens, Sloane Square, London, SW1 8DJ. ☎ **0171/824-8415.** Fax 0171/730-4830. 19 rms (all with bath). TV TEL. £74 ($114.70) single; £96–£102 ($148.80–$158.10) double. All rates include English breakfast. AE, DC, MC, V. Tube: Sloane Square.

A mansard roof and bay windows give character to this well-restored Victorian London town house hotel, complete with its own garden. Rooms have been recently renovated; some are lavishly decorated with tented fabric treatments above the beds. Complimentary newspapers are provided. A hospitality tray comes with biscuits and coffee or tea. Some of the larger doubles have refrigerators. Hair dryers.

Where To Eat

An 18th-century visitor to London dismissed English cuisine, saying that there were 40 religions in England but only one sauce. If he were to return today, he might still argue that the national cuisine still suffers from this lack, but he would celebrate the variety (and value) of the cuisines that are now offered by London's many international communities. At last they and their chefs have given the city tasty, exciting food and stirred the Brits into doing the same.

1 Best Bets for the Frugal Traveler

- **Cafe Bruno** (63 Frith St.; ☎ **0171/734-4545**): A renowned chef turns out innovative, affordable French cuisine in an attractive dining room in Soho.
- **Café in the Crypt** (at St. Martin-in-the-Fields; ☎ **0171/ 839-4342**): An atmospheric cafeteria in the church's brick-vaulted crypt. Sandwiches and hot meals.
- **Wagamama** (4 Stretham St., off Coptic Street; ☎ **0171/ 323-9223**): Health-conscious food and a stylish noodle bar. Not for romance, though.
- **The Greenhouse Basement** (16 Chenies St.; ☎ **0171/ 637-8038**): A candlelit basement in Bloomsbury with fine vegetarian cuisine.
- **The Eagle** (159 Farringdon Rd.; ☎ **0171/827-1353**): A new-wave pub with Mediterranean cuisine.
- **The French House** (49 Dean St.; ☎ **0171/437-2477**): Classic French food upstairs at a popular Gallic pub.
- **De Hems** (11 Macclesfield St.; ☎ **0171/437-24940**): Great Dutch food in a friendly Dutch pub.
- **Gopal's** (12 Bateman St.; ☎ **0171/434-2477**): Distinctive Indian food in Soho.
- **Plummers** (33 King St.; ☎ **0171/240-2534**): A great three-course meal for only £14.70. The casseroles are extraordinary.
- **Pollo** (20 Old Compton St.; ☎ **0171/734-5917**): Everyone comes to this Soho spot for the pasta, though the restaurant's name and menu suggest its specialty is chicken.
- **Sydney Street Café** (Chelsea Farmer's Market, 125 Sydney St.; ☎ **0171/352-5600**): Wonderful for a light meal in summer outdoors.

- **The Rock & Sole Plaice** (47 Endell St.; ☎ 0171/836-3785): Not much of a decor at this Covent Garden shop, but great batter on the fish and good chips to accompany it.
- **Le Shop** (329 Kings Rd.; ☎ **0171/352-3891**): Crepes galore, both savory and sweet.
- **Pizza Express** (30 Coptic St.; ☎ **0171/636-3232**): A sophisticated pizza parlor. Their crust is just right, and multiple toppings are offered. Jazz, played some nights, is a bonus.
- **Café Delancey** (3 Delancey St.; ☎ **0171/387-1985**): Love their rosti at this Camden brasserie.

DINING NOTES

Many restaurants automatically add a 12.5%–15% service charge to the bill, so look for this and avoid double tipping. Tax is always included in the prices.

At London's finer restaurants—only a few of these more upscale restaurants are listed in this budget guide—reservations are accepted; these are essential on weekends and recommended throughout the week at fashionable spots.

2 London's Bill of Fare

Gone is the sodden cabbage and the gray meat that used to be on every English dinner plate. London finally has thrilling international cuisine prepared by chefs from all over the world. Challenged by foreigners, the English have responded by improving and reinterpreting their own food. Suffice to say that the late humorist George Mikes's comment that "the Continentals have good food; the English have good table manners" is no longer deserved. Even Michelin agrees and has awarded some of its coveted stars to a handful of English restaurants.

Meals & Dining Customs Mealtimes in England are much the same as in the United States. England is still famous for its huge breakfast—bacon, eggs, grilled tomato, and fried bread. Toast will be served cold in toast racks—another strange British habit that persists at finer dining establishments. Other traditional breakfast dishes are kippers or smoked herring. The finest kippers come from the Isle of Man, Whitby, and Loch Fyne in Scotland. The herrings are split open, placed over oak chips, and smoked slowly to produce a nice pale-brown smoked fish. Most hotel rates include breakfast, which is usually served from about 7 to 9am (later on weekends).

Lunch, usually eaten between noon and 2pm, is often taken at the pub or consists of a sandwich on the run. Pub fare may include bangers and mash, and a variety of other hot dishes like curry or lasagne. Cornish pasties—a pastry envelope filled with seasoned chopped potatoes, carrots, and onions—was traditionally taken down the mines or to fisheries by Cornishmen. The Scotch egg, another pub dish, is a hard-boiled egg surrounded by breaded sausage meat. A pub favorite, the ploughman's, is a plate of cheese, bread, and pickles.

Afternoon tea, still enjoyed by many, may be limited to a simple cup of tea, or tea with biscuits or cakes. A more formal affair may start with tiny delicate, crustless cucumber or watercress sandwiches, followed by scones or crumpets with jam and possibly cream, and finished with a selection of cakes and pastries, all accompanied by a properly brewed pot of tea. Class distinctions even exist here: Whether you put your milk in the cup before or after the tea will indicate your status in the world.

Dinner is served anytime between 5:30 and 11pm; unlike the majority of Continentals, Britons dine early—usually by 8pm. Supper is traditionally a late-night meal, usually eaten after the theater.

British Cuisine   You don't have to travel around England to experience regional English dishes—you can find them all in restaurants throughout London. On any pub menu, you're likely to encounter such dishes as shepherd's pie, a deep dish of chopped cooked beef mixed with onions and seasoning, covered with a layer of mashed potatoes and served hot. You might also find Lancashire hot pot, a stew of mutton, potatoes, onions, and carrots; it's the English equivalent of a *pot au feu.*

Among appetizers the most typical are potted shrimp (small buttered shrimp preserved in a jar); prawn cocktail; and smoked salmon, served with lemon and brown bread. You might also be served pâté or fish pie, which is a very light fish pâté. If you're an oyster lover, try some of the famous Colchester variety. Most menus will also feature a variety of soups including cock-a-leekie (chicken soup flavored with leeks, actually Scottish in provenance); a game soup, like turtle that has been flavored with sherry; or any number of others.

The most traditional main course is roast beef and Yorkshire pudding—the pudding is made with a flour base and cooked under the joint to absorb the fat flavor from the meat. The beef might be a large rolled sirloin, which was named by James I (not Henry VIII, as some claim) when he was a guest at Houghton Tower, Lancashire. "Arise Sir Loin," he cried as he knighted the joint with his dagger, so the story goes. Another dish that makes similar use of a flour-based batter is toad-in-the-hole, in which sausages are cooked. Game is also a staple on English tables, especially pheasant and grouse.

On any menu, you'll find fresh seafood—cod, haddock, herring, plaice, or that aristocrat of flat fish, Dover sole, delicious served on the bone. Cod and haddock are the most popular for traditional fish and chips. Chips, of course, are fried potatoes, or thick french fries. The true Briton covers them with salt and vinegar.

The East End of London has quite a few interesting old dishes, among them tripe and onions. East Enders can still be seen on Sunday at the jellied eel stall by Petticoat Lane, devouring their share of eel or cockles, mussels, whelks, and winkles—all small shellfish or snails eaten with a touch of vinegar. Eel-pie and mash shops can still be found in London. These purvey what is really a minced beef pie topped with flaky pastry and served with mashed potatoes and a portion of jellied eel.

The British call desserts "sweets" or "pudding." Topping the list is trifle, which consists of sponge cake soaked in sherry or brandy, coated with fruit or jam, and topped with a cream custard. A "fool," such as "gooseberry fool," is a light cream dessert whipped up from seasonal fruits. Other old favorites are bread-and-butter pudding and the traditional British plum pudding. Served at Christmas, plum pudding is suet and dried fruit and other ingredients, all steamed together and enriched with brandy or a similar liquor. A variation of this is a richly sweet treacle pudding.

Cheese is traditionally served after dessert as a savory. The best-known regional cheese is Cheddar. (One of the best places to view and taste England's regional cheeses is Neal's Yard Dairy in Neal's Yard; they have a number of extra-special goat cheeses.) County cheeses include Cheshire, Leicester, Double Gloucester, and many more. Caerphilly, a mild, crumbly cheese, comes from Wales. Stilton, the king of British cheeses, is a blue-veined cheese, often enriched with port; it comes from Leicestershire, Derbyshire, and Nottinghamshire.

From Tea to Beer to Claret   The quintessential British drink is tea, of course. The British have been known to use a cup of tea to assuage any and all problems. Tea is served and brewed in a pot, properly warmed. Afternoon tea is still one of the great British rituals.

Beer is an Englishman's solace. Primarily, there's lager and bitter. Lager is what Americans are used to, light, slightly carbonated, and served cold. Most of the Brits prefer bitter, which is higher in alcohol, more flavorful, less carbonated, and usually served at room temperature.

In recent years, the English started a campaign for real ale to protest the centralization and standardization of beers by the large breweries. Many pubs now offer these "real" ales, distinguishable at the bar by hand-pumps that must be "pulled" by the barkeep. Real ales are natural "live" beers, allowed to ferment in the cask.

Cocktails are not mixed quite in the same way as they are in America, but simple drinks like whisky and soda and gin and tonic are common. In summer, a great thirst quencher—although it sounds awful—is the shandy, which is half lager and half lemonade or ginger beer. A lager and lime is 90% lager and 10% or less Rose's lime juice. Other unique British combinations include the Black Velvet—Irish, in this case—made of Guinness and champagne. A rum and black is dark rum with black currant juice added. A drink associated with special summer occasions is a Pimms cup, which consists of Pimms mixed with lemon or other ingredients. Cider is also served. Then, there's something called "scrumpy," extraordinarily powerful stuff, produced in the West Country.

The English have long had a reputation for being great wine connoisseurs, primarily because they controlled the Bordeaux wine region for so many centuries. Then claret was their wine of choice, but today wines from all over the world are available. Port is still passed around at traditional dinners. The English do make their own wines, but these are the fruity variety, made from such ingredients as elderberry.

Soft drinks, of course, are also available. If you order water in a restaurant, specify whether you want tap or bottled; if you want bottled water, say whether you want it with or without carbonation.

3 Restaurants by Cuisine

AFRICAN/CARIBBEAN

Calabash (Covent Garden & the Strand)
Cottons Rhum Shop (Camden)

AFTERNOON TEA

Brown's Hotel (Mayfair)
Fortnum & Mason (Piccadilly)
Ritz Hotel (Mayfair)

AMERICAN

Big Easy (Chelsea)
Ed's Easy Diner (A chain throughout London)
The Exchange Bar Diner (The Strand)
Hank's Bar & Grill (Chelsea)
Texas Lone Star Saloon (Paddington & Bayswater)

BRASSERIE

Café Delancey (Camden)
Tuttons (Covent Garden & the Strand)

CHINESE

Chuen Cheng Ku (Soho)
Dragon Inn (Soho)
Fung Shing (Soho)
Happy Wok (Covent Garden & the Strand)
Harbour City (Soho)
Ming (Soho)
Wong Kei (Soho)
Young Cheng (Soho)

CONTINENTAL

Gaby's Continental Bar (Soho)
Palms (Covent Garden)
Pelican (Covent Garden & the Strand)

CREPES

L'Ecluse (Camden Town)
My Old Dutch Pancakes (Chelsea & throughout London)

DESSERT

Maison Bertaux (Soho)
Patisserie Valerie (Soho)

ENGLISH

Andrew Edmunds Wine Bar & Restaurant (Soho)
The Café (Paddington & Bayswater)
Café in the Crypt (Covent Garden & the Strand)
The English House (Chelsea)
Ferrari's (the City)
French House (Soho)
The Green Café (Victoria)
Minories Restaurant (the City)
Piccolo (the City)
Plummers (the Strand)
Porters English Restaurant (Covent Garden & the Strand)
The Star Café (Soho)
Steph's (Soho)
Stockpot (Soho & throughout London)

FISH & CHIPS

Johnnie's Fish Bar (Chelsea)
North Sea Fish Bar (Bloomsbury)
The Rock and Sole Plaice (Covent Garden & the Strand)

FRENCH

Brasserie du Coin (Bloomsbury/Euston)
Cafe Bruno (Soho)
Chez Marc (Camden)
L'Escargot (Soho)
Le Metro (Knightsbridge)
Pelican (Covent Garden)
Pitcher & Piano (Soho)
Pret à Manger (Leicester Square & throughout London)
Le Shop (Chelsea)
Thierry's (Chelsea)

GREEK

Daphne (Camden)
Jimmy's (Soho)
Kalamaras (Bayswater)
Konaki (Bloomsbury/Euston)
Lemonia (Camden)
Nontas (Camden Town)

INDIAN

Aladin (Aldgate East)
Anwar's (Bloomsbury)

Clifton Restaurant (Aldgate East)
Gopal's (Soho)
Grand Indian (Covent Garden & the Strand)
Khan's (Paddington & Bayswater)
Red Fort (Soho)
Royals (Covent Garden & the Strand)
Salwa (Paddington & Bayswater)

INDONESIAN

Batavia (Soho)

INTERNATIONAL

Camden Brasserie/Underground Café (Camden)
Dell Ugo (Soho)

ITALIAN

Amalfi (Soho)
Arts Theatre Café (Covent Garden)
La Bersagliera (Chelsea)
Bertorellis (Covent Garden & the Strand)
Cosmoba (Bloomsbury)
Pollo (Soho)
Signor Zilli (Soho)
Trattoria Cappucetto (Soho)

JAPANESE

Wagamama (Bloomsbury/Euston)

LEBANESE

Byblos (Kensington)

LIGHT FARE

Bar Italia (Soho)
Cafe Boheme (Soho)
Café San Martino (Covent Garden & the Strand)
Café Valerie (Covent Garden & the Strand)
Chelsea Kitchen (Chelsea)
Cyberia Cyber Cafe (Soho)
Diana's Diner (Covent Garden & the Strand)
Farmer Brown's (Covent Garden & the Strand)
Kettners (Soho)
Mille Feuille (Covent Garden & the Strand)

Neal's Yard Beach Café (Covent
    Garden & the Strand)
October Gallery Café (Bloomsbury)
Patisserie Valerie (Soho)
Sydney Street Café (Chelsea)
Wooley's Health Foods
    (Bloomsbury)
Zoe (Oxford Street/Great Portland
    Street)

MALAYSIAN

Nusa Dua (Soho)
Rasa Sayang Restaurant (throughout
    London)

MEDITERRANEAN

The Eagle (Clerkenwell)

MEXICAN

The Exchange Bar Diner (the Strand)

NEPALESE

Great Nepalese (Bloomsbury/Euston)

PIZZA

Kettners (Soho)
Pizza Express (Holborn & throughout
    London)

POLISH

Daquise (South Kensington)

PORTUGUESE

O Fado (Brompton)

PUBS

The Australian (Chelsea)
The Black Friar (the City)
The Eagle (Clerkenwell)
De Hems (Soho's Chinatown)
The Lamb and Flag (Covent
    Garden)
The Sun (Bloomsbury)

TAPAS

Meson Dona Ana (Notting Hill)

THAI

Bahn Thai (Soho)
Sri Siam (Soho)

VEGETARIAN

Cranks (a chain throughout London)
Food for Thought (Covent Garden
    & the Strand)
The Greenhouse Basement
    (Bloomsbury)
The Place Below at St. Mary Le Bow
    (the City)

VIETNAMESE

Saigon (Soho)
Vietnamese (Soho)

---

4 Meals for Less Than £7.50 ($11.60)

IN & AROUND SOHO

Batavia

Frith Street, between Old Compton and Romilly. ☎ **0171/439-1835**. £3.95–£6.95 ($6.10–$10.75). No credit cards. Daily noon–3pm, 6pm–midnight. Tube: Leicester Square. INDONESIAN.

Batavia is the old name given to Indonesia, and traditional cuisine from those archipelago islands of Borneo, Java, and Sumatra is what you'll find here, including the hot sambals, like beef in sambal sauce. Other dishes include king prawn curry, fish cutlets in green chili, and chicken in coconut gravy—all palate-tingling dishes.

Chuen Cheng Ku

17 Wardour St., W1. ☎ **0171/437-1398**. £4.50–£8.40 ($7–$13). AE, DC, MC, V. Daily 11am–11:45pm; dumplings served until 5:45pm. Tube: Leicester Square. CHINESE.

This huge restaurant serves 21 kinds of steamed, fried, or boiled dim sum (dumplings). Favorites include steamed pork buns and shrimp dumplings, both £1.75 ($2.70). It takes a few servings here to satisfy the appetite, but it can be done for about £6.50 ($10.05).

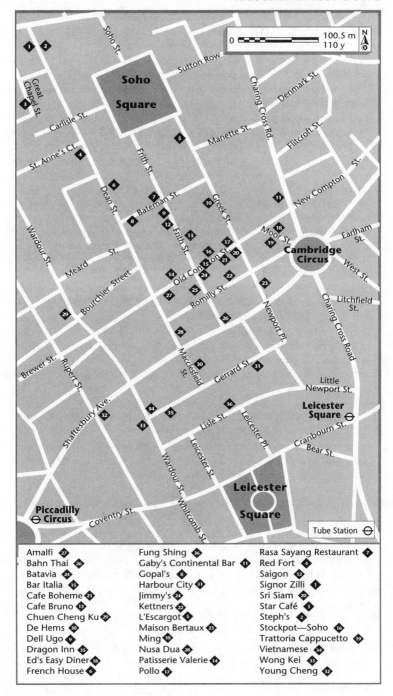

Restaurants: Soho

0 ━━━━━━ 100.5 m
        110 y

N

Soho St.

Sutton Row

Soho Square

Great Chapel St.

Charing Cross Rd.

Denmark St.

Carlisle St.

Manette St.

Flitcroft St.

St. Anne's Ct.

Frith St.

St.

Dean St.

Bateman St.

Greek St.

New Compton

Wardour St.

Meard   St.

Bourchier Street

Frith St.

Old Compton St.

Moor St.

Earlham St.

Cambridge Circus

West St.

Romilly St.

Newport Pl.

Litchfield St.

Brewer St.

Rupert St.

Shaftesbury Ave.

Macclesfield St.

Gerrard St.

Charing Cross Road

Little Newport St.

Leicester Square

Lisle St.

Leicester Pl.

Cranbourn St.

Bear St.

Wardour St.

Whitcomb St.

Leicester St.

Leicester Square

Piccadilly Circus

Coventry St.

Tube Station ⊖

Amalfi ㉗	Fung Shing ㊱	Rasa Sayang Restaurant ❼
Bahn Thai ㉖	Gaby's Continental Bar ⓫	Red Fort ❹
Batavia ㉔	Gopal's ❽	Saigon ⑫
Bar Italia ⑮	Harbour City ㉛	Signor Zilli ❶
Cafe Boheme ㉑	Jimmy's ㉔	Sri Siam ⑳
Cafe Bruno ⑬	Kettners ㉒	Star Café ❸
Chuen Cheng Ku㉙	L'Escargot ❺	Steph's ❾
De Hems ㉚	Maison Bertaux ㉓	Stockpot—Soho ⑯
Dell Ugo ❾	Ming ❿	Trattoria Cappucetto ⑲
Dragon Inn ㉟	Nusa Dua ㉘	Vietnamese ㉞
Ed's Easy Diner ⑱	Patisserie Valerie ⑭	Wong Kei ㉝
French House ❻	Pollo ⑰	Young Cheng ㉜

Dragon Inn
12 Gerrard St., W1. ☎ **0171/494-0870.** Main courses £5.80–£10 ($9–$15.50). AE, MC, V. Daily 11am–midnight. Tube: Leicester Square. CHINESE.

Far from fancy, this small, low-ceilinged restaurant offers some great Chinese food. Baked chicken in soya sauce, prawn with cashew nuts, steamed fish with chili and black bean sauce, and duck flavored with ginger and pineapple are among the fine dishes on the broad menu.

Gaby's Continental Bar
30 Charing Cross Rd., WC2. ☎ **0171/836-4233.** £5–£8 ($7.75–$12.40). No credit cards. Mon–Sat 8am–midnight, Sun 11am–10pm. Tube: Leicester Square. CONTINENTAL.

This restaurant just off Leicester Square has good-value food. A fine assortment of home-cooked specialties like stuffed eggplant and rolled cabbage are displayed in the window and will make your mouth water even before you walk through the door. Most dishes are under £6 ($9) and are usually served with salad or rice. There is no guarantee that a particular dish will be on the menu the day you visit, because everything is made fresh daily according to the chef's mood. The restaurant is also known for its sandwiches, especially salt beef (England's approximation of corned beef), cheapest when you buy it to take away for about £3 ($4.65). Gaby's is fully licensed.

Harbour City
46 Gerrard St., W1. ☎ **0171/439-7859.** Main courses £5.20–£11 ($8.05–$17.05). AE, DC, V. Daily noon–midnight Tube: Leicester Square. CHINESE.

One of the most comfortable restaurants in Chinatown. Downstairs is a candlelit dining room; upstairs the tables are set with crisp white tablecloths and have black lacquered chairs. More than a dozen soups are offered, plus a variety of noodle, meat, and seafood dishes like duck in lemon sauce, moo shu pork, and Singapore-style vermicelli.

Jimmy's
23 Frith St., W1. ☎ **0171/437-9521.** £4.50–£8 ($7–$12.40). No credit cards. Mon–Sat 12:30–3pm and 5:30–11:30pm. Tube: Leicester Square. GREEK/CYPRIOT.

Across from Ronnie Scott's jazz club (see Chapter 9), Jimmy's is a popular basement bistro with good Greek/Cypriot food. Kleftico (baked lamb), moussaka, and other distinctive Mediterranean dishes cost about £5.50 ($8.50).

Nusa Dua
11 Dean St., W1. ☎ **0171/437-3559.** £4–£7 ($6.20–$10.85). AE, MC, V. Mon–Fri 12:30–2:30pm; Mon–Sat 6:30–midnight, Sun 6–9:30pm. Tube: Leicester Square. MALAYSIAN.

The fare is hot and spicy and includes a variety of dishes from the Malay Peninsula—chicken with spicy coconut, chicken Sumatra-style, Malaysian beef curry, and lamb chop in chili sauce. The fish dishes are extra-special; these include fried fish with pineapple in hot green chili sauce or steamed fish with spring onion in ginger and oyster sauce. My favorite, though, is the pomfret with shallots in a sweet soy sauce.

✪ Pollo
20 Old Compton St., W1. ☎ **0171/734-5917.** £3.40–£7 ($5.25–$10.10). No credit cards. Mon–Sat 11:30am–11:30pm. Tube: Leicester Square. ITALIAN.

Despite its name, locals flock here for the tasty pasta dishes, and you're likely to find a long line stretching out the door. The bustling atmosphere is appealing, and the prices are embarrassingly low. As for the pasta sauces, fiorentina, romana, slavia, Alfredo—you name it, they serve it—and the helpful staff is happy to explain it all in plain English. Chicken, though, is the specialty of the house, and it's served in a variety of ways—Valdostana, cacciatore, principessa (with asparagus), and milanese.

Upstairs there are small round, marble-top tables, while downstairs there's a small, attractive restaurant. The list of Italian desserts includes a fair tiramisu.

Saigon
45 Frith St., W1. ☎ **0171/437-7109.** £4.30–£7.65 ($6.65–$11.85); set menu £14.40 ($22.30). AE, DC, V. Mon–Sat noon–11:30pm. Tube: Leicester Square/Tottenham Court Road. VIETNAMESE.

This small, low-lit restaurant offers wonderful Vietnamese food. Try the spiced crab with garlic, lemongrass, and herbs or the sliced duck with coriander in a special sauce. Also exciting is the spiced lamb with satay sauce, stir-fried prawns with spring onion and chili, and rice noodle with spring onion and mixed meat.

Sri Siam
16 Old Compton St., W1. ☎ **0171/434-3544.** £6–£8 ($9.30–$12.40). AE, DC, V. Mon–Sat noon–3pm and 6–11:15pm, Sun 6–10:30pm. Tube: Leicester Square. THAI.

This long, narrow dining room is softly lit with sconce lighting. Black lacquer chairs are set at tables decked with fine white tablecloths. The dishes are well spiced and nicely presented. Try the marinated fish grilled in banana leaf and served with two sauces (chili or tamarind plum). Stir-fried pork with basil, chili, and garlic; diced chicken with lemon grass and red chili; mee krob and other traditional curry. Thai noodle dishes like pad thai are worth trying, too.

The Star Café
22 Great Chapel St., W10. ☎ **0171/437-8778.** £4–£5.50 ($6.20–$8.50). MC, V. Mon–Fri 7am–6pm, Sat 10:30am–4:30pm. Tube: Tottenham Court Road. ENGLISH.

This greasy spoon is a favorite of film and media folk working in the area—it's just off Oxford Street near the Tottenham Court Road Underground. The café is good for breakfast and its daily luncheon specials such as roast chicken with crispy bacon stuffing, steak and onion pie, or salmon fillet with broccoli. Pasta, salads, and a vegetarian dish of the day are offered, too.

Vietnamese
34 Wardour St., W1. ☎ **0171/494-2592.** £3.70–£6 ($5.75–$9.30); set menus from £6.20 ($9.60). AE, DC, JCB, MC, V. Mon–Sat 11:30am–11:30pm, Sun 11am–11pm. Tube: Leicester Square. VIETNAMESE.

The decor is minimal but the food is good and cheap. Choose from the 16 soups and as many noodle and rice dishes. Also on the menu are sweet-and-sour chicken or prawns, beef with ginger and onions, sizzling beef with chili and black-bean sauce, or stuffed tofu with aubergine (eggplant) and peppers.

Wong Kei
41–43 Wardour St., W1. ☎ **0171/437-8408.** £3–£7 ($4.65–$10.85); set menus from £5.80 ($9). No credit cards. Daily noon–11:30pm. Tube: Leicester Square or Piccadilly Circus. CHINESE.

Wong Kei is one of the most inexpensive restaurants in the area. The menu is extensive, featuring lemon chicken, beef with ginger and green onion, braised duck with assorted vegetables, and baked crab in black bean sauce. Dine upstairs or downstairs at cloth-covered tables with glass overlays. Sarah Bernhardt laid the foundation stone and fellow actor Henry Irving the coping stone of the building in 1905.

Young Cheng
76 Shaftesbury Ave., W1. ☎ **0171/437-0237.** £4.80–£8 ($7.45–$12.40); set menus from £6 ($9.30). AE, MC, V. Daily noon–11:20pm. Tube: Leicester Square. CHINESE.

Small and plain with Formica-topped tables. The menu is limited—Szechuan chicken, tofu with prawn and spicy sauce, chicken with black-bean sauce, and sweet-and-sour pork—but the quality is high.

CAFÉS IN SOHO

Cafés, or "caffs," are coming into fashion in London, and a host of Soho-based, old-time java joints are once again at the center of this city's new-found café culture. In addition to the following, see gay section in Chapter 9, "London After Dark" for **The Box** and **Freedom Cafe**.

Bar Italia
22 Frith St., W1. ☎ **0171/437-4520.** Cappuccino £1.10 ($1.70); pastry £1.50 ($2.35); sandwiches £1.50–£2.50 ($2.35–$3.90). No credit cards. Daily 24 hours. Tube: Tottenham Court Road. LIGHT FARE.

Soho's most authentic Italian café features great espresso served in a loud and busy atmosphere. Parma ham and cheese sandwiches can be had at the bar, eaten standing up, or served at one of the few sit-down tables, all of which are usually taken on weekends.

Cafe Boheme
13 Old Compton St., W1. ☎ **0171/734-0623**. Mon–Sat 8am–3am, Sun 10am–10:30pm. Tube: Leicester Square. LIGHT FARE.

One of my favorite Soho hangouts. Full of atmosphere. Very crowded at night when it seems you can watch the whole world drift in and out. More relaxing during the day but still very cool, funky, and relaxed. Worthy of its name.

Cyberia Cyber Cafe
39 Whitfield St., W1. ☎ **0171/209-0982**. From 85p ($1.30). Mon–Fri 11am–10pm, Sat–Sun 10am–9pm. Tube: Goodge Street. LIGHT FARE.

This café has eight computers which you can reserve ahead of time at £2.50 per half hour to get onto the Internet. While you're wating for your turn at the keyboard you can sample coffee, tea, pastries, and sandwiches, although this isn't really why you're here. T-shirts, e-mail, and training are all part of the service.

Maison Bertaux
28 Greek St., W1. ☎ **0171/437-6007.** Pastry £1.35–£2.25 ($2.10–$3.50). No credit cards. Mon–Sat 9am–7pm, Sun 9:30am–1pm and 3:30–6:30pm. Tube: Leicester Square. DESSERT.

One of London's top French bakeries. Maison Bertaux draws in passersby with rich aromas and a window displaying pastries, brioches, and buns. Everything is freshly prepared on the premises. The goods are served at small tables, occupying two floors. Meat-and-cheese-stuffed croissants and other light snacks are offered, too.

Patisserie Valerie
44 Old Compton St., W1. ☎ **0171/437-3466.** Pastry £1–£2.50 ($1.55–$3.90); main dishes £4.50–£6 ($7–$9.30). No credit cards. Mon–Sat 8am–8pm, Sun 10am–6pm. Tube: Tottenham Court Road. DESSERT/LIGHT FARE.

This eternally crowded bakery is the Soho café to see and be seen in. Frequented by local film and theater types, Valerie is not the cheapest place for coffee and cake, but its chocolate truffle cake is almost world-famous. Delectable, too, are the florentines, lemon tarts, croissants, and brioches. Sandwiches, salads, omelets, and pasta dishes are also available.

THE CITY

Almost everyone in the square mile of the City of London goes home by 6pm, and restaurant workers are no exception. Below are some good lunch selections.

Ferrari's
8 W. Smithfield, EC1. ☎ **0171/236-7545.** £2.50–£6 ($3.90–$9.30). No credit cards. Mon–Fri 5:15am–3pm. Tube: St. Paul's. ENGLISH.

Restaurants: The City

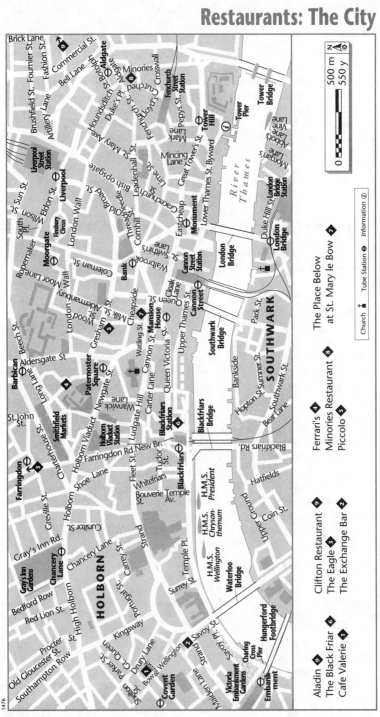

Aladin **9**
The Black Friar **6**
Cafe Valerie **1**

Clifton Restaurant **9**
The Eagle **3**
The Exchange Bar **2**

Ferrari's **4**
Minories Restaurant **8**
Piccolo **5**

The Place Below
at St. Mary le Bow **7**

Church ✝   Tube Station ⊖   Information ①

For a somewhat nicer meal in the same area as Piccolo (see below), turn left at the Museum of London, and then right onto Little Britain Street, until you reach the Smithfield Market, London's wholesale meat center (about six blocks from St. Paul's Underground). This restaurant is just across the square. Although small and plain, Ferrari's is famous for its very unusual sandwich menu that includes selections like Norwegian prawn and farmhouse pâté and a very moderately priced sirloin and vegetable main dish. The shop's cakes are irresistible, too. Ferrari's is located in London's financial district, but don't expect to hear the latest share prices here. Most of the customers are meat porters from across the street.

Minories Restaurant

105A The Minories, EC3. ☎ **0171/702-1658.** £3.50–£6.50 ($5.45–$10.10). No credit cards. Mon–Fri 8am–3pm. Tube: Tower Hill. ENGLISH.

Under a railway bridge, Minories may have the most unusual location of any restaurant in London—arched ceiling and all. It's a good-quality budget choice, only about 150 yards north of the Tower of London. The small menu features roast beef with chips and peas and other home-cooked British standards. The cheerful owner, Mr. Novani, will make you feel at home.

Piccolo

7 Gresham St., EC2. ☎ **0171/606-1492.** £2–£3 ($3.10–$4.65). No credit cards. Mon–Sat 6am–6pm, Sun 6am–2pm. Tube: St. Paul's. ENGLISH.

This is just a sandwich bar with fewer than a dozen stools all facing the street. It's perfect for a quick bite before or after a visit to St. Paul's Cathedral. Piccolo offers the widest range of sandwiches I've ever come across. Bacon and turkey, roast chicken, and all the standards are priced well below £2.50 ($3.90). The shop is just off Martin's Le Grand Street, between St. Paul's Underground and the Museum of London.

The Place Below at St. Mary Le Bow

Cheapside, EC2. ☎ **0171/329-0789.** £5.95–£6.50 ($9.25–$10.10). No credit cards. Mon–Fri 7:30am–2:30pm. Tube: St. Paul's. VEGETARIAN.

This atmospheric, self-service café situated in the Norman crypt offers fine vegetarian cuisine. The menu changes daily but you'll always find a hot dish of the day like the delicious aubergine and almond filo pie and a quiche. When I was last there the quiche was especially full of flavor, combining the tartness of Stilton with the earthiness of field mushrooms. Salads are also always available, and you can finish off with the chocolate cake inspired by California's own Alice Waters. Take-out is available at slightly lower prices. No smoking.

COVENT GARDEN & THE STRAND

✪ Café in the Crypt

St Martin-in-the-Fields, WC2. ☎ **0171/839-4342.** £1.75–£2.20 ($2.70–$3.40) rolls & sandwiches; £5.50–£6.10 ($8.50–$9.45) main dishes. Mon–Sat 10am–8pm, Sun noon–7pm. Tube: Charing Cross. ENGLISH.

Set in the church's brick-vaulted crypt, this self-service cafeteria offers nicely prepared meals. Choices range from rolls filled with ham and cheese to more substantial hot dishes like salmon with a lemon-lime butter, chicken supreme in a white wine and asparagus sauce, or spinach and nut roulade. The salads are excellent. Among the dessert selections there might be apple crumble, or bread-and-butter pudding (bread soaked in eggs and milk with currants or sultanas and then oven-baked). A good stop for coffee and breakfast. It's atmospheric and classical music plays in the background.

Late-Night Eating

Unlike many other cities, London's late night dining is extremely limited. Some of the restaurants that stay open until midnight or after include: **Bar Italia** *(p. 98)*, **Big Easy** *(p. 116)*, **Clifton** *(p. 118)*, **Ed's Easy Diner** *(p. 120)*, **O Fado** *(p. 124)*, and **Pelican** *(p. 114)*.

Café San Martino

57 St. Martin's Lane, WC2. (**No phone**). 60p–£2 (93¢–$3.10). Mon–Sat 11am–8pm. Tube: Charing Cross. LIGHT FARE.

Office workers and others line up at this tiny Italian take-out place for the big variety of sandwiches or any of the hot dishes like gnocchi, lasagne, or jacket potatoes. It's an additional 20p to eat in.

Café Valerie

8 Russell St., WC2. ☎ 0171/240-0064. £2.95–£5.95 ($4.55–$9.20). MC, V. Mon–Sat 8am–11:30pm, Sun 9am–6pm. LIGHT FARE.

This attractive café has a variety of light casual fare—bagels, pastries, and toasted sandwiches like a Rueben. It also offers more substantial dishes including a tasty chicken cordon bleu.

Calabash

The Africa Centre, 38 King St., WC2. ☎ 0171/836-1976. £5–£8.50 ($7.75–$13.15). AE, DC, V. Mon–Fri 12:30pm–2:30pm; Mon–Sat 6–10:30pm. Tube: Covent Garden. AFRICAN/CARIBBEAN.

The spices of Africa flavor the food here, which includes dishes from East, West, and North Africa. Try the Yassa (chicken cooked in lemons with pepper and onions), the chicken with plantain, sweet potatoes, and hot sauce, or the lamb stew Dioumbre cooked in palm oil with okra. Couscous and fried fish with tahini are also favorites. There's little decor to speak of.

Diana's Diner

39 Endell St., WC2. ☎ 0171/240-0272. £3–£6 ($4.65–$9). No credit cards. Mon–Sat 7am–8pm, Sun 8am–6pm. Tube: Covent Garden. PASTA/LIGHT FARE.

Plain and simple with bentwood chairs. Pasta is the order of the day—spaghetti carbonara, penne arrabbiata, lasagne, and fusilli amatriciana—but there's also subtly flavored scampi, roast lamb, and steaks.

Farmer Brown's

4 New Row, WC2. ☎ 0171/240-0320. £4–£7 ($6.20–$10.85) salads; £1.50–£4 ($2.30–$3.55) sandwiches. Mon–Wed 7:30am–7:30pm, Thurs–Sat 7:30am–8:30pm. Tube: Covent Garden. LIGHT FARE.

An atmospheric spot with salami hanging from the ceiling. All sorts of salads and sandwiches—such as smoked salmon—are available. Make your selection from the blackboard menu behind the counter and sit at the banquettes and polished wood tables.

Food for Thought

31 Neal St., WC2. ☎ 0171/836-9072. £2–£6 ($3.10–$9). No credit cards. Mon–Tues 9:30am–8pm, Wed–Sat 9:30am–9:30pm, Sun 10:30am–4pm. Tube: Covent Garden. VEGETARIAN.

Good vegetarian food at great prices. This smoke-free place is somewhat cramped, but the daily selections of salads, quiche, pies, stews, and stir-frys are worth stopping for.

Restaurants: Mayfair & St. James's

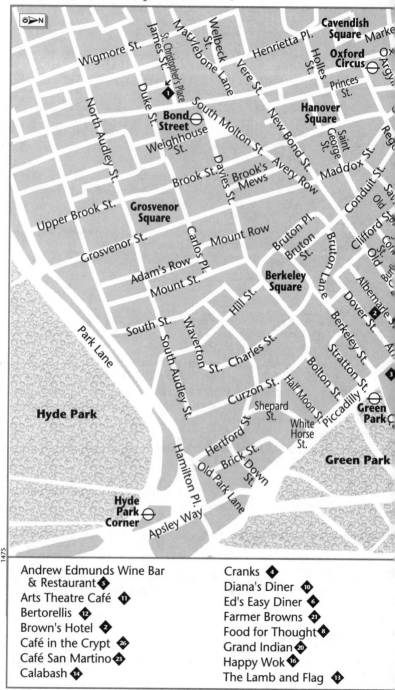

Andrew Edmunds Wine Bar
& Restaurant ⑤

Arts Theatre Café ⑪

Bertorellis ⑫

Brown's Hotel ②

Café in the Crypt ㉖

Café San Martino ㉓

Calabash ⑭

Cranks ④

Diana's Diner ⑩

Ed's Easy Diner ⑥

Farmer Browns ㉑

Food for Thought ⑧

Grand Indian ⑳

Happy Wok ⑯

The Lamb and Flag ⑬

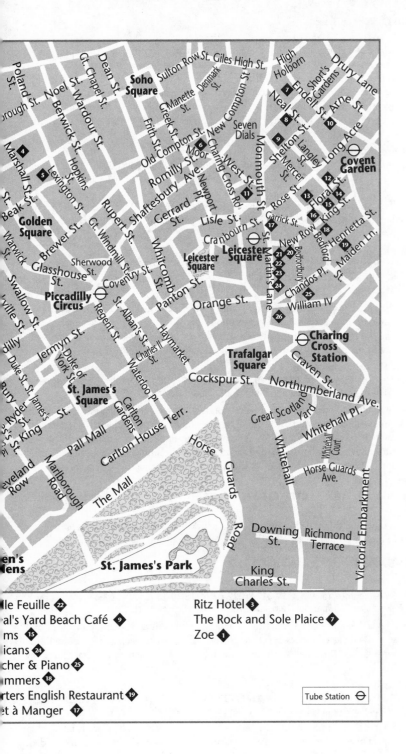

Soho Square

Poland St.
borough St.
Noel St.
Berwick St.
Wardour St.
Gt. Chapel St.
Dean St.

Sutton Row St. Giles High St.
High Holborn
Endell St.
Short's Gardens
Drury Lane

Manette St.
Dennmark St.
Neal St.
Arne St.

Greek St.
New Compton St.
7
8
10

Old Compton St.
Frith St.
Seven Dials
Shelton St.
Langley St.
Long Acre
9

Marshall St.
Hopkins St.
Lexington St.
4
5
Romilly St.
Moor St.
Charing Cross Rd.
West St.
Monmouth St.
Mercer St.
Covent Garden

Beak St.
6
Shaftesbury Ave.
Newport Pl.
Rose St.
12
13
Flora**14**
15
King St.

Golden Square
Brewer St.
Gt. Windmill St.
Rupert St.
Gerrard St.
Lisle St.
11
16
Henrietta St.

Warwick St.
Sherwood St.
Whitcomb St.
Cranbourn St.
Carrick St.
17
New Row
18
Bedford St.
Maiden Ln.
19

Glasshouse St.
Coventry St.
Leicester Square
Leicester Square
St. Martin's Lane
Bedfordbury
Chandos Pl.

Swallow St.
Piccadilly Circus
Panton St.
Orange St.
21
20
22
23
24
25
William IV

ville St.
St. Alban's St.
Haymarket
26
Charing Cross Station

dilly
Jermyn St.
Regent St.
Charles II St.
Waterloo Pl.
Trafalgar Square
Craven St.

Duke of York St.
Duke St. St. James's
St. James's Square
Carlton Gardens
Cockspur St.
Northumberland Ave.

bury
Ryder St.
King St.
Pall Mall
Carlton House Terr.
Great Scotland Yard
Whitehall Pl.

's St.
's Pl.
eveland Row
Marlborough Road
The Mall
Horse
Guards Road
Whitehall
Whitehall Court
Horse Guards Ave.
Victoria Embankment

en's
dens
St. James's Park
Downing St.
Richmond Terrace

King Charles St.

---

lle Feuille **22**

al's Yard Beach Café **9**

ms **15**

icans **24**

cher & Piano **25**

mmers **18**

rters English Restaurant **19**

t à Manger **17**

Ritz Hotel **3**

The Rock and Sole Plaice **7**

Zoe **1**

Tube Station ⊖

The menu changes daily, but there might be roasted eggplant and fennel in a tomato sauce, a shepherd's pie made with leeks, mushrooms, swede (rutabaga), turnips, carrots, and lentils, or spinach and broccoli quiche. A good selection of healthful desserts, too, like banana and strawberry scrunch and fresh fruit. Feel free to bring your own wine. The decor is simple with pine tables and fresh flowers and original art on the fresh whitewashed walls. Neal Street is across from the Covent Garden Underground.

Grand Indian

6 New Row, WC2. ☎ **0171/240-0785.** Main courses £4.90–£10.95 ($7.60–$17); seven-dish set menu £7.50 ($11.60). AE, DC, MC, V. Daily noon–3pm, 5pm–midnight. Tube: Covent Garden. INDIAN.

This pleasant restaurant offers a wide variety of vegetable and meat dishes, from a very hot beef vindaloo and rogan josh, to chicken jalfrezi, masala and Madras, and subtle prawn biryani.

Mille Feuille

39 St. Martin's Lane, WC2. ☎ **0171/836-3035.** £1.75–£3.50 ($2.70–$5.40). Mon–Sat 11am–8pm. Tube: Charing Cross. LIGHT FARE.

A small place with tables covered by lace cloths and glass tops. The display case in the back showcases the fresh salads and sandwiches—avocado and prawn, chicken tandoori, or smoked salmon, for example. The quiches, chili, and lasagne are tasty and filling About 15 or so pastries are offered too, including a decent rendering of California carrot cake, several cheesecakes, and, naturally, mille feuilles.

Neal's Yard Beach Café

13 Neal's Yard, WC2. ☎ **0171/240-1168.** £3.75–£5 ($5.80–$7.75). No credit cards. Mon–Sat 9:30am–8pm, Sun 9:30am–7:30pm. Tube: Covent Garden. LIGHT FARE.

Brilliantly colored murals and palm fronds transport you to tropical climes at this ground-floor courtyard café. And so does the food—an array of salads and foccacia sandwiches, such as the one with smoked guacamole and pane farcito, filled with Mozzarella, spinach, tomato, and avocado. Large, healthful, and well-priced. Carrot, apple, celery, and other juices are available. Better than average ice cream, too.

✪ The Rock and Sole Plaice

47 Endell St., WC2. ☎ **0171/836-3785.** £5–£7 ($7.75–$10.85). No credit cards. Mon–Sat 11:30am–10:30pm. Tube: Covent Garden. FISH & CHIPS.

A tarted-up fish-and-chip spot outfitted with wood tables, white-tiled walls, and lots of theater posters. Select from haddock, plaice, cod, and many more.

PADDINGTON & BAYSWATER

The Café

106 Westbourne Grove, W2. ☎ **0171/229-0777.** £3.30–£5 ($5.10–$7.75). No credit cards. Mon–Sat 7am–7:15pm, Sun 7am–6pm. Tube: Bayswater. ENGLISH.

The Café looks like an American diner. Sit at a booth and open the menu to find soup, sandwiches, pasties, meat pies (such as steak and kidney), and ice-cream dishes for 60p (95¢). All that's missing is the jukebox. The restaurant is near Chepstow Road.

Khan's

13–15 Westbourne Grove, W2. ☎ **0171/727-5420.** £4–£7 ($6.20–$10.85). AE, DC, MC, V. Daily noon–3pm and 6pm–midnight. Tube: Bayswater. INDIAN.

Khan's is said to have the best Indian food in Bayswater. The place is famous, so expect a wait. Don't anticipate a gracious leisurely meal; the scene is crowded,

Restaurants: Marylebone to Maida Vale

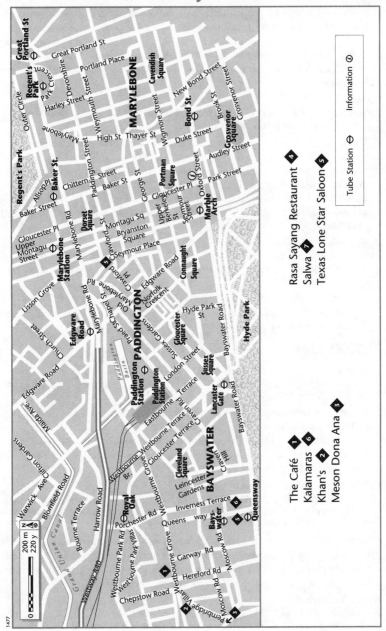

The Café ◆ 1
Kalamaras ◆ 6
Khan's ◆ 2
Meson Dona Ana ◆ 3

Rasa Sayang Restaurant ◆ 4
Salwa ◆ 7
Texas Lone Star Saloon ◆ 5

Tube Station ⊖   Information ⓘ

rushed, and noisy with people constantly coming and going. The menu, which features dozens of tandoori specialties plus a variety of lamb, chicken, and seafood curries, assures that only *halal* meat is used, thus conforming to the Muslim dietary code. Curry dishes cost about £3 ($4.65). A whole tandoori chicken is under £5 ($6.20) and is probably enough for two. Turn left onto Westbourne Grove from Queensway.

Salwa

4 Crawford Place, W1. ☎ **0171/262-3356.** £4.30–£5.50 ($6.66–$8.55). No credit cards. Daily 11:30am–midnight. Tube: Edgware Road. INDIAN.

Where can you get the most authentic Indian food in London? The competition is tough, but Salwa may take the prize. Don't expect the Taj Mahal—this is a small take-out place that's almost literally a hole in the wall. Behind an open kitchen are three small tables. Try the chicken curry at £4.50 ($6.95), a plate of pilau rice for £1.50 ($2.30), and a paratha (traditional Indian bread) for £1 ($1.55), and you'll be well satisfied. The restaurant is just east of Edgware Road, about seven blocks north of Oxford Street.

Texas Lone Star Saloon

117A Queensway, W2. ☎ **0171/727-2980.** £5.95–£12.45 ($9.20–$19.30). V. Mon–Fri noon–2:45pm and 6:30pm–midnight; Sat noon–midnight, Sun noon–11:15pm. Tube: Bayswater or Queensway. AMERICAN.

For all of those dying for American food and American-sized portions, this is the place to go for ribs, fried chicken, burritos, and burgers. Checkered tablecloths, ceiling fans, and country music set the tone.

BLOOMSBURY

Anwar's

64 Grafton Way, W1. ☎ **0171/387-6664.** £3–£5 ($4.65–$7.75). No credit cards. Daily noon–11pm. Tube: Warren Street. INDIAN.

Anwar's not only maintains very high standards of quality but is one of the cheapest Indian restaurants in London. Few dishes top £4 ($6.20), and most cost just £3 ($4.65). Select from a wide choice of meat and vegetable curries and other Indian specialties, such as tandoori chicken. Service is cafeteria-style; help yourself and bring your meal to a basic Formica-covered table.

✪ The Greenhouse Basement

16 Chenies St., WC1. ☎ **0171/637-8038.** £1–£3.70 ($1.55–$5.75) salads, pizza, and quiches; £3.95 ($6.10) main courses. No credit cards. Mon 10am–6pm, Tues–Sat 10am–9pm. Tube: Goodge Street. VEGETARIAN.

Candles on the harvest tables and fresh flowers make for a pretty atmosphere. At the counter, choose from a variety of salads and vegetarian dishes. Chickpea or bean-sprout salad might be offered, and perhaps lasagne or a mixed-vegetable masala with black-eyed peas. Teas and vegetable and fruit juices are available.

North Sea Fish Bar

7–8 Leigh St., WC1. ☎ **0171/387-5892.** £6–£7.50 ($9.30–$11.60). AE, DC, V. Mon–Sat noon–2:30pm and 5:30–10:30pm. Tube: Russell Square or King's Cross. FISH & CHIPS.

Locals love this chippie offering, of course, the national dish. Cod, scampi, skate, and many other selections offered for take-out. One of the best.

October Gallery Café

24 Old Gloucester St., WC1. ☎ **0171/242-7367.** Main courses £3.50–£5 ($5.40–$7.75). Tues–Sat 12:30–2:30pm. Tube: Holborn. LIGHT FARE.

Restaurants: Bloomsbury to the Strand

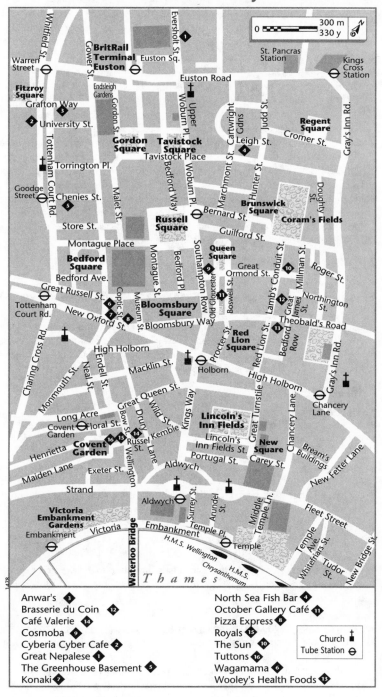

Anwar's ◆ 3
Brasserie du Coin ◆ 12
Café Valerie ◆ 14
Cosmoba ◆ 9
Cyberia Cyber Cafe ◆ 2
Great Nepalese ◆ 1
The Greenhouse Basement ◆ 5
Konaki ◆ 7

North Sea Fish Bar ◆ 4
October Gallery Café ◆ 11
Pizza Express ◆ 8
Royals ◆ 15
The Sun ◆ 10
Tuttons ◆ 16
Wagamama ◆ 6
Wooley's Health Foods ◆ 13

Church	†
Tube Station	⊖

Walk through the October Gallery to this café with its polished pinewood floors and tables. The menu changes daily, but will most likely include a vegetarian and meat dish and a salad or two, plus dessert. Get here early, as the food usually runs out before 2pm.

Wooley's Health Foods

33 Theobalds Rd., WC1. ☎ **0171/405-3028.** 95p–£1.50 short quick roll; £1.85–£2.50 ($2.85–$3.85) long roll; 70p–£3.30 ($1.10–$5.10). Mon–Fri 7:30am–3:30pm. Tube: Holborn. LIGHT FARE.

This is a first-rate take-out salad and sandwich place, which unfortunately offers no seating. The food is freshly prepared daily, and each week two special sandwiches and a special salad are offered—a St. David sandwich made with leeks, sweet red pepper, and a semi-soft cheese from Wales, and a new potato, lemon, and mint salad the week I stopped by. The soups are delicious. About 19 or so sandwiches are offered, ranging from tuna salad or avocado and bacon, to beef and smoked salmon. In addition there are baked potatoes with several different fillings—ratatouille or beans and mushrooms. The ten or so salads range from potato and leek to pasta shells with red kidney beans, sweet corn, and cheese in a tomato dressing.

AROUND VICTORIA

The Green Café

16 Eccleston St., SW1. (**No phone**). £3–£5 ($4.65–$7.75). No credit cards. Mon–Fri 6am–6:30pm, Sat 6:30am–noon. Tube: Victoria. ENGLISH.

Located between Buckingham Palace Road and Ebury Street, this café really is green, both inside and out. With only seven tables, it offers hearty daily specials—braised lamb, fish and chips, shepherd's pie, lasagne al forno, or steak-and-kidney pie—for £3 ($4.65). À la carte selections are also available.

CHELSEA

Chelsea Kitchen

98 Kings Rd., SW3. ☎ **0171/589-1330.** £2–£3.20 ($3.10–$4.95). Set meals from £3. No credit cards. Mon–Sat 8am–11:45pm, Sun 10am–11:45pm. Tube: Sloane Square. LIGHT FARE/DINER.

The British version of a coffee shop. The wide menu offers everything from spaghetti bolognese, braised lamb chops, and goulash. The usual diner fare like omelets, burgers, and salads are served, too. Polished wood tables and booths make up the decor.

Hank's Bar & Grill

195–7 Kings Rd., SW3. ☎ **0171/352-9255.** £5.25–£6.25 ($8.15–$9.70). AE, MC, V. Mon–Sat 11:45am–11pm; Sun noon–10:30pm. Tube: Sloane Square. AMERICAN.

If you're a homesick American, then this is one place to visit. Festooned with commercial signs, it offers chili dogs, nachos, a variety of burgers, and all those other familiar fast-food favorites.

La Bersagliera

372 Kings Rd., SW3. ☎ **0171/352-5993.** £6.10–£11.20 ($9.45–$17.35); £5.10–£6.60 ($7.90–$10.23) for pasta. No credit cards. Mon–Sat 12:30–3pm and 7pm–midnight. Tube: Sloane Square. ITALIAN.

Murals of Italy, marble-topped tables, and rush-seat gateback chairs create an Italian atmosphere. The dishes range from steak pizzaiola made extra-piquant by the use of capers, to veal in marsala finished off with artichoke hearts. All the favorite pasta dishes are available (cannelloni, lasagne, spaghetti carbonara). Daily specials are offered, too.

✪ Le Shop

329 Kings Rd., SW3. ☎ **0171/352-3891.** £4–£8 ($6.20–$12.40). Daily noon–midnight. Tube: Sloane Square. FRENCH.

Galettes (pancakes from Britanny) are the specialty here. These can be filled with ham, cheese, and spinach; chicken and asparagus; and prawn and ratatouille; or many other ingredients. Sweet fillings can be had, too. Round wooden tables, brick walls, and poster art make for a pleasant atmosphere.

✪ Sydney Street Café

Chelsea Farmer's Market, 125 Sydney St., SW3. ☎ **0171/352-5600.** £7.50–£10.50 ($11.60–$16.30). MC, V. Summer daily 9:30am–5:30pm and 7pm–midnight; winter Tues–Sun 11am–3pm and 6pm–midnight. Tube: South Kensington or Sloane Square. Bus: 11. LIGHT FARE.

Located in Chelsea Farmer's Market—where in summer you can sit outside at the wrought-iron tables in a patio-like setting—this popular spot offers a variety of sandwiches and light fare like chicken on a baguette and bacon, lettuce, and tomato sandwiches. Steak, seafood and pasta dishes are offered in the evening.

CAMDEN/PRIMROSE HILL/REGENT'S PARK

L'Ecluse

3 Chalk Farm Rd., NW1. ☎ **0171/267-8116.** Main courses £4.65–£9 ($7.20–$13.95); 3-course lunch/dinner £9.95 ($15.40). AE, V. Mon–Fri noon–11pm, Sat 11am–11pm, Sun 10am–10:30pm. Tube: Camden Town or Chalk Farm. CREPES.

At L'Ecluse, the specialty is crepes, both savory and sweet, like *basquaise* or *forestiere* (with mushrooms) or lemon chocolate. Other dishes are available, too, such as chicken in mushroom sauce, leg of lamb with rosemary, and pork in a spicy sauce. Brick walls and floral-printed tablecloths make for a rustic French atmosphere.

Nontas

14–16 Camden High St., NW1. ☎ **0171/387-4579.** £5.50–£6.25 ($8.50–$9.70). AE, DC, MC, V. Mon–Sat noon–2:45pm, 6–11:30pm. Tube: Camden Town. GREEK.

There's a 1960s flavor to this spot with its wooden tables lit by drop lamps. The food is mostly Greek—pork, lamb, chicken and fish kebabs, moussaka, lamb cutlets, and rump steak.

4 Meals for Less Than £10 ($15.50)

SOHO

Amalfi

29–31 Old Compton St., W1. ☎ **0171/437-7284.** Pasta £5.25–£5.75 ($8.15–$8.90), pizza £5–£7 ($7.75–$10.85), main courses £5.95–£11.95 ($9.20–$18.55). AE, DC, V. Mon–Sat noon–11:15pm, Sun 10am–10pm. Tube: Leicester Square or Tottenham Court Road. ITALIAN.

One side of Amalfi is an espresso bar serving delicious pastries. The restaurant part has tile-topped tables, lanterns, and plants. Its menu offers five different kinds of pasta with a choice of sauces, such as napoletana and amatriciana. More substantial main courses include the veal dishes—marsala, milanese, and limone—steak pizzaiola with garlic and anchovy sauce, or steak cacciatore.

Andrew Edmunds Wine Bar & Restaurant

46 Lexington St., W1. ☎ **0171/437-5708.** £5.25–£7.25 ($8.15–$11.25). V. Mon–Sat 12:30–3pm, Sun 1–2:30pm; daily 6–10:45pm. Tube: Oxford Circus or Piccadilly Circus. NEW ENGLISH.

Restaurants: Kensington to Belgravia

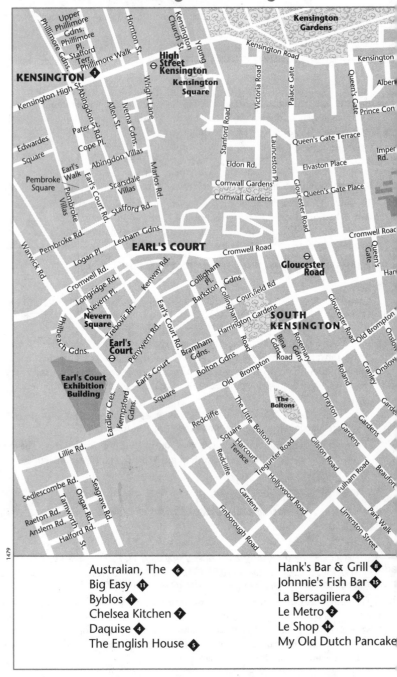

Australian, The ❻

Big Easy ⓫

Byblos ❶

Chelsea Kitchen ❼

Daquise ❹

The English House ❺

Hank's Bar & Grill ❽

Johnnie's Fish Bar ⓯

La Bersagiliera ⓭

Le Metro ❷

Le Shop ⓮

My Old Dutch Pancake

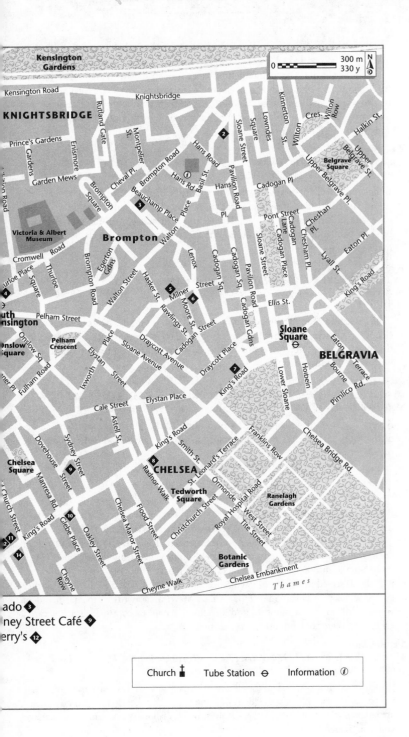

ado ❸
ney Street Café ❾
erry's ⓬

Church ⛪   Tube Station ⊖   Information ⓘ

Small and atmospheric with a low, wood-slatted ceiling, the dining room features butcher paper–covered tables lit by candles in wine bottles. Fresh is the keyword to describe the cuisine. The menu might offer a confit of duck with gratin dauphinoise, wild rabbit stew with mash and roast swede (rutabaga), baked cod fillet with sweet potatoes, peppers, and salsa verde, or parma ham ravioli with basil butter. For dessert try the tiramisu, plum and almond tart, or a portion of Stilton. Among the appetizers, opt for the smoked salmon.

✪ Cafe Bruno

63 Frith St., W1. ☎ **0171/734-4545.** £4.50–£8.50 ($7–$13.15). AE, DC, V. Mon–Fri 12:15–2:30pm; Mon–Sat 6:15–11:30pm. Tube: Leicester Square or Tottenham Court Road. FRENCH.

Budget diners will have to select from the limited café menu, but this is no hardship. On it, you might find steak and frites, a roast poussin au gratin dauphinois, or fish cake with mushy peas and a salad. The setting is attractive, with rush-seated chairs, brightly painted wood tables, and polished wood floors. At night the sconce lighting is soft.

Kettners

29 Romilly St., W1. ☎ **0171/734-6112.** Main courses £6.25–£12.95 ($9.70–$20.05). AE, DC, V. Daily 11am–midnight. Tube: Leicester Square or Tottenham Court Road. PIZZA/ LIGHT FARE.

Haute cuisine atmosphere but down-home food sums up Kettners. Retaining its paneled walls, mirrors, and sconce lighting from its days as an elegant French restaurant, this place serves a broad selection of dishes, from steaks, pizza and pasta to chili, burgers, and sandwiches.

Pitcher & Piano

40–42 William IV St., W2. ☎ **0171/240-6180.** Main courses £5–£8 ($7.75–$12.40). AE, V. Mon–Sat noon–11pm; Sun noon–10:30pm. Tube: Charing Cross. FRENCH.

A very large room with polished wood floors and a grand piano at the center of the room. Steak frites and other traditional bistro fare are offered at reasonable prices.

Red Fort

77 Dean St., W1. ☎ **0171/437-2525.** £6–£15 ($9.30–$23.25). AE, DC, V. Daily noon–2:45pm, 6–11:30pm. Tube: Leicester Square or Piccadilly Circus. INDIAN.

Refreshingly different from the traditional Indian restaurant decor. The chairs are well upholstered with rich, red cushions setting off the pink tablecloths. Here you can experience a true Indian treat—pomfret marinated in caraway seeds and spiced yogurt, then roasted or spiced with whole red chilli, coconut, and lemon juice. Other more familiar dishes include murg tikka (chicken baked with mild spices) and rogan josh (lamb served in a tomato-based sauce and garnished with fresh herbs). Another extra-special dish is the Shah Jahan's Last Stew, made with lamb marinated in yogurt with mace, cardamom, and apricot and cooked to a medium hot taste. Of course, there are tandoori specialties, too.

Signor Zilli

41 Dean St., W1. ☎ **0171/734-3924.** £7–£11.50 ($10.85–$17.80). AE, DC, V. Daily noon–3pm and 5:30–11:30pm. Tube: Tottenham Court Road. ITALIAN.

Burled wood, mirrors, and gold walls set an elegant tone to this café bar. Classic Italian pastas like gnocchi and spaghetti bolognese are offered. Also found on the menu are chicken in lemon with parsley; lamb in wine, shallots, and rosemary; or sausage and bean casserole.

🕈 Family-Friendly Restaurants

Anwar's *(see p.106)*   Since meals are served cafeteria-style, children can see the dishes before choosing. The food here is both good and cheap.

Ed's Easy Diner *(see p. 120)*   Faithfully re-creates a 1950s-style American diner. Giant burgers, authentic fries, and thick shakes are featured.

North Sea Fish Bar *(see p. 106)*   One of the best places for traditional fish and chips. Children love the crispy batter, and they may even develop a taste for french fries doused with vinegar rather than ketchup.

Porters English Restaurant *(see p. 114)*   In the heart of bustling Covent Garden, Porters is a fun place to sample typical English fare. On Sundays, the entire restaurant takes on a festive air.

The Star Café *(see p. 97)*   A playful English eatery located on a colorful Soho corner. Irish stew, beef casserole, a variety of meat pies, and other pastry-covered English specialties will please the whole family.

Le Shop *(see p. 109)*   The sweet and savory Brittany pancakes should tickle the kids' fancy, and it won't cost too much to keep everyone happy.

Steph's
39A Dean St., W1. ☎ **0171/734-5976**. £6.50–£15 ($10.05–$23.25). AE, MC, V. Mon–Fri noon–3pm; Mon–Thurs 5:30–11:30pm, Fri–Sat 5:30–12:30pm. Tube: Leicester Square or Piccadilly Circus. NEW ENGLISH.

A fun spot, the walls are painted with frolicking flamingos. The eclectic menu offers bangers and mash, pie of the day, burgers, swordfish with tomato and pesto, or a lime-flavored chicken breast, as well as steaks. Desserts include a fine key lime pie and the ubiquitous bread-and-butter pudding. Start with baked mushrooms with Stilton.

Trattoria Cappucetto
17 Moor St., W1. ☎ **0171/437-2527**. £5–£12.50 ($7.75–$19.40). AE, MC, V. Daily noon–3pm, 5:30–11pm. Tube: Tottenham Court Road or Leicester Square. ITALIAN.

Small and intimate both upstairs and downstairs. The food is well prepared, particularly the veal dishes—*saltimbocca alla romana, carciofo, funghetto, limone,* or *marsala.* Other dishes like *pollo cacciatore* and *pollo sorpresa* stuffed with cheese, ham, and garlic and butter, steak in barolo sauce, and scampi and calamari round out the menu.

COVENT GARDEN/STRAND

Bertorellis
44A Floral St., WC2. ☎ **0171/836-3969**. £5.25–£8.25 ($8.15–$12.80). AE, DC, MC, V. Mon–Sat noon–3pm; Mon–Sat 5:30–11:30pm. Tube: Covent Garden. ITALIAN.

Head to the café downstairs here because the dining room upstairs is more expensive. Select from the pizzas and pasta dishes like spaghetti bolognese or cannelloni. Among the secundi piatti are such dishes as salmon and horseradish fish cakes on spinach leaves; roast chicken with grilled marinated squash and roasted pepper pesto; or richly flavored wild mushrooms and leeks with baked polenta topped with Mozzarella cheese. There's another Bertorelli's at 19–23 Charlotte St. W1 (☎ **0171/636-4174**) serving similar fare (except for the risotto selections) at slightly higher prices.

Happy Wok

52 Floral St., WC2. ☎ **0171/836-3696.** £5.80–£11 ($9–$17.05). AE, DC, V. Mon–Fri noon–
2:30pm and 5:30–11:30pm, Sat 5:30–midnight. Tube: Covent Garden. CHINESE.

Go for the crab in the shell with spring onions and ginger, the Szechuan prawn, or
the chicken with chili sauce. If you want something more bland, try the sweet-
and-sour chicken or chicken with cashew nuts.

Palms

39 King St., WC2. ☎ **0171/240-2939.** £4.95–£8 ($7.65–$12.40); 2-course lunch £5.95
($9.20); pre- and posttheater dinner menu £6.95 ($10.80). MC, V. daily noon–midnight. Tube:
Covent Garden. CONTINENTAL.

A pleasant bistro. The menu offers traditional bistro fare such as steak with frites,
tarragon chicken, and char-grilled tuna fish in a piquant tomato sauce. About ten
pastas are also available, including a wonderfully tart penne arrabiatta flavored with
chili and basil.

Pelican

45 St. Martin's Lane, WC2. ☎ **0171/379-0309.** Main courses £9–£15 ($13.95–$23.25);
2-course fixed price £9.95 ($15.40). AE, MC. Mon–Sat noon–midnight, Sun noon–10pm.
FRENCH/CONTINENTAL.

A very French brasserie with a long bar and café-style chairs. The menu features typical bistro dishes like *boeuf bordelaise.* Vegetarians will appreciate the *gratin de poireaux,
celeriac, et pleurottes*—layers of oyster mushrooms, celeriac, and leeks, gratinéed and
served with a tomato basil coulis.

Porters English Restaurant

17 Henrietta St., WC2. ☎ **0171/836-6466.** £7.80–£8 ($12.10–$12.40); set meal £15.75
($24.40) for a pie or winter warmer plus pudding, tea/coffee and ¹/₂ bottle of wine. AE, DC,
MC, JCB, V. Daily noon–11:30pm. Tube: Covent Garden. ENGLISH.

Unless you really like English food, don't come here because the selections run from
pies and heritage dishes to traditional winter warmers like steak and kidney pie, toad
in the hole (sausages in batter pudding), bangers and mash, and turkey and chestnut pie. Conclude the meal with equally British horrors like spotted dick and bread
and butter pudding, or more happily with banana split or sherry trifle. The atmosphere is publike, and the dining rooms are encrusted with signboards and other fake
historiana.

Royals

8 Bow St., WC2. ☎ **0171/379-1099.** £5.95–£9.50 ($9.25–$14.70). DC, JCB, MC, V. Mon–
Sat noon–2:30pm; Sun–Thurs 5:30–11:30pm, Fri–Sat 5–11pm. Tube: Covent Garden. INDIAN.

This comfortable Indian restaurant is conveniently located near the Royal Opera
House. Tables are decked with crisp white tablecloths, and the chairs are upholstered
in handsome fabric. Fine tandoori dishes—prawn masala, lamb or chicken biryani,
and chicken korma—are just a few of the choices on the extensive menu.

Tuttons

11–12 Russell St., WC2. ☎ **0171/836-4141.** Main courses £6.90–£11.50 ($10.70–$17.80);
fixed-price 2-course lunch £8.90 ($13.80); 2-course dinner £11.50 ($17.80); snacks £3–£3.80
($4.65–$5.90). AE, MC, V. Sun–Thurs 9:30am–11:30pm, Fri–Sat 9:30am–midnight. Tube:
Covent Garden. BRASSERIE.

A great eatery at the corner of the market piazza for breakfast, lunch, afternoon tea,
or dinner. The decor is "elegant café," with a tile floor and high ceilings. Main courses
run from burgers with french fries to salmon with sorrel sauce to tagliatelle
with smoked salmon and red pepper sauce. Several set afternoon teas are offered,

featuring sandwiches and scones priced from £3.50–£4 ($5.40–$6.20). Just add the pastry/dessert of your choice.

OXFORD STREET/GREAT PORTLAND STREET

Zoe
St. Christopher's Place, W1. ☎ **0171/224-1122.** Main courses £5.95–£11 ($9.25–17.05); set price lunch or dinner £10 ($15.50). AE, DC, MC, V. Mon–Sat 11am–11pm. Tube: Bond Street. LIGHT FARE.

Frenetic and noisy, it's popular with businesspeople and shoppers, because they can obtain an imaginative three-course meal here for £10. The ground-floor café offers soup and sandwiches, while the restaurant downstairs has good, occasionally inspired food for fair prices. You might find on the menu a rustic roast chili-rubbed chicken with deep-fried okra and garlic potatoes. Sandwiches are creative combinations, such as one with smoked salmon with ricotta, red onions, and capers.

BLOOMSBURY/EUSTON

Brasserie du Coin
54 Lamb's Conduit, WC1. ☎ **0171/405-1717.** £6.90–£11.90 ($10.70–$18.45); fixed price £11.50 ($17.80). AE, DC, MC, V. Mon–Fri noon–3pm; Mon–Sat 6–11:30pm. Tube: Holborn or Russell Square. FRENCH.

This classic bistro offers traditional filet mignon and béarnaise, duck in orange sauce, and scampi Provençale, along with pastas and sandwiches like croque monsieur.

Cosmoba
9 Cosmo Place (off Southampton Row), WC1. ☎ **0171/837-0904.** Pasta £4.40–£4.90 ($6.80–$7.60); main courses £5.50–£11.95 ($8.50–$18.50). MC, V. Mon–Sat 11:30am–3pm and 5–11pm. Tube: Russell Square. ITALIAN.

Small and cozy up front with a dining room in the back. Choose a pasta (tagliatelle, penne, spaghetti), and then select one of the many sauces (arrabbiata, vongole, bolognese). Cannelloni and risotto are also available. Main dishes include scampi fritti, pollo arrosto, pollo Kiev, steak pizzaiola, escalope of veal Valdostan, and saltimbocca à la romana.

Great Nepalese
48 Eversholt St., NW1. ☎ **0171/388-6737.** £4.25–£7.95 ($6.60–$12.30); set meal £10.95 ($16.95). AE, DC, MC, V. Daily noon–2:45pm, 6–11:45pm. Tube: Euston. NEPALESE.

A unique spot to sample authentic Nepalese dishes and traditional Indian cuisine. Vegetable mamocha, Bhutuwa chicken, fish masala, and the excellent value thali are just some of the choices. No ambience, though.

Konaki
5 Coptic St., WC1. ☎ **0171/580-9730.** £5.90–£10.50 ($9.15–$16.30). AE, DC, V. Mon–Fri noon–3pm and 6–11:30pm, Sat 6pm–midnight. Tube: Holborn or Tottenham Court Road. GREEK.

Behind the façade with its white classical pillars lies a comfortable dining room with a beamed ceiling. The food is good. Appearing on the menu are traditional Greek favorites such as moussaka and both meat and fish souvlaki. There's also lamb cooked in tomato sauce in a casserole with green beans *(lamb fassolaki)*. Afelia is pork marinated in red wine and cooked with coriander and spices. Start with hummus or taramosalata and finish with a filling baklava.

✪ Wagamama
4 Streatham St. (off Coptic Street), WC1. ☎ **0171/323-9223.** £3.80–£6.80 ($5.90–$10.55). No credit cards. Mon–Fri noon–2:30pm, Sat 1:30–3pm, Sun 1:30–3pm; Mon–Sat 6–11pm, Sun 6–10pm. Tube: Tottenham Court Road. JAPANESE.

This is currently one of London's hot spots. Essentially, it's a noodle house. Stone stairs lead down to a dining room with long, family-style tables and a long counter. You select your order and it's brought to you, but don't expect everything to be co-ordinated so that you and your dining partner are eating at the same time. Try the yaki soba with chicken, prawn, onions, eggs, green peppers, carrots, bean sprouts, and green onions garnished with sesame seeds; or the ramen with seafood; or the chili beef ramen. Other dishes like chicken katsu curry are also available. No smoking.

Another equally sleek branch is located on Lexington Street in Soho.

KNIGHTSBRIDGE/SOUTH KENSINGTON & CHELSEA

Big Easy
332–34 King's Rd., SW3. ☎ **0171/352-4071.** £6–£10 ($9.30–$15.50), £16–£20 ($24.80–$31) for steaks. V. Sun–Thurs noon–midnight, Fri–Sat noon–12:30. Tube: Sloane Square. AMERICAN.

Another retreat for homesick Americans. Business cards cover the walls and paper lays over the wooden tables. The fare is typically American—burgers, barbecue ribs, crab claws, and serious steaks.

Byblos
262 Kensington High St., W8. ☎ **0171/603-4422.** Set menus from £7.50–£10 ($11.60–$15.50); main dishes £5–£10 ($7.75–$15.50). Daily noon–11:30 pm. Tube: High Street or Kensington. LEBANESE.

Pick from a variety of traditional dishes starting with hummus, falafel, or tabbouleh, and follow with any one of several kebabs or the fun Lebanese hamburger served inside Lebanese bread with pickles and salad.

Daquise
20 Thurloe St., SW7. ☎ **0171/589-6117.** £4.50–£9 ($6.95–13.95). No credit cards. Daily 10am–11pm. Tube: South Kensington. POLISH.

Daquise is one of the best finds in South Kensington; it's near the major museums and just steps from the South Kensington Underground. This Polish restaurant features cabbage in many guises. Stuffed with meat or served with veal escalope, it will cost under £4 ($6.20). The ingredients in the chlodiak soup (ham stock with beetroot, cream, and pickled cucumber) may seem strange, but the combination tastes great. Other dishes include potato pancakes, stuffed peppers, shashlik, and wiener schnitzel. A variety of Polish vodkas and beers is also served. Oilcloths cover the tables. On the wall, a picture of horses on the steppe evokes memories of Eastern Europe.

Le Metro
28 Basil St., SW3. ☎ **0171/589-6286.** £7–£10 ($10.85–$15.50). MC, V. Mon–Sat 8am–10:30pm. Tube: Knightsbridge. FRENCH.

Around the corner from Harrods, this basement eatery consistently offers fresh food at reasonable prices. Fettuccine with langoustine sauce and grilled herring with sun-dried tomatoes and olives are just two examples of possible daily specials.

Thierry's
342 King's Rd., SW3. ☎ **0171/352-3365.** £10–£15 ($15.50–$23.25); 2-course lunch £10, 3-course lunch £13. AE, DC, V. Mon–Sat 12:30–3:45pm and 7–10:45pm, Sun 12:30–3pm and 7–10:15pm. Tube: Sloane Square. FRENCH.

Dark burgundy walls, gilt-framed pictures, and wood tables make an elegant atmosphere at Thierry's. The cuisine is classic French bistro—entrecôte bordelaise, coq au vin, and beef bourguignon. At lunch quiches, casse croute, and croque monsieur are all under £4 ($6.20).

Fish & Chips

Fast-food restaurants have replaced many a chippie, as the British call them, but they can still be found fairly easily. Nowadays, fish and chips may be served along with Chinese or Middle Eastern takeout, but the most authentic joints won't have a kebab in sight. Several kinds of fish are offered, but all taste similar—cod is the cheapest.

Sitting down will raise the price of the meal considerably, so do as the locals do, and take it away—wrapped in a paper cone, doused with malt vinegar, and sprinkled with salt. The bill should never top £3 ($4.65).

Two of the most popular chippies are: **Johnnie's Fish Bar,** 494 King's Rd., SW10 (☎ **0171/352-3876**), just past the World's End Pub in Chelsea, open Monday through Saturday 11am to 11pm; and **North Sea Fish Bar** (see its listing above in this chapter under Bloomsbury).

NOTTING HILL/PORTOBELLO

Meson Dona Ana

37 Kensington Park Rd., W11. ☎ **0171/243-0666**. 95p–£5.25 ($1.50–$8.15). MC, V. Daily noon–11:30pm Tube: Ladbroke Grove. TAPAS.

This cheerful wine bar with a colorful Spanish decor serves a large selection of tapas. The reasonably priced dishes include tuna croquettes, potato with chili sauce, and prawn with aïoli. Some good Spanish wines can accompany your meal.

CAMDEN

✪ Café Delancey

3 Delancey St., NW1. ☎ **0171/387-1985**. £4.90–£12.25 ($7.60–$18.60). MC, V. Daily 9:30am–11pm. Tube: Camden Town. BRASSERIE.

This very popular place is great for breakfast, which is served all day. Delicious main courses include rack of lamb with parsley and herb sauce; chicken in mushroom sauce; and sausage and onions with rosti potatoes. Salads and sandwiches like croque monsieur are available, too. The large tiled dining rooms are furnished with round, marble-topped tables and bentwood chairs. At night the tables are covered and the rooms are transformed into charming candlelit spaces. In summer you can sit outside. Away from the main action of the market, it's a pleasant retreat.

Camden Brasserie/Underground Café

214–216 Camden High St., NW1. ☎ **0171/482-2114**. £7–£11 ($10.85–$17.05). MC, V. Mon–Sat noon–3pm and 6–11:30pm, Sun noon–4:30pm and 5:15–10:30pm. Tube: Camden Town. INTERNATIONAL.

A large popular bistro with a long, light oak bar. The antiqued walls are decorated with photographs and other art. On the wide-ranging menu, you'll find chicken rosemary, salmon hollandaise, lamb fillet with mint sauce, and rib-eye steak with béarnaise.

Chez Marc

7 Plender St., NW1. ☎ **0171/388-0402**. £7.90–£10.50 (12.25–$16.25); fixed price 2-course lunch £5.50 ($8.50). AE, MC, V. Tues–Fri noon–2pm, Tues–Sat 7–10:30pm. Tube: Camden Town. FRENCH.

On a side street, this small, pretty bistro has tables covered with salmon-pink cloths. The food is always fresh and the menu changes daily. An excellent two-course meal is offered. When I visited, puff pastry with mushroom or duck liver pâté were starters. Main course selections included lamb provençale; breast of chicken with garlic, olive oil, and soy sauce; or wood pigeon with plantains. À la carte dishes might include pheasant flambéed and served with apples; rack of lamb with Dijon mustard; and casserole of lentils and beans.

Cottons Rhum Shop
55 Chalk Farm Rd., NW1. ☎ **0171/482-1096**. £6.95–£11.95 ($10.75–$18.50). AE, DC, V. Daily 11:45am–11:45pm (lunch til 3:30pm; dinner from 6:30pm). Tube: Chalk Farm. AFRICAN/ CARIBBEAN.

Spicy Jamaican cuisine is what you'll find at this attractive restaurant with antiqued walls and wood tables. Try the okra and breadfruit curry, the jerk chicken, or the goat curry—a true specialty. Get high on the Caribbean atmosphere. Real reggae.

Daphne
83 Bayham St., NW1. ☎ **0171/267-7322**. £6.25–£7.50 ($9.70–$11.60). MC, V. Mon–Sat noon–2:30pm and 6–11:30pm. Tube: Camden Town. GREEK.

This small restaurant has a tiny outdoor terrace overgrown with vines. Inside, the tables are covered with green gingham and the walls are decorated with scenes of Greece. Lamb cutlets; chicken baked with oil, lemon, and oregano; baby squid; and lamb and chicken shashlik are the order of the day. Of course, souvlaki and dolmades are offered, too.

Lemonia
89 Regent's Park Rd., NW1. ☎ **0171/586-7454**. £6.50–£12.75 (10.10–$19.75). V. Mon–Fri noon–3pm; Mon–Sat 6–11:30pm. Tube: Chalk Farm. GREEK.

This large restaurant with polished wood tables offers a classic Greek menu with many grilled meat and fish dishes. It's very popular, but still a pleasant dining experience.

ELSEWHERE

Aladin
132 Brick Lane, E1. ☎ **0171/247-8210**. £3.50–£4 ($5.40–$6.20) No credit cards. Sun–Thurs 11am–11:30pm, Fri–Sat 11:30am–midnight. Tube: Aldgate East. INDIAN.

This is one of the best choices along this street of Bangladeshi joints. The portions are large, the prices excellent, and the quality good for everything from curries to tandoori dishes. Bring your own wine, and don't focus on the plain decor and synthetic pine tables.

Clifton Restaurant
126 Brick Lane, E1. ☎ **0171/377-9402**. Dishes £4–£8.25 ($6.20–$12.80); fixed-price dinner £5.50 ($8.55). AE, MC. Daily noon–1am. Tube: Aldgate East. INDIAN.

Lined with restaurants serving Indian food, Brick Lane is a "little Bangladesh"—the equivalent of East 6th Street in Manhattan. The Clifton, one of the street's original restaurants, has been redecorated with gray carpeting and mirrors. The food is pretty standard—vindaloos, bhunas, masalas, and kormas. If you've never tried Indian food before, I recommend onion bhaji appetizer, followed by chicken bhuna or tikka masala, with a side of pilau rice and naan bread. The entire à la carte meal will cost less than £11 ($17.05); fixed-price meals are even cheaper.

The Exchange Bar Diner
450 The Strand, WC2. ☎ **0171/839-7980**. Meals £5.95–£16 ($9.20–$24.80). AE, DC, MC. Mon–Sat noon–10pm, Sun noon–4pm. Tube: Charing Cross. MEXICAN/AMERICAN.

The Exchange opened in 1993 in the former home of Lyons Corner House Tea Room. Located on an island in the middle of the Strand, the structure is exceptional from an architectural viewpoint. On two levels with big windows are a full bar and dining areas with comfortable wooden tables and chairs. Here, Americans and others can get their dose of Tex-Mex food—hard to find in London. Enchiladas, fajitas, chimichangas, burritos, and other guacamole-topped dishes are served. Admittedly, the food's not as good as at most Houston holes-in-the-wall, but consider that you're an ocean away.

Kalamaras

76–78 Inverness Mews, W2. ☎ **0171/727-9122.** £6–£10 ($9.30–$15.50). MC, V. Mon–Fri noon–2:30pm, 5:30pm–midnight. Tube: Bayswater. GREEK.

Authentic and unique Greek cuisine is served in a traditional atmosphere of white-washed walls adorned with rugs and other Greek objets d'arts. The menu features close to 30 meze dishes, including salt cod and filo stuffed with lamb and spinach. The real specialties are the fish dishes.

THE CHAINS

The following eateries are popular with Londoners. They are conveniently located in the center of the city.

Cranks

8 Marshall St., W1. ☎ **0171/437-9431.** £5.75–£9 ($8.90–$13.95). No credit cards. Mon–Sat 9:30am–8pm, Sun 10am–7pm. Tube: Oxford Circus. VEGETARIAN.

Pub Fare

Pub fare can vary from snacks at the bar to a complete meal, but it's usually cheap, good, and filling. Most pubs offer food, and as there are so many pubs in the city, if you don't like what you see in one, you can always move on to the next. Don't hesitate to take a look at the food before purchasing—it's usually displayed under glass. When it's not, ask the bartender for a menu. Popular items include Scotch eggs (a hard-boiled egg surrounded by sausage meat and encased in bread crumbs), bangers and mash (sausages and mashed potatoes), meat pies (especially during colder months), and a ploughman's lunch (bread, cheese, salad, and pickles). Wash it all down with a beer.

The best pubs make their own dishes and keep the food hot on hotplates. Others only offer factory-made pasties (meat-filled pastry) and microwave them on demand. Note that food and drink are ordered and paid for separately. A good pub lunch will run from £3.50 to £6 ($5.40–$9.30), and careful ordering can cut that amount almost in half.

Many popular pubs are listed in Chapter 9. Pubs known especially for their food include: **The Australian,** 29 Milner St., Chelsea, SW3 (☎ **0171/589-3114**), which has won numerous awards for its excellent food; **The Black Friar,** 174 Queen Victoria St., EC4 (☎ **0171/236-5650**), near the Blackfriars Underground in The City; ✪ **De Hems,** 11 Macclesfield St., W1 (☎ **0171/437-2494**), in Soho's Chinatown; **The Eagle,** 159 Farringdon Rd., EC1 (☎ **0171/837-1353**); **The Lamb and Flag,** 33 Rose St., WC2 (☎ **0171/497-9504**), by Covent Garden Market; and **The Sun,** 63 Lamb's Conduit St., WC1 (☎ **0171/405-8278**), between Russell Square and Holborn Underground stations.

When Cranks opened their first health-oriented vegetarian restaurant in the early 1960s, the British public laughed. Today, more than half a dozen of these places serve no-longer-snickering Londoners innovative, high-quality cuisine at good prices. Cheesy lasagne, lentil-and-spinach quiche, satay vegetables, and other tasty dishes are well presented. The surroundings are modern, airy, and even decorous. A wide selection of herb teas, at about £1 ($1.55) per pot, is available. There's a good choice of reasonably priced organic wines.

This Cranks is three blocks east of Regent Street in Soho. Other downtown locations include the following: 8 Adelaide St., WC2 (☎ 0171/836-0660), where the Strand meets Trafalgar Square; the Market, Covent Garden, WC2 (☎ 0171/379-6508); 9–11 Tottenham Street, W1 (☎ 0171/631-3912), two blocks from Goodge Street Underground off Tottenham Court Road; 23 Barret Street, W1 (☎ 0171/495-1340), across Oxford Street from the Bond Street Underground.

Ed's Easy Diner
12 Moor St., W1. ☎ 0171/439-1955. £4.50–£8.50 ($6.95–$13.15). MC, V. Sun–Thurs 11:30am–midnight, Fri–Sat 11:30am–1am. Tube: Leicester Square. AMERICAN.

Ed's Easy Diners are re-creations of 1950s-style American diners, complete with bobby-soxed waitresses and dime (5p) jukeboxes. A good gimmick, but the burgers aren't for real unless you've been away for a real long time. With fries and a cola or a milk shake, a burger will cost about £7.50 ($10.10).

Other central London locations include: 362 King's Rd., SW3 (☎ 0171/352-1956), past the fire station in Chelsea; and 16 Hampstead High St., NW3 (☎ 0171/431-1958).

My Old Dutch Pancakes
221 King's Rd, SW3. ☎ 0171/352-6900. £2.95–£6.20 ($4.55–$9.60). AE, DC, MC, V. Daily noon–11pm. Tube: Sloane Square. CREPES.

A Dutch ambience prevails at these establishments with wooden chairs and tables. The menu features a host of savory and sweet pancakes and waffles. I recommend the simple pancakes with lemon and sugar, or a stack accompanied with mandarin orange and curaçao, or those with pineapple, or chocolate sauce and cinnamon. The savory versions range from chili to vegetable. My favorite is the old Dutch savory filled with chicken, ham, bacon, sweet peppers, sweet corn, cheese, and mushrooms. Daily specials and a variety of special Dutch beers, too. Also at 132 High Holborn WC1 (☎ 0171/242-5200).

✪ Pizza Express
30 Coptic St., WC1. ☎ 0171/636-3232. £3.40–£5.65 ($5.27–$8.75). AE, V. Daily noon–midnight. Tube: Holborn. PIZZA.

Some of the best pizza in London. Black-tiled floors and black faux-marble tables create an elegant setting. The pies range from simple margarita to the veneziana with sultanas, capers, olives, onions, and pine nuts. Simple desserts are available. There are too many of these places to list—check the phone directory.

Pret à Manger
77–78 Upper St. Martins Lane, WC2. ☎ 0171/379-5335. £1.75–£5 ($2.30–$7.75). No credit cards. Mon–Tues 7:45am–10pm, Wed–Fri 7:45am–10:30pm, Sat 7:45am–11pm, Sun 10am–8pm. Tube: Leicester Square or Charing Cross. FRENCH.

A very successful chain of sandwich, salad, and dessert bars. Crisp and clean in look. Using superfresh and good-quality ingredients, they make up a variety of sandwiches—salmon; watercress; pastrami with mustard mayonnaise; Brie and tomatoes; and tarragon chicken, to name only a few—on a variety of breads. Some branches have tables; others are strictly takeout. There are too many of these to list—check the telephone directory for the nearest one.

Rasa Sayang Restaurant
10 Frith St., W1. ☎ **0171/734-8720**. £5.50–£8.80 ($8.55–$13.65). AE, DC, MC, V. Daily noon–11:15pm (sometimes varies by location). Tube: Tottenham Court Road. MALAYSIAN/ SINGAPOREAN.

These spic-and-span establishments were some of the first Southeast Asian eateries on London's dining scene. Though plain, they're extremely popular. Main dishes will tweak the palate—Singapore beef curry, lemon chicken, gado gado, nasi goreng, and most of all the sambals (try the prawn version). On Sunday, a Malaysian buffet is served from 1 to 7pm for only £6.50 ($10.05).

The other central London location is 38 Queensway, W2 (☎ **071/229-8417**), diagonally across from the Bayswater Underground station.

Stockpot—Soho
18 Old Compton St., W1. ☎ **0171/287-1066**. £3–£5 ($4.65–$7.75). No credit cards. Daily 9am–11pm (sometimes varies by location). Tube: Leicester Square. ENGLISH.

The Stockpot restaurants feature contemporary decor and follow a generous, budget-minded philosophy. Menus change daily, but regularly feature two homemade soups for 95p ($1.45) each; a dozen main-course selections such as chili, roast chicken, fish and chips, and liver and bacon for £2.60 to £3.95 ($4 to $6.10); and an excellent selection of desserts for under £1.70 ($2.65). The food is good and the prices make all the 'Pots popular.

Central London locations include: 273 King's Rd., SW3 (☎ **0171/823-3175**), in Chelsea, a few blocks past the fire station; 6 Basil St., SW3 (☎ **0171/589-8627**), in ultrafashionable Knightsbridge, between Harrods and Sloane Street; and 40 Panton St., SW1 (☎ **0171/839-5142**), just off Haymarket, one block south of Piccadilly Circus.

5 Afternoon Tea

Afternoon tea can consist of a pot of tea and a pastry taken at **Richoux of London** or, better yet, at **Maison Bertaux** or **Patisserie Valerie**. Either way, afternoon tea is still very much a British tradition and makes for a mini-meal in the mid-afternoon. A proper tea will include a pot of choice tea, accompanied by scones, wafer-thin sandwiches minus their crusts, and a selection of pastries and cakes. Don't confuse this with high tea, which is a working person's supper consisting of a hot dish, followed by dessert or cookies—high tea is mostly had in Northern England and Scotland. In my opinion, afternoon tea on a grand scale is not really worth it, but if it's part of your dream London vacation, then by all means go ahead and blow the £20 on the places listed here. Alternatively, you can drop into **Fortnum and Mason** at 181 Piccadilly (☎ **0171/734-8040**), where you can enjoy a formal tea accompanied by music in St. James's Restaurant for around £12 or decent cream teas in the Patio or Fountain restaurants for anywhere from £6 to £9. It's certainly a quintessentially English name too.

Brown's Hotel
Albemarle and Dover Streets, W1. ☎ **0171/493-6020**. Reservations required for 3pm seating. £16 ($24.80) per person. AE, DC, MC, V. Daily 3–6pm. Tube: Green Park.

This quintessentially understated hotel—so English—has a reputation for its afternoon tea. It's served in the sitting room/lounge. Tailcoated waiters will bring tomato, cucumber, and meat sandwiches, as well as scones and pastries. Choose from a variety of teas from India and Southeast Asia.

Ritz Hotel
Piccadilly, W1. ☎ **0171/493-8181.** Reservations are essential; make them at least a week in advance. £17.50 ($27.10) per person. Daily sittings at 2–6pm. Tube: Green Park.

The elaborate affair of afternoon tea at the Ritz is probably the most famous tea in the world. It's accompanied by a pianist or harpist. There are two sittings daily.

6   Worth a Splurge

Arts Theatre Café
6–7 Great Newport St., WC2. ☎ **0171/497-8014.** £8–£12.50 ($12.40–$19.35). 2-course meal £10 ($15.50), 3 courses £12.50 ($19.35). No credit cards. Mon–Fri noon–11pm, Sat 6–11pm. Tube: Covent Garden. ITALIAN.

Small, candlelit, and comfortable. The menu changes daily but might feature such pasta dishes as pasta tossed with broccoli, anchovy, garlic, and chili, as well as such main dishes as liver with balsamic vinegar and sage, or bourrida, a fish stew containing prawns, mussels, squid, mullet, and scallops. Save room for a dessert like the chilled zabaglione with vin santo whipped cream and raspberry sauce. Good Italian wine list.

Bahn Thai
21A Frith St., W1. ☎ **0171/437-8504.** £8–£17 ($12.40–$26.35). AE, DC, MC, V. Mon–Fri noon–2:45pm; Mon–Sat 6–11:15pm, Sun 6:30–10:30pm. Tube: Tottenham Court Road. THAI.

Right in the middle of Soho is one of the best Southeast Asian restaurants in London. Decorative wall hangings give this exceptional place a totally authentic feel, but it's the food you've come for, and you won't be disappointed. Excellent soups, seafood, and rice dishes are featured on the huge and creative menu. Try the crispy fried pomfret. Frith Street is near Tottenham Court Road Underground, just south of Soho Square.

Dell Ugo
56 Frith St., W1. ☎ **0171/734-8300.** £8–£12 ($12.40–$18.60). AE, V. Downstairs Mon–Sat 11:30am–11:30pm; upstairs Mon–Fri noon–3pm and Mon–Sat 7pm–12:30am. Tube: Leicester Square. INTERNATIONAL.

Fashionable decor and food. On the walls are wildly colorful abstract murals, and seating is at black tables and chairs. The menu is broad. It ranges from pasta (farfalle with Gorgonzola, spinach and pine nuts; gnocchi with chorizo, olives, and tomatoes) to plain (rump steak and frites; lamb shank with flageolets, garlic, and rosemary). For dessert, there's an enticing double chocolate terrine with coffee and a lemon tart. A tapas menu is offered in the cafe downstairs.

✪ The Eagle
159 Farringdon Rd., EC1. ☎ **0171/837-1353.** £7–£10 ($10.85–$15.50). No credit cards. Mon–Fri 12:30–2:30pm and 6:30–10:30pm. Tube: Farringdon. MEDITERRANEAN.

Celebrated for its food, this pub, which is more like a café-restaurant than a traditional pub, is packed at lunch. The fresh ingredients are displayed in baskets at the bar. Always on hand is a hearty soup. A variety of Mediterranean-flavored delights come out of the kitchen, like salt cod Lisbon-style or steak sandwich in ciabatta. A three-course meal can be had for £12 or less.

The English House
3 Milner St., SW3. ☎ **0171/584-3002.** Reservations recommended. £11.50–£15.50 ($17.80–$24); set lunch (Mon–Fri) £15.75 ($24.40); 3-course set lunch (Sun) £15.75 ($24.40), dinner

(Sun) £20.75 ($32.15). AE, DC, MC, V. Daily 12:30–2:30pm; Mon–Sat 7:30–11:30pm, Sun 7:30–10pm. Tube: South Kensington or Sloane Square. ENGLISH.

Set on a beautiful back street in Chelsea, the English House looks like an ideal country home. As a fire roars in the cozy dining room, patrons are treated to beautifully prepared dishes, served by an expert staff. Despite the fact that tables are too close together, dining here is romantic. The menu will feature a couple of traditional English dishes like the fish pie or the liver with smoked bacon and horseradish mash, along with such items as confit of duck with braised red cabbage or salmon Wellington with leek cream sauce. On the dessert list, sticky toffee pudding with cream and butterscotch sauce is the biggest English hit. A traditional three-course English lunch is served Sundays.

✪ French House
49 Dean St., W1. ☎ **0171/437-2477.** £8.50–£10 ($13.15–$15.50). AE, DC, V. Daily 12:30–3pm; Mon–Sat 6:30–11:30pm, Sun 6:30–10:30pm. Tube: Leicester Square or Piccadilly Circus. NEW ENGLISH.

In this plain dining room over a popular pub, a classic French menu is served. Start with frog legs, leeks, and olives or snails. Follow with one of the select main courses— boiled ham with sweded mash, rabbit with mustard and shallots, or roast pigeon and celeriac bake. Desserts can be English (like a pear tart or rhubarb and apple crumble) or continental (such as walnut and Armagnac ice cream). Oak paneling, polished wood floors, and brass gas-style lamps make up the decor.

Fung Shing
15 Lisle St., WC2. ☎ **0171/437-1539.** £7.50–£13 ($11.60–$20.15). Set meals from £12.50 ($19.35). MC, V. Daily noon–11:30pm. Tube: Leicester Square. CHINESE.

This is one of the best Cantonese restaurants in the city—not the cheapest but worth the splurge. Making up the menu are a whole range of dishes—about 150 items. Try the scallops with soy sauce or the stewed duck with yam in a pot, or one of the sizzling dishes. It's much more comfortable here than at most Chinatown restaurants.

✪ Gopal's
12 Bateman St., W1. ☎ **0171/434-0840.** £6–£12.50 ($9.30–$19.35). AE, DC, V. Daily noon–3pm; 6–11:30pm. Tube: Piccadilly Circus or Tottenham Court Road. INDIAN.

The atmosphere here is pleasant with cane-backed upholstered chairs and tables covered with salmon-pink cloths. The food is not drenched in ghee or oil as at so many Indian restaurants, and the spice flavors are distinctive. A substantial number of traditional vegetarian, seafood, and meat dishes are featured. Two specialties of the house are dum ka murg (steamed chicken cooked on the bone in a sealed pot with Hyderabadi spices and herbs) and mutton xacutti (a Goan dish of hot lamb cooked with coconut, vinegar, and spices).

L'Escargot
48 Greek St., W1. ☎ **0171/437-2679.** Lunch £10.50 ($16.30); main courses £12.50–£16 ($19.35–$24.80). AE, DC, V. Mon–Fri 12:15–2:15pm; Mon–Sat 6–11:15pm. Tube: Leicester Square or Tottenham Court Road. FRENCH.

Outside the town house restaurant of l'Escargot, a snail graces the wrought-iron railing and another is depicted in a mosaic on the front step. Inside, cream-colored walls, fresh flower arrangements, and handsome table settings set an elegant tone. Among the appetizers you're likely to find are tuna niçoise and cassoulet de poissons. The short menu features such dishes as entrecôte with roast pepper mousseline, duck confit with red cabbage and Madeira gravy, or saddle of lamb with rosemary au jus. A traditional peach melba or chocolate tart with orange sorbet is usually among the desserts. There's a fine, extensive wine list.

Ming

35–36 Greek St., W1. ☎ **0171/734-2721.** Main courses £6–£8.50 ($9.30–$13.15); set meals from £13 ($20.15); pretheater menu served until 7pm £10 ($15.50). AE, DC, V. Mon–Sat noon–11:45pm. Tube: Leicester Square. CHINESE.

Light and airy and decorated in pink and jade, Ming offers fine Chinese cuisine. Most popular are the sizzling dishes—prawns with fresh mango or lamb with leeks. The traditional crowd-pleasers include grilled fish with chili, Mongolian lamb, Szechuan shredded beef, and a flavorsome shredded duck with ginger.

O Fado

49–50 Beauchamp Place, SW3. ☎ **0171/589-3002.** £6.20–£8.95 ($9.60–$13.85). AE, MC, V. Daily noon–3pm; Mon–Sat 6:30–12:30am, Sun 6:30–11:30pm. Tube: Knightsbridge or South Kensington. PORTUGUESE.

If you choose a meat dish rather than fish, you can dine here on a modest budget. Tables covered with white cloths are paired with bentwood chairs for comfortable dining. Try the lamb cutlet, liver and onions, or chicken in wine sauce. For a real Portuguese treat, splurge on the cod cooked with clams and tomatoes.

✪ Plummers

33 King St., WC2. ☎ **0171/240-2534.** Set menus 1-course £8.90 ($13.80), 2-course £12.15 ($18.85), 3-course £15.40 ($23.85). AE, DC, V. Mon–Fri noon–2:30pm; Mon–Sat 5:30–11:30pm, Sun 6–10pm. Tube: Covent Garden or Leicester Square. ENGLISH.

A comfortable restaurant that is definitely worth a splurge. Start with an apple and Stilton soup, the terrine of salmon and smoked trout, or melon and orange with a raspberry coulis. The casserole dishes are excellent, such as venison in ginger and Madeira, or the chicken breast in pimento and chili sauce. Fish, too, is available, such as salmon and crab cakes. Finish with a chocolate Grand Marnier mousse or the poached pears in red wine with black currants. The decor is calming—gray chairs, gray chintz wallpaper, and English prints hung on the walls.

What to See & Do in London

To paraphrase Samuel Johnson, the great English lexicographer: When one is tired of London, one is tired of life, for London offers all that life can afford. It would take a lifetime to explore every alley and court, each street and square in this vast city. For the first-time visitor, the question is never what to do, but what to do *first*. The "Suggested Itineraries" listed below and "The Top Attractions" will help.

Americans are notorious for whizzing around Europe's major sights trying to squeeze in as many of the "hits" as their brief vacations will allow. Europeans, who enjoy longer holidays, often poke fun at the hectic pace of vacationing Americans. Yet, when you only have a few days, moving at a fast clip is in order. If you prefer a slower pace, simply modify the itineraries below.

SUGGESTED ITINERARIES

If You Have 1 Day

Take the tube to Charing Cross or Embankment (they are within one block of each other) and cross into Trafalgar Square, London's most famous square and the city's unofficial hub. Here, the commercial West End meets Whitehall, the main street of government, and The Mall, the regal road that leads to Buckingham Palace. In the center of the square is Nelson's Column. The National Gallery is on the northern side of the square, while the northeast side is dominated by the Church of St. Martin-in-the-Fields.

Turn down Whitehall and enter the Banqueting House, in the middle of the block, to view the nine magnificent, allegoric ceiling paintings by Rubens. Across the street from the Banqueting House, visit the home of the Queen's Life Guards, to see the Changing of the Guard, Monday through Saturday at 11am and on Sunday at 10am and 4pm (not to be confused with the larger affair at Buckingham Palace). Farther down Whitehall, in the middle of the street, you'll see the Cenotaph, dedicated to the citizens of the United Kingdom who died in the two world wars. Just opposite it is 10 Downing St., the official residence of the British prime minister. At the foot of Whitehall lies Parliament Square, site of Big Ben and the spectacular Houses of Parliament. The famous Westminster Abbey is just across Parliament Square.

What's Special About London

The Flea Markets
- Especially Camden High Street and Portobello Road, the granddaddy of them all, which seems to go on forever and offers a full day of fun.

British Fare
- Harrods Food Hall, a food market that doubles as a museum.
- Pubs, for their good-value grub and their role as social centers.

Museums
- The celebrated British Museum, the touchstone for other major museums of the world.
- MOMI (The Museum of the Moving Image), one of the city's newest, is as easy to view as a classic flick.
- The Tate, for its Blakes and Turners.
- The Victoria and Albert, a monumental storehouse of decorative arts and one of the world's finest collections of Indian art.

Spectacles
- A visit to any one of the government institutions—the House of Commons, the House of Lords, the Old Bailey, or the Royal Courts of Justice.
- Speaker's Corner, where anarchists, stand-up comics, religious fanatics, and would-be politicians spout their opinions and grievances on all subjects every Sunday.

Attractions
- The Tower of London—a medieval fortress-palace, prison, and royal menagerie—possessing a lurid past.
- Westminster Palace, with the Houses of Parliament and the tower topped by Big Ben, both symbols of London.

Special Events
- Chelsea Flower Show, the rose of England's garden shows, on the grounds of the Chelsea Royal Hospital.
- Notting Hill Carnival, one of Europe's largest street festivals, featuring Caribbean music, food, and fun.
- Wimbledon Lawn Tennis Championship, the most prestigious event in tennis.

Evening Entertainment
- Great theater—offering a wide variety of productions.

After a late lunch and a short rest, take the tube into The City and visit St. Paul's Cathedral.

If You Have 2 Days

Follow the itinerary described above but at a more leisurely pace. During your Whitehall stroll, cross the beautiful St. James's Park to arrive at Buckingham Palace for the 11:30am Changing of the Guard. Save St. Paul's for the morning of your second day.

You could begin your walk of Whitehall from Parliament Square and end up at the National Gallery in Trafalgar Square. After visiting the gallery, continue north along Charing Cross Road, turn right on Long Acre, and visit Covent Garden. In the afternoon of your second day, visit one of the museums listed in "The Top Attractions," below.

If You Have 3 Days

Spend days one and two as described above. On your third day, visit the City of London and its host of interesting financial, legal, religious, and historical sights. Attractions include the Stock Exchange, the Royal Exchange, the Old Bailey, St. Paul's Cathedral, and St. Bride's Church, on Fleet Street. Try to time your sightseeing so that you are at St. Bride's for a free lunchtime recital (Tuesday, Wednesday, and Friday at 1:15pm, or Sunday at 11am and 6pm).

In the afternoon of your third day, visit the Museum of the Moving Image on the South Bank, then stroll over to the adjacent South Bank Arts Centre for a late-afternoon drink.

If You Have 5 Days

Spend your first three days as described above.

An extra couple of days will give you a chance to stop and explore London's historic neighborhoods or to enjoy the city's cultural scene. If you like museums, make sure you make a pilgrimage to South Kensington. In addition to the Victoria and Albert Museum, no fewer than six other museums are found in this area, including the Natural History Museum, the Science Museum, the Geological Museum, and the Museum of Instruments. Also worth a stop is Kensington Palace, in Kensington Gardens.

1   The Top Attractions

✪ British Museum

Great Russell Street, WC1. ☎ **0171/636-1555;** 0171/580-1788 for recorded information. Main galleries free; £1 ($1.55) donation requested. Special exhibitions £3 ($4.65) adults, £2 ($3.10) students, seniors, and children under 16. Mon–Sat 10am–5pm, Sun 2:30–6pm. Tube: Holborn, Russell Square, or Tottenham Court Road.

Behind its classical facade, this museum is one of the richest storehouses of antiquities, prints, drawings, manuscripts, and objets d'art in the world. From a core collection purchased from Sir Hans Sloane in 1753, the museum has grown through acquisition and gifts. Celebrated objects and collections include the **Rosetta Stone** acquired from Napoleon after his defeat at Alexandria, **Lord Elgin's marbles** from the Parthenon and Erechtheum, **George III's library** (with almost 13,000 volumes), **Lady Raffle's Javanese collection, James Cook's South Sea Islands collection,** and the **Halicarnassus sculptures** obtained by Sir Stratford Canning from Constantinople.

So much more is showcased today, too—the **Sutton Hoo** treasure hoard from the 7th century, Egyptian mummies, Assyrian friezes, Babylonian astronomical instruments, the Diamond Sutra, and the world's oldest printed document found in northern China.

To the right of the museum's entrance, on the ground floor, are the **British Library Galleries.** From the library's collection of more than eight million books, temporary exhibits are set up. Included in the permanent exhibit are two copies of the **Magna Carta** (1215), **Shakespeare's First Folio** (1623), the **Lindisfarne Gospels,** and the **Gutenberg Bible** (ca. 1453), the first book ever printed with movable—that is to say, reusable—type. Autographed works by Bach, Mozart, and Handel are also on view.

British Museum

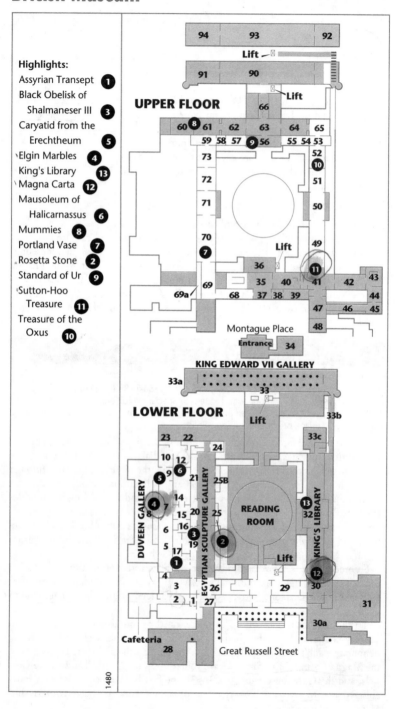

Highlights:
Assyrian Transept **1**
Black Obelisk of
  Shalmaneser III **3**
Caryatid from the
  Erechtheum **5**
Elgin Marbles **4**
King's Library **13**
Magna Carta **12**
Mausoleum of
  Halicarnassus **6**
Mummies **8**
Portland Vase **7**
Rosetta Stone **2**
Standard of Ur **9**
Sutton-Hoo
  Treasure **11**
Treasure of the
  Oxus **10**

UPPER FLOOR

Lift

Lift

Lift

Montague Place

Entrance **34**

KING EDWARD VII GALLERY

LOWER FLOOR

Lift

DUVEEN GALLERY

EGYPTIAN SCULPTURE GALLERY

READING ROOM

KING'S LIBRARY

Lift

Cafeteria

Great Russell Street

The adjacent **British Library Reading Room** (constructed from 1852 to 1857), with its copper dome, is an extraordinarily beautiful place and has been used by numerous scholars and writers, including Thomas Carlyle, Virginia Woolf, Mahatma Gandhi, Lenin, George Bernard Shaw, and others. Karl Marx wrote *Das Kapital* here. Visitors are admitted with a guide only at 2:15 or 4:15pm, Monday through Friday.

Buckingham Palace

The Mall, SW1. ☎ **0171/930-4832.** Tours of the State Rooms £8.50 ($13.15) adults, £6.50 ($10.10) seniors, £4.50 ($6.95) children 5–17. Daily 9:30–5:30pm from second week in August to nearly the end of September. Queen's Gallery £3.50 ($5.40) adults, £2.50 ($3.85) seniors, £2 ($3.10) children 5–17. Daily 9:30am to 4pm. Royal Mews £3.50 ($5.40) adults, £2.50 ($3.85) seniors, £2 ($3.10) children 5–17. Usually from Apr–Aug Tues–Thurs noon–4pm; Aug–Sept Mon–Thurs noon–4pm; Oct–Mar Wed only; times are very tentative so call ahead. Combined Gallery and Mews: £6 ($9.30) adults, £4 ($6.20) seniors, and £3 ($4.65) children 5–17. Physically disabled visitors (only) can reserve tickets for palace tours directly from the palace (☎ **0171/839-1377).** Tube: Victoria, St. James's Park, or Green Park.

Buckingham Palace is the official London residence of Her Majesty the Queen; her personal standard flies when she is in residence. There are 600 rooms in the palace. The queen and the Duke of Edinburgh occupy a suite of just twelve rooms, and the remainder are used by the royal household or for affairs of state. During the summer, the queen gives three famous parties in the 45-acre gardens. Attractively landscaped, the garden has one remaining mulberry tree planted by James I.

Buckingham House is reported to be the queen's least favorite residence. Originally, it was the London home of the Duke of Buckingham. In 1762, King George III bought it and moved here with Queen Charlotte. King George IV later commissioned John Nash to add grandeur to the palace—which he did by adding wings at the front and extending those at the back, all for the astonishing sum of £700,000. Neither George IV nor his brother William IV lived here, though. By the time Queen Victoria came to the throne, the house was in a very poor state of repair: The drains clogged, doors would not close, windows would not open, and bells would not ring. Nash was dismissed, and Edward Blore completed the repair work for Queen Victoria, who made it her official residence. It quickly became too small for the queen, and in 1847 the East Front, which faces The Mall, was constructed. At that time, the Marble Arch, which had stood in the palace's forecourt, was moved to its present position at the top of Park Lane. In 1913, a facade designed by Sir Aston Webb was placed here in the forecourt.

In 1962, the **Queen's Gallery** in the south wing was opened to the public. On view here are artworks from the royal collection—some of the finest pieces in the world. A recent show featured more than 400 pieces of Fabergé.

The **Royal Mews** is one of the finest working stables in the world today. Housed here are the gilded and polished state carriages—such as the gold state coach used at every coronation since 1831—along with the horses that draw them.

In 1993, the queen opened the **State Rooms** at Buckingham Palace to the public to help raise money for the repair of Windsor Castle, extensively damaged in a fire. Occupying the West Front, these include the **Throne Room** and other chambers in which ceremonial events take place. They are open during August and September when the royal family is on holiday. Overlooking the gardens, they are decorated with some of the finest pictures, tapestries, and furnishings from the royal collections. The queen's famous **picture gallery** is really worth seeing—it's a cache that includes Rembrandt's *The Shipbuilder and His Wife,* as well as works by Hals, Rubens, Van Dyke, and Claude Lorrain. Eager tourists start lining up at the palace gates at sunrise, and an hour-long wait is the rule. You must purchase a timed-entrance ticket on the same day you wish to take the palace tour.

The **Changing of the Guard** takes place daily from April through July at 11:30am, and on alternate days August through March. The ceremony is canceled during bad weather and for major state events. Always check ahead so you're not disappointed.

✪ Hampton Court Palace

East Molesey, Surrey. ☎ **0181/781-9500** for recorded information or 0181/781-9666. Admission £8.50 ($13.20) adults, £5.95 ($9.20) seniors, £5.20 ($8.05) children 5–15. Mid-Mar–mid-Oct Mon 10:15am–6pm, Tues–Sun 9:30am–6pm; mid-Oct–mid-Mar Mon 10:15–4:30pm, Tues–Sun 9:30–4:30pm. Closed Dec 24–26, Jan 1. Train: From London Waterloo to Hampton Court (about 30 minutes). River launch: from Westminster Dock, Richmond, or Kingston. The journey takes from 3 to 4 hours one-way, depending on the tide. Tickets cost £7 ($10.85) one-way, £10 ($15.50) round-trip for adults, £4 ($6.20) one-way and £7 ($10.85) round-trip for children under 15. Bus: 111, 131, 216, 726, R68. Green Line Coach: 415, 718.

On the banks of the Thames, about 15 miles southwest of London, sits this magnificent country palace. It was first opened to the public in 1838 by Queen Victoria. Hampton Court was originally built in 1515 by Cardinal Wolsey as a retreat from the poisonous air and water and other inconveniences of London. He had it built to meticulous specifications. His plan called for 280 rooms and a staff of 500. When he fell into disfavor in 1525, he offered it to Henry VIII, who confiscated all the cardinal's property, regardless of his gesture. Today, a visit to the Wolsey rooms and the Renaissance Picture Gallery will give you the aura of the period.

Henry turned Hampton Court into an even grander pleasure palace by constructing new courtyards and gardens, kitchens, galleries, a library, a covered tennis court, and a guard room. He also rebuilt the Great Hall where plays were regularly performed; it remains a splendid example of Tudor carving and artistry. The banquets the king presided over at Hampton Court were immense—a glimpse of the Tudor kitchens will give visitors some idea. Today, in the state apartments, a video shows what life was like at the Tudor court.

Queen Elizabeth I came to live at Hampton Court in 1559, conducting both state business and private matters. It was at this palace that she decided upon Mary's fate, and she celebrated Christmas here with great pomp and festivity. The Virgin Queen personally tended the gardens and planted them with new plants brought back by Drake and Raleigh, such as tobacco and potatos. At the time, one foreign visitor described the queen sitting surrounded by tapestries encrusted with gold and precious stones, finely crafted furnishings, and musical instruments.

During the Stuart period, especially under Charles I, the palace was further adorned with hundreds of paintings and other lavish objets d'art. Cromwell lived here, too, from 1651–58. When Charles II moved in, the palace was once again buoyed up with a lively court. Pepys and Evelyn were regular visitors, as were the king's many mistresses.

When William and Mary ascended the throne, they found the palace apartments old-fashioned and uncomfortable. The royal couple commissioned Sir Christopher Wren to make improvements and asked such artists as Grinling Gibbons, Jean Tijou, and Antonio Verrio to decorate the rooms. Later, Anne redid the chapel and commissioned Thornhill and Verrio to paint murals in the drawing rooms. Under George I and II, restoration work continued, but with little personal attention from these monarchs. George II was the last monarch to live here. Supposedly, his successor, George III, hated the place ever since his grandfather boxed his ears as a boy in the State Apartments. Among the highlights of the palace are Henry VIII's apartments and the Tudor kitchens, the King's Apartments, as well as the Wolsey Rooms and Renaissance Picture Gallery. See, for example Andrea Mantegna's masterpiece, the *Triumphs of Caesar*.

Attractions: Westminster & Victoria

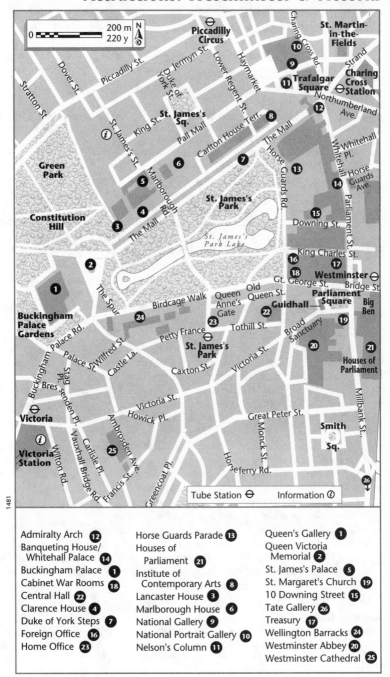

Admiralty Arch	12
Banqueting House/ Whitehall Palace	14
Buckingham Palace	1
Cabinet War Rooms	18
Central Hall	22
Clarence House	4
Duke of York Steps	7
Foreign Office	16
Home Office	23

Horse Guards Parade	13
Houses of Parliament	21
Institute of Contemporary Arts	8
Lancaster House	3
Marlborough House	6
National Gallery	9
National Portrait Gallery	10
Nelson's Column	11

Queen's Gallery	1
Queen Victoria Memorial	2
St. James's Palace	5
St. Margaret's Church	19
10 Downing Street	15
Tate Gallery	26
Treasury	17
Wellington Barracks	24
Westminster Abbey	20
Westminster Cathedral	25

The gardens are splendid. Don't miss the famous maze and the recently restored Privy Garden. Capability Brown, who designed the gardens, planted the Great Vine in 1769.

A fire in 1986 destroyed the south wing around the Fountain Court, but this was restored in 1992. Three dining facilities are available for anything from a full meal to a snack.

✪ Houses of Parliament

(☎ **0171/219-4272** for information.) Free admission. House of Commons: public admitted Mon, Tues, Thurs starting at 4:15pm, Wed from 10am and Fri from 9:30am; House of Lords: public admitted Mon–Wed from about 2:30pm, Thurs from about 3pm, and on some Fridays from 11am. Line up at St. Stephen's entrance, just past the statue of Oliver Cromwell. Debates usually run into the night, and lines shrink after 6pm. Tube: Westminster.

Located in the Palace of Westminster, the Houses of Parliament, along with their trademark clock tower, are the ultimate symbol of London. Before the Norman Conquest of 1066, a palace built for Edward the Confessor stood on this site; it remained the home of the monarchy and the court until Henry VIII's time. Westminster Hall (1097) is the only part of that palace still standing today, but it's not open to the general public. The current Gothic Revival buildings date from 1840 and were designed by Charles Barry. (The earlier buildings were engulfed in flames in 1834—a fire to burn the tally sticks that had been used to keep the Exchequer accounts got out of control.) Assisting Barry was Augustus Welby Pugin, who designed the paneled ceilings, tiled floors, stained glass, clocks, fireplaces, umbrella stands, and even inkwells. There are more than 1,000 rooms and two miles of corridors. The clock tower at the eastern end houses the world's most famous timepiece. **"Big Ben"** refers not to the clock tower, as many people assume, but to the largest bell in the chime, which weighs close to 14 tons and is named for the first commissioner of works. At night, a light shines in the tower whenever Parliament is in session.

Visitors may observe parliamentary debates from the **Strangers' Galleries** in both the Commons and the Lords—the Commons being of the greatest interest. Sessions usually begin in mid-October and run to the end of July, with recesses at Christmas and Easter.

Most visitors are struck by how small the **Commons chamber** is. When it was rebuilt in 1950 after being destroyed during the Blitz in 1941, the chamber was re-created in precise detail. Only 437 of its 651 members can sit at any one time, the rest must crowd around the door and the **Speaker's chair.** The ruling party and the opposition sit facing one another, two sword lengths' apart, and on the table of the House sits the **mace,** a symbol of Parliament's authority.

Opulently decorated with frescoes and mosaics, the **House of Lords** seems almost sacrosanct. Debates here are not as interesting or lively as those in the Commons, but the line for admission is usually shorter. A visit here will give you an appreciation for the pageantry of Parliament. In front of the throne is the **Woolsack,** seat of the lord chancellor, who presides over the house; it's a reminder of the source of Britain's original great wealth.

National Gallery

Trafalgar Square, WC2. ☎ **0171/839-3321.** Main galleries free; Sainsbury wing, £2–£5 ($3.10–$7.75) during some special exhibitions. Mon–Sat 10am–6pm, Sun 2–6pm (June–August Wed until 8pm). Closed Dec 24–26, Jan 1, and Good Friday. Tube: Charing Cross or Leicester Square.

This gallery houses Britain's collection of more than 2,200 paintings dating from the early Renaissance to the early 20th century. The **Impressionist collection** in the East Wing includes works by Monet, Van Gogh, Rousseau, Cézanne, and Seurat. The

early Renaissance works are displayed in the Sainsbury Wing (van Eyck, Piero della Francesca, Botticelli, Raphael, and Leonardo da Vinci). The **16th-century master-works** are shown in the West Wing (Titian, Michelangelo, Veronese, and El Greco); while **art of the 17th century** (Rubens, Velázquez, Van Dyck, Rembrandt) is found in the North Wing.

An audio guide to every painting on the main floor (about 1,000) is now available for rent for only £3. Free guided tours are given, too. In the Sainsbury Wing, stop in the Micro Gallery and use one of the 12 workstations to view the visual encyclopedia of the collection. Look for special temporary shows from the museum's collection and visiting exhibits.

✪ Natural History Museum

Cromwell Road, South Kensington, SW7. ☎ **0171/938-9123.** Admission £5.50 ($8.50) adult, £3 ($4.65) seniors, £2.80 ($4.35) children 5–17. Mon–Sat 10am–6pm, Sun 11am–6pm. Closed Dec 23–26, Jan 1, and Good Friday. Tube: South Kensington.

With towers, spires, and a huge navelike hall, this terra-cotta building is a wonder in itself. Designed by Alfred Waterhouse and opened in 1881, the museum is one of the finest of its kind. The core of the collection came from Sir Hans Sloane. Today, only a fraction of the museum's natural treasures—fossils, animal and plant life exhibits, and minerals—can be displayed. Among the highlights are the **dinosaurs** in the main hall, the **Human Biology exhibit** that features many interactive displays, and an **ecology exhibit.** There's also an **earthquake simulator** and an **insect display.**

✪ St. Paul's Cathedral

Ludgate Hill, St. Paul's Churchyard, EC4. ☎ **0171/248-2705.** Cathedral and crypt, £4 ($6.20) adults, £3.50 ($5.40) students and seniors, £2 ($3.10) children 6–16. Mon–Sat 8:30am–4pm. Sun for worship only. Tube: St. Paul's or Mansion House.

After Old St. Paul's was destroyed in the Great Fire, Christopher Wren cleared the site with a battering ram and set about rebuilding. More than 515 feet long and 365 feet high, the building's construction took from 1675 to 1710. Anticipating that the commissioners overseeing the project might insist on economy, rather than starting at one end or the other, Wren constructed the base first and worked from the ground up. Wren's anxiety was justified. He was constantly harassed by the commission, which cut his salary in half and obstructed his genius at every turn.

The **outer dome** of St. Paul's is so huge and heavy that Wren devised a smaller interior dome and a brick cone, sandwiched between the two, to support it. The cross on top is 365 feet above the sidewalk.

The **inner dome** is embellished with **frescoes depicting the life of St. Paul** by Sir James Thornhill. One day while painting these, Thornhill stepped back to contemplate his work. He was, of course, high up on scaffolding. Seeing Thornhill about to plunge to the church floor, an assistant smeared the wet paint of the fresco with a brush, and this caused Thornhill to jump forward angrily and safely back to the platform, the story goes. These frescoes are best viewed from the **Whispering Gallery,** famous for its acoustics that enable a whisper to be heard 107 feet away on the opposite side of the gallery.

From the Whispering Gallery, a second steep climb leads to the **Stone Gallery.** Here visitors are presented with a fine view of the city. An additional 153-step climb brings you to the **Inner Golden Gallery** at the top of the inner dome and an even more dramatic view.

The two **west towers** were added as an afterthought. The southern one contains the famous **Great Tom,** which is rung when a member of the royal family, a Bishop of London, the Dean of St. Paul's, or the serving Lord Mayor dies.

St. Paul's Cathedral

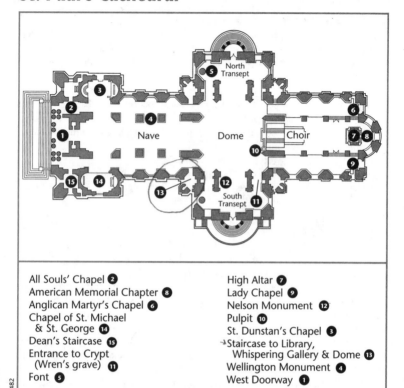

All Souls' Chapel **2**
American Memorial Chapter **8**
Anglican Martyr's Chapel **6**
Chapel of St. Michael
  & St. George **14**
Dean's Staircase **15**
Entrance to Crypt
  (Wren's grave) **11**
Font **5**

High Altar **7**
Lady Chapel **9**
Nelson Monument **12**
Pulpit **10**
St. Dunstan's Chapel **3**
Staircase to Library,
  Whispering Gallery & Dome **13**
Wellington Monument **4**
West Doorway **1**

The cathedral's ornamentation was completed by several artists. Grinling Gibbons carved the choir screens and stalls and the organ case. Francis Bird sculpted the statues of St. Paul, St. Peter, and St. James that grace the west front pediment. Tijou is responsible for the gates to the chancel aisles. Caius Gabriel Cibber executed the phoenix above the motto Resurgam on the pediment of the south door. The master mason William Kempster designed the Geometrical Staircase in the southwest tower.

It's amazing to think that Wren completed this masterpiece at the same time that he was working on 50 or more other churches. He's buried in **the crypt.** On his tombstone is inscribed *"Lector, si monumentum requiris, circumspice"* ("Reader, if you seek his monument, look around you"). Nelson is also buried in the crypt, marked by a sarcophagus that was originally created for Cardinal Wolsey. Wellington rests here, too. In the ambulatory, the American Memorial Chapel pays tribute to the American soldiers who lost their lives during World War II.

The cathedral has been the setting of some dramatic ceremonies, notably a thanksgiving in 1704 for the victory at Blenheim and another celebration a century later for Waterloo; the funerals of Nelson (1806), Wellington (1852), and Winston Churchill (1965), and the marriage of the Prince of Wales to Lady Diana Spencer (1981).

✪ Royal Botanic Gardens at Kew

Richmond, Surrey. ☎ **0181/940-1171**. Information: Visitor Centre at Victoria Gate. Palace and Gardens £5 ($7.75) adult, £3.50($5.40) seniors, £2.50 ($3.90) children 5–15; Palace and Queen

Charlotte's Cottage £1 ($1.55) adults, seniors and children 5–15. Garden, daily 9:30am–4pm in winter, to 6:30pm in summer. Palace, Apr–Sept daily 11am–5:30pm. Queen Charlotte's Cottage, summer Sat–Sun and Bank Holidays only 11am–5:30pm. Tube: Kew Gardens. Train: From Waterloo to Kew Gardens or Kew Bridge. Bus: 65, 391. River Launch: from Westminster Pier (☎ **0171/930-2062**) to Kew Pier (☎ **0181/940-3891**).

More than 40,000 plants from all over the world grow at this 300-acre garden. The most famous of the several glasshouses is the **Palm House** (1844–48) built by Decimus Burton and engineer Richard Turner. The newest and largest glasshouse is **the Princess of Wales Conservatory** (1987). The gardens are dotted with a variety of temples and sculptures, including the ten-story **Pagoda,** which was designed by Sir William Chambers. Most notable are the **Aquatic Gardens** and the **Orangery,** also designed by Chambers (1761). **Queen Charlotte's Cottage,** a timber-and-frame house with a thatched-roof, dates from around 1771; it was first opened to the public in 1899. On the garden's eastern border, don't miss the **Marianne North Gallery,** which houses more than 800 oil paintings by this artist with an enthusiasm for botany.

Also found within the gardens, **Kew Palace** (☎ 0181/940-3321) is the smallest of the royal palaces. Originally known as the Dutch House, it was the favorite residence of King George III and Queen Charlotte. Here in the Queen's Drawing Room, they were entertained by J. C. Bach on the harpsichord that is on display today.

✪ Science Museum

Exhibition Road, SW7. ☎ **0171/938-8000.** Admission £5 ($7.75) adult, £2.60 ($4.05) seniors and children 5–17. Daily 10am–6pm. Closed Dec 24–26. Tube: South Kensington.

Among the most notable exhibits here are naval models; the Puffing Billy (1813), one of the oldest locomotives still in existence; Stephenson's Rocket (1829); Arkwright's spinning machine; Wheatstone's electric telegraph; Fox Talbot's first camera; Edison's original phonograph; the Vickers "Vimy" aircraft, which made the first Atlantic crossing in 1919; and Sir Frank Whittle's turbo-jet engine. Three new galleries are designed to appeal to children. The garden provides water, construction, sound and light shows and games for 3- to 6-year-olds. The other two galleries appeal to 7- to 12-year-olds, allowing them to play on networked terminals and also to investigate the way things work through interactive exhibits.

✪ Tate Gallery

Millbank, SW1. ☎ **0171/887-8000.** Permanent collection free; temporary exhibits £4–£7 ($6.20–$10.85). Mon–Sat 10am–5:50pm, Sun 2–5:50pm. Tube: Pimlico.

Founded in 1897 and endowed by sugar magnate Sir Henry Tate, this gallery displays two major collections. The first is a collection of **British art from the 16th to the late 19th centuries.** It consists of paintings, sculptures, and engravings by such major artists as Hogarth, Joshua Reynolds, John Constable, Thomas Gainsborough, William Blake, and the Pre-Raphaelites. This collection includes more than 300 brilliant oils and 30,000 watercolors by Turner—these are exhibited on a rotating schedule in the **Clore Gallery.** The second, the **Modern Collection,** includes works by British artists from 1880, as well as painting and sculpture done by international artists, from the Impressionist period and beyond. The Tate's permanent galleries are rehung every year to rotate the collection. Dine at the museum restaurant, which sports decorations by Rex Whistler.

Tower Bridge

SE1. ☎ **0171/378-1928.** Admission £5 ($7.75) adults, £3.50 ($5.40) seniors and children 5–15. Apr–Oct, daily 10am–6:30pm; Nov–Mar, daily 9:30am–6pm. Last entry is an hour and a quarter before closing. Closed Dec 24–26, Jan 1, and the 4th Wed in January. Tube: Tower Hill.

The Ceremony of the Keys

Plan in advance to attend the **Ceremony of the Keys** at the Tower of London. Every night for the past 700 years, the gates of this ancient fortress have been ceremoniously locked. At ten o'clock, the chief yeoman warder marches out across the causeway to the entrance gate, which he locks. From there the guard returns, locking the gates of the Byward Tower. As they approach the Bloody Tower, the sentry on duty confronts them and demands, "Halt, who goes there?" The chief yeoman warder replies "The Keys." "Whose keys?" demands the sentry. "Queen Elizabeth's keys," replies the chief warder. The sentry presents arms. The chief warder removes his Tudor bonnet and yells, "God preserve Queen Elizabeth." To which the whole guard replies, "Amen." You can watch this half-hour-long ritual if you request permission in writing at least one month in advance. Tickets are free. Write to: The Resident Governor, Operations Department, HM Tower of London, London EC 3N 4AB. Include an International Reply Coupon.

Here's a lyrical London landmark you can't miss—possibly the most celebrated and most photographed bridge in the world. It's the one that a certain American thought he'd purchased instead of the one that spanned the Thames farther upriver. Despite its Gothic appearance, the bridge was built in 1894. The two towers are steel, clad in stone. Inside the towers, exhibitions trace the history of its construction. Visitors may ascend to the pedestrian walkways that have great views up- and downriver to St. Paul's, the Tower, and in the distance, the House of Parliament.

Electrical power now raises and lowers the drawbridges, but the original hydraulic system (pre-1976) was preserved. In the south tower, you can see how that system worked—unless you're a dedicated engineer, it might not thrill you that much. The drawbridges are raised several hundred times a year to allow vessels to pass—in summer, about five times each day. Opening times change daily and are only announced one day in advance; call for information.

Tower of London

EC3. ☎ **0171/709-0765.** Admission £8.30 ($12.85) adults, £6.25 ($9.70) students and seniors, £5.50 ($8.50) children 5–15. March–Oct Mon–Sat 9am–6pm, Sun 10am–6pm; Nov–Feb Mon–Sat 9–5pm, Sun 10–5. Last tickets sold one hour before closing. Last entry to buildings 30 minutes before closing. Visitors should allow at least 2 hours to tour. Tours are given every half hour, starting at 9:30am. Closed Dec 24–26 and Jan 1. Tube: Tower Hill. Bus: 15, 25, 42, 78, 100, D1, D9, D11. DLR: Tower Gateway.

This perfect medieval fortress was initially built by William I to protect London and to awe his subjects. Each succeeding monarch added to it until the outer walls, built by Edward I, enclosed 18 acres. Royal palace and prison, the Tower has also contained the royal mint, royal menagerie, royal armories, and the royal observatory.

The massive impregnable tower at its center, dubbed the **White Tower** after a 1240 whitewashing, has walls 15 feet thick. It was probably built about 1078 by order of William I. This tower remains one of the finest examples of Norman military architecture anywhere. It contained prison cells on the first floor, soldiers' and servants' quarters on the second floor, a banqueting hall, the St. John chapel and nobles' quarters on the third floor, and royal bedrooms and the council chambers. Today, the White Tower houses the Royal Armouries Collection, an impressive array of armor—including a suit made to accommodate the massive girth of Henry VIII—artillery, weapons, and instruments of torture.

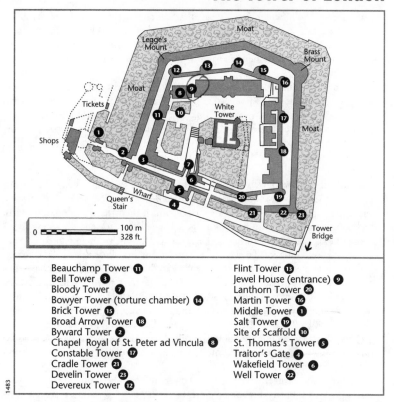

Beauchamp Tower **11**

Bell Tower **3**

Bloody Tower **7**

Bowyer Tower (torture chamber) **14**

Brick Tower **15**

Broad Arrow Tower **18**

Byward Tower **2**

Chapel Royal of St. Peter ad Vincula **8**

Constable Tower **17**

Cradle Tower **21**

Develin Tower **23**

Devereux Tower **12**

Flint Tower **13**

Jewel House (entrance) **9**

Lanthorn Tower **20**

Martin Tower **16**

Middle Tower **1**

Salt Tower **19**

Site of Scaffold **10**

St. Thomas's Tower **5**

Traitor's Gate **4**

Wakefield Tower **6**

Well Tower **22**

The **Bloody Tower** has a gruesome history worthy of its name, which it received when the two royal princes, the 10- and 12-year-old sons of Edward IV, disappeared *Jewel House #9* ichard of Gloucester was off at Westminster having himself d III. The bodies of two children were later found near the 4. Many notables passed through **Traitor's Gate** on the mprisoned in the Bloody Tower. Sir Walter Raleigh spent 13 his family and writing his *History of the World* before he was

e kept in **Beauchamp Tower.** Its interior walls are covered with most moving of which is "Jane," thought to have been carved dley of his beloved, Jane Grey, the "Nine Days' Queen." King oned in **Wakefield Tower** in 1464. Rescued by Warwick the ter recaptured and returned to the Tower, where he was killed

ost frequent during the Reformation. The majority took place on Tower Hill. 535, John Fisher, Bishop of Rochester, and Sir Thomas More were both put to death here for refusing to sign the Oath of Supremacy making Henry VIII head of the Church. Fisher was so weak he had to be carried to the scaffold. Only a few were allowed the privacy and seclusion of being executed on Tower Green, including Henry VIII's second wife, Anne Boleyn, whose pretty head rolled in 1536. Losing favor with Henry for arranging his marriage to Anne of Cleves, Thomas Cromwell, who had brought the adultery charges against Anne, was beheaded in 1540. Sentenced to death that same year, the Countess of Salisbury, mother of Cardinal Pole, refused to place her head on the block. She ran screaming until she was dispatched standing up—or "fetched off slovenly," as it was described at the time. In 1542, Catherine Howard was beheaded for her adultery with Thomas Culpepper.

Before she became queen, Elizabeth I was briefly imprisoned in the **Bell Tower** after being implicated in a plot against Mary. Later, the Earl of Essex was executed for his aborted rebellion, as was the Duke of Monmouth, who chastised the executioner because the ax blade was so dull that it took three attempts to complete the deed. In the 18th century, numerous Jacobites were executed, except for lucky Lord Nithsdale, who escaped in 1716 dressed as his wife's maid.

After some valuables were stolen from Westminster Palace while King Edward I was away, the **Crown jewels** were moved to the Tower in 1303. Today, they're displayed in the ✪ **Jewel House** (1994). The collection includes several magnificent crowns, including the Imperial State Crown, which is encrusted with 3,200 jewels, including a ruby given to the Black Prince. In the late 17th century, an extraordinary attempt was made to steal the Crown jewels by an Irishman named Captain Blood and an accomplice. They posed as a parson and his wife, befriended the keeper, and then proposed to introduce their nephew to the keeper's daughter for a possible marriage. At this introduction, they requested to see the Crown jewels, attacked the keeper, and tied him up. The heist was foiled when the keeper's son returned unexpectedly, and the robbers were chased and captured. Charles II, though, was so charmed by Blood that he pardoned him, granted him estates in Ireland, and settled a £500 pension upon him. Some say that the king, who was short of money at the time, was in on the plot. Today visitors can also see a video of the 1953 coronation of Queen Elizabeth II.

The **yeoman warders** who guard the Tower are not to be confused with the yeoman guard, established sometime before 1485. They are not and never should be referred to as "beefeaters." They are all highly decorated retired warrant officers or noncommissioned officers.

The **legendary ravens** are all that remain of the **royal menagerie,** which was kept at the Tower for hundreds of years. This zoo was begun in 1235 when the Holy Roman Emperor gave Henry III three leopards. Later, a polar bear was presented by the king of Norway and an elephant from King Louis IX of France. In 1834, when it was removed to Regent's Park and became London Zoo, the menagerie had almost 60 animals.

The **Chapel of St. John** in the White Tower is a fine example of a Norman chapel; it's only 55 feet long and 36 feet wide. With their cubiform capitals, the massive columns supporting the nave are typically Romanesque. In the **subcrypt,** 600 Jews were imprisoned in 1278 for supposedly clipping the coinage. Of them, 267 were hanged, and the rest were banished. During the Peasants' Revolt in 1381, the king's ministers were dragged from the chapel's altar to Tower Hill and beheaded. In the hall off the chapel, Henry IV initiated the Ceremony of the Bath on the night before his coronation; an elite core took baths and were invested into the knighthood Order of the Bath.

Among those buried at the Royal Chapel of St. Peter ad Vincula (St. Peter in Chains) are John Fisher, Thomas More, Anne Boleyn, Catherine Howard, and Lady Jane Grey.

Every three years on Ascension Day, a ceremony called the **Beating of the Bounds** is conducted. The tower is not under the jurisdiction of the city, so its liberties have to be confirmed and its boundaries set by a painter who marks them on the ground.

During its long and bloody history, torture played a major part. Today, the instruments used are on display: bilboes that shackled ankles; thumbscrews; the Scavenger's Daughter that fastened the neck, wrists, and ankles; and the rack that reduced Guy Fawkes to confession in 30 minutes.

See the box, **"The Ceremony of the Keys,"** above for information on attending the Tower's nightly ceremony.

✪ Victoria & Albert Museum

Cromwell Road, SW7. ☎ **0171/938-8500** (8441 for general information; 8349 for current exhibitions). Free admission. Suggested donation £4.50 ($6.95) adults, £1 ($1.55) children. There is also a charge for special exhibitions. Mon noon–5:50pm, Tues–Sun 10am–5:50pm. Closed all major holidays. Tube: South Kensington.

Named after Queen Victoria and her consort, the V&A is an enormous treasure house devoted to the decorative and fine arts. Huge, in both size and scope, the museum has seven miles of galleries. They hold fabulous collections of sculpture, furniture, fashion, textiles, paintings, silver, glass, ceramics, and jewelry—from Britain and all over the world. The **Dress Court** shows the history of fashion from 1500 to the present day. (Check out Vivienne Westwood's gigantic blue mock-crocodile platform shoes from which supermodel Naomi Campbell fell during a Paris fashion show.) The **Furniture Collection** has pieces by designers from Chippendale to Charles Rennie Mackintosh. **The National collection of British watercolors** has one of the finest collections of Constables. The **Devonshire Hunting Tapestries** date from the 15th century. The **Medieval Treasury** includes the Gloucester Candlestick (1105). Of the museum's collection of Renaissance and Victorian sculpture, the most valued piece to date is *The Three Graces* by Antonio Canova, for which £7.6 million was paid. Special collections feature the work of William Morris, the Arts and Crafts movement, and the Pre-Raphaelites. The **Great Bed of Ware** is here; it's referred to by Shakespeare in *Twelfth Night*. Raphael's famous *Cartoons* are beautiful—seven designs for tapestries commissioned by Pope Leo X in 1514 to hang in the Sistine Chapel. The Nehru Gallery of Indian Art displays Shah Jahan's jade cup. The Tsui gallery is rich in Chinese art. The 20th-century gallery is devoted to contemporary art and design. The Glass Gallery displays 7,000 objects, among them ancient Egyptian perfume bottles and the Luck of Eden Hall Vase, which had a curse laid on it when it was brought to England from the Holy Land by a 14th-century crusader. The Ironwork Gallery displays English and continental decorative ironwork spanning eight centuries—everything iron from balconies to cookie tins. Another gallery is devoted to Frank Lloyd Wright.

The collections are displayed in two ways. The Art and Design Galleries are arranged by place or date showing their visual relationships and cultural influences; the Materials and Techniques Galleries trace the developments in form, function, or technique of the particular material.

The café here offers fine cuisine and an appealing ambience.

✪ Westminster Abbey

Dean's Yard, SW1. ☎ **0171/222-5152.** Nave and cloisters free; Royal Chapels, £4 ($6.20) adults, £2 ($3.10) seniors, students, £1 ($1.55) children under 16 (Note: Wed 6–7:45pm is the only time that photography is permitted); Abbey, Mon–Sat 8am–6pm; Royal Chapels, Mon–Fri 9:20am–4pm, Sat 9:20am–2pm and 3:45–5pm. Brass rubbing center open Mon–Sat 9am–5pm. For times of daily services call **0171/222-5152.** Comprehensive "Super Tours" are given by the abbey's vergers for £7 ($10.85) per person. Apr–Oct they leave weekdays at 10, 10:30, and 11am, and 2, 2:30, and 3pm (except Fri), Sat at 10 and 11am and 12:30pm. Nov–Mar, they leave weekdays 10 and 11am and 2 and 3pm, Sat at 10, 11am, and 12:30pm. Tube: Westminster/St. James's Park.

Neither a cathedral nor a parish church, Westminster Abbey is a "royal peculiar," under the jurisdiction of a dean and chapter and subject only to the sovereign. An architectural masterpiece, the Gothic abbey dates largely from the 13th to 16th centuries. The first church on the site was built in the 7th century by King Sebert of the East Saxons, on the instruction of St. Peter—who is said to have materialized at its consecration given by Mellitus, the first bishop of London. In 1050, Edward I built his palace and a church here in Westminster. Much of what visitors see today, however, dates from the reign of Henry III, who began rebuilding the existing edifices around 1245. Every coronation since 1066 has taken place at Westminister Abbey, and so have many great events in the life of the nation. The nave and the cloisters of this house of worship, with regularly scheduled services, can be seen for free.

The **nave** soars 106 feet, the highest in Britain. It contains the **grave of the Unknown Warrior,** representative of all those who fell in World War I. The soldier was buried here in 1920 in soil that was brought from French battlefields, and the stone is from Belgium. Today, the nave is lit by six Waterford chandeliers, donated by the Guinness family to celebrate the abbey's 900th anniversary.

The **cloisters,** which were rebuilt after a fire in 1298, contain illuminated panels by David Gentleman on the East Walk. These show the various stages in the abbey's construction. Today, visitors can make a rubbing at the cloister's **Brass Rubbing Center** (☎ 0171/222-2085). Also in the east cloister is the **Chapter House** (1245–55). The king's great council gathered here for the first time in 1257, during the reign of Henry III. From the middle of the 14th century to 1547, the Chapter House was used as a Parliament House for the Commons. Close by is the **Pyx Chamber,** where the standards for the coinage were kept. It displays the plate of the abbey and of St. Margaret's Church.

The **Norman Undercroft** houses a display of famous royal and nonroyal effigies, which were carried on top of coffins in funeral processions. Other exhibits include replicas of the coronation regalia.

In the south transept, **Poets' Corner** contains a veritable literary history of Britain. It was originated in 1400, when Geoffrey Chaucer was buried here with a simple memorial. He was, in fact, interred here not because he was a famous poet, but because he worked for the abbey. Among other famous literary figures buried here are Ben Jonson (standing upright), Dryden, Samuel Johnson, Sheridan, Browning, and Tennyson. The practice of placing memorials to literary greats began in earnest in the 18th century. The first was the full-length figure of Shakespeare. The others that followed are to Eliot, Auden, Dylan Thomas, Lewis Carroll, William Blake, and more recently Virginia Woolf (1991), and Oscar Wilde, whose memorial window was unveiled finally in 1995.

Many other famous people are buried or memorialized throughout the abbey. The politicians Castlereagh, Canning, Peel, Palmerston, and Gladstone are all buried here. The ashes of politicians Andrew Bonar Law, Neville Chamberlain, Clement Attlee, and Ernest Bevin are ensconced here, too. Scientists resting here include Sir Isaac Newton, Lord Rutherford, Robert Stephenson, and Thomas Telford. So, too, are the architects Robert Adam, Sir William Chambers, Charles Barry, and Sir George Gilbert Scott. The explorer David Livingston and theatrical greats David Garrick and Henry Irving lie here. Yet, there's only one painter, Godfrey Kneller.

Behind the high altar stands the **Shrine of Edward the Confessor,** who founded the abbey. He died only a few days after it was consecrated on December 28, 1065. The shrine was built by Henry III. Buried near the shrine are five kings and four queens, including Henry III, Edward III, and Richard II. The **Henry VII Chapel** (1519) has an extraordinary Tudor vaulted roof. Since 1725, it's been used as the

Westminster Abbey

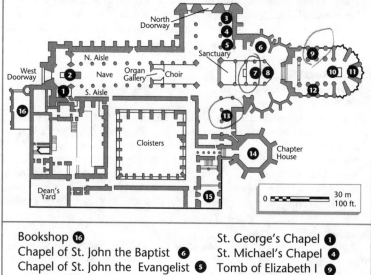

Bookshop **16**
Chapel of St. John the Baptist **6**
Chapel of St. John the Evangelist **5**
Chapter House **14**
Henry V's Chantry **8**
Poets' Corner **13**
RAF Chapel **11**
St. Andrew's Chapel **3**
St. Edward's Chapel (Coronation Chair) **7**

St. George's Chapel **1**
St. Michael's Chapel **4**
Tomb of Elizabeth I **9**
Tomb of Henry VII **10**
Tomb of Mary Queen of Scots **12**
Tomb of Unknown Warrior/ Memorial to Churchill **2**
Undercroft Museum **15**

Chapel of the Order of the Bath; their colorful banners, crests, and mantlings adorn the wooden stalls, which have beautifully carved misericords underneath their seats. In the north aisle of this chapel is the **grave of Elizabeth I,** who lies in the same vault as her half-sister Mary. The white marble effigy is reckoned a faithful likeness of the queen. Behind the altar is the final resting place of King Henry VII and his consort, Elizabeth of York, marked by a monument by Torrigiani. At the east end is the **Royal Air Force Chapel,** containing a memorial window that incorporates the crests of the 68 Fighter Squadrons which took part in the Battle of Britain in 1940.

The **Coronation Chair,** an oak chair made for King Edward I by Master Walter of Durham, was designed to hold the ancient **Stone of Scone,** seized from the Scots in 1296. The stone, on which Scottish kings were crowned, has been stolen back by Scottish nationalists several times—most recently in the 1950s—but it's always been recovered. The chair has been used at every coronation since 1308.

2 More Attractions

ARCHITECTURAL HIGHLIGHTS

Banqueting House

Opposite Horse Guards Parade, Whitehall, SW1. ☎ **0171/930-4179.** Admission £3 ($4.65) adults, £2.25 ($3.50) seniors and students, £2 ($3.10) children. Mon–Sat 10am–5pm. Closed Sun, Dec 24–26, Jan 1, Good Friday. Note, too, that it is often closed at short notice for government functions, so always check the hours ahead of time. Tube: Charing Cross or Embankment.

This is all that remains of the great palace of Whitehall. A masterpiece of English Renaissance (1619–22) architecture, it was designed by Inigo Jones. In the main hall, see the nine magnificent, allegorical paintings by Rubens depicting the Divine Right of Kings—they're fantastic. Designed for sumptuous royal banquets, balls, and concerts, it is still used for many functions today.

Chelsea Royal Hospital

Royal Hospital Road, SW3. Free admission. Mon–Sat 10am–noon and 2–4pm, Sun 2–4pm. Tube: Sloane Square.

This dignified institution was founded by Charles II in 1682 for veteran soldiers and designed and completed by Sir Christopher Wren in 1692. There's been little change to Wren's design, except for minor work done by Robert Adam in the 18th century and the addition of the stables, designed by Sir John Soane in 1814. The main block containing the hall and chapel is flanked by east and west wings that are dormitories. The Duke of Wellington lay in state in the hall here from November 10–17, 1852. So many people thronged to see him that two were crushed to death.

Guildhall

Off Gresham Street, EC2. ☎ **0171/606-3030.** Free admission. Daily 10am–5pm (Mon–Sat only in winter). Closed Dec 24–26, Jan 1, Good Friday, and Easter Monday, and for ceremonial occasions. Tube: Bank.

Dating from 1411, Guildhall is the city's most important secular Gothic structure. It's been restored—once after the Great Fire and again after the Blitz. It's the seat of the City of London's local government, and City council meetings are presided over by the lord mayor. These meetings are open to the public; they're held at 1pm on the third Thursday of each month.

Lloyd's of London Building

Lime Street, EC3. ☎ **0171/623-7100.** Tube: Monument.

Designed by Richard Rogers (coarchitect of the Pompidou Center in Paris), the Lloyd's of London Building opened in 1986 to much critical attention. All the "guts" of the building (elevators, water pipes, electrical conduits) are on the exterior. Cranes are permanently stationed on the roof—ready to help with further expansion, should it become necessary. At night, special lighting lends an extraterrestrial quality. Unfortunately, it's currently closed to visitors for security reasons.

Queen's House

Romney Road, Greenwich, SE10. ☎ **0181/858-4422.** Admission £5.50 ($8.50) adults, £4.50 ($7) seniors, £3 ($4.65) children, includes National Maritime Museum and Old Royal Observatory. Daily 10am–5pm. Train: From Charing Cross to Maze Hill. DLR: Island Gardens.

Designed by Inigo Jones, Queen's House (1616) is a fine example of this architect's innovative style. It is most famous for the cantilevered tulip staircase, the first of its kind. Carefully restored, the house contains a collection of royal and marine paintings and other objets d'art.

St. Pancras Station

Euston Road, NW1. Tube: St. Pancras.

The London terminus for the Midland Railway, St. Pancras Station (1863–67) is a masterpiece of Victorian engineering. Designed by W. H. Barlow, the 689-foot-long glass-and-iron train shed spans 240 feet in width. It rises to a peak of 100 feet above the rails. The platforms were raised 20 feet above the ground because the tracks ran over the Regent's Canal before entering the station. The pièce de résistance, though, is Sir George Gilbert Scott's fanciful Midland Grand Hotel. Done in high Gothic style, it's graced with pinnacles, towers, and gables; it now functions as office space. The facade runs 565 feet and is flanked by a clock tower and a west tower.

CEMETERIES

Highgate Cemetery

Swain's Lane, N6. ☎ **0181/340-1834.** East side, £2 ($3.10); west side, £4 ($6.20). Apr–Sept, daily 10am–5pm; Oct–Mar, daily 10am–4pm. Tours at 12, 2, and 4pm weekdays, every hour on weekends, although do call ahead and make an appointment before trekking out to Highgate. Avoid Sunday, when it's very crowded. Tube: Archway.

Serpentine pathways wind through this beautiful cemetery, laid out around a huge, 300-year-old cedar tree. Lined with tombs, **Egyptian Avenue** stretches beyond an archway—supported by two Egyptian columns and obelisks—to the **Circle of Lebanon.** This circular passageway is lined with catacombs. The cemetery was so popular and fashionable in the Victorian era that it was extended on the other side of Swain's Lane in 1857. Among the famous buried in the old western cemetery—which is only accessible if you take a guided tour, given hourly in summer—are scientist **Michael Faraday** and poet **Christina Rossetti.** In the eastern cemetery lie **Karl Marx,** marked by a gargantuan bust; novelist **George Eliot;** and philosopher **Herbert Spencer.** The grave of Marx is popular with government delegations visiting from China; in fact, the Chinese government helps pay for its upkeep. The cemetery is still very much in use and the proper respect is appropriate. *Note:* No children under 8 are allowed into the cemetery. Only small cameras are permitted, at the discretion of the wardens.

CHURCHES & CATHEDRALS

Many of the churches listed below offer free **lunchtime concerts**—it's customary to leave a small donation. A full list of churches offering lunchtime concerts is available from the London Tourist Board.

All Hallows Barking by the Tower of London

Byward Street, EC3. ☎ **0171/481-2928.** Free admission. Museum Mon–Fri 11am–4:30pm; Church Mon–Fri 11am–6pm, Sat–Sun 10am–5pm. Tube: Tower Hill.

Through excavation work, archeologists have determined that a church has stood here since Saxon times. In 1644, William Penn was baptized here. The following year, Archbishop Laud was buried here after he was executed; later his body was removed to St. John's College, Oxford. In 1797, John Quincy Adams got married at All Hallows. Bombs destroyed the church in 1940, leaving only the tower and walls standing. Rebuilt from 1949 to 1958, the church now has a brass rubbing center.

St. Bride's Church

Fleet Street, EC4. ☎ **0171/353-1301.** Free admission. Weekdays 8:30–4:30pm; weekends 9am–4:30pm. Concerts at 1:15pm. Tube: Blackfriars.

Known as the "the church of the press," St. Bride's is a remarkable landmark. The current church is the eighth one that has stood here. After it was bombed in 1940, an archeologist excavated the crypts and was able to confirm much of the site's legendary history: A Roman house was found preserved in the crypt, and it was established that St. Brigit of Ireland had founded the first Christian church here. Among the famous parishioners have been writers John Dryden, John Milton, Richard Lovelace, and John Evelyn. The diarist Samuel Pepys and his eight siblings were all baptized here. The novelist Samuel Richardson and his family are buried here. After the Great Fire destroyed it, the church was rebuilt by Sir Christopher Wren for £11,430 5s 11d, excluding the spire. This was added later and has been described as

Attractions: The City

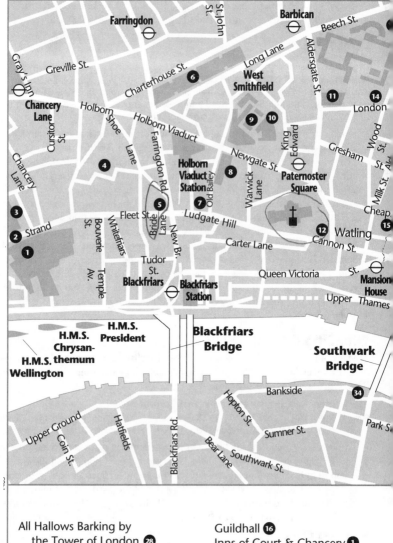

All Hallows Barking by
  the Tower of London **28**
Bank of England Museum **17**
Barbican Centre **13**
H.M.S. *Belfast* **31**
Cheshire Cheese **7**
Docklands **33**
Dr. Samuel Johnson's House **4**
Fishmonger's Hall **21**
Geffrye Museum **16A**

Guildhall **16**
Inns of Court & Chancery **1**
Lloyd's of London **25**
London Bridge **22**
London Dungeon **24**
Mansion House **19**
Museum of London **11**
National Postal Museum **10**
New Globe Theatre **34**

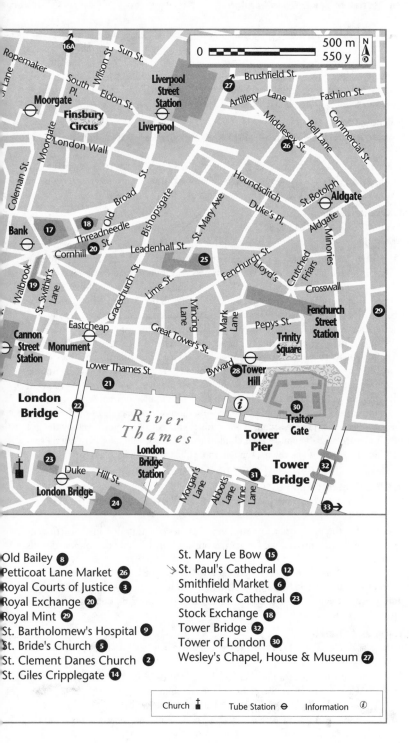

Old Bailey **8**

Petticoat Lane Market **26**

Royal Courts of Justice **3**

Royal Exchange **20**

Royal Mint **29**

St. Bartholomew's Hospital **9**

St. Bride's Church **5**

St. Clement Danes Church **2**

St. Giles Cripplegate **14**

St. Mary Le Bow **15**

St. Paul's Cathedral **12**

Smithfield Market **6**

Southwark Cathedral **23**

Stock Exchange **18**

Tower Bridge **32**

Tower of London **30**

Wesley's Chapel, House & Museum **27**

Church **†**   Tube Station **⊖**   Information **ⓘ**

a "madrigal in stone." The spire has four octagonal tiers capped by an obelisk that's topped off with a ball and vane. This soaring confection (234 feet tall) supposedly inspired the wedding cakes of a pastry cook who lived in Fleet Street in the late 17th century. The crypts had been used as burial chambers and a charnel house for centuries; today, they're a museum. **Concerts** are given on Tuesday and Friday, and an **organ recital** is given on Wednesday.

✪ Brompton Oratory

Brompton Road, SW7. ☎ **0171/589-4811.** Free admission. Daily 6:30am–8pm. Tube: South Kensington.

Done in the Italian Renaissance style, this Roman Catholic church is famous for its **musical services.** Its organ has nearly 4,000 pipes. After Westminster Cathedral and York Minster, this is the widest nave in England.

St. Clement Danes

Strand, WC2. ☎ **0171/242-8282.** Free admission. Daily 9am–5pm. Tube: Temple.

It's not known for certain why Danes is part of the church's name, but we do know that there was a Saxon church on this site. In the late 10th century, that wooden church was rebuilt in stone. Although the church survived the Great Fire, it was declared unsafe, and Sir Christopher Wren was commissioned to rebuild it. The spire was designed by James Gibbs. The interior is decorated with ornate plasterwork. Samuel Johnson attended services here regularly. Robert Cecil, later Earl of Salisbury, was baptized here in 1563. Bishop George Berkeley and the wife of poet John Donne are buried here. The Blitz totally gutted the church, and it was rebuilt in the late 1950s. Today, this is the central church of the RAF. It contains memorials to the British, Commonwealth, and American airmen who flew in World War II. Among its more famous rectors is William Webb Ellis who, as a schoolboy playing soccer at Rugby, infringed soccer rules when he picked up the ball and ran with it, thereby inventing the game of rugby. Oranges and lemons say the bells of St. Clements, according to the nursery rhyme. Today this rhyme is still memorialized by the gift of an orange and a lemon to each child of the attached primary school after a special annual service. (The rhyme, though, more likely refers to St. Clement Eastcheap, located on the riverfront where citrus fruits were unloaded.)

St. Giles Church Cripplegate

Corner of Fore and Wood Streets, London Wall, EC2. ☎ **0171/606-3630.** Free admission. Mon–Sat 10am–5pm, Sun for services. Tube: Moorgate or Barbican.

Named for the patron saint of cripples, St. Giles was founded in the 11th century. The church survived the Great Fire, but the Blitz left only the tower and walls standing.

Betrothed here in 1620 was Oliver Cromwell to Elizabeth Bourchier. John Milton, author of *Paradise Lost,* was buried here in 1674. More than a century later, someone opened the poet's grave, knocked out his teeth, stole a rib bone, and tore hair from his skull.

St. James's Church

197 Piccadilly, W1. ☎ **0171/734-4511.** Free admission. Recitals Wed–Fri at 1:10pm. Tube: Piccadilly Circus.

When the aristocratic area known as St. James was developed in the late 17th century, Sir Christopher Wren was commissioned to build its parish church. Diarist John Evelyn wrote of the interior, "There is no altar anywhere in England, nor has there been any abroad, more handsomely adorned." The reredos, the organ case, and the font were all carved by Grinling Gibbons. As might be expected, this church has rich historical associations. Baptized here were the poet William Blake and William Pitt, the first Earl of Chatham who became England's youngest prime minister at age 24. Caricaturist James Gillray, auctioneer James Christie, and coffeehouse founder Francis White are all buried here. One of the more colorful marriages celebrated here was that of explorer Sir Samuel Baker and the woman he had bought at a slave auction in a Turkish bazaar.

Lunchtime recitals are given; inexpensive evening concerts, too.

St. Martin-in-the-Fields

Trafalgar Square, WC2. ☎ **0171/930-1862.** Free admission. Daily 8am–7:30pm. Tube: Charing Cross, Leicester Square, or Embankment.

Famous for its music, this is one of London's most beautiful and best loved churches. Handel played on its first organ. Mozart performed here, too, it's said. Today, **free lunchtime concerts** are given Monday through Wednesday and Friday beginning at 1:05pm. **Candlelit evening concerts** are performed, too. (Tickets cost around £12 ($18.60). For information, ☎ **0171/839-8362.**) The three Sunday services offer great **choral music,** often featuring choirs visiting from other countries. If I had to choose one quintessential Anglican service, it would be **Evensong,** usually at 5pm.

A place of worship has stood here since 1220; the current church, designed by James Gibbs, was completed in 1726. Its simple nave is enhanced by an intricate plasterwork ceiling. Curiously, the parish boundary passes through the middle of Buckingham Palace, and the names of many royal children appear on the baptismal registry. The Queen Mother, who resides at Clarence House, is also a parishioner.

In the crypt, there's an atmospheric café, shop, and the **London Brass Rubbing Centre** (open Mon–Sat 10–8pm, Sun noon–6pm).

St. Mary Le Bow

Cheapside, EC2. ☎ **0171/248-5139.** Free admission. Mon–Thurs 6:30am–6pm, Fri 6:30am–4pm. Tube: St. Paul's/Bank.

A true Cockney is said to be born within hearing distance of the famous Bow bells of this church. Destroyed in the Blitz, those bells have been replaced. This church certainly hasn't been blessed by the series of disasters that mark its sometimes gruesome history. The first occurred in 1091, when its roof was ripped off in a storm. When the church tower collapsed in 1271, twenty people were killed. In 1331, Queen Philippa and her ladies-in-waiting fell to the ground when a wooden balcony collapsed during a joust celebrating the birth of the Black Prince. The Great Fire engulfed the church, and it was rebuilt by Wren. The church was rededicated in 1964 after extensive restoration work.

St. Paul's, The Actors Church

Covent Garden, WC2. Free admission. Tube: Covent Garden.

As the Drury Lane Theatre, the Theatre Royal, and the Royal Opera House are all within its parish, St. Paul's has long been associated with the theatrical arts. Inside, you'll find scores of memorial plaques dedicated to such luminaries as Vivien Leigh, Laurence Harvey, Boris Karloff, Margaret Rutherford, and Noël Coward, to name only a few. Designed by Inigo Jones in 1631, this church has been substantially altered over the years, but it retains a quiet garden-piazza in the rear. Among the famous who are buried here are woodcarver Grinling Gibbons, writer Samuel Butler, and actress Ellen Terry. Landscape painter J. M. W. Turner and librettist W. S. Gilbert were both baptized here.

Southwark Cathedral

Montague Close, London Bridge, SE1. ☎ **0171/407-2939.** Free admission. Suggested donation £1 ($1.55). Daily Mon–Sat 8:30am–6pm. Tube: London Bridge.

There has been a church on this site for more than a thousand years. The present one dates from the 15th century; it was partly rebuilt in 1890. The previous one was the first Gothic church (1106) to be built in London. In the heart of London's first theatrical district, Shakespeare and Chaucer worshipped at services here. A Shakespeare birthday service is held annually. Inside is a carved memorial to the playwright (1912). A wooden effigy of a knight dates from 1275. In 1424, James I of Scotland married Mary Beaufort here. During the reign of Mary Tudor, Stephen Gardiner, the Bishop of Winchester, held a consistory court in the retro choir. This court condemned seven of the Marian martyrs to deaths. Later, the same retro choir was rented to a baker and even used to house pigs.

Lunchtime concerts are regularly given on Monday and Tuesday. Call for exact times and schedules.

Wesley's Chapel, House & Museum

49 City Rd., EC1. ☎ **0171/253-2262.** Chapel is free; house and Museum £4 ($6.20) adult, £2 ($3.10) children 5–17. House and museum Mon–Sat 10am–4pm (closed Thurs from 12:45–1:30). Tube: Old Street or Moorgate.

John Wesley, the founder of Methodism, established this church in 1778 as his London base. The man who rode on horseback throughout the English countryside and preached in the open air is buried in a grave behind the chapel. (He lived at no. 47 City Road.) Surviving the Blitz, the church later fell into serious disrepair; major restoration was completed in the 1970s. In the crypt, the museum traces the history of Methodism to today. Across the road in Bunhill Fields is the Dissenters Graveyard where Daniel Defoe, William Blake, and John Bunyan are buried.

Westminster Cathedral

Ashley Place, SW1. ☎ **0171/798-9055.** Cathedral free; tower, £2 ($3.10). Cathedral, daily 7am–8pm; tower, Apr–Nov, daily 9am–1pm, 2–5pm; otherwise Thurs–Sun only. Tube: Victoria.

This spectacular brick-and-stone church (1903) is the headquarters of the Roman Catholic Church in Britain. Done in high Byzantine style, it's massive—360 feet long and 156 feet wide. One hundred different marbles compose the richly decorated interior. Eight dark-green marble columns support the nave. The huge balacchino over the high altar is lifted by eight yellow marble columns. Mosaics emblazon the chapels and the vaulting of the sanctuary. Visitors can climb to the top of the 273-foot-tall campanile; they're rewarded with a sweeping view over Victoria and Westminster. In 1903, composer Sir Edward Elgar conducted the first performance of his celebrated choral work, the oratorio setting of Cardinal Newman's *The Dream of Gerontius* here (a piece initially regarded as a failure but later acclaimed).

HISTORIC BUILDINGS/MONUMENTS

✪ Cabinet War Rooms

Clive Steps, King Charles Street, SW1. ☎ **0171/930-6961.** Admission. £4.40 ($6.80) adults, £3.20 ($4.95) students and seniors; £2.20 ($3.40) children 5–16. Daily 10am–5:50pm (last admission 5:15pm). Tube: St. James's Park or Westminster.

These underground rooms served as the British government's headquarters during World War II. The Cabinet Room, Map Room, Churchill's Emergency Bedroom, and the Telephone Room (where numerous calls to Roosevelt were made) have been restored to their 1940s appearance.

Kensington Palace State Apartments and Court Dress Collection

Kensington Gardens. ☎ **0171/937-9561.** Admission £5.50 ($8.55) adults; £4.10 ($6.35) seniors and students; £3 ($4.65) children 5–15. [*Author's note:* The palace will be open only

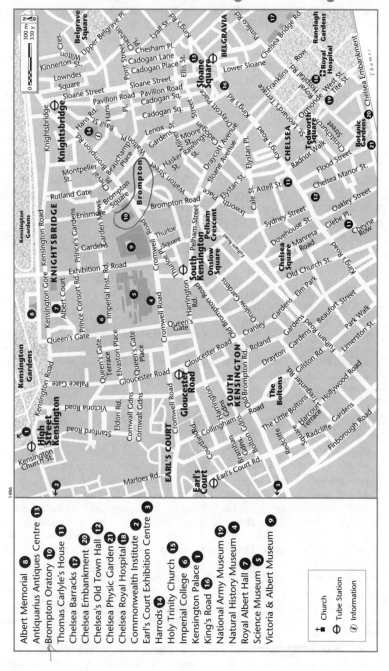

Albert Memorial **8**
Antiquarius Antiques Centre **13**
Brompton Oratory **10**
Thomas Carlyle's House **11**
Chelsea Barracks **17**
Chelsea Embankment **20**
Chelsea's Old Town Hall **12**
Chelsea Physic Garden **21**
Chelsea Royal Hospital **18**
Commonwealth Institute **2**
Earl's Court Exhibition Centre **3**
Harrods **14**
Holy Trinity Church **15**
Imperial College **6**
Kensington Palace **16**
King's Road **16**
National Army Museum **19**
Natural History Museum **4**
Royal Albert Hall **7**
Science Museum **5**
Victoria & Albert Museum **9**

✝ Church
Ⓣ Tube Station
ⓘ Information

May 1–Sept 30 in 1997 Mon–Sat 9am–5pm, Sun 11am–5pm. Closed for renovation during the winter.] Tube: Queensway or Bayswater.

The air of Whitehall aggravated the asthma of King William III, and so he and his wife Mary purchased this home from the Earl of Nottingham in 1689. The royal couple commissioned Sir Christopher Wren to make some alterations. Queen Anne, who succeeded William III in 1702, found the palace comfortable, too. Anne laid out the gardens in English style; she had the Orangery House built after designs of Nicholas Hawksmoor. The queen spent many happy times at Kensington Palace with her friend Sarah Churchill, the Duchess of Marlborough, until the duchess complained that she had been "kept waiting like a Scotch lady with a petition." The queen asked her to put it in writing; the duchess did and they never associated again. Queen Anne died here in 1714 from apoplexy brought on by overeating. The first two Georges lived at the palace, but George III preferred Buckingham House, so the palace fell into disrepair. Edward, duke of Kent, the fourth son of George III, did have apartments here, though. His daughter, the future Queen Victoria, was born here on May 24, 1819. On June 27, 1837, the archbishop of Canterbury and the Lord Chamberlain roused her from sleep to inform her that she had succeeded her uncle William IV to the throne. That night, she slept outside her mother's room for the first time in her life. Three weeks later, she moved into Buckingham Palace. Today, the Princess of Wales, Princess Margaret, the Duke and Duchess of Gloucester, and Princess Michael of Kent all have apartments here.

Only the **State Apartments** and **Court Dress Collection** are open to the public. Among the highlights in the first are the Cupola Room, where Queen Victoria was baptised and where she was told that she was queen, and the King's Gallery, which features among others seven ceiling paintings depicting the journeys of Ulysses. The dress collection displays court fashions and uniforms from 1760 to 1950. The gardens and parkland surrounding the palace are beautiful, and you can have lunch or tea in the Orangery.

Mansion House

Bank, EC4. ☎ **0171/626-2500.** Free admission. Tours given on Tues, Wed, and Thurs at 11am and 2pm. Tube: Mansion House.

This is the official residence of the lord mayor of London during his one-year term of office. The original plans of this impressive Palladian building were executed by George Dance. The foundation stone was laid in 1739. The 103-foot-wide facade has a raised portico supported by six Corinthian columns. On the pediment, sculptures depict London trampling Envy and leading in Plenty, while Father Thames stands by. In 1768, when John Wilkes was elected to Parliament, a mob of his supporters broke the windows and chandeliers of Mansion House because the lights were not illumined to celebrate his victory. The house has several prison cells, one of which housed suffragette Emmeline Pankhurst in 1914 for demonstrating outside Buckingham Palace. Today the Mansion House houses the staff of the Lord Mayor's Office.

Spencer House

27 St. James's Place, SW1. ☎ **0171/499-8620.** Admission £6 ($9.30) adults, £5 ($7.75) seniors and children under 16; children under 10 not allowed. Sun 10:45am–4:45pm. Closed August and January. Tube: Green Park.

This is one of the city's most beautiful buildings. It was built in 1766 for the first Earl Spencer, heir to Sarah Churchill, Duchess of Marlborough. By 1927, it was no longer a private residence and has experienced a checkered history since then. At various times, it was used by the Ladies' Army and Navy Club, Christie's, and British Oxygen Gases Ltd. Finally, it was restored and opened as a museum in 1990.

INSTITUTIONS AS ENGLISH AS SHEPHERD'S PIE

Law Courts

Strand, WC2. Free admission. During sessions Mon–Fri 10:30am–1pm and 2–4pm. Tube: Holborn or Temple.

At these 60 or more courts presently in use, all civil and some criminal cases are heard. Designed by G. E. Street, the neo-Gothic buildings (1874–82) contain more than 1,000 rooms and 3.5 miles of corridors. Sculptures of Christ, King Solomon, and King Alfred grace the front door; Moses is depicted at the back entrance. On the second Saturday in November, the annually elected lord mayor is sworn in by the lord chief justice.

Lord's Cricket Ground

St. John's Wood, NW8. ☎ **0171/266-3825** or 289-1611. Tickets £8–£40 ($12.40–$62). Box office, Mon–Fri 9:30am–5:30pm. Tube: St. John's Wood or Marylebone.

This is the elegant home of English cricket, where the first test against the Australians was played in 1884. Originally, Thomas Lord founded the Marylebone Cricket Club in 1787 on a site in Dorset Square. In 1811, the club was relocated to St. John's Wood, and it came to its current location in 1816. For complete information, see the "Spectator Sports" section, below.

✪ Old Bailey

Newgate Street, EC4. ☎ **0171/248-3277**. Free admission. Mon–Fri 10:30am–1pm and 2–4pm. Tube: St. Paul's.

This is the nation's Central Criminal Court, affectionately known as the Old Bailey after a street that runs nearby. Today, it's a fascinating experience to observe the bewigged barristers presenting their cases to the high court judges, who include the lord chancellor and the lord chief justice.

Built on the site of Newgate Prison, it opened in 1907. Added to in the 1970s, it now has 19 courtrooms and holding cells for 70 prisoners. Oscar Wilde was among the famous defendants tried here.

Note: No cameras, electronic equipment, or food. No children under 14. These rules are strictly adhered to.

MARITIME/WATERFRONT SIGHTS

Butlers Wharf

On the South Bank of the Thames, SE1. Tube: Tower Hill.

Near Tower Bridge, this complex of shops and restaurants has river views.

Cutty Sark

King William Walk, Greenwich, SE10. ☎ **0181/858-3445**. Admission £3.25 ($5.05) adults, £2.25 (3.50) children. Mon–Sat 10am–6pm (5pm in winter). Sun noon–6pm (to 5pm in winter). Closed Dec 24–26. DLR: Island Gardens. River launches: Greenwich Pier.

This 19th-century sailing clipper is the most famous of those that made regular tea runs to China. Built in Dumbarton, it covered almost 400 miles of sea per day. Its name is derived from Rabbie Burns's poem "Tam O' Shanter." Restored in 1922, the ship has been in dry dock since 1954. Highlights aboard include a fine collection of mastheads and maritime paintings and prints.

Gipsy Moth IV

Cutty Sark Gardens, Greenwich, SE10. ☎ **0181/858-3445**. Admission 60p (95¢) adults, 40p (60¢) children. Mon–Sat 10am–6pm (5pm in winter); Sun noon–6pm (to 5pm in winter). Closed Nov–March. DLR: Island Gardens. River launches: Greenwich Pier.

Attractions: Mayfair & St. James's

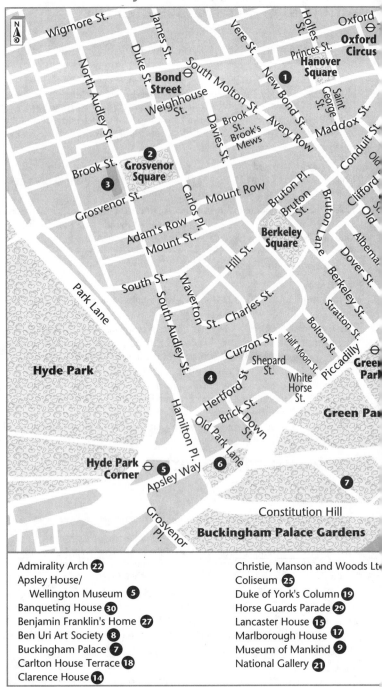

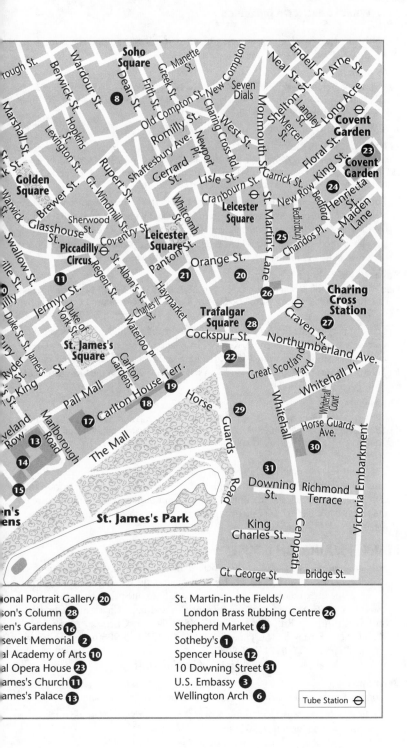

Soho Square

Golden Square

Leicester Square

Piccadilly Circus

St. James's Square

Trafalgar Square **28**

St. James's Park

Charing Cross Station **27**

Covent Garden **23**

Covent Garden **24**

8

11

21 **20**

25

26

22

29

30

31

17 **18** **19**

13

14

15

Soho Square · Manette St. · Greek St. · New Compton St. · Neal St. · Endell St. · Arne St.

Wardour St. · Berwick St. · Dean St. · Frith St. · Old Compton St. · New Compton St. · Seven Dials · Shelton St. · Langley St. · Mercer St. · Monmouth St. · Long Acre

Marshall St. · Hopkins · Lexington St. · Rupert St. · Shaftesbury Ave. · Romilly St. · West St. · Charing Cross Rd. · Floral St. · King St.

Brewer St. · Gt. Windmill St. · Gerrard St. · Newport Pl. · Lisle St. · Garrick St. · New Row · Bedford · Henrietta St. · Maiden Lane

Glasshouse St. · Sherwood St. · Coventry St. · Whitcomb St. · Cranbourn St. · St. Martin's Lane · Bedfordbury · Chandos Pl.

Swallow St. · Regent St. · Leicester Square · Panton St. · Orange St.

Jermyn St. · St. Alban's St. · Haymarket · Charles II St. · Waterloo Pl.

Duke of York St. · Duke St. · St. James's St. · King St. · Ryder St.

Pall Mall · Carlton Gardens · Carlton House Terr. · Cockspur St. · Great Scotland Yard · Northumberland Ave. · Craven St.

Cleveland Row · Marlborough Road · The Mall · Horse Guards Road · Whitehall · Whitehall Pl. · Whitehall Court · Horse Guards Ave. · Victoria Embankment

Downing St. · Richmond Terrace · King Charles St. · Cenotaph · Gt. George St. · Bridge St.

153

This is the boat in which Sir Francis Chichester sailed solo around the world from August 27, 1966, to May 28, 1967.

HMS *Belfast*

Morgan's Lane, Tooley Street, SE1. ☎ **0171/407-6434.** Admission £4.50 ($6.95) adults, £3.20 ($4.95) seniors, £2.20 ($3.40) children 5–17. Daily 10am–6pm. Closed Dec 24, 25, 26. Tube: Tower Hill or London Bridge. River launches: Tower Pier.

A World War II cruiser with seven decks to explore.

✪ National Maritime Museum

Romney Road, Greenwich, SE10. ☎ **0181/858-4422.** Admission £5.50 ($8.50) adults, £4.50 ($6.95) seniors, £3 ($4.65) children 5–16. Daily 10am–5pm. Closed Dec 24–26. Rail: Charing Cross to Maze Hill. DLR: Island Gardens. Bus: 177, 180, 188.

This museum adjoining the Queen's House is undergoing reconstruction. The new Nelson gallery displays many priceless items associated with Horatio Nelson, including the coat with the hole made by the bullet that killed him. The 20th-century gallery shows modern naval warfare illustrated with videos, paintings, and ship models both merchant and military.

Royal Naval College

King William Walk, off Romney Road, Greenwich, SE10. ☎ **0181/858-2154.** Free admission. Daily 2:30–5pm. Closed Dec 24–26, Good Friday. Rail: Maze Hill Riverbus to Greenwich. Bus: 177, 180, 188.

This complex designed by Sir Christopher Wren in 1696 occupies four blocks named after King Charles, Queen Anne, King William, and Queen Mary. Formerly, Greenwich Palace stood here from 1422 to 1640. See the magnificent Painted Hall by Thornhill where the body of Nelson lay in state in 1805 and also the Georgian chapel of St. Peter and St. Paul.

Thames Barrier

Unity Way, Woolwich, SE18. ☎ **0181/854-1373.** Admission £2.50 ($3.85) adults, £1.55 ($2.40) seniors or children 5–17. Daily Mon–Fri 10:30am–5pm; Sat–Sun 10:30am–5:30pm. Bus: 177, 180. River launches: From Westminster, Charing Cross, Tower, and Greenwich piers.

This giant feat of engineering opened in 1984 to protect London from flooding. It consists of four huge gates, each weighing 3,000 tons, and six smaller ones. When closed, these ten gates seal the upper river off from the sea. The Visitor Centre on the south bank has exhibits that illustrate the operation of London's tidal flood defenses.

MARKETS/AUCTION HOUSES

Auction houses are great fun to visit. Before the auction, you can inspect the merchandise; during it, you can share in the excitement of the bidding and buying. Items on sale at the three houses listed below may range from fine paintings, furniture, and jewelry to wines, stamps, cars, toys, valentines, and fans. Check out: **Christie's,** 85 Old Brompton Rd., SW7 (☎ **0171/581-7611**); **Christie, Manson and Woods Ltd.,** 8 King St., St. James's, SW1 (☎ **0171/839-9060**); and **Sotheby's,** 34 New Bond St. (☎ **0171/493-8080**).

As for markets, here's a very short list of London's best.

Bermondsey

Bermondsey Square, Fri only 5am–1pm. SE1. Tube: Elephant & Castle or Borough.

Get here early (it opens at 5am) to uncover the bargains at this antique market. It's been going strong for almost 50 years.

Billingsgate
North Quay, West India Docks Road, Isle of Dogs, E14. Tues–Sat 5–8:30am. DLR: West India Quay.

This ancient fish market, which has operated since Saxon times, relocated to a warehouse here in 1962. Although the porters no longer wear their "bobbing" hats (so named after the amount they charged to carry the boxes of fish from the wholesaler to the retailer), it's still a fascinating place to come early in the morning. Forklifts now do the duties that were performed by porters wearing leather and wood hats that were supposedly modeled after the helmets bowmen wore at the Battle of Agincourt.

Camden Lock
NW1. Mon–Fri 10–6pm, Sat–Sun 9–6pm. Tube: Camden Town.

A London youth scene. On weekends—especially Sunday—this market is flooded with young people checking out the stalls featuring crafts, bric-a-brac, clothes (a lot of leather, jeans, tie-dyed items, Doc Martens, etc.), and furniture. The market is held in a courtyard off Camden High Street. Tucked away on the sidestreets at the east end of Camden High are some decent restaurants.

Greenwich Antiques Market
Greenwich High Road (opposite St. Alfeges Church), SE10. Sat–Sun 8am–4pm. Rail: Greenwich.
DLR: From Tower Gateway to Island Gardens then cross river via pedestrian tunnel.

This market has everything—books, furniture, crafts, and all kinds of bric-a-brac. A fun experience.

Leather Lane
EC1. Mon–Fri 10–2:30pm. Tube: Chancery Lane.

This lively lunchtime market is close to Hatten Garden. It's London's diamond center.

New Caledonian
Tower Bridge Road, SE1. Fri only 6am–2pm. Tube: Borough or London Bridge.

A favorite antique market. Come early to find the gems.

New Covent Garden
Nine Elms, SW8. Mon–Fri 3:30–10:30am. Tube: Vauxhall.

The old Covent Garden market moved here in 1974 and became new. It's the biggest wholesale fruit, vegetable, and flower market in the nation and still worth visiting.

Petticoat Lane
Middlesex Street, E1. Sun only 9–2pm. Tube: Liverpool Street or Aldgate.

Not what it used to be, now that London has Sunday shopping and other events to draw the crowds. Still a London scene, though.

Portobello Road Market
Portobello Road, W11. Mon–Wed 8am–5pm, Thurs 8am–1pm, Fri–Sat 8am–6pm. Flea market at the northern end on Fri and Sat. Tube: Ladbroke Grove or Notting Hill Gate.

Atmospheric and fun. Antiques, clothes, and bric-a-brac along a road that never seems to end. The daily market features fruits and vegetables. Saturday is the antiques day. Check out the many antique stores along Portobello Road, too.

MUSEUMS & GALLERIES

Apsley House/Wellington Museum
149 Piccadilly, Hyde Park Corner, W1. ☎ **0171/499-5676.** Admission £3 ($4.65) adults, £1.50 ($2.30) children. Tues–Sun 11am–5pm. Closed Dec 24–26, Jan 1, May 1. Tube: Hyde Park Corner.

This was the London palace of the first Duke of Wellington. It houses his magnificent collection of paintings, silver, porcelain, and sculpture, which are displayed within the Robert Adam and Benjamin Dean Wyatt interiors. The eighth Duke of Wellington and his son retain private apartments in the house, making it one of the great town houses in London where the collections remain intact and the family is still in residence. The house was built by Robert Adam between 1771 and 1778 for the second Earl of Bathurst, Baron Apsley, which is when it acquired its nickname as Number One, because it was the first house beyond the tollgate at the top of Knightsbridge. It was here that Wellington returned after his triumphant military career, which culminated in his victory over Napoleon at Waterloo. The collection of more than 200 paintings includes major works by Velazquez, Goya, Brueghel, and Steen. Note the huge nude statue of Napoleon by Canova in the vestibule.

Bank of England Museum

Threadneedle Street, EC2. ☎ **0171/601-5545.** Free admission. Summer Mon–Fri 10am–5pm; winter Mon–Fri 10am–4pm. Closed Dec 25, 26, and Jan 1. Tube: Bank.

This museum housed in the Bank of England provides insight into the institution that's long been the powerhouse of England's empire. It traces the history of the bank from its foundation by Royal Charter in 1694 to its role today as the nation's central bank. Displays include gold bars, bank notes, and pikes and muskets used to defend the bank. A video presentation reveals some of the workings of the central bank.

Barbican Art Gallery

Barbican Centre, EC2. ☎ **0171/382-7105,** 0171/588-9023 for recorded information. Admission £5 ($7.75) adults, £3 ($4.65) students, seniors, and children; reduced admission from 5pm weekdays, £3 ($4.65). Mon, Wed–Sat 10am–6:45pm, Tues 10am–5:45pm, Sun noon–6:45pm. Tube: Moorgate, Barbican, St. Paul's, Bank. The main entrance is on Silk Street.

In the brutally ugly Barbican Centre, this gallery has major exhibitions. A recent one was *Impressionism in Britain.*

Ben Uri Art Society

21 Dean St., 4th floor, W1. ☎ **0171/437-2852.** Free admission. Mon–Thurs 10–5pm, Sun 2–5pm. Tube: Tottenham Court Road.

This museum has regular exhibitions of works by Jewish artists and is the home of the Ben Uri collection of more than 700 works, including paintings by David Bomberg and Mark Gertler, and sculpture by Sir Jacob Epstein.

British Library

Great Russell Street, WC1. ☎ **0171/323-7111.** Free admission. Hours vary, depending on the particular reading room. Tube: Tottenham Court Road.

In 1973, three institutions—the British Museum Library, the National Central Library, and the National Lending Library for Science and Technology—were combined to form the British Library. Its main reading room is currently in the British Museum, although it's not formally part of the museum. The reference division alone contains nearly ten million books, plus ancillary collections of maps, charts, ancient papyri, and more. At the end of 1996, the library will relocate to new buildings near St. Pancras, but will not actually open until 1998.

Commonwealth Institute

Kensington High Street, W8. ☎ **0171/603-4535.** Admission £1 ($1.55) adults, 50p (75¢) children. Mon–Sat 10am–5pm, Sun 2–5pm. Tube: High Street Kensington.

This organization has exhibits on the culture and history of the 50 commonwealth countries. The galleries, which are currently closed, will reopen in the spring of 1997.

Courtauld Institute Galleries

Somerset House, the Strand, WC2. ☎ **0171/873-2526.** Admission £3 ($4.65) adults, £1.50 ($2.35) students, children 5–15, and seniors. Mon–Sat 10am–6pm, Sun 2–6pm. Closed Dec 24–26, Jan 1. Tube: Temple or Covent Garden.

Named for its chief benefactor, textile mogul Samuel Courtauld, who collected Impressionist and post-Impressionist paintings, this museum is housed in the elegant Somerset House, a neoclassical masterpiece itself. Some fine Renaissance paintings are on view, including the intense *Master of Flemalle Triptych* and works by Tintoretto and Veronese. Among the remarkable works are Bruegel's *Christ and the Woman Taken in Adultery* and Cranach's *Adam and Eve.* Almost a whole gallery is devoted to Rubens. The collection also includes works by Gainsborough, Raeburn, Ramsay, Romney, and Turner (watercolors) as well as paintings by Ben Nicholson, Graham Sutherland, and Larry Rivers, but they are not currently on display.

The glory of this collection, though, is the Impressionist works—Manet's *Bar at the Folies Bergère;* Monet's *Banks of the Seine at Argenteuil; Lady with Parasol* by Degas; *La Loge* by Renoir; Van Gogh's *Self-Portrait with Bandaged Ear;* and a number of Cézannes, including *The Card Players.*

Design Museum

28 Shad Thames, London, SE1. ☎ **0171/378-6055.** Admission £4.50 ($6.95) adults, £3.50 ($5.40) students and children. Weekdays 11:30am–6pm; weekends noon–6pm. Tube: Tower Hill (then walk over the bridge) or London Bridge (then walk along Tooley Street). DLR: Tower Gateway (then walk over the bridge). Bus: 15, 78, 47, 42, or 188.

Part of the new Docklands development, this museum displays all kinds of manufactured products that have won love and acclaim for their design. The Volkswagen Bug and the anglepoise lamp are just two examples. The museum shop has everything from designer socks to sleek alarm clocks.

Dulwich Picture Gallery

College Road, SE 21. ☎ **0181/693-5254.** Admission £2 adults, £1 seniors and students, free for children under 16; free on Friday. Tues–Fri 10am–5pm, Sat 11am–5pm, Sun 2–5pm. Closed ... Sunday. Tube: Brixton then P4 bus. Train: West Dulwich.

Freud's Couch

... e gallery in England, it houses a fine collection of Old Mas- ... Canaletto, Gainsborough, Poussin, Rembrandt, Rubens, and

0171/435-3471. Admission £3.60 ($5.60) adults, £1.80 ($2.80) ... m; Apr–Oct, Sat–Sun 11am–5:30pm, Wed–Fri 2–5:30pm. Closed

... of historic homes will want to visit this home built in 1693. ... 8th century by a merchant named Fenton. In the 1950s, the ... ational Trust by then owner Lady Binning to display her col- ... d porcelain. Also on exhibit is a collection of musical instru- ... rder, including a 1612 harpsichord that was probably used by Handel.

Freud Museum

20 Maresfield Gardens, Hampstead, NW3. ☎ **0171/435-2002.** Admission £3 ($4.65) adults, £1.50 ($2.35) students; free for children under 12. Wed–Sun noon–5pm. Tube: Finchley Road.

This was the London home of Sigmund Freud, the founder of psychoanalysis. Freud lived, worked, and died here after he and his family left Nazi-occupied Vienna as refugees in 1938. On view are rooms containing Freud's furniture, paintings, photographs, letters, and personal effects. Of particular interest is Freud's study and library with his famous couch and his large collection of Egyptian, Roman, and Oriental antiquities. Archive film programs are also given.

Geffrye Museum

Kingsland Road, E2. ☎ **0171/739-9893.** Free admission. Tues–Sat 10am–5pm, Sun and holidays 2–5pm. Closed Good Friday, Dec 24–26, and Jan 1. Garden open April–Oct. Tube: Liverpool St. Bus: 22A, 22B, or 149 from Bishopsgate.

This museum is worth a visit for its architecture alone, for it's housed in the former almshouses of the Ironmongers' Company, a harmonious grouping of 18th-century buildings. The gardens in front, especially the herb garden, are used to enhance the period rooms. A series of period rooms traces the history of English domestic interior design from 1600 to the present—from Jacobean oak through fine Georgian and ornate Victorian to art deco and postwar utility. Special exhibitions explore a wide variety of themes. In December, the rooms sparkle with festive decorations, as 400 years of Christmas tradition comes to life.

Hayward Gallery

South Bank Centre, SE1. ☎ **0171/928-3144.** Admission varies. Mon, Thurs–Sun 10am–6pm; Tues–Wed 10am–8pm. Tube: Waterloo or Embankment.

Part of the South Bank Centre, this gallery puts on a variety of contemporary, historical, and international shows. Call for schedule of exhibits.

Imperial War Museum

Lambeth Road, SE1. ☎ **0171/416-5000.** Admission £4.10 ($6.35) adults, £3.10 ($4.80) seniors, £2.05 ($3.20) children 5–16. Daily 10–6pm. Closed major holidays. Tube: Lambeth North or Elephant & Castle.

This museum is dedicated to war history since 1914, with exhibits on both World Wars I and II. The Blitz, life in the trenches, and flying on Operation Jericho are simulated. Art is displayed, too.

The museum occupies an 1815 building that was part of Royal Bethlehem Hospital (Bedlam), where "distracted" patients were kept chained to the walls, dunked in water, or whipped when they became violent. In the 17th and 18th centuries, Bedlam was one of the major London "sights," and visitors paid a hefty entrance fee.

Institute of Contemporary Arts (ICA)

The Mall, SW1. ☎ **0171/930-6393** for recorded information. Galleries, £1.50 ($2.35). Mon noon–11pm, Tues–Sat noon–1am, Sun noon–11pm Tube: Piccadilly Circus or Charing Cross.

Publicly assisted, ICA is a major forum for arts. It maintains a theater, cinema, café, bar, bookshop, lecture program, and two galleries for the avante-garde. See also "Fringe Theater," in Chapter 9 for more information.

Jewish Museum

129 Albert Street, Camden Town, NW1. ☎ **0171/284-1997.** Admission £3 ($4.65) adults, £1.50 ($2.30) seniors and children. Apr–Sept Sun, Tues–Thurs 10am–4pm; Oct–Mar Tues–Thurs 10am–4pm, Sun 10am–1pm. Tube: Euston or Russell Square.

This museum aims to tell the story of Jewish life in Britain. On display are silver Torah bells made in London and two loving cups presented by the Spanish and Portuguese Synagogue to the lord mayor in the 18th century.

London Canal Museum

12–13 New Wharf Rd., King's Cross, N1. ☎ **0171/713-0836.** Admission charged. Tues–Sun 10am–4:30pm. Closed Dec 25, 26, and Jan 1. Tube: King's Cross.

Life on London's canals—trade and the barges that traveled them—is shown here.

London Transport Museum

Floral Market, Covent Garden, WC2. ☎ **0171/379-6344.** Admission £4.25 ($6.70) adults, £2.50 ($3.85) seniors and children 5–15. Daily 10am–6pm. Closed Dec 24, 25, 26. Tube: Covent Garden or Charing Cross.

With a collection of omnibuses, paintings, and models, this museum traces 200 years of London transport history. The story is enlivened by several interactive video exhibits—you can put yourself in the driver's seat of a bus or tube train. A good gift shop, too.

Madame Tussaud's

Marylebone Road, NW1. ☎ **0171/935-6861.** Admission £9 ($13.95) adults, £6.25 ($9.70) children 5–15, £7 ($10.85) seniors. July–Aug, daily 9am–5:50pm; Sept–June, Mon–Fri 10am–5:30pm, Sat–Sun 9:30am–5:30pm. Closed Dec 25. Tube: Baker Street. Bus: 2,13, 18, 27, 30, 74, 82, 113, 159, 176.

Eerily lifelike figures have made this century-old waxworks world-famous. The figures from the original molds of Voltaire and members of the French court, to whom Madame Tussaud had direct access, are fascinating. Unfortunately, however, this "museum" gives the lion's share of its space to images of modern superstars like Michael Jackson and political figures like George Bush. The dungeon-level Chamber of Horrors, which features the likenesses of Charles Manson, Jack the Ripper, Dracula, as well as audio-visual tableaux of Joan of Arc being burned at the stake and Guy Fawkes being hung, drawn, and quartered, is the stuff tourist traps are made of. Despite the fact that Madame Tussaud's is expensive and somewhat overrated, it attracts more than 2.5 million visitors annually. If you go, get there early to get a jump on the crowds.

Museum of Garden History

St. Mary-at-Lambeth, Lambeth Palace Road, SE1. ☎ **0171/401-8865.** Free admission. Mon–Fri 10:30am–4pm, Sun 10:30am–5pm (closed Sat). Closed second Sun of Dec to the first Sun in March. Tube: Waterloo or Victoria, then bus 507.

The garden at this museum is planted according to a 17th-century plan and contains many rare plants introduced into the country by the Tradescants, royal gardeners to Charles I. Another garden inspired by Persian gardens of old is open on Wednesdays and the first Sunday of the month. The museum houses a collection of garden tools and artifacts. It's located south of the Thames, in a historic church and churchyard. Morning coffee and lunchtime snacks served daily.

✪ Museum of London

150 London Wall, EC2. ☎ **0171/600-3699.** Admission £3.50 ($5.40) adults, £1.75 ($2.70) children, £8.50 ($13.15) families (valid for three months). Free from 4:30pm. Tues–Sat 10am–5:50pm, Sun noon–5:50pm. Tube: Barbican, Moorgate, St. Paul's. Bus: 4, 56, 172.

For anyone interested in the city's history, this is the place to begin. Two floors of ← exhibits trace the city's development from Roman times to today. Appropriate background music makes for an evocative tour. Among the highlights are a bedroom in a merchant's house from the Stuart period; the lord mayor's coach; an audio-visual presentation on the Great Fire, as described by the diarist Samuel Pepys; a Victorian barber's shop; and the original elevators from Selfridges department store.

Museum of Mankind

6 Burlington Gardens, W1. ☎ **0171/437-2224.** Free admission. Mon–Sat 10am–5pm, Sun 2:30–6pm. Tube: Piccadilly Circus or Green Park.

Cultural artifacts from Australia, the Pacific Islands, North and South America, Africa, and Asia are on display here—native houses, modes of transport, clothes, and tools. A fine collection of African art is showcased. Note the nine-foot-high Easter Island statue brought back to England by Captain Cook. Home of the ethnographic department of the British Museum.

○ Museum of the Moving Image (MOMI)

National Film Theatre, South Bank, SE1. ☎ **0171/928-3535**, 0171/401-2636 for recorded information. Admission £5.95 ($9.25) adults, £4.85 ($7.50) students and seniors, £4 ($6.20) children 5–16. Daily 10am–6pm; last admission 5pm. Tube: Waterloo is closer, but the short walk over Hungerford Bridge from the Embankment Underground station is more scenic.

This lively, "hands-on" celebration of film and television is one of the city's best museums. Fifty chronologically organized exhibits are designed to captivate. They're staffed with outgoing, costumed actors, who never step out of character. Visitors can read the news from a TelePrompTer, create their own animated strip, and play around with many interactive exhibits. Films are shown daily. A good insight into British culture.

National Army Museum

Royal Hospital Road, Chelsea, SW3. ☎ **0171/730-0717**. Free admission. Daily 10am–5:30pm. Closed Dec 24, 25, 26, Jan 1, Good Friday, early May public holiday. Tube: Sloane Square.

This museum tells the story of the British army from the raising of the Yeoman of the Guard in 1485 to the U.N. peacekeeping troops of today. Displays include medals (including 30 original Victoria Crosses), paintings of battle scenes, weapons, and uniforms. A model of the Battle of Waterloo has more than 70,000 model soldiers. Video presentations are given. Even the skeleton of Napoleon's horse is on view.

National Portrait Gallery

St. Martin's Place, WC2. ☎ **0171/306-0055**. Free admission. Mon–Sat 10am–6pm, Sun noon–6pm. Closed Dec 24–26, Jan 1, Good Friday, May 1. Tube: Trafalgar Square or Leicester Square.

This gallery has more than 9,000 paintings and 500,000 photographs in its collection. Those on display are in chronological order. Some have been painted by great artists like those of Henry VII, Henry VIII, and Sir Thomas More by Holbein, or the one of T. S. Eliot by Sir Jacob Epstein. Others have been done by amateurs, including one of Jane Austen by her sister.

National Postal Museum

King Edward Building, King Edward Street, EC1. ☎ **0171/239-5420**. Free admission. Mon–Fri 9:30am–4:30pm. Closed all bank holidays. Tube: St. Paul's, the Barbican. Bus: 4, 8, 22B 25, 172, 501, 521, 11, 15, 17, 23,26, 76, 172.

In 1840, Britain introduced the world's first postage stamp, the Penny Black, but for 200 years before that a postal service of sorts was operating. In the main gallery, all the stamps of Britain are on display. One exhibit shows original art compared with the issued stamps. Also displayed are valentines and other greeting cards; scales and handstamps; and letter boxes, which were introduced by the Post Office surveyor and novelist Anthony Trollope in 1852.

Old Royal Observatory

Flamsteed House, Greenwich Park, SE10. ☎ **0181/858-4422**. Admission £5.50 ($8.50) adults, £4.50 ($6.95) students, £3 ($4.65) children 5–16 (includes National Maritime Museum and Queens House). Daily 10am–5pm. Closed Dec 24–26. Rail: Charing Cross to Maze Hill. DLR: Island Gardens. Bus: 177, 180, 188.

Located high on a hill overlooking the Thames, this is the original home of Greenwich Mean Time. The observatory has the largest refracting telescope in the United Kingdom and a collection of historic timekeepers and astronomical instruments. You can stand astride the meridian and set your watch precisely by the falling time-ball. Wren designed the Octagon Room. Here the first royal astronomer, Flamsteed, made

Attractions: Above Hyde Park

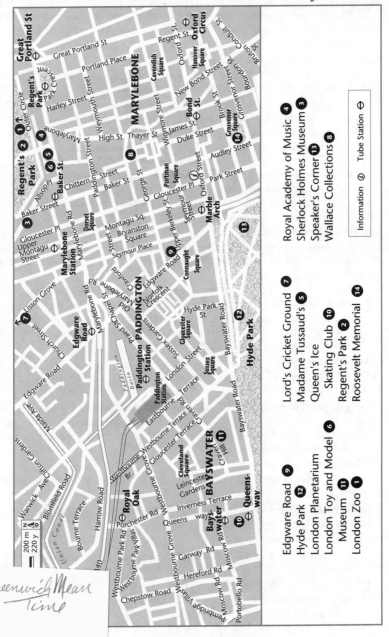

Greenwich Mean Time

Edgware Road 9
Hyde Park 12
London Planetarium
London Toy and Model 6
Museum 11
London Zoo 1

Lord's Cricket Ground 7
Madame Tussaud's 5
Queen's Ice
Skating Club 10
Regent's Park 2
Roosevelt Memorial 14

Royal Academy of Music 4
Sherlock Holmes Museum 3
Speaker's Corner 13
Wallace Collections 8

Information ⓘ   Tube Station ⊖

his 30,000 observations that formed the basis of his *Historia Coelestis Britannica*. Edmond Halley, who discovered Halley's Comet, succeeded him. In 1833, the ball on the tower was hung to enable shipmasters to set their chronometers accurately.

Percival David Foundation of Chinese Art

53 Gordon Square, WC1. ☎ **0171/387-3909.** Free admission. Mon–Fri 10:30am–5pm. Closed bank holidays. Tube: Russell Square, Euston Square, Euston, Goodge Street.

Sir Percival David presented this fine collection of Chinese ceramics to the University of London in 1950. The more than 1,700 objects date mainly from the 10th to 18th centuries. They're not only exquisitely beautiful, but some bear important inscriptions by such emperors as Qianlong (1736–95). The stonewares from the Song (960–1279) and Yuan (1279–1368) dynasties are exceptional, and include examples of rare Ru and Guan wares. Most familiar are the blue-and-white porcelains. Polychrome wares are also represented, including examples of the doucai wares from the Chenghua period (1465–87) as well as a group of 18th-century porcelains known as Gu yue xuan.

Royal Academy of Arts

Burlington House, Piccadilly, W1. ☎ **0171/439-7438.** Admission varies, depending on the exhibition. Daily 10am–6pm. Closed Dec 24–26, Good Friday. Tube: Piccadilly Circus or Green Park.

Created in 1768 during the reign of George III, the academy included Sir Joshua Reynolds, Thomas Gainsborough, and Benjamin West among its founding members. Since its beginning, each academician had to donate a work of art, so over the years the academy has built up a sizable collection. The annual exhibition has been held for more than 200 years. The Sackler Galleries opened in 1991.

✪ Saatchi Gallery

98A Boundary Rd., NW8. ☎ **0171/624-8299.** Admission £3.50($5.40), free Thurs. Thurs–Sun 12–6 pm. Tube: St. John's Wood.

In the world of contemporary art, this collection is unparalleled. Charles Saatchi is one of Britain's greatest private collectors, and this personal museum features rotating displays from his vast holdings. Enter through the unmarked metal gateway of a former paint warehouse.

Sherlock Holmes Museum

221B Baker St., NW1. ☎ **0171/935-8866.** Admission £5 ($7.75) adults, £3 ($4.65) children 7–16. Daily 10am–6pm. Tube: Baker St.

Dedicated Holmes fans will want to visit the literary address of their hero-detective who "resided" here from 1881 to 1904.(23?*u*)

✪ Sir John Soane's Museum

13 Lincoln's Inn Fields, WC2. ☎ **0171/430-0175.** Free admission (donation requested). Tues–Sat 10am–5pm; first Tues of each month also 6–9pm. Tube: Holborn.

John Soane (1753–1837) was the son of a bricklayer who apprenticed himself to George Dance the Younger and Henry Holland before opening an architectural practice of his own. He married into great wealth and began collecting the things displayed in this wonderful house, which he designed and where he resided. Architectural fragments, casts, bronzes, sculpture, and cork models are displayed throughout his neoclassical home. The collection of paintings includes works by Turner, three Canalettos, and two series of paintings by Hogarth, *An Election* and *The Rake's Progress*. Other works, including a wonderful group of Piranesi drawings, are ingeniously hung behind special movable panels in the Picture Room. Of special note is the sarcophagus of Seti I (Pharaoh 1303–1290 B.C.), which Soane bought for

£2,000—a price so steep that it deterred the British Musem from its purchase. A new gallery opened in April 1995 displays changing exhibitions of architectural drawings from Soane's collection of over 30,000, which includes works by Dance, Sir Christopher Wren, Sir William Chambers, and Robert and James Adam.

Theatre Museum

Russell Street, WC2. ☎ **0171/836-7891.** Admission £3.50 ($5.40) adults, £2 ($3.10) seniors and children 5–17. Tues–Sun 11am–7pm. Closed Dec 25, 26, and Jan 1. Tube: Covent Garden or Charing Cross.

A branch of the Victoria and Albert Museum, it contains the national collections of the performing arts encompassing theater, ballet, opera, music hall pantomime, puppets, circus, and rock and pop music. Daily make-up demonstrations and costume workshops are run using costumes from the Royal Shakespeare Company and the Royal National Theatre. The museum also has a major Diaghilev archive.

Wallace Collections

Hertford House, Manchester Square, W1. ☎ **0171/935-0687.** Free admission (donation requested). Mon–Sat 10am–5pm, Sun 2–5pm. Tube: Bond Street.

Beginning in the 18th century, four generations of the Marquesses of Hertford amassed this varied and discriminating collection of beautiful and fine things. Sèvres porcelain, Limoges enamels, 17th-century Dutch paintings, 18th-century British paintings, 18th-century French art (Watteau, Fragonard, and Boucher), and Italian majolica are displayed in their large home.

NEIGHBORHOODS/BOROUGHS/VILLAGES

Bloomsbury

Bloomsbury is a great neighborhood to explore if you appreciate bookish and intellectual pursuits. Of course, it's most often associated with the Bloomsbury group of artists and intellectuals. (The area is bounded by Tottenham Court Road on the west, Euston Road on the north, Gray's Inn Road on the east, and Bloomsbury Way and Theobalds Road on the south.) The focal points of this neighborhood are the British Museum and the University of London. Elegant town houses edge the neighborhood's famous squares—Russell, Gordon, Tavistock, Bedford, and Bloomsbury. Antiquarian book and map shops, art galleries, and small affordable hotels fill the area.

According to the Domesday book, a survey of England written by officials of William the Conqueror in 1086, the area had vineyards and woods for 100 pigs. In the 13th century, the land became part of the manor Blemondsburi. Edward III gave the land to the Carthusian monks of Charterhouse in the 14th century. Later, it was acquired by the Earl of Southampton. The fourth earl laid out Southampton Square, which today is Bloomsbury Square, and constructed a magnificent home. Other aristocrats built similar homes in the neighborhood, including Montague House, now the British Museum. Until the 18th century, Bloomsbury was a rural retreat.

Among the great names associated with the area are Thomas Gray, the poet, who lived on Southhampton Row; Sir Hans Sloane, physician and British Museum benefactor; diarist and novelist Fanny Burney, who lived on Queen Square; Lord Chief Justice Mansfield, whose house was sacked during the Gordon Riots (the ringleaders were hanged in Bloomsbury Square); and that celebrated group of friends including art critic Clive Bell, married to Vanessa, Virginia Woolf's sister; novelist and R.A.F. pilot David Garnett; novelist E. M. Forster; artist and art critic Roger Fry, founder of the Omega Workshop that encouraged young modern designers; painter Duncan Grant, a pioneer of abstract art who lived with Vanessa Bell; Lytton Strachey, biographer of Queen Victoria; economist and author John Maynard Keynes; and novelist Virginia and her husband Leonard Woolf, author, editor, and art critic. The Bloomsbury group subscribed to G. E. Moore's dictum that "by far the most valuable things are the pleasures of human intercourse and the enjoyment of beautiful objects." Not a bad philosophy of life.

Chelsea

Even though Chelsea no longer officially exists as an independent borough—it was formally amalgamated with Kensington in 1965—it retains a character of its own. The origin of its name is uncertain, although early references to *Chelched* suggest that it may mean chalk wharf. Its reputation was firmly established when Thomas More built a retreat here. That was followed by homes for the Duke of Norfolk and King Henry VIII.

In the 17th and 18th centuries, Chelsea attracted a great number of writers and intellectuals, including Swift, Addison, Carlyle, and Leigh Hunt. Its association with art and artists began with the foundation of the Chelsea Porcelain works (1745–84) and the illustrations done for the publications of the Chelsea Physic Garden. In the late 19th century, such dramatic figures as Whistler and Rossetti gave the district a great reputation for style.

Although many of the 19th-century Chelsea homes have been replaced by ugly, blasted modern blocks, there are still residential streets with elegant town houses and well-tended front gardens to stroll along and enjoy.

Covent Garden

Long Acre, St. Martin's Lane, Drury Lane, and the Strand mark the boundaries of today's Covent Garden. Originally, it belonged to the Convent of St. Peter at Westminster, but after the dissolution of the monasteries, it was granted to John Russell, first Earl of Bedford, and it has remained in this family's hands. In 1627, the fourth earl hired Inigo Jones to lay out a new square consisting of St. Paul's Church and three sides of a square of tall terraced houses. Considered odd at the time, the houses had front doors that opened on vaulted arcades, but they were soon occupied by fashionable tenants. In the middle of the 17th century, a market developed here, encouraging some of the more fashionable folks to move to the new and more attractive district of St. James. The market continued to grow and new, more substantial shops were built. In the mid-18th century, coffeehouses opened up, too, and these were frequented by such literary figures as Fielding, Boswell, Goldsmith, Pope, Garrick, Sheridan, and Walpole. The Bedford was the most famous coffeehouse. The area has always been associated with the theater, and many of the early 18th-century theater actors and managers lived here.

By the mid-18th century, cheap lodging houses, gambling dens, and brothels dotted the area. Dubbing Covent Garden the Square of Venus, Magistrate John Fielding said, "One would imagine that all the prostitutes in the kingdom had picked upon the rendezvous." By the early 19th century, the market had become so disorderly that the Duke of Bedford applied to Parliament for authority to collect tolls and to build a new market building. Constructed in the early 1830s, the new market now shelters a variety of stores; it's been recently refurbished. The market thrived. Nearly 1,000 porters were employed when the market was at its height, earning between 30 and 45 shillings a week. It was still very disorderly, and the eleventh Duke of Bedford eventually sold it in 1918 to a private group. Although it was condemned in 1920, the market continued to operate here until 1974. The Flower Market (1870) is now occupied by the National Transport Museum. The Jubilee Market (1904) now features a covered street market.

Attractions: Bloomsbury & Beyond

The Architectural
  Association 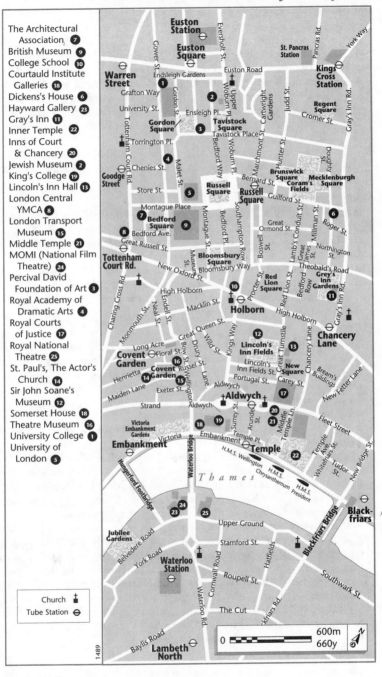⑦
British Museum ⑨
College School ⑩
Courtauld Institute
  Galleries ⑱
Dickens's House ⑥
Hayward Gallery ㉓
Gray's Inn ⑪
Inner Temple ㉒
Inns of Court
  & Chancery ⑳
Jewish Museum ②
King's College ⑲
Lincoln's Inn Hall ⑬
London Central
  YMCA ⑧
London Transport
  Museum ⑮
Middle Temple ㉑
MOMI (National Film
  Theatre) ㉔
Percival David
  Foundation of Art ③
Royal Academy of
  Dramatic Arts ④
Royal Courts
  of Justice ⑰
Royal National
  Theatre ㉕
St. Paul's, The Actor's
  Church ⑭
Sir John Soane's
  Museum ⑫
Somerset House ⑱
Theatre Museum ⑯
University College ①
University of
  London ⑤

Church ✝
Tube Station ⊖

1489

0   600m
     660y

Docklands, Isle of Dogs

In the 1970s, the dockers fought stubbornly against containerization and in a few short years most London docks, except for Tilbury, had closed. When they died, the 55 miles of waterfront between the Tower of London and Greenwich were redeveloped by the government. Begin your visit of this large area at the **London Docklands Visitor Centre** (☎ 0171/512-1111) in Limeharbour, Isle of Dogs. A 16-minute video recaps the area's redevelopment. *Financial Times* walking-tour maps are available at the center; you can explore the area either by foot or bicycle. **Canary Wharf** is a shopping and office complex that incorporates **Cesar Pelli's dramatic tower.** Old sugar warehouses stand at Port East.

To get there, take the Docklands Light Railway (DLR) from Tower Gateway station or catch it from Bank or Tower Hill tube stations to Crossharbour. Travelcards are valid on the DLR.

✪ Greenwich

Henry VIII, and later his daughter Elizabeth I, ruled England from a medieval palace in Greenwich. Today, the area is architecturally harmonious and home to the **Royal Naval College** (1694); the elegant **Queen's House;** and the **Old Royal Observatory** (see individual listings above in this chapter). The **Greenwich Tourist Information Centre** is at 46 Greenwich Church St., SE10 (☎ 0181/858-6376); it's open daily from 10am to 5pm. To get to Greenwich, take the Network Southeast train from Charing Cross or Cannon Street; trip time is 20 minutes. Launches on the river can be had from Westminster, Charing Cross, and Tower piers.

✪ Hampstead

Since earlier times, especially during the Great Plague, Hampstead has been a pristine rural escape for Londoners. In the late 17th century, London taverns served water from Hampstead, and this helped to make the area fashionable. In 1700, John Duffield built a pump room in Well Walk, and stylish society began to flock to the tearooms, racetrack, and taverns of Hampstead.

Among its diverse residents have been navigator Martin Frobisher; Prime Minister William Pitt; poet and essayist Leigh Hunt; the romantic poets Byron and Keats; landscape painter John Constable; Kate Greenaway (at no. 39 Frognal); father of psychoanalysis Sigmund Freud (at no. 20 Maresfield Gardens); Nobel Prize-winning author Rabindranath Tagore (at no. 3 Villas on the Heath); ballet star Anna Pavlova (at Ivy House North End Road); biologist Julian Huxley; writers D. H. Lawrence, H. G. Wells, Katherine Mansfield, and John Galsworthy (at Grove Lodge); photographer and designer Cecil Beaton; and rock star Boy George.

The **800-acre heath** has been left to the public in perpetuity and is a wonderful place to walk or fly a kite. Great views are had from **Parliament Hill.** You could spend the day just strolling the village streets or visiting Heathside pubs, which include **Jack Straw's Castle,** the **Spaniards,** and the **Old Bull and Bush.** Specific sights to see include **Keats House** and **Freud Museum** (see individual listings for both of these in this chapter). The **Iveagh Bequest Kenwood,** at Hampstead Lane (☎ 0181/348-1286), is Lord Iveagh's collection of paintings; this includes works by Rembrandt, Vermeer, Turner, and Reynolds. It's open daily 10am–6pm in summer, 10am to 4pm in winter; admission is free.

Highgate

This area was named for a tollgate high up on one of its hills. In the 14th century, a poor boy named Dick Whittington, resting at the bottom of that hill, heard the famous call to "Turn again, Whittington, Lord Mayor of London," the legend goes.

Hampstead

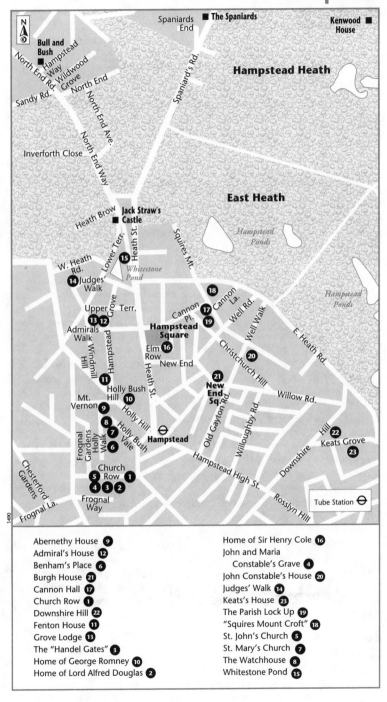

Abernethy House 9
Admiral's House 12
Benham's Place 6
Burgh House 21
Cannon Hall 17
Church Row 1
Downshire Hill 22
Fenton House 11
Grove Lodge 13
The "Handel Gates" 3
Home of George Romney 10
Home of Lord Alfred Douglas 2

Home of Sir Henry Cole 16
John and Maria
   Constable's Grave 4
John Constable's House 20
Judges' Walk 14
Keats's House 23
The Parish Lock Up 19
"Squires Mount Croft" 18
St. John's Church 5
St. Mary's Church 7
The Watchhouse 8
Whitestone Pond 15

Impressions

In people's eyes, in the swing, tramp, and trudge; in the bellow and uproar; the carriages, motor cars, omnibuses, vans, sandwich men shuffling and swinging; brass bands; barrel organs; in the triumph and the jingle and the strange high singing of some aeroplane overhead was what she loved; life; London; this moment in June.

—Virginia Woolf, *Mrs. Dalloway*

The young man went to London with only his cat, believing the streets were paved with gold and silver. He became a cloth merchant and then thrice the lord mayor of London. Today, Highgate is discreet, low-key, WASPy, and right-wing. The streets are lined with elegant Georgian, terraced Victorian, and Edwardian homes. The district is known for its wealth of intellectual societies—debating, reading, and choral singing. The famous cemetery of the same name was laid out in the 19th century (see individual listing, above in this chapter). The poets A. E. Housman and John Betjeman and ethnologist Mary Kingsley are among the village's famous sometime residents.

✪ Soho

A cosmopolitan neighborhood with a fascinating history, Soho was used for hunting in the Tudor era. This may explain its name, as *So ho!* was a common hunting cry. Residential development began in the early 17th century and accelerated in the 1670s. In the 18th century, many French Huguenots settled in the area, giving it a Gallic ambience. So much so that in 1749 William Maitland wrote that in Soho, you could easily imagine yourself in France. To this day, some fine charcuteries can be found in the district. While Soho's wealthier residents eventually moved on, its foreign communities remained and were joined by artists. In the 19th century, Soho became one of the most densely populated areas of London. Cholera and other epidemics swept through the neighborhood and onto other parts of London. Yet, at this time, Soho was London's entertainment center, filled with theaters, music halls, and some more disreputable pursuits.

In *The Forsyte Saga* (1922), John Galsworthy described Soho as: "Untidy, full of Greeks, Ishmaelites, cats, Italians, tomatoes, restaurants, organs, colored stuffs, queer names, people looking out of upper windows, it dwells remote from the Body Politic."

Soho's reputation as a fashionable but inexpensive dining area was well established by the 1920s. People flocked to restaurants and new theaters along Shaftesbury Avenue and Charing Cross Road. In the 1960s, sex clubs proliferated and Soho gained an unsavory reputation. The few residents who did remain fought to save their neighborhood. A series of police corruption trials and a law requiring the licensing of sex clubs has reduced their number—dramatically. Today, Soho is one of the liveliest and interesting areas of London. Wander along Dean and Frith Streets and into Soho Square (see also Chapter 5 for Soho restaurants) to absorb the flavor of the area.

ZOOS

London Zoo

Regent's Park, NW1. ☎ **0171/722-3333**, 0891/505-767 for recorded information. Admission £7.50 ($11.60) adults, £6.50 ($10.10) students and seniors, £5.50 ($8.50) children 4–14. Apr–Oct daily 10am–5:30pm; Nov–Mar 10am–4pm. Closed Dec 25. Tube: Camden Town,

Regent's Park. Waterbus: Service operates along Regent's Canal between Camden Lock or Little Venice and the zoo. From April to the end of September the boat departs on the hour 10am to 5pm. In winter there is less frequent daily service.

The most recent excitement at London Zoo (population 8,000) has been the opening of the children's zoo (in August 1994). Other highlights include the Elephant House, the Penguin Pool, Lion Terraces, the Aquarium, and the invertebrate (primarily insects) house. When you enter pick up a copy of the daily events guide, check it out for demonstrations at the Amphitheatre or the feeding times of your favorite animals. The zoo has six places to eat.

3   Parks & Gardens

Founded in 1673, the **Chelsea Physic Garden,** at 66 Royal Hospital Rd., SW3 (☎ 0171/352-5646), is the second-oldest botanical garden in England. Behind its high walls is a rare collection of exotic plants, shrubs, and trees, many more than 100 years old. Originally founded by the Society of Apothecaries to teach their apprentices how to identify medicinal plants, the garden has since expanded to include rare species from the New World. Its resident English Gardening School holds lectures throughout the summer; call for details. Admission is £3 ($4.65) for adults and £1.80 ($2.80) for students and children. It's open April through October, on Wednesday 2–5pm and Sunday from 2 to 6pm. Take the tube to Sloane Square.

Behind Kensington High Street is **Holland Park,** a quiet oasis of lawns and gardens with roaming peacocks. Also found here are the Japanese Kyoto Garden, the Orangery, and Ice House Galleries. Take the tube to High Street Kensington.

Of all the city's parks, ✪ **Hyde Park** (☎ 0171/298-2100) is the most popular and most identified with London. The aptly named Serpentine Lake is the 340-acre park's most notable feature. The small Serpentine Gallery (☎ **0171/402-6075**) exhibits contemporary art. It's open daily from 10am to 6pm.

As in other Royal Parks, wood-and-cloth deck chairs are scattered throughout Hyde Park, and fee collectors seem to appear from nowhere to extract 60p (95¢) from seated visitors who are usually ignorant of this cost. It's free to sit on the benches and grass. On Sunday the park really comes alive, when artists hang their works along the Bayswater Road fence. The northeast corner, near Marble Arch, becomes "Speaker's Corner." Anyone can stand on a soapbox here and speak on any subject. Although this tradition is often touted as an example of Britain's tolerance of free speech, few people realize that this ritual began several hundred years ago when condemned prisoners were allowed some final words before they were hung on Tyburn gallows, which stood on the same spot. Take the tube to Hyde Park Corner.

Originally a private hunting ground of Henry VIII, today **Regent's Park** (☎ 0171/486-7905) is London's playground, famous for its zoo, concerts, and open-air theater in the summer. A band plays free beside the lake twice daily from May through August. Get there by tube to Regent's Park, Baker Street, or Camden Town (to Camden Town for the zoo).

With its trademark Round Pond, **Kensington Gardens** (☎ 0171/298-2100) merges with Hyde Park's westernmost side. Fronting Kensington Palace, the gardens are more formal and distinctive than those in the neighboring park. The famous statue of Peter Pan with attending bronze rabbits is the garden's most popular feature for children.

Opposite Buckingham Palace, **St. James's Park** (☎ 0171/930-1793) is perhaps the most beautiful of all of London's parks. It's centrally located, near the West End.

Picnic Supplies

Most of the supermarkets in London offer picnic fixings. For a treat of a grocery-shopping experience, though, go to **Harrod's Food Hall,** 87–135 Brompton Rd., SW1 (☎ **0171/730-1234,** Tube: Knightsbridge); or **Fortnum & Mason,** 181 Piccadilly, W1(☎ **0171/734-8040,** Tube: Piccadilly Circus or Green Park). In Soho, **Randall & Aubin,** on the north side of Brewer at no. 16, is a characterful boucherie/charcuterie. Here you can make up a feast of bread, cheese, and sausage.

If you're in Hampstead and want to take a picnic up to the Heath, then head to the **Rosslyn Hill Deli.** It ain't cheap, but you can splurge a little on a picnic, no?

For a Chinese-inspired picnic, try the big and fascinating **Loon Fung Super-market** at 42–44 Gerrard St., W1 (☎ **0171/437-7332**), right in the heart of Soho's Chinatown. The most adventurous will try the black jelly fungus. The rest of us will enjoy dried cuttlefish, a traditional snack. Loon Fung is open daily from 10am to 7pm.

Swans glide on the water and geese frolic, giving the park a romantic atmosphere. A beautiful lake and plentiful benches make this park perfect for picnicking. Take the tube to St. James's Park.

Named for its absence of flowers (except for a short time in spring), **Green Park** (☎ **0171/930-1793**) provides ample shade from tall trees that makes it a picnic bower.

4 Guided Tours

Although the image of a tour group is repugnant to most independent travelers, guided tours do offer benefits, especially as an introductory orientation or for visitors with limited time.

WALKING TOURS

London's most interesting streets are best explored on foot, and several inexpensive walking-tour companies will lead you on a fascinating route. One of the most popular tours is **Discovery Walks' On the Trail of Jack the Ripper;** it leaves Aldgate East Underground station nightly at 8pm (☎ **0171/256-8973**). Reservations are not required. Other excellent walks are offered by **City Walks,** 147C Offord Rd., London N1 1LR (☎ **0171/700-6931**); and **The Original London Walks,** P.O. Box 1708, London NW6 4LQ (☎ **0171/624-3978**). Both companies operate regularly scheduled, thematically based tours around the city on a daily basis; write or phone for a free brochure.

Original London Walks offers an amazing array of themes, from the Beatles to pub walks to ghosts to literary heroes. Their Jack the Ripper walk (which leaves daily at different times from Tower Hill Underground) is led twice a week by Donald Rumbelow, a retired member of the City Police force and an authority on the subject. This company also offers several tours of prominent city museums as well as **Explorer Day** tours to such places as Oxford and Bath. Tours generally cost £4 to £5 ($6.20 to $7.75) and represent one of the best bargains in London.

For a few dollars more, author and historian **Richard Jones,** 67 Chancery Lane, London WC2A 1AF (☎ **0171/256-8973**), will escort you on one of his Discovery Walks. He offers more than 30 different itineraries for £4.50 ($6.95) per person.

Among the most popular is the London Theatrical Ghost Walk led by the spooky guide Thomas Bodie. Private walks costing £12 ($18.60) per person with a minimum of three people are also available.

One of London's most popular walks follows the route from Trafalgar Square to Parliament Square and is outlined in Chapter 8. Other enjoyable walks are also described in that chapter, as well as in *Frommer's Walking Tours: London* (Macmillan Travel).

BUS TOURS

If your time is more limited than your budget, a comprehensive bus tour may be your best bet. The **Original London Sightseeing Tour** operated by London Coaches is a 90-minute tour that departs from Piccadilly Circus, Victoria, Baker Street, or Marble Arch. The cost is £10 ($15.50) for adults, £5 ($7.75) for children, and tickets can be purchased on board or any London Transport or London Tourist Board office. The **London Plus Tour** (same price) allows you to get on and off at about 20 stops.

Do-it-yourselfers should purchase a **travelcard** (see "Getting Around," in Chapter 3) and climb aboard a red double-decker bus. Two of the more scenic routes are bus nos. 11 and 53. The first passes King's Road, Victoria Station, Westminster Abbey, Whitehall, Horse Guards, Trafalgar Square, the National Gallery, the Strand, Law Courts, Fleet Street, and St. Paul's Cathedral. Bus no. 53 passes Regent's Park Zoo, Oxford Circus, Regent Street, Piccadilly Circus, the National Gallery, Trafalgar Square, Horse Guards, Whitehall, and Westminster Square.

BOAT TOURS

Several companies offer boat tours on the Regent's Canal. **Jason's Trip** (☎ 0171/286-3428; Tube Warwick Avenue) operates a 90-minute tour in narrow boats from Little Venice, with a pick-up at Camden Lock. The price is £5.50 ($8.50) for adults and £4 ($6.20) for children. Lunch and dinner cruises are offered, too. **London Waterbus Company** (☎ 0171/482-2660; take Warick Avenue or Camden Town tube) operates similar trips and cruises on the River Lea and to Limehouse. These canal trips operate from April to Sept only.

5 Especially for Kids

Kidsline (☎ 0171/222-8070) offers advice on current happenings for youngsters. **Circusline** (☎ 0522/681591) is a 24-hour updated recording on circuses around town. Consult the special childrens' pages of *Time Out* for special events.

Obvious choices for children include touring the **Tower of London,** seeing Buckingham Palace's **Changing of the Guard,** climbing to the top of both **Tower Bridge** and **St. Paul's Cathedral,** and visiting the **Museum of the Moving Image.**

Other hits are (see above in this chapter) the *Cutty Sark;* HMS *Belfast;* the Imperial War Museum; London Transport Museum; the London Zoo; Madame Tussaud's; the Natural History Museum; and the Science Museum.

STILL MORE HITS FOR CHILDREN

Bethnal Green Museum of Childhood

Cambridge Heath Road, E2. ☎ **0181/980-2415.** Free admission. Mon–Thurs, Sat 10am–5:50, Sun 2:30–5:50. Closed Fri, Dec 25, 26, Jan 1, and May Bank Holiday. Tube: Bethnal Green.

A great collection of toys, dolls, dollhouses, games, puppets, children's costumes, and other kids' items.

✪ Little Angel Theatre

14 Dagmar Passage, Islington, N1. ☎ **0171/226-1787.** Tickets £4–£6.50. Tube: Angel, Highbury or Islington.

A unique puppet theater, featuring a variety of puppet and marionette groups. Performances are given on weekends at 11am and 3pm and during school holidays.

↳ London Brass Rubbing Centre

In the crypt of St. Martin-in-the-Fields Church, Trafalgar Sq., WC2. ☎ **0171/930-9306.** Free admission. Brass rubbings cost from £2 ($3.10). Mon–Sat 10am–6pm, Sun noon–6pm. Closed Dec 25 and Good Friday. Tube: Charing Cross.

Inside one of London's landmark churches, both adults and children can make rubbings of about 100 replicas of medieval church brasses—knights, ladies, kings, merchants, and heraldic animals—or any of several unusual Celtic designs and early woodcuts of the zodiac. It's fun, historical, and artistic. Materials and instruction are provided. The gift shop stocks Celtic jewelry as well as model knights and other mementos.

London Dungeon

28–34 Tooley St., SE1. ☎ **0171/403-7221.** Admission £8 ($12.40) adult, £6.50 ($10.05) seniors, £5 ($7.75) children 5–14. Daily Apr–Sept, 10am–5:30pm; Oct–Mar, 10am–4:30pm. Closed Dec 24, 25, 26. Tube: London Bridge.

Some children may appreciate this state-of-the-art horror chamber. The Theatre of the Guillotine and the Jack the Ripper Experience are special spine-chilling shows. This place may frighten and upset other children.

London Planetarium

Marylebone Road, NW1. ☎ **0171/486-1121.** Admission £5.45 ($8.45) adult, £4.30 ($6.65) seniors, £3.60 ($5.60) children 5–17. Daily with shows beginning at 12:20pm (10:20am on weekends). Tube: Baker Street.

Next door to Madame Tussaud's, the shows at the planetarium explore the mysteries of the stars and the night sky. The most recent show starts with sunrise over Stonehenge and travels through superclusters, past distant galaxies and even down the optic nerve of the human eye to show how our perception of the universe has changed. There are also several interactive exhibition areas that relate to planets and space. Visitors can also hear Stephen Hawking talk about the mysterious black holes and also experience what shape or weight they would be on other planets.

Polka Theatre for Children

240 The Broadway, SW19. ☎ **0181/543-4888.** Tickets £5–£8.50 ($7.75–$13.20). Tues–Fri 9:30–4:30pm, Sat 11am–5:30pm. Closed Sept, Dec 25, Jan 1. Tube: South Wimbledon on Northern Line.

This company presents plays for young people and special shows for those from 3 to 13 years old.

Quasar

Trocadero Centre, Piccadilly Circus, W1. ☎ **0171/734-8151.** Mon–Thurs £6 ($9.30) adult, £5 ($7.75) seniors, £4.50 ($6.95) children 5–17; Fri–Sun £7 ($10.85), £6 ($9.30), £5 ($7.75) respectively. Daily 10am–midnight. Tube: Piccadilly Circus.

A military game for kids and adults. Armed with a laser gun and body armor, the participants have half an hour to hit as many of the opposing team as possible. At the end, a personal score sheet is given to each player. Children must be 7.

Rock Circus

London Pavilion, Piccadilly Circus, W1. ☎ **0171/734-7203.** Admission £7.50 ($11.60) adult, £6.50 ($10.05) seniors/students, £5.50 ($8.50) children 5–15. Sun–Mon, Wed–Thurs

11am–9pm, Tues noon–9pm, Fri–Sat 11am–10pm. Extended hours in summer 10am–10pm except Tues noon–9pm. Closed Dec 25 Tube: Piccadilly Circus.

An audio-animatronic show that tells the story of rock from the 1950s to today.

Unicorn Arts Theatre

6–7 Great Newport St., WC2. ☎ **0171/379-3280**; box office 0171/836-3334. £4–£7.50 ($6.20–$11.60). Tube: Covent Garden.

With a season from September to June, this theater presents plays for 4- to 12-year-olds. The plays may be adaptations of old favorites or specially commissioned new plays. Performances are given Saturday and Sunday morning and afternoon.

6 Special-Interest Sightseeing

FOR ART AND LITERARY ENTHUSIASTS

England has a long and rich literary tradition, and walking the streets of London can bring you to homes of writers and artists and to the setting of scenes from novels that have become part of our personal myths. The curious may want to secure a guide to all the blue plaques in London, marking historically significant spots. Geoffrey Chaucer lived above Aldgate, in the easternmost part of the city, until 1386. Playwright Joe Orton lived on Noel Road in Islington until his death in 1967. Oscar Wilde, Dylan Thomas, George Orwell, D. H. Lawrence, George Bernard Shaw, Rudyard Kipling, William Blake—the list of writers who made London their home goes on and on. Usually, the blue plaque is, unfortunately, all that's left to mark the past, but there are some exceptions.

Dickens's House

48 Doughty St., WC1. ☎ **0171/405-2127**. Admission £3 ($4.65) adults, £2 ($3.10) students and seniors, £1 ($1.55) children, £6 ($9.30) families. Mon–Sat 10am–5pm. Tube: Russell Square.

Home to Victorian London's quintessential chronicler, this terraced house is on the outskirts of Bloomsbury. Dickens only lived here for two years (1837–39), but in that time, he produced some of his best-loved works, including *The Pickwick Papers, Nicholas Nickleby,* and *Oliver Twist.* The author's letters, furniture, and first editions are displayed in glass cases. The rooms have been restored to their original appearance.

Dr. Johnson's House

17 Gough Sq., Fleet Street, EC4. ☎ **0171/353-3745**. Admission £3 ($4.65) adults, £2 ($3.10) students and seniors, £1 ($1.55) children over 10. May–Sept, Mon–Sat 11am–5:30pm; Oct–Apr, Mon–Sat 11am–5pm. Tube: Blackfriars, Temple or Holborn.

The house where famous lexicographer Samuel Johnson (1709–84) lived and compiled the world's first English dictionary is now a shrine to him. His original dictionary is on display in the long attic where it was produced.

Keats House

Wentworth Place, Keats Grove, NW3. ☎ **0171/435-2062**. Free admission. Apr–Oct, Mon–Fri 10am–1pm and 2–6pm, Sat 10am–1pm and 2–5pm; Sun 2–5pm; Nov–Mar, Mon–Fri 1–5pm, Sat 10am–1pm and 2–5pm, Sun 2–5pm. Closed Dec 24–26, Jan 1, Good Friday, Easter Eve, and May 1. Tube: Hampstead.

Romantic poet John Keats (1795–1821) lived and worked in this unassuming home in tranquil Hampstead. "Ode to a Nightingale" was penned here, and a first edition of this is displayed along with books, diaries, letters, memorabilia, and some original furnishings.

Leighton House

12 Holland Park Rd., W14. ☎ **0171/602-3316.** Free admission. Mon–Sat 11am–5:30pm. Closed Sun and major holidays. Tube: High Street Kensington.

This fine example of high Victoriana, the former home of Lord Leighton (1830–96), contains a collection of Pre-Raphaelite and late 19th-century art. If features a magnificent studio, where Leighton worked, and a stunning Arab hall complete with fountain, mosaic floor, and brilliant antique Middle Eastern tiles.

Linley Sambourne House

18 Stafford Terrace, W8. ☎ **0181/994-1019.** Admission £3 ($4.65) adult, £2.50 ($3.85) seniors £1.50 ($2.30) children under 16. Mar–Oct only, Wed 10–4pm, Sun 2–5. Tube: High Street Kensington.

Sambourne (1844–1910) was a leading cartoonist for *Punch* magazine. The house retains most of the original decor and late Victorian paintings.

Thomas Carlyle's House

24 Cheyne Row, SW3. ☎ **0171/352-7087.** Admission £3 ($4.65) adults, £1.50 ($2.30) children under 17. Apr–Oct, Wed–Sun 11am–5pm. Closed Nov–Mar. Tube: Sloane Square.

At this 18th-century town house, located on a beautiful street in Chelsea, Carlyle lived for 47 years, until his death in 1881. His house remains virtually unaltered, to the extent that some of the rooms are without electric light. The surrounding neighborhood is now one of the most expensive residential areas in the city; the sublime silence of this enclave creates a wonderful counterpoint to the bustle of nearby King's Road.

William Morris Gallery

Lloyd Park, Forest Road, Walthamstow, E17. ☎ **0181/527-3782.** Free admission. Tues–Sat and first Sun of each month 10am–1pm and 2–5pm. Closed Mon and all bank holidays.

Designer, socialist, poet, publisher, and manufacturer of furniture and wallpaper, William Morris was an extraordinarily talented man. Fascinated by the medieval period, he was a founder of the Arts and Crafts movement. Fans of Morris will not want to miss the permanent collection here. Temporary exhibits highlight the work of his circle, the Pre-Raphaelite artists, such as Edward Burne-Jones and Dante Gabriel Rossetti.

FOR VISITING AMERICANS

Grosvenor Square, W1, has strong U.S. connections and is referred to by some as "Little America." John Adams lived on the square when he was the American ambassador to Britain, a statue of Franklin Roosevelt stands in the center of the square, General Eisenhower headquartered here during World War II, and the entire west side is occupied by the U.S. Embassy.

The former **home of Benjamin Franklin,** 36 Craven St., WC2 (steps from Trafalgar Square), is just one of many houses formerly occupied by famous Americans. For a complete list, pick up *Americans in London* (Queen Anne Press, 1988), by Brian Morton, an excellent anecdotal street guide to the homes and haunts of famous Americans.

7 Staying Active

Two organizations can help you find places to keep up an exercise routine: the **Sports Council,** 16 Upper Woburn Place, WC1 (☎ **0171/388-1277**) has information on sports centers, while **Sportsline** (☎ **0171/ 222-8000**) will answer any and all questions about sports in general.

CHESS

Amateurs and grand masters lock horns at the Durham Castle, Alexander Street, in Paddington (no phone). Sets and clocks can be rented from the bar for £1 ($1.55) plus a £5 ($7.75) returnable deposit, and there's always someone looking for a game. The club is open during pub hours. Tube to Bayswater.

SWIMMING/FITNESS

Brittania Leisure Centre

40 Hyde Rd., N1. ☎ **0171/729-4485.** Admission 60p (93¢) adults, 30p (45¢) children. Mon–Fri 9am–8:15pm Sat–Sun 9am–5:45pm. Tube: Old Street.

A modern public sports facility with a swimming pool, badminton and squash courts, and soccer and volleyball fields.

Chelsea Sports Centre

Chelsea Manor Street, SW3. ☎ **0171/352-6985.** Pool £2.10 ($3.10). Call for prices on other facilities. Pool, Mon 7:30am–7pm, Tues–Wed and Fri 7:30am–10pm, Thurs 7:30am–2pm and 3–8pm, Sat 8am–5pm and 6–10pm, Sun 8am–6:30pm. Tube: Sloane Square.

A community fitness center, this tri-level spa has a pool, sauna, solarium, and badminton, squash, basketball, and volleyball courts. Aerobics classes are given.

London Central YMCA

112 Great Russell St., WC1. ☎ **0171/637-8131.** Admission £15 ($23.25) per day, £40 ($62) per week. Mon–Fri 7am–10:30pm, Sat–Sun 10am–9pm. Tube: Tottenham Court Road.

Snazzy for a Y, this top facility has a pool, weight room, cardiovascular equipment, sauna, and solarium. Beauticians, massage therapists, and other specialized staff members are also on hand.

HORSEBACK RIDING

Hyde Park Riding Stables, 63 Bathurst Mews, W2, ☎ **0171/723-2813,** and **Ross Nye,** 8 Bathurst Mews, W2, ☎ **0171/262-3791.** These are the places to go if you want to join a group horseback ride around Hyde Park. Hyde Park charges £25 ($37.20) per hour, Ross Nye costs the same. Both get booked up early for weekends. No galloping or jumping is allowed. Get there by tube to Lancaster Gate or Paddington.

ICE SKATING

Broadgate Ice

The Arena office, Broadgate Circle, 3 Broadgate, EC2. ☎ **0171/588-6565.** Admission £7 ($10.85) including skate rental Nov–Apr, Mon–Thurs noon–2:30pm and 3:30–6pm, Fri noon–2:30pm, 3:30–6pm and 7–10:30pm. Sat–Sun 11am–1pm, 2–4pm, and 5–7pm. Tube: Liverpool Street.

You can also glide to the hits at England's only open-air rink. This tiny but modern rink is surrounded by wine bars and features a state-of-the-art sound system that will knock your skates off.

Queen's Ice Skating Club

Queensway, W2. ☎ **0171/229-0172.** Admission £5 ($7.75) adults, £3.50 ($5.40) children 5–15. There are three sessions daily; call for exact times. Tube: Bayswater or Queensway.

Weekend disco nights are especially crowded at this large indoor rink right in the heart of Bayswater. The basement-level rink can handle about 1,000 skaters, and often does. Monday and Wednesday are student nights when the charge is only £4 and skate rental is free. Otherwise, skates can be rented for £1.50.

8 Spectator Sports

The English are passionate about sport and fair play and there is no better way to get to know and understand them than to watch them at play. The list that follows will help you in this endeavor. Questions about any spectator or participatory London sport will be answered free of charge by **Sportsline** (☎ **0171/222-8000**), Monday through Friday from 10am to 6pm. A good start is to drop by Regent's Park on a weekend and just ask to join one of the casual soccer or other games you'll find being played there.

CRICKET

Cricket is played at Lord's and the Oval. County games and international test series against a variety of countries—Australia, India, South Africa, the West Indies and New Zealand, for example, are played during the summer. Check the newspapers or call Sportsline (see above) or the tourist board for information on current matches.

The Foster's Oval Cricket Ground

The Oval Kennington, SE11. ☎ **0171/582-6660.** Tickets £7–£40 ($10.85–$62). Box office, Mon–Fri 9:30am–5pm. Tube: Oval.

The less classy cricket ground, the Oval, is also less stodgy (and less pretty) than Lord's. Home to Surrey CCC, this field hosts matches during summer months only. Again, for international tests, you'll need to book tickets in advance.

Lord's Cricket Ground

St. John's Wood Road, NW8. ☎ **0171/289-1611;** box office 289-8979. Tickets £8–£40 ($12.40–$62). Box office, Mon–Fri 9:30am–5:30pm. Tube: St. John's Wood.

England's most important matches are played here. Some of the games are considered society events, but everyone is welcome, if seats are available and you can afford a ticket. You'll need to reserve tickets for international tests, but for the county matches (Middlesex plays here) you can purchase tickets at the gate. Guided tours are given. Call for information.

FOOTBALL (SOCCER)

England's soccer (called "football") season runs from August to April and attracts fiercely loyal fans. Games usually start at 3pm and are great to watch, but the stands can get very rowdy, so think about splurging for seats. Centrally located first-division football clubs include: **Arsenal,** Arsenal Stadium, Avenell Road, N5 (☎ **0171/226-0304,** box office **354-5404**), tube to Arsenal; **Tottenham Hotspur,** 748 High Rd., N17 (☎ **0181/365-5000,** box office 396-4567), tube to Seven Sisters; and **Chelsea,** Stamford Bridge, Fulham Road, SW6 (☎ **0171/385-5545,** box office 0891 121011), tube to Fulham Broadway. Tickets cost £15 to £32 ($23.25 to $49.60), and games are usually played on Saturday.

GREYHOUND RACING

There is no horse racing in London proper, but **Ascot, Epsom,** and **Sandown** are within easy reach. Bettors may also want to try one of the greyhound dog tracks below, for an exciting alternative night out. Races run throughout the year.

Catford Stadium

Ademore Road, SE26. ☎ **0181/690-8000.** Tickets £2.50–£3.50 ($3.85–$5.40). BritRail: Catford.

A party atmosphere prevails at Catford, one of London's busiest tracks. There are usually ten races on Monday, Wednesday, and Saturday, the first one beginning at 7:30pm.

Wembley Stadium

Wembley. ☎ **0181/902-8833;** box office 0181/900-1234. Tickets £3–5 ($4.65–$7.75) for the dogs; £12–30 ($18.60–$46.50) for major events. Tube: Wembley Park.

The soccer field is partitioned every Monday, Wednesday, and Friday to make way for the dogs. The first race usually begins at 7:30pm. At other times this is a venue for major national and international sports events of all sorts. Guided tours are given of the stadium—call for information.

RUGBY

Twickenham

Whitton Road, T. W. 2. ☎ **0181/892-8161.**

The headquarters of the amateur Rugby Football Union where local and international games are played. The season lasts from September to April. Big games are expensive and sell out far in advance, but tickets for smaller matches start from £20 ($31). Take the tube to Richmond, then the Southern Railway.

TENNIS

Center-court seats for the **Wimbledon Championships** are sold by lottery. Write between August and December of the preceding year for an application form for inclusion in the ticket ballot. Alternatively, **Keith Prowse, Inc.,** 234 W. 44th St., Ste. 1000, New York, NY 10036 (☎ **212/398-1430**), offers Wimbledon packages, which include accommodations. Also, a (very) few center-court seats are sold on the day of the match. To get these seats, camping out in line the night before might be in order; prices range from £21 to £42 ($32.55 to $65.10).

Tickets for the outside courts, where you can see all the stars in earlier rounds of play, are usually available at the gate. Ground entrance for these outside courts costs £7–£8 ($10.85–$12.40). For further information, write or call the **All England Lawn Tennis and Croquet Club,** Church Road, Wimbledon, SW19 5AE (☎ **0181/946-2244**). To get there, take the tube to Wimbledon.

7

Strolling Around London

Despite heavy traffic, never-ending construction, and confusing streets, London is a walker's city. The walking tours outlined below are designed to acquaint you with different parts of the city and the divergent aspects of city life. For alternative itineraries, consult *Frommer's Walking Tours: London* (Macmillan Travel), or take one of the excellent guided walks offered daily by a number of specialized companies *(see "Guided Tours," in Chapter 6).*

WALKING TOUR 1
Political London

Start: Trafalgar Square.
Finish: Parliament Square.
Time: 1.5 hours, not including museum stops.
Best Times: When the museums are open, Monday to Saturday between 10am and 5:30pm, Sunday between 2 and 5:30pm.
Worst Times: Early Sunday, when the museums are closed.

Whitehall, a single, long road that connects Trafalgar Square with Parliament Square, is London's primary street for government. The entire length of the road was once fronted by the Old Palace of Whitehall (formerly York Palace, home of Cardinal Wolsey), until it burned down in 1698. Today, the Home and Foreign Offices have a Whitehall address, as do a host of other government buildings. The official residence of the prime minister is just steps away on Downing Street, and the spectacular Houses of Parliament are at the end of the block, towering over Parliament Square.

　　Start your tour in Trafalgar Square, which is easily reached by tube to the Charing Cross or Embankment Underground stations (each within one block of the other). Watch out for speeding cars and cross the street into:

1. **Trafalgar Square.** You are now standing in the heart of London. To the east is The City, London's financial center. To the north are Leicester Square and the commercial West End, London's entertainment and shopping areas. To the west is The Mall, the royal road that leads to Buckingham Palace. And to the south is Whitehall, the city's thoroughfare of government. In the center of the square is:

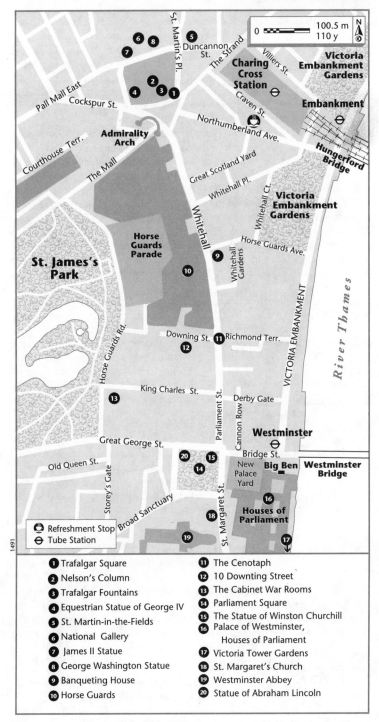

Political London

Refreshment Stop
Tube Station

1. Trafalgar Square
2. Nelson's Column
3. Trafalgar Fountains
4. Equestrian Statue of George IV
5. St. Martin-in-the-Fields
6. National Gallery
7. James II Statue
8. George Washington Statue
9. Banqueting House
10. Horse Guards
11. The Cenotaph
12. 10 Downting Street
13. The Cabinet War Rooms
14. Parliament Square
15. The Statue of Winston Churchill
16. Palace of Westminster, Houses of Parliament
17. Victoria Tower Gardens
18. St. Margaret's Church
19. Westminster Abbey
20. Statue of Abraham Lincoln

2. **Nelson's Column,** one of the most famous monuments in London. Commemorating the victorious naval commander who died at the Battle of Trafalgar (1805), the 145-foot column is topped by the figure of Lord Nelson. The statue itself stands 16 feet high and is made of stone. It is so heavy it had to be hoisted up in three different pieces. At the base of the column are the famous:

3. **Trafalgar Fountains.** Surrounded by oversized bronze lions, the square and the fountains are the annual site of London's largest New Year's Eve party. Of the three other statues in Trafalgar Square, the most interesting is of:

4. **George IV,** on horseback. This equestrian statue was originally intended to top Marble Arch, which stands at the northeast corner of Hyde Park. One wonders why the king rides without boots, on a horse without stirrups or saddle. Look to the northeastern corner of the square, toward:

5. **St. Martin-in-the-Fields.** This popular London church is famous for its spire-topped classical portico. Begun in 1722, the church contains several famous tombs, including those of the actress-mistress of Charles II, Nell Gwynne, highwayman Jack Sheppard, furniture maker Thomas Chippendale, and painters William Hogarth, Sir Joshua Reynolds, and Nicholas Hilliard. The church's grand interior can be combined with a visit to the Brass Rubbing Centre *(see Chapter 6),* or with a free lunchtime concert *(see Chapter 6).* Occupying the entire north side of the square is the:

6. **National Gallery.** *(See Chapter 6.)* Designed by William Wilkins in 1832–38, the gallery houses Britain's best collection of historical paintings by world-class masters. The museum's entrance is guarded by the:

7. **James II Statue,** sculpted by Grinling Gibbons, one of England's greatest. Made in 1686, this is one of London's best statues. Also outside the gallery is the:

8. **George Washington Statue.** A gift from the state of Virginia, the statue is a replica of the one by Houdon, which sits in the state capitol building in Richmond.

   With your back toward the National Gallery, cross Trafalgar Square and begin your walk down Whitehall.

☕ **TAKE A BREAK** If you're ready for a light snack or a pint, make your second left turn off Whitehall, into Great Scotland Yard. Cross Northumberland Avenue to **The Sherlock Holmes,** 10 Northumberland St. In the upstairs dining room of this popular "theme" pub you will find a re-creation of Holmes's fictional living room at 221b Baker St. The head of the hound of the Baskervilles and other relevant "relics" decorate the downstairs bar.

   Back on Whitehall, continue walking for three blocks. On your left you will see:

9. **Banqueting House,** on the corner of Horse Guards Avenue. Modeled on Sansovino's Library in Venice, and completed by Inigo Jones in 1622, this opulent eating hall is the only extant part of the Old Palace of Whitehall, which stretched almost the entire way from Trafalgar Square to Parliament Square. Commissioned by Charles I, the interior ceiling was painted by Rubens in 1635, and portrays the benefits of wise rule. Ironically, that same king was beheaded outside Banqueting House in 1649. You can enter Monday to Saturday

Impressions

London itself perpetually attracts, stimulates, gives me play, a story and a poem without any trouble, save that of moving my legs through the streets.

—Virginia Woolf, 1928

from 10am to 5pm. Admission is £3 ($4.16). Directly across Whitehall from Banqueting House is:

10. **Horse Guards,** home to the queen's ceremonial guards. Two brightly suited mounted guards stand watch—solely for the benefit of tourists—daily from 10am to 4pm. There is a small, relatively crowd-free changing-of-the-guard ceremony here Monday to Saturday at 11am, Sunday at 10am. The best show is probably the guard dismount, which takes place daily at 4pm.

Farther down Whitehall, in the middle of the street, you'll see the:

11. **Cenotaph,** dedicated to the citizens of the United Kingdom who died during the two world wars. Often surrounded by flowers and wreaths, the monument was designed by Sir Edwin Lutyens in 1919. Just opposite it is:

12. **10 Downing St.,** the official residence of the British prime minister. Unlike most of the big government buildings on Whitehall, which were built in the 19th century, Downing Street is small in scale, lined with homes dating from 1680 to 1766. Number 10, down on the right-hand side, has been home to prime ministers since 1731. Number 11 is the office and home of the Chancellor of the Exchequer. Although they look small, these rather plain fronts hide sizable rooms and offices. Because of a rise in terrorist threats, we can no longer enter Downing Street, but must content ourselves with viewing it from behind a tall gate.

Turn right at the next corner, and leave Whitehall for a short walk down King Charles Street. At the far end of the street are:

13. **The Cabinet War Rooms.** *(See Chapter 6.)* Here, in the British government's World War II underground headquarters, you can see the Cabinet Room, Map Room, Churchill's Emergency Bedroom, and the Telephone Room (where calls to Roosevelt were made). They have all been restored to their 1940s appearance, accurate down to an open cigarette pack on the table.

Return to Whitehall, turn right, and continue one block into:

14. **Parliament Square.** Laid out in the 1860s by Charles Barry, the designer of the new Houses of Parliament, the square was remodeled earlier this century when the center of the square was turned into a traffic island. Several statues sit around the square; most depict British prime ministers and generals. The first one you will encounter is the:

15. **Statue of Sir Winston Churchill.** Sculpted in 1973 by Ivor Roberts-Jones, the bronze statue is fitted with a small electrical current to discourage pigeons from sitting on the prime minister's head.

It's probably hard for you to concentrate on statues when one of the world's most famous buildings, and a spectacular architectural wonder as well, is towering above you.

16. **The Palace of Westminster,** now occupied by the **Houses of Parliament,** is a stunning example of Victorian engineering. *(See Chapter 6 for complete information.)* The site has been home to royalty and government since Edward the Confessor occupied a palace here, before the Norman Conquest of 1066. The oldest remaining part of the building is **Westminster Hall,** a rectangular banqueting room, noted for its magnificent oak hammerbeam roof. Rebuilt in 1394–1402 for Richard II, the hall was regularly used for high treason trials, including those of Anne Boleyn, Sir Thomas More, Guy Fawkes, and Charles I. Oliver Cromwell was proclaimed lord protector here (his statue stands outside), and more recently, this is where Sir Winston Churchill lay in state. Unfortunately, since a bomb killed an MP in 1979, entrance to Westminster Hall is difficult; tickets are available, on a limited basis, from your embassy *(see Chapter 3 for information).* The current 19th-century Gothic Revival Houses of Parliament buildings contain over 1,000 rooms

and two miles of corridors. The 316-foot-high Clock Tower is the palace's most striking feature. Inside is **Big Ben,** a 28,000-pound bell that first chimed in 1858.

Just past the Houses of Parliament, on your left-hand side, fronting the Thames is:

17. Victoria Tower Gardens. Filled with benches, this small park is a great place for a picnic. At the park's entrance is a replica of Rodin's *Six Burghers of Calais.* The large bronze statue depicts the men who surrendered to Edward III in order to save their city from destruction in the Hundred Years' War. Exiting the park, and turning back to Parliament Square, you face:

18. St. Margaret's Church, a grand 15th-century structure that is often initially mistaken for Westminster Abbey. St. Margaret's is in fact the parish church of the House of Commons, and is most famous for its beautiful and enormous east window, a stained-glass masterpiece made to commemorate the marriage of Catherine of Aragon to Prince Arthur, the brother of Henry VIII. William Caxton, Sir Walter Raleigh, and John Pym are buried here. Samuel Pepys, John Milton, and Sir Winston Churchill were all married here. Behind the church, on the south side of Parliament Square, is:

19. Westminster Abbey. *(See Chapter 6 for complete information.)* Originally called Westminster (West Monastery) after its location west of The City, this was the site of a Benedictine abbey as early as A.D. 750. The present building was started by Henry III in 1245 and now contains his tomb. The main structure was completed by the end of the 14th century; Henry VII's chapel was built during the beginning of the 16th century, the west towers were constructed in 1735, and the exterior underwent a drastic restoration in the 19th century.

Back on Parliament Square, take a close look at the many statues. Do you recognize anyone? You may be surprised to find the statue of:

20. Abraham Lincoln, on the side of the square farthest from the Parliament, the only depiction of a non-Briton on the square. It was donated by the city of Chicago and is an exact replica of the one in Lincoln Park.

WALKING TOUR 2
Aristocratic London

Start: Trafalgar Square.
Finish: Piccadilly Circus.
Time: Approximately two hours, not including shopping stops.
Best Times: Mornings, when you can be at Buckingham Palace in time for the Changing of the Guard (usually at 11:30am).
Worst Times: After 6pm and on Sunday, when the shops of St. James's and Piccadilly are closed.

The small corner of London nestled between Green Park and St. James's Park has long been a favorite of the aristocracy. St. James's Palace was a royal residence as early as 1660, and Queen Victoria made Buckingham Palace her home when she took the throne in 1837.

Start your tour in Trafalgar Square *(see Walking Tour 1, above),* and proceed through:

1. Admiralty Arch, on the eastern side of the square, the striking entranceway to:

2. The Mall, a straight half-mile strip that connects Trafalgar Square with Buckingham Palace. Closed to traffic on Sunday and during important state

Walking Tour—Aristocratic London

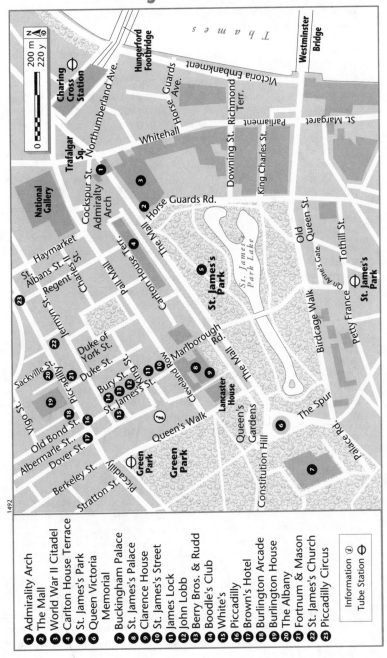

1 Admirality Arch
2 The Mall
3 World War II Citadel
4 Carlton House Terrace
5 St. James's Park
6 Queen Victoria
   Memorial
7 Buckingham Palace
8 St. James's Palace
9 Clarence House
10 St. James's Street
11 James Lock
12 John Lobb
13 Berry Bros. & Rudd
14 Boodle's Club
15 White's
16 Piccadilly
17 Brown's Hotel
18 Burlington Arcade
19 Burlington House
20 The Albany
21 Fortnum & Mason
22 St. James's Church
23 Piccadilly Circus

Information ⓘ
Tube Station ⊖

visits, The Mall takes its name from a similarly named ballgame that was once played on a long court here. Near the entrance to The Mall, Admiralty Arch is flanked by the:

3. World War II Citadel, on the south side, a bomb-proof communications center, and:

4. Carlton House Terrace, to the north. Built in 1837 by John Nash, the large Regency structure was home to Prime Ministers Gladstone and Palmerston. It also housed the offices of the Free French forces from 1940 to 1945, under the leadership of Charles de Gaulle. The terrace now houses the Institute of Contemporary Arts *(see Chapter 6 for complete information).* Bordering the entire south side of The Mall is:

5. St. James's Park, the oldest of London's Royal Parks, was opened by Henry VIII in 1532. One of London's prettiest parks, St. James's once contained an aviary, from which Birdcage Walk on the other side of the park takes its name. From 1662 to 1990, the park was home to a family of pelicans. Although these big birds have been removed to the Regent's Park Zoo, St. James's centrally located wrench-shaped lake still supports more than 20 species of waterfowl. After a stroll (and maybe even a picnic) in the park, continue along The Mall to its terminus at the:

6. Queen Victoria Memorial. Now enclosed by an iron fence, in the center of a busy traffic circle, the massive 1911 statue depicts the queen with golden horses. Just behind the memorial is:

7. Buckingham Palace, originally home to the duke of Buckingham, and later converted into a royal residence by George IV. *(See Chapter 6 for complete information on the palace and the Changing of the Guard.)* John Nash, one of London's most prolific architects, led the renovation. Rebuilding was far from finished when Queen Victoria took up residence in 1837. Successive modifications have enlarged the palace to almost 600 rooms. Although tourists have a good view only of the rather plain neo-Georgian east front (added by Sir Aston Webb in 1913), the best view is said to be from the back, where the queen's famous garden parties are held. The Changing of the Guard is performed by five rotating regiments of the Queen's Foot Guards.

Backtrack one block up The Mall, turn left on Stable Yard Road, and after one more block, turn right, around the corner of:

8. St. James's Palace. Built in the 1530s by Henry VIII, this pretty but understated palace has lent its name to the fashionable area that surrounds it. Since it was originally built in the 16th century, the Tudor residence has been successively modified by illustrious craftsmen and architects, including Grinling Gibbons and Christopher Wren. Although it is no longer home to the reigning monarch, foreign ambassadors to London are still called "ambassadors to the Court of St. James's."

Walk to the front of the palace, just ahead of you. Although you cannot enter it:

9. Clarence House, the residence of the Queen Mother, is located through the big front gates, just behind the palace. Here, facing the south end of St. James's Street, guards in tall, black bearskin hats stand guard with bayoneted machine guns—weapons that have only relatively recently replaced the sword. With your back to the palace gates, walk up:

10. St. James's Street, one of the city's most opulent roads. This short stretch is home to some of London's most famous gentlemen's clubs. For centuries, these bastions of the aristocracy have provided lodging, food, drink, and good company for the well-born and well-connected. Only recently have women been admitted and then only to some clubs. None displays its name; if you don't know where they are, you probably weren't meant to. On the right-hand side are many shops boasting storefronts that haven't changed substantially since the 18th century. These are some of the most exclusive stores anywhere. For instance:

11. **James Lock,** 6 St. James's St., has long supplied handmade hats to wealthy, aristocratic ladies and gentlemen. Heads are measured for made-to-order hats that can take up to two months to create. It is said that the traditional bowler was invented here, and it can still be purchased for about £100 ($155). You might just want to window-shop. Nearby is:

12. **John Lobb,** 9 St. James's St., one of the world's fanciest shoemakers. Members of the royal family have been coming here for handcrafted footwear for more than 140 years; their exact foot measurements are all kept here. To make sure the shoe fits, John Lobb will take a cast of your foot, and create the shoe around it. The simplest styles start from about £1,000 ($1,550), and you will have to wait about half a year. A few doors down is:

13. **Berry Bros. & Rudd,** a wine shop that has changed little since it first opened as a grocery store in 1699. As you have probably guessed, however, this is no ordinary liquor store. Behind the dark black exterior are an enormous pair of scales, wheelback Windsor chairs, and, curiously, no wine—the bottles are kept downstairs in the cellars. The list is extensive, however, and in addition to an excellent selection of French, German, and American wines, the store sells malts, cognacs, sherries, and vintage ports that date back to the turn of the century.

Continue walking up St. James's Street, until you reach:

14. **Boodle's Club,** 28 St. James's St., on the right-hand side, flanked by two towerlike wings. You might be able to steal a peek into this old gentlemen's club—a gathering place for politicians and gentry since 1783—through the large, street-level windows.

Farther up St. James's, two doors past Jermyn Street, at no. 37, is:

15. **White's,** one of London's most famous clubs for wealthy gentlemen. Founded in 1775 as a chocolate house—in the years when cocoa was fashionable and expensive—White's began as a club for Tories, conservatives who supported George III. Continue walking up St. James's to its end at:

16. **Piccadilly,** a main street reputedly named for a 17th-century dressmaker who invented the frilly collars called "picadills." Once the address of many of London's largest aristocratic mansions, Piccadilly is now one of the city's major commercial thoroughfares. Just ahead, nestled between Albemarle and Dover Streets is:

17. **Brown's Hotel,** an ultratraditional, oak-paneled hostelry of the rich and famous.

☕ **TAKE A BREAK** If you're in the area between 3pm and 6pm and would like to get a taste of the aristocratic lifestyle, enter Brown's Hotel (☎ **0171/ 493-6020**) for the best-set tea in London. While you relax in an overstuffed chair under stained-glass windows, tailcoated waiters will serve you an endless supply of sandwiches and scones. If you can, make advance reservations *(see Chapter 5).*

Cross Piccadilly, turn right, and almost immediately on your left you will see the:

18. **Burlington Arcade,** one of London's first malls. There are no chain stores here, however. This elegant Regency shopping arcade has been filled with small, expensive boutiques since 1819. Tailcoated watchmen, called "beadles," continue to enforce the promenade's conservative code of behavior, making sure visitors don't run, yell, or whistle. Next to the arcade is:

19. Burlington House, home of the Royal Academy of Arts (☎ **0171/439-7438**), England's oldest fine arts society. Founded in 1768, the academy boasts a collection including works by Constable, Gainsborough, Reynolds, Stubbs, and Turner, and sculpture by Michelangelo. The society is best known for its annual summer exhibition, in which contemporary works are displayed and (often) sold. The academy is open daily from 10am to 6pm, and admission varies depending on the show. Beside Burlington House is:

20. The Albany, a 1770 Georgian apartment building, with a reputation as London's most prestigious address.

Cross Piccadilly. Directly across from the Burlington House, at the corner of Duke Street, is:

21. Fortnum & Mason, 181 Piccadilly, a fancy department store famous for its food hampers and ground-floor food market. Founded in 1705, Fortnum's is reputed to be the oldest extant shop in Piccadilly. Look on the building's exterior and notice the Royal Warrants: coats-of-arms awarded by the royal family to show that they shop here, too. Higher up on the wall is an ornately decorated glockenspiel. If you arrive on the hour, you can see the clock put on a show.

Continue down Piccadilly one block to:

22. St. James's Church, a postwar reconstruction of one of Sir Christopher Wren's prettiest designs. Enter the courtyard and notice the outdoor pulpit atop a short flight of carved stairs. Inside, the church boasts a beautifully carved baptismal font and organ case, by master sculptor Grinling Gibbons. Our tour ends three blocks ahead at:

23. Piccadilly Circus, a confusing confluence of the West End's major thoroughfares. Best at night, when the enormous neon advertising signs are in full glow, the circus is best known for its center-island **statue of Eros.** Cast in 1893, this small aluminum angel is not the cherub of love, but was made to represent Christian charity, in honor of Victorian philanthropist Lord Shaftesbury.

☕ **A FINAL BREAK** If you'd like to end your tour with lunch or dinner, head for the **New Piccadilly Restaurant,** 8 Denman St. (☎ **0171/437-8530**). Located one block north of Piccadilly Circus, just off the bottom of Shaftesbury Avenue, this no-nonsense English restaurant offers good, inexpensive meals in one of London's most heavily touristed areas. There is no liquor license; patrons are encouraged to bring their own. *(See Chapter 5 for complete details.)*

WALKING TOUR 3
Legal London

Start: Trafalgar Square.
Finish: St. Paul's Cathedral.
Time: About two hours, not including museum stops.
Best Times: Weekdays, when the streets and Inns of Court are full of activity.
Worst Times: Weekends, when The City becomes a virtual ghost town.

England's fascinating, but sometimes complex, legal system is centered around four powerful legal societies; Lincoln's Inn, Gray's Inn, Middle Temple, and Inner Temple. Called "Inns of Court," the origins of these important fraternities are shrouded in history.

Until the 18th century, many lawyers were forced to decline professional advancements and judgeships because they could not afford to throw the requisite banquet

Walking Tour—Legal London

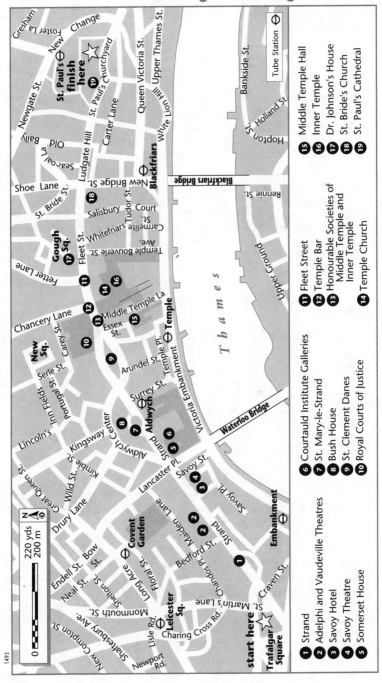

1. Strand
2. Adelphi and Vaudeville Theatres
3. Savoy Hotel
4. Savoy Theatre
5. Somerset House
6. Courtauld Institute Galleries
7. St. Mary-le-Strand
8. Bush House
9. St. Clement Danes
10. Royal Courts of Justice
11. Fleet Street
12. Temple Bar
13. Honourable Societies of Middle Temple and Inner Temple
14. Temple Church
15. Middle Temple Hall
16. Inner Temple
17. Dr. Johnson's House
18. St. Bride's Church
19. St. Paul's Cathedral

for their fraternity. The enforcement of these traditions allowed the class-conscious inns to keep wealthy landholders in the highest positions. It wasn't at all covert. In the early 17th century, a mandate by James I actually denied admission to the Inns of Court to anyone who was not a gentleman by descent.

Although they are no longer the sole dispensers of legal education, the powerful societies still provide lectures to aspiring barristers and maintain complete control over admissions to the bar. Before they are allowed to practice, law students are required to serve an apprenticeship for two years at one of the four Inns of Court.

This walk will take you along one of London's oldest and busiest thoroughfares, through several churches, and into several sanctuaries of law—some of the most mysterious and least-known parts of the city.

Start your tour in Trafalgar Square *(see Walking Tour 1, above)*, and walk east along the right-hand side of the:

1. **Strand,** meaning "sandy bank." This long stretch used to hug the Thames, in the days before the Embankment narrowed the river. The Strand has long been the address of elegant residences and has been associated with lawyers for over six centuries. As you begin your walk, you'll notice the:

2. **Adelphi and Vaudeville Theatres,** on your left, known for musicals and dramas, respectively.

Stay on the right, however, where one of the first buildings you will encounter, just past Carting Lane, is the:

3. **Savoy Hotel.** This was London's most prestigious hostelry when it first opened in 1889. Notice the long driveway, into and out of which taxis continually move. This may be the only place in London where cars drive on the right-hand side. The adjacent:

4. **Savoy Theatre** was home to several of Gilbert and Sullivan's first comic operas.

Two blocks ahead, just past Lancaster Place (which crosses Waterloo Bridge) is:

5. **Somerset House,** a huge Palladian structure dating from 1776, housing the Internal Revenue Ministry and the:

6. **Courtauld Institute Galleries,** a small museum with a fine collection of impressionist and postimpressionist art. *(See Chapter 6 for complete information.)*

After exiting the galleries, return to the Strand, and almost immediately you come upon the church:

7. **St. Mary-le-Strand,** lodged on an island in the middle of the street. Consecrated in 1724, the exterior Ionic portico hides a baroque interior, complete with intricate floral moldings. Famous parishioners included Sir Isaac Newton and the parents of Charles Dickens, who were married here in 1809.

Opposite the church, under the arches of Aldwych, on the north (left) side of the Strand is:

8. **Bush House,** a 1935 building that has been home to BBC Radio's World Service since 1940.

About three blocks ahead stands another center-island church, that of:

9. **St. Clement Danes.** Although it survived the Great Fire of 1666, the church was condemned soon afterward, and rebuilt by Christopher Wren in 1682. The 50-foot baroque steeple was added in 1719 by architect James Gibbs. After suffering heavy damage during the Battle of Britain, the interior was renovated, and the church was rededicated in honor of the Royal Air Force. The building's exterior remains damaged by shrapnel, a reminder of the hits it took from German bombs. The interior contains several Shrines of Remembrance, filled with names of airmen who died in action. Included are many Americans who were killed while fighting

for Britain. The Welsh slate floors are inlaid with 750 brass badges of RAF squadrons. Lexicographer Samuel Johnson worshipped here seated in the north gallery in seat no. 18, which also accounts for the statue of him that stands out front.

Just outside the church, it's hard to ignore the elaborately ornamented building in front of you. It's not a cathedral, it's the:

10. **Royal Courts of Justice,** one of London's most architecturally stunning Victorian buildings. Construction of the Law Courts, as they are also called, was begun in 1874. The design is the result of an architectural competition won by George Street, an expert in 13th-century Gothic styles. Inside the main hall of this highest English court is a small exhibition of the legal costumes worn by judges and barristers. You are free to walk around the building and peek into the courtrooms. Here, and in the halls, you can still see lawyers and judges dressed in ermine-trimmed robes and full-bottomed wigs.

☕ **TAKE A BREAK** Take time out to rub elbows with judges and lawyers and pop into **The George,** 213 The Strand, an old timbered inn opposite the Royal Courts of Justice. This bi-level pub serves traditional ales on the ground floor and full lunches upstairs. It is known for its particularly good carved meats, served with the requisite potatoes and two vegetables.

Just past the Law Courts, the Strand becomes:

11. **Fleet Street,** named for a river—now covered—which used to flow from Hampstead. Fleet Street is synonymous with journalism, and was once home to the printing facilities and offices of most of London's newspapers. Since the *Daily Telegraph* and the *Daily Express* left their respective buildings several years ago, there are no longer any newspapers headquartered here. The monument in the middle of the street is:

12. **Temple Bar,** which marks the entrance to the City of London, and stands at the point in the road where the Strand becomes Fleet Street. Topped by a dragon and surrounded by statues of royalty, the bar was erected in 1880, and is actually a memorial to two previous gates that occupied this spot for hundreds of years. The monument, and much of the area surrounding you, is named for its proximity to Temple Church, an ancient church belonging to the order of the Knights Templar *(see below)*.

On your right, about 50 yards up Fleet Street, is a pretty, half-timbered house at no. 17. Turn right under the house (Inner Temple Lane) and walk through the gateway into the grounds of the:

13. **Honourable Societies of Middle Temple and Inner Temple.** This single compound used to house the Knights Templar, a powerful religious brotherhood popular in the Middle Ages. The site is now home to two of London's four Inns of Court. The 14th-century inns were so called because they provided room and board to the students. Today, tradition still requires legal apprentices to eat with their fraternity 24 times before they are admitted to the bar. Practicing barristers must also continue to eat with the society, at least three times during each law term, in order to maintain their membership. Although they overlap somewhat, the Inner Temple has most of its buildings to the left of the walk you are now standing on, while most of Middle Temple's buildings are to your right.

Walk about 40 yards and turn left after the doorway marked no. 2. Just through this passageway, on your right, is:

14. **Temple Church,** an unusual round church designed using both Norman and Gothic models. Styled after the Dome of the Rock, in Jerusalem, this stone

church was consecrated in 1185 and is one of the oldest in London. Inside, the nine life-size statues lying on the church floor are effigies of rich patrons of the Templars. A few steps south of the church is:

15. **Middle Temple Hall,** which dates from 1570, and was long the site of Middle Temple's mock trials. The hall used to have regular visiting hours, but has recently been closed to the public. Try knocking on the door. If the guard is in he might let you sneak a peek. Inside is London's most fantastic double hammerbeam oak roof, and the walls are almost completely covered with coats of arms of former Middle Temple members. It is said that this hall hosted the first performance of Shakespeare's *Twelfth Night,* in 1601, a show which, most probably, was attended by the Bard himself. Queen Elizabeth I was also in the audience and later gave the hall an oak table made of a single 29-foot plank. It still sits at the hall's far end.

   To the east of Middle Temple Hall, just across the lawn, are the buildings of:

16. **Inner Temple,** the society with which Margaret Thatcher was associated, before turning to politics.

   Exit the temple grounds the same way you came in. Cross Fleet Street, turn right, and take the second left after Fetter Lane, onto Johnson Court. Just steps ahead is Gough Square, site of:

17. **Dr. Johnson's House.** *(See Chapter 6 for complete information.)* Now a museum, this is the house where journalist and lexicographer Samuel Johnson (1709–84) lived and worked, compiling the world's first English dictionary.

   ☕ **TAKE A BREAK** Ye Olde Cheshire Cheese Pub, located on the north (left) side of Fleet Street, in a narrow passageway called Wine Office Court, has been serving since 1667. This historical wooden pub is where Dr. Johnson took his tipple, and is a sightseeing attraction in its own right. You'll have to duck through the low doors, which, along with the long bar and wooden benches, are unchanged since the 17th century. *(See Chapter 5 for complete information.)*

   Crossing Fleet Street once again, you soon arrive at:

18. **St. Bride's Church,** hiding on your right, in a courtyard just before Ludgate Circus. Look at the tiered spire. It's said that this stunning steeple was the inspiration for the traditional wedding cake, first created by a baker across the way. On December 30, 1940, German bombs destroyed the church and revealed the ruins of seven previous reconstructions on the same site. Most of what was uncovered is now on display in a small museum downstairs. If you arrive at 1:15pm on Tuesday, Wednesday, or Friday, stop in for a free classical-music concert. *(See Chapter 6 for full details.)*

   Our walk now takes us across busy Ludgate Circus, for the ¹/₄-mile walk up Ludgate Hill to the City of London's most spectacular masterpiece:

19. **St. Paul's Cathedral,** the only building in London that would not be out of place in Rome or Venice. *(See Chapter 6 for complete information.)* If you have the strength, climb the stairs to the uppermost gallery, and you will be rewarded with an unrivaled view of London. Looking west, you can trace your steps all the way back to Trafalgar Square.

   ☕ **TAKE A BREAK** If you're in the mood for a quick bite before heading back to the West End or continuing on to the Tower of London, stop in at Piccolo, 7 Gresham St., a simple sandwich bar with a cheap and extensive menu. The shop is two blocks northeast of St. Paul's, just off Martin's Le Grand Street, between St. Paul's Underground and the Museum of London. *(See Chapter 5 for complete information.)*

London is a great shopping city, but it no longer offers the shopping bargains that it used to. Everything in London is terribly expensive. In fact, the Brits now come to New York to seek their bargains. Even though budget travelers probably won't make any purchases at the traditional English stores—like Locke, Lobb, Turnbull & Asser, and Asprey—it's fun to window-shop and see the still carefully crafted merchandise. Going to an auction house or strolling through a market won't cost a quid, either—unless, of course, you alight upon an object of your desire and can't resist it.

HOURS

Stores are usually open daily from 10am to 6pm, but most stay open at least one extra hour one night during the week. Shops in Knightsbridge usually remain open until around 7pm on Wednesday, while stores in the West End are open late on Thursday. Some shops around touristy Covent Garden stay open until 7 or 8pm nightly. If you are planning on visiting a particular store, always call ahead to check.

RECLAIMING VALUE-ADDED TAX (VAT)

A VAT refund scheme for overseas visitors exists. Unfortunately, not all stores participate, and if they do they may impose minimum purchase amounts. To reclaim your VAT, you need to show identification at the store and fill out a VAT form. Make sure you keep your receipt and form. On your departure, show your form and receipt to British customs and they will stamp it. Then mail the stamped form back to the store and eventually you'll receive a refund. For more information contact the BTA.

TRADITIONAL SALES

January sales are as British as Christmas pudding—and this dessert is usually reduced by 30% after the holiday, too. All the big department stores start their annual sales just after Christmas; the smaller shops usually follow suit. For Londoners, the January sales are a rite. Visitors are certainly not immune to this shopping fever. Offering one or two remarkable specials, Harrods and Selfridges may have people lined up all night long to get in the doors the morning of the sale. Buyer beware: Some goods are shipped into the stores especially for sales, and these goods may not be of as high a quality as what's carried year-round.

1 The Shopping Scene

The **West End** is the heart of London shopping; its main artery is mile-long **Oxford Street,** lined with stores including John Lewis, Selfridges, and Marks & Spencer. At its midpoint, Oxford Street is crossed by **Regent Street,** a more elegant shopping street, which is noted for such clothiers as Aquascutum, Austin Reed, and Burberry. **Old Bond Street,** which changes its name to **New Bond Street,** heads north from **Piccadilly** to **Oxford Street;** this lane is wonderful for gazing at fine antiques,art, and jewelry at such stores as Asprey's. Sotheby's auction house is also on the street.

At Piccadilly Circus, Regent Street meets **Piccadilly,** which, along with **St. James's Street, Jermyn Street,** and the **Burlington Arcade,** makes up one of the classiest shopping districts in the entire world. Here you'll find Hatchard's for books; Swaine, Adeney Brigg & Sons for fine leather goods, riding equipment, and umbrellas; and Fortnum & Mason, a department store with a renowned food hall. Jermyn Street is well known for shirtmakers; its other fine shops include Paxton & Whitfield, a specialist cheesemonger, and Floris, which has been blending perfume since 1730.

Anchored by Harrods department store, **Brompton Road** in Knightsbridge has a variety of fashionable boutiques for both men and women.

Sloane Street is one of London's fanciest for high fashion. Connecting Knightsbridge with Chelsea, it's lined with designer boutiques like Joseph, Armani, Valentino, and Kenzo.

King's Road bisects Chelsea and straddles the fashion fence between trendy and tradition. In the 1970s, this was the center of punk fashion. Things have quieted down somewhat, but mainstream boutiques are still mixed with a healthy dose of the avant-garde.

Young fashion flourishes, too, on **Kensington High Street** in general, and in Hyper-Hyper (see "Fashion, Contemporary," below) and the Kensington Market in particular. See listings below for information on specific shops.

MARKETS

Outdoor markets are where knowledgeable Londoners and bargain-hunting visitors shop for food, clothing, furniture, books, antiques, crafts, and, of course, junk. Dozens of markets cater to different communities. For shopping or just browsing, markets offer a unique and exciting day out. Only a few stalls officially open before sunrise, but that doesn't stop the flashlight-wielding professionals who'll snap up gems even before they reach the display table. During wet weather, stalls may close early. See below for detailed information on specific London markets.

2 Shopping A to Z

ANTIQUES

In addition to looking in the outdoor markets listed below, serious and casual antique hunters should check out three stall-filled "malls" along Chelsea's King's Road. **Antiquarius,** 131 King's Rd. (☎ **0171/351-5353**), features more than 120 sellers hawking everything from books and prints to scientific instruments, glass, and jewelry. **Chelsea Antique Market,** 253 King's Rd. (☎ **0171/352-5689**), has been around since 1964 and is known for good prices on decorative objects, jewelry, books, and film and theater memorabilia. **Chenil Galleries,** 181 King's Rd. (☎ **0171/351-5353**), is more upscale and specializes in oil paintings, furniture, and an eclectic collection of 19th-century applied arts and crafts. These venues are open Monday through Saturday from 10am to 6pm; take the tube to Sloane Square or South Kensington.

The streets around Portobello are lined with antique stores, especially Westbourne Grove between Portobello and Ladbroke.

BOOKS/MAGAZINES

London is one of the best places in the world for books—new, used, and antiquarian—but the prices are no longer as cheap as they used to be. A great many of the city's 1,000 or so booksellers are clustered in and around **Charing Cross Road.** Look for entire shops devoted to art, science fiction, religion, medicine, cookery, crime, government, sport, and travel. Browsers should start from the Leicester Square tube station and work their way north along Charing Cross Road. Don't ignore side streets like St. Martin's Court and Cecil Court. Bloomsbury, too, has many booksellers, especially scholarly antiquarian dealers.

To find specialist shops, check the phone book or ask a local bookseller.

Ballantyne & Date
38 Museum St., WC1. ☎ **0171/242-4249.** Tube: Holborn.

This store specializes in antiquarian and new books on art design, architecture, photography, and the decorative and applied arts. It also sells prints, some of which can be purchased for as little as £15 ($23.25).

Books for Cooks
4 Blenheim Crescent, W11. ☎ **0171/221-1992.** Tube: Ladbroke Grove.

A cook's paradise. This store stocks books on practically every ethnic cuisine in the world, as well as classic books on entertaining and more. Small café in the back, too.

✪ Compendium Bookshop
234 Camden High St., NW1. ☎ **0171/485-8944.** Tube: Camden Town.

A terrific shop with exhaustive sections on politics, psychology, women's issues, and New Age. All the alternative magazines.

✪ Dillons the Bookstore
82 Gower St., WC1. ☎ **0171/636-1577.** Tube: Goodge Street.

An extremely helpful staff, terrific indexing, and almost a quarter of a million books makes Dillons one of the best bookshops in the world. New books only.

Foyles
119 Charing Cross Rd., WC2. ☎ **0171/437-5660.** Tube: Leicester Square or Tottenham Court Road.

The largest bookseller on the strip, famous Foyles has the best-sellers along with a good collection of hard-to-find titles. Once the best in town, and still very well stocked, but today it has been surpassed at least in efficiency by such chains as Waterstones and Dillons.

Hatchards
187 Piccadilly, W1. ☎ **0171/439-9921.** Tube: Piccadilly Circus or Green Park.

A holder of all four Royal Warrants, Hatchards has been trading for nearly 200 years. It carries all the latest releases and popular fiction and nonfiction titles.

Jarndyce
46 Great Russell St., WC1. ☎ **0171/631-4220.** Tube: Tottenham Court Road.

An antiquarian bookseller with a specialty collection of 19th-century English literature. Also in the same building upstairs, **Fine Books Oriental** has just that, a superb collection of Orientalia.

Offstage Theatre and Film Bookshop
37 Chalk Farm Rd., NW1. ☎ **0171/485-4996.** Tube: Camden Town or Chalk Farm.

A great selection of books on drama and film, including screenplays and plays. Special sections on stagecraft, cinematography, circus, and commedia del arte. A large secondhand department, too.

Stanfords
12–14 Long Acre, WC2. ☎ **0171/836-1321.** Tube: Covent Garden.

One of the best travel bookshops in the world, Stanfords is known for its exhaustive collection of travel guides and travel literature, as well as tons of maps and atlases.

The Travel Bookshop
13–15 Blenheim Crescent, W11. ☎ **0171/229-5260.** Tube: Ladbroke Grove.

Carries a variety of literary titles and guidebooks, both old and new.

Ulysses
31 Museum St., WC1. ☎ **0171/637-5862.** Tube: Holborn.

A great store selling rare travel books. Wonderful stock in good condition.

There's another branch at 40 Museum Street (☎ **0171/831-1600**), which carries a large stock of modern first editions and illustrated books. Rare and fine books are a specialty, but there are also less expensive books in the basement.

Vintage Magazine Shop
39 Brewer St., at Great Windmill St., W1. ☎ **0171/439-8525.** Tube: Piccadilly Circus.

A great place to pick up a gift book at a bargain price. Classical music, newspapers, and other magazines. Prices start at £3 ($4.65). There's another branch at 247 Camden High St.

✪ Waterstones
In Harrods, 87–135 Brompton Rd., SW1. ☎ **0171/730-1234.** Tube: Knightsbridge.

This is my favorite chain bookstore in London. They have a tremendous stock and the service is swift, expert, and friendly. The store makes special recommendations and holds frequent author signings. Other branches can be found at 9–13 Garrick St., WC2 (☎ **0171/836-6757**); 121 Charing Cross Rd., WC2 (☎ **0171/434-4291**); 193 Kensington High St., W8 (☎ **0171/937-8432**); 99 Old Brompton Rd., SW7 (☎ **0171/581-8522**); and 128 Camden High St., NW1 (☎ **0171/284-4948**).

CHARITY SHOPS

Don't overlook charity shops (i.e., thrift shops), especially those in well-heeled neighborhoods. The stock can be exceptional in quality. Check out Imperial Cancer Research Fund, Unicef, and Oxfam.

CRAFTS & GALLERIES

Galerie Singleton
40 Theobalds Rd., WC1. ☎ **0171/831-6928.** Tube: Holborn.

A good selection of modern art and crafts items—night-lights for under £10, pewter, glass, and ceramic objects, and picture frames.

The Kasbah
8 Southampton St. ☎ **0171/240-3538.** Tube: Covent Garden or Charing Cross.

Good-quality Moroccan leather, glass, textiles, rugs, clothing, and furniture. A set of six decorated tea glasses is about $30. There's also a wide selection of affordable boxes—metal, juniper wood, and camel bone.

Tibet Shop
10 Bloomsbury Way. ☎ **0171/405-5284.** Tube: Holborn.

Filled with jewelry, rugs, crafts, musical instruments, Thangka paintings, books, and cards. Proceeds go to help the Tibetan cause.

DEPARTMENT STORES

Department stores are the city's most famous shopping institutions, and a handful stand out as top visitor attractions as well.

✪ Harrods
87–135 Brompton Rd., SW1. ☎ **0171/730-1234.** Tube: Knightsbridge.

By many estimates, Harrods is the largest department store in the world, selling everything from pins to pianos. The store claims that anything in the world can be bought here. Even if you're not in a shopping mood, the incredible ground-floor food halls are definitely worth a visit.

Liberty
210–214 Regent St., W1. ☎ **0171/734-1234.** Tube: Oxford Circus.

London's prettiest department store. In addition to colorful clothing separates with the famous Liberty imprint, this old-world store features an incomparable Asian department and fashion by well-known designers.

Marks & Spencer
458 Oxford St., W1. ☎ **0171/935-7954.** Tube: Marble Arch.

England's largest and best-known department store chain is headed by this flagship store in the heart of Oxford Street. Mid-priced British designs run the gamut from traditional to trendy. The store is most famous for its excellent underwear and intimate apparel departments.

Selfridges
400 Oxford St., W1. ☎ **0171/629-1234.** Tube: Marble Arch or Bond Street.

Selfridges seems almost as big as, and more crowded than, its chief rival, Harrods. Opened in 1909 by Harry Selfridge, a salesman from Chicago, this department store revolutionized retailing with its variety of goods and dynamic displays. The ground-floor perfumery is one of London's best. The upper floors are well stocked with top designer fashions.

FASHION
CONTEMPORARY

The following listings are "warehouse" shops, each encompassing dozens of small, individually owned and managed stalls.

Hyper-Hyper
26–40 Kensington High St., W8. ☎ **0171/938-4343.** Tube: High Street Kensington.

At Hyper-Hyper, young British designers operate their own stands on their way to the big time. Not cheap, this bi-level emporium is chock-full of England's most in- teresting and esoteric fashions—definitely worth a visit. Some stalls accept credit cards.

Kensington Market
49–53 Kensington High St., W8. No phone. Tube: High Street Kensington.

Located diagonally across the street from Hyper-Hyper. The fashion here is on the cutting edge of street fashion. Look for the latest in nightclub fashions, hard-impact postpunk designs, period clothing, and chunky "heavy metal" accessories. Even after a recent reorganization, the multilevel emporium is labyrinthine. It's often packed. Some stalls accept credit cards.

DISCOUNT

Designer Sale Studio

201 King's Rd., SW3. ☎ **0171/351-4171.** Tube: Sloane Square.

Armani, Versace, Bagutta, Aspesi, and other high-fashion designer womens' wear are sold here for 60% off their original ticket price. Younger looks from Byblos, Complice, and Moschino, too. Much of the stock is made up of hits from last season, though current samples and timeless accessories are also usually on hand. There's also a menswear department.

Shop 70

Lamb's Conduit St., WC1. ☎ **0171/430-1533.** Tube: Holborn.

Primarily an outlet for men's clothes, it sells overstock from the top designers' less conservative lines. Giorgio Armani and Paul Smith are labels that you'll frequently come across here, along with Moschino and Stone Island. Knowledgeable salespeople and contemporary ambience.

GIFTS/SPECIALTIES

Anything Left Handed

57 Brewer St., W1. ☎ **0171/437-3910.** Tube: Oxford Circus.

"Righties" will be amazed at how much they take for granted when they visit this unusual shop. Scissors, rulers, kitchenware, corkscrews, mugs, and books—all made for the southpaw. It's off Regent Street, four blocks south of Oxford Circus.

Architectural Components Ltd.

4–8 Exhibition Rd., SW7. ☎ **0171/581-2401.** Tube: South Kensington.

Ever yearned for those very English hearth implements, door knockers, snuffers, fireplace implements, and shaving stands? Here's where to find them. Some are quite reasonably priced.

The Back Shop

24 New Cavendish Sq., W1. ☎ **0171/935-9120.** Tube: Bond Street.

The Back Shop claims to stock the largest range of products for backache sufferers in Europe—chairs, pillows, massage equipment, writing slopes, and other comfort-inducing devices.

British Museum Shop

Great Russell Street, WC1 ☎ **0171/323-8624.** Tube: Tottenham Court Road.

Like most museum shops, this is an inspired place to find a gift. Jewelry, books, reproductions, and replicas are all beautifully crafted.

Coincraft/Lobel

45 Great Russell St., WC1. ☎ **0171/636-1188.** Tube: Tottenham Court Road.

For an unusual gift, check out some of the coins and archaeological objects here. You can pick up a Victorian silver sixpence dated 1887 for as little as £10 ($15.50), a genuine 1,600-year-old Roman oil lamp for only £30 ($46.50) or a small Roman vase for £45 ($69.75).

The Filofax Centre

21 Conduit St., W1. ☎ **0171/499-0457.** Tube: Oxford Circus.

Nothing was more emblematic of the booming 1980s than the Filofax loose-leaf organizers found under almost every Yuppie arm. They're not cheap, but they're handy.

Here at the British headquarters, you can pick up every insert ever made for the filers. There's another branch at 69 Neal St., Covent Garden WC2 (☎ **0171/ 836-1977**).

Garden Treats
Sydney St., SW3. No phone.

This store offers a wide variety of functional and decorative items for the garden. Among the selections are pretty herb labels and huge candles that look like birch logs.

London Tourist Board Shop
In the Tourist Information Centre, Victoria Station Forecourt, SW1. No phone. Tube: Victoria.

A variety of books, gifts, and souvenirs, such as T-shirts, key rings, teapots, and coasters.

London Transport Museum Shop
The Piazza, Covent Garden. ☎ **0171/379-6344.** Tube: Covent Garden.

A wide selection of souvenir items: T-shirts, models, toys, posters, and reproductions of Underground maps the size you see in the station.

MUSIC

HMV
150 Oxford St., W1. ☎ **0171/631-3423.** Tube: Tottenham Court Road or Oxford Circus.

HMV is known for its particularly vast collection of international music and spoken-word recordings, downstairs. Look for contemporary sounds from Europe, Africa, India, and the Caribbean. The ground floor has a decent selection of pop music.

Tower Records
1 Piccadilly Circus, W1. ☎ **0171/439-2500.** Tube: Piccadilly Circus.

A veritable warehouse of sound, Tower has four floors of records, tapes, and compact discs. Pop, rock, classical, jazz, bluegrass, folk, country, sound tracks and more—all in separate departments. Downstairs you'll find a broad selection of international music magazines.

Virgin Megastore
14–16 Oxford St., W1. ☎ **0171/631-1234.** Tube: Oxford Circus or Tottenham Court Road.

In many ways the best record supermarket, Virgin is particularly strong on new releases. Customers can listen to their selections on headphones before paying. The store now carries videos and has a Virgin Atlantic airline ticket office.

OUTDOOR MARKETS
Please note additional markets are listed in Chapter 6.

Brixton Market
Electric Avenue, SW9. Tube: Brixton.

Brixton is the heart of African-Caribbean London, and the Brixton Market is its soul. Electric Avenue (immortalized by Jamaican singer Eddie Grant) is lined mostly with exotic fruit and vegetable stalls. If you continue to its end and turn right, you'll see a terrific selection of the cheapest secondhand clothes in London. Take a detour off the avenue through the enclosed **Granville Arcade** for African fabrics, traditional West African teeth-cleaning sticks, reggae records, and newspapers oriented to the African-British community. Open Monday to Tuesday and Thursday to Saturday 8am to 5:30pm, Wednesday 8am to 1pm.

Camden Markets

Along Camden High Street, NW1. Tube: Camden Town.

Don't confuse Camden Markets with the Camden Passage Market (below). This trendy collection of stalls—in parking lots and empty spaces along Camden High Street all the way to Chalk Farm Road—specializes in original fashions by young designers and junk that appeals to people of all ages. Cafés and pubs (some offering live music) line the route, making for an enjoyable day out. When you've had enough of shopping here, turn north and walk along the peaceful and pretty Regent's Canal. Open Saturday and Sunday 8am to 6pm only.

Camden Passage Market

Off Upper Street, N1. Tube: Angel.

The Market at Camden Passage is smaller than Portobello and usually cheaper, too. Wednesday and Saturday are the best days to pick up bargain jewelry, trinkets, and antiques. Open daily 8:30am to 3pm.

Petticoat Lane

Middlesex Street, E1. Tube: Liverpool Street or Aldgate.

Located in the East End, this is London's best market for inexpensive fashions. A terrific variety of new, contemporary styles hang on racks all along the street. Visitors also flock here to experience the Cockney scene and try jellied eel, the local delicacy. Open Sunday 9am to 2pm only.

✪ Portobello Market

Along Portobello Road, W11. Tube: Notting Hill Gate (ask anyone for directions from there).

Along a road that never seems to end, Portobello Market is the granddaddy of all of London's markets. It's famous for its overflow of antiques and bric-a-brac. As at all antique markets, bargaining is in order here. Saturday between 8am and 4pm is the best time to come; during the week this is mostly a fruit and vegetable market.

SHOES

Shoe stores almost outnumber pubs and churches in London. In general, check Brompton Road and Sloane Street for high fashion, King's Road for trendy styles, and Oxford Street for mid-priced popular footwear.

Natural Shoe Store

21 Neal St., WC2. ☎ **0171/836-5254.** Tube: Covent Garden.

Not the most beautiful shoes in the world, but the most comfortable. Full lines of Dexter, Birkenstock, Arche, and Timberland. Shoes with specialized contours, arches, and soles are carried.

TOILETRIES

The Body Shop

32–34 Great Marlborough St., W1. ☎ **0171/437-5137.** Tube: Oxford Circus.

Now famous internationally, this British chain sells organically based lotions, shampoos, and beauty aids. Prices on some popular products are lower here than in the U.S.

Crabtree & Evelyn

6 Kensington Church St., W8. ☎ **0171/937-9335.** Tube: High Street Kensington.

Fans of Beatrix Potter and Laura Ashley are also undoubtedly loyal to this purveyor of fanciful English-design toiletries. Pastel-colored soaps, powders, and potpourri are beautifully packaged.

Neal's Yard Remedies
15 Neal's Yard, W2. ☎ **0171/379-7222.** Tube: Covent Garden.

London's best shop for packaged herbal medications, aromatherapy oils, homeopathic hair remedies, and other nonprescription medications. Except for gift boxes, everything is under £5 ($7.75). The store is located at the end of a short cul-de-sac off Short's Gardens, two blocks north of Covent Garden Market.

TOYS

✪ Hamley's
188–196 Regent St., W1. ☎ **0171/734-3161.** Tube: Oxford Circus or Piccadilly Circus.

Its antecedent was named Noah's Ark and founded in 1760 by William Hamley. On seven floors, Hamley's has more than 35,000 toys, games, models, dolls, stuffed animals, and electronic cars—one of the largest, if not the largest toy store in the world.

TRADITIONAL BRITISH GOODS

Frank Johnson Sports
189 Ferndale Rd., SW9. ☎ **0171/733-1722.** Tube: Brixton.

Darts fans and other sports enthusiasts will want to visit this most British of sports shops. All types of darts and accessories are sold. Boards can be shipped home from the store. Open Mon–Sat 9:30am–6pm.

James Smith & Sons
53 New Oxford St., WC1. ☎ **0171/836-4731.** Tube: Tottenham Court Road.

Few things are more British than the umbrella, and James Smith & Sons is one of London's premier purveyors. Traditional "brollies" come in nylon or silk, and they're stretched over wood or metal frames. Prices start from about £30 ($46.50). A fancy umbrella or cane can set you back £300 ($465) or more.

Lawleys
154 Regent St., W1. ☎ **0171/734-3184.** Tube: Piccadilly Circus.

A venerable English store that stocks a very broad selection of English bone china— Royal Doulton, Minton, Derby, Wedgwood, and Aynsley for starters.

Reject China Shop
33 Beauchamp Pl., SW3. ☎ **0171/581-0737.** Tube: Knightsbridge.

These stores carry a wide range of English china. As the name suggests, most of the stock is seconds. Shoppers who know the going prices in the United States may pick up some bargains here. Other branches are at 183 Brompton Rd. and 134 Regent St.

The Scotch House
2 Brompton Rd., SW1. ☎ **0171/581-2151.** Tube: Knightsbridge.

Good-quality sweaters and vests begin at about £50 ($77.50). Prices go up with the quality and complexity of design. The emphasis here is on hand-knit Shetlands and cashmeres, as well as machine-made woolens. Kilts, hats, socks, and scarves can be bought off-the-rack or made-to-order with your desired pattern.

The Tea House
15 Neal St., WC2. ☎ **0171/240-7539.** Tube: Covent Garden.

Besides teapots and tea balls, this wonderful-smelling shop sells more than 70 varieties of tea from India, China, Japan, and the rest of the world. Available loose or in bags, traditional English blends make excellent, light, and inexpensive gifts.

Waterford Wedgwood

173 Piccadilly, W1. ☎ **0171/629-2614.** Tube: Piccadilly Circus or Green Park.

Waterford crystal and Wedgwood china share the same table at this upscale shop. Fine cut-glass vases, platters, and objets d'art in a wide range of prices. Complete sets of the famous powder-blue-and-white Jasper china are available, along with many other styles and patterns.

The flagship store, which is at 158 Regent St. (☎ **0171/734-7262**) stocks an even wider selection and is open seven days a week.

Whittard of Chelsea

184 King's Rd., SW1 ☎ **0171/351-3381.** Tube: Sloane Square.

Everything you need to make tea or to accompany it. Other branches are at: 33 Bedford St., WC2; 43 Carnaby St., W1; and 209 Kensington High St., W8.

WINE

Oddbins

With more than 50 branches, this chain of wine stores carries a broad range of reasonably priced wines from all over the world. Centrally located stores include: Brewer Street, W1; Brompton Road, SW3; Ebury Street, SW1; and Southampton Row, WC1.

9

London After Dark

London's reputation for the arts is renowned, especially for its theater and musical life. The best source of information about what's on is *Time Out* magazine. The arts section of the weekend *Independent* is also a good reference.

1 London Theater

TICKETS   Attending a play in London is an experience that should not be missed. More theatrical entertainment is offered here than in any other city, and at prices that are below those in New York. About 40 West End stages compete for audiences with comedies, musicals, and dramas. Tickets range from £12 to £32.50 ($18.60 to $50.40); tickets for musicals are the most expensive since the demand for them is highest. Discounts are available. Many of the major theaters offer reduced-price tickets to documented students on a standby basis. When available, these tickets are sold 30 minutes prior to curtain time; line up early for popular shows.

The **Society of London Theatre** (☎ **0171/836-0971**) operates a **discount ticket booth** in Leicester Square, where tickets for many shows are available at half price, plus a £2 ($3.10) service charge. Tickets are sold only on the day of performance, and there is a limit of four per person. You cannot return tickets, and no credit cards are accepted. The booth is open Monday through Saturday from noon on matinee days (which vary with individual theaters), and from 2:30 to 6:30pm for evening performances. All West End theaters are closed Sunday. Beware of ticket scalpers that work the crowds outside theaters; they will sell you tickets at horrendously inflated prices. Should you fall victim to this practice, report it to the Society of London Theatres.

MAJOR COMPANIES

Three major world-class theater companies can be enjoyed in London—the Royal Shakespeare Company, the Royal National Theatre, and the Royal Court Theatre. Try to fit at least one of them into your schedule.

Barbican Theatre—Royal Shakespeare Company
Barbican Centre, Silk Street, EC2. ☎ **0171/638-8891.** Barbican Theatre £8–£25 ($12.40–$38.75); The Pit £16–£17 ($24.80–$26.35). Tube: Barbican or Moorgate.

This is the London home of the world-renowned Royal Shakespeare Company. Its actual base is in Stratford-upon-Avon, the bard's birthplace, where many of its productions originate. (See Chapter 10, "Easy Excursions from London.") The company stages the classics in the Barbican's 1,200-seat main auditorium. It also performs the works of other playwrights, standard and new, in a smaller studio space called The Pit. Box office open daily 9am to 8pm.

✪ Royal Court Theatre

Sloane Square, SW1. ☎ **0171/730-1745/2554.** Tickets £5–£18 ($7.75–$27.90); Mon evenings, all seats are £5 ($7.75). Tube: Sloane Square.

Contemporary world drama is the specialty of the Royal Court. It was here that the works of the angry young playwrights of the 1950s were staged. Whatever the current production, it will most likely be controversial and excitingly staged.

✪ Royal National Theatre

South Bank, SE1. ☎ **0171/928-2252** box office; 0171/633-0880 information and backstage tours. Tickets £7.50–£22.50 ($11.60–$34.90). Box office open Monday to Saturday 10am to 8pm. Tube: Waterloo.

An evening spent here at Britain's national drama house is a wonderful experience (you can even dine at the Mezzanine Restaurant). The lobby is filled with musical performers and people browsing the bookstore or enjoying coffee or dinner in the restaurants. Others are outside strolling the riverfront terrace. The center contains three performance spaces: the two large Olivier and Lyttelton theaters and the smaller, studio-style Cottesloe. At any one time, as many as six different plays are being performed, from new stagings of classics to premieres of contemporary plays, from musicals to shows for young people. A limited number of cheaper tickets are always available on the morning of the performance at all three theaters. Any unsold tickets are available shortly before the performance on a standby basis for as little as £8.50 or £6.50. Box office open Monday to Saturday 10am to 8pm.

FRINGE THEATER

Some of the best theater in London is performed on the "fringe"—at the dozens of so-called fringe theaters devoted to "alternative" plays, revivals, contemporary dramas, and even musicals. These shows are often more exciting than established West End productions; they are also consistently lower in price. Expect to pay from £4 to £7 ($6.20 to $10.85). Most theaters offer discounted seats to students and seniors.

These theaters are scattered around London. Check the weekly listings in *Time Out* for schedules and show times. Some of the more popular and centrally located fringe theaters are listed below. Call for details on current productions.

✪ Almeida Theatre

Almeida Street, N1. ☎ **0171/359-4404.** Tickets £6.50–£15.50 ($10.05–$24). Tube: Angel or Highbury.

Home to the annual Festival of Contemporary Music, also known as Almeida Opera, from mid-June to mid-July, the Almeida is also known for adventurous stagings of new and classic plays. The theater's legendary status means consistently good productions at lower-than-average prices. Among the more recent celebrated productions have been *Hamlet* with Ralph Fiennes and *Medea* with Dame Diana Rigg, both of which transferred to Broadway. Performances are usually held Monday through Saturday. Box office open Monday to Saturday 10am to 6pm.

Central London Theaters

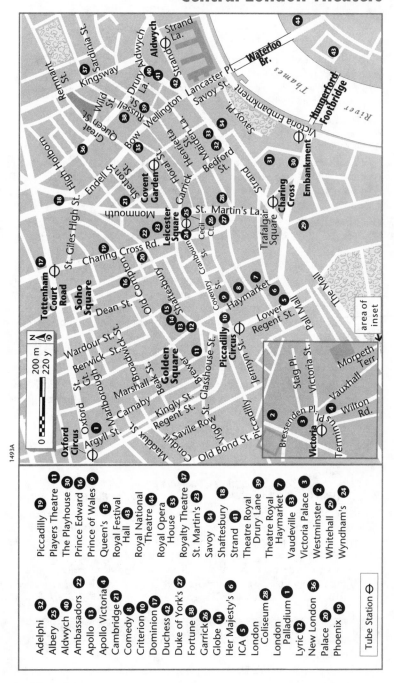

Adelphi **32**
Albery **25**
Aldwych **40**
Ambassadors **22**
Apollo **13**
Apollo Victoria **4**
Cambridge **21**
Comedy **8**
Criterion **10**
Dominion **17**
Duchess **42**
Duke of York's **27**
Fortune **38**
Garrick **26**
Globe **14**
Her Majesty's **6**
ICA **5**
London Coliseum **28**
London Palladium **1**
Lyric **12**
New London **36**
Palace **20**
Phoenix **19**

Piccadilly **19**
Players Theatre **11**
The Playhouse **30**
Prince Edward **16**
Prince of Wales **9**
Queen's **15**
Royal Festival Hall **43**
Royal National Theatre **44**
Royal Opera House **35**
Royalty Theatre **23**
St. Martin's **23**
Savoy **34**
Shaftesbury **18**
Strand **41**
Theatre Royal Drury Lane **39**
Theatre Royal Haymarket **7**
Vaudeville **33**
Victoria Palace **3**
Westminster **2**
Whitehall **29**
Wyndham's **24**

Tube Station ⊖

203

Gate Notting Hill

In the Prince Albert Pub, 11 Pembridge Rd., W11. ☎ **0171/229-0706.** Tickets £5–£10 ($7.75–$15.50). No credit cards. Tube: Notting Hill Gate.

This tiny room above a pub in Notting Hill is one of the best alternative stages in London. Popular with local cognoscenti, the theater specializes in translated works by foreign playwrights. Performances are usually held nightly at 7:30pm. Box office open Monday to Friday 11am to 6pm, Saturday 2 to 6pm.

ICA Theatre

The Mall, W1. ☎ **0171/930-3647.** Average tickets £7 ($10.85). Tube: Charing Cross or Piccadilly Circus.

In addition to a cinema, café, bar, bookshop, and two galleries, the Institute of Contemporary Arts (ICA) has one of London's top theaters for experimental work. The fact that ICA is subsidized by the government usually means good, high-quality performances. Box office open daily noon to 9:30pm.

The King's Head

115 Upper St., N1. ☎ **0171/226-1916.** Tickets £10–£11 ($15.50–$17.05). No credit cards. Tube: Angel.

Arguably London's most famous fringe venue, the King's Head is also the city's oldest pub-theater. Despite its tiny stage, the popular theater is heavy on musicals; some that originated here have gone on to become successful West End productions.

Both matinee and evening performances are usually held Tuesday through Friday. Evening performances only on Saturday. Box office open Monday to Friday 10am to 6pm, Saturday 10am to 8pm, Sunday 10am to 4pm.

Young Vic

66 The Cut, SE1. ☎ **0171/928-6363.** Tickets £8–£14 ($12.40–$21.70). Tube: Waterloo.

Adjacent to the Old Vic, a major venue that once was home to the Royal National Theatre, the Young Vic endeavors to give new talent a stage. The seating, around a central stage, is as unusual as the theater's eclectic variety of productions. Box office open Monday to Saturday 10am to 6pm.

A RE-CREATED CLASSIC

✪ New Globe Theatre

New Globe Walk, Bankside, SE1. ☎ **0171/928-6406.** Tours: £5 ($8) adults, £3 ($4.80) children, £14 ($22.40) family ticket. Daily 10am–5pm. Tube: Mansion House.

This recently reconstructed replica of Shakespeare's original theater-in-the-round— on its original site—is now the premier London showcase of the Bard's works. The theater itself is a duplicate of the original, destroyed by fire in 1613. The New Globe was painstakingly recreated, utilizing a combination of plans from period theaters, and staying as close to the original plans as possible. Performances are staged exactly as in Elizabethan times, without lighting or scenery, or such luxuries as cushioned seats and a roof over the audience. Ticket prices vary depending on the performance.

2 The Performing Arts

OPERA/BALLET

London has a long and venerable opera history. The first theater at Covent Garden was built in 1734, and Handel wrote several operas and oratorios that were performed there. Under the musical direction of Covent Garden's Henry Bishop, Mozart was performed in English for the first time in 1817. It wasn't until 1849 that the theater became devoted exclusively to opera. Adelina Patti made her English debut at Covent Garden in *La Somnambula* in 1861. Since then, most, if not all, of the great opera singers have performed there. The London premieres of works by several British composers, notably, Sir Arthur Bliss, Sir Ralph Vaughan Williams, Sir Benjamin Britten, Sir Michael Tippett, and Sir William Walton have been performed here. The two major companies are the Royal Opera, which was granted a charter in 1968, and the English National Opera.

Ballet has had a venerable history in London, too, although recently the scene has changed, leaving the city with only one major ballet company, the Royal Ballet. The old Sadler's Wells Ballet moved out to Birmingham; it's now called the Birmingham Royal Ballet. The only other ballet company performing in London is the Rambert Dance Company (formerly the Ballet Rambert); it doesn't have a city home base but tours the United Kingdom and internationally. Of course, many international dance companies perform regularly in London, too.

The English National Opera

London Coliseum, St. Martin's Lane, WC2. ☎ **0171/836-3161.** Tickets £5–£48 ($7.75–$74.40). AE, DC, MC, V. Tube: Trafalgar Square.

The English National Opera (ENO) is an innovative company that continually thrills enthusiasts and rocks traditionalists. Operas are always sung in English, and many productions have been transported to Germany, France, and the United States. The ENO performs in the 2,350-seat London Coliseum. Their season lasts from August to May.

✪ The Royal Ballet

In the Royal Opera House, Bow Street, Covent Garden, WC2. ☎ **0171/304-4000** box office. Tickets £13–£64 ($20.15–$99.20). Tube: Covent Garden.

Britain's leading ballet company performs in one of the capital's most glamorous theaters, the Royal Opera House. Currently under the direction of Anthony Dowell, the company performs a variety of the ballet repertory with a tilt toward the classics and works by its earlier choreographer-directors Sir Frederick Ashton and Kenneth Macmillan.

✪ The Royal Opera

In the Royal Opera House, Bow Street, Covent Garden, WC2. ☎ **0171/240-1066,** 0171/836-6903 for unsold seat information. Tickets £7–£150 ($35.65–$232.50). Tube: Covent Garden.

England's most elite opera company performs the international repertoire including productions of Wagner's *Ring Cycle*. Performances are usually sung in the original language, but supertitles are projected, translating the libretto for the audience. The best seats are expensive, but there are several budget options. At £2–£7 ($3.10–$10.85), the upper-level benches are a bargain. Usually available on the day of the performance, these restricted-view seats are quite far from the stage.

Standing room, in the rear of the stalls, may be available 1 to 1½ hours before the performance. At £7 to £14 ($10.85–$21.70), it's a relatively inexpensive way to see a production in one of the world's foremost theaters.

Finally, about 65 amphitheater seats are sold from 10am on the day of the performance. Line up before dawn if Pavarotti or Plácido Domingo is in town. Box office open Monday to Saturday 10am to 8pm.

CLASSICAL MUSIC

Currently, London supports five major orchestras—the **London Symphony,** the **Royal Philharmonic,** the **Philharmonia Orchestra,** the **BBC Symphony,** and the **BBC Philharmonic**—several choirs, and many smaller chamber groups and historic instrument ensembles. Among them look out for the **London Sinfonietta,** the **English Chamber Orchestra,** and the **Academy of St. Martin-in-the-Fields.** Performances take place in the South Banks Arts Centre and the Barbican. For smaller recitals, there's Wigmore Hall and St. John's Smith Square.

Tickets usually range in price from £6–£30 ($9.30–$46.50). The **British Music Information Centre,** 10 Stratford Place, W1 (☎ **0171/499-8567**), is the city's clearinghouse and resource center for "serious" music. The center provides free telephone and walk-in information on current and upcoming events. Free recitals are offered here weekly, usually on Tuesday and Thursday at 7:30pm; call for exact times. Take the tube to Bond Street.

London Symphony Orchestra

Barbican Centre, Silk Street, EC2. ☎ **0171/638-8891.** Tickets £6–£30 ($9–$46.50). Tube: Barbican or Moorgate.

London's top orchestra is currently under the musical direction of Sir Colin Davis. Reduced-price student standby tickets are sometimes available 90 minutes prior to show time.

DANCE

Dance in London is downright cheap in many instances. The major houses all offer inexpensive standby seats (sold on the day of performance only), while prices at fringe theaters rarely top £6 ($9) at any time. Dance venues include: **The Place,** 17 Duke's Rd., WC1 (☎ **0171/387-0031**); **ICA,** The Mall, SW1 (☎ **0171/930-3647**); **South Bank Centre,** South Bank, SE1 (☎ **0171/928-8800**); and **Sadler's Wells Theatre,** Rosebery Ave., EC1 (☎ **0171/713-6000**). For ballet information see above.

Contemporary Dance Theatre

At The Place, 17 Duke's Rd., WC1. ☎ **0171/387-0031.** Tickets £8–£11 ($12.40–$17.05). Tube: Euston.

This showplace usually offers good performances and cheap tickets. The space is small; as you can see from the mirrors and bars, it's used by a dancing school during the day. Box office open Monday to Friday (and Saturday performance days) 10am to 6pm.

Dance Umbrella

20 Chancellor's Street, W6. ☎ **0181/741-4040.** Tickets £9–£25.

This company's fall season showcase become the contemporary dance event in London. During its six-week season, new works by up-and-coming choreographers are featured. Performances are given at a variety of theaters.

MAJOR CONCERT HALLS & ALL-PURPOSE AUDITORIUMS

✪ Barbican Centre

Silk Street, EC2. ☎ **0171/638-8891.** Reduced-price student standby tickets sometimes available. Tube: Barbican or Moorgate.

Reputedly the largest arts complex in Europe, the Barbican is so mazelike that yellow lines have been painted on the sidewalk to help visitors negotiate their way from the Underground to the box office. The architecture of the sprawling center has long been the object of critical attention, most of it negative.

Even its detractors, however, agree that the Barbican has an acoustically excellent concert hall that is home to the London Symphony Orchestra. It hosts festivals and other large-scale events when the orchestras are not performing. It's also the

London home of the Royal Shakespeare Company. The complex contains two theaters, two art galleries, three cinemas, and several dining facilities.

Free concerts are performed in the foyer weekdays from 5:30 to 7:30pm. The program, which alternates between classical and jazz, is repeated on Sunday from 12:30 to 2:30pm. Box office open daily 9am to 11pm.

London Coliseum
St. Martin's Lane, WC2. Box office ☎ **0171/632-8300.** Tube: Leicester Square or Charing Cross.

Home to the English National Opera, the Coliseum is one of London's most architecturally spectacular houses. During summer and other times when the opera is off or out of town, visiting companies (often dance) perform. Box office open Monday to Saturday 10am to 8pm.

Royal Albert Hall
Kensington Gore, SW7. ☎ **0171/589-3203;** box office 0171/589-8212. MC, V. Tube: South Kensington or Kensington High Street.

For 124 years, the 5,000-seat Royal Albert Hall has been host to some of the finest international talent in the world from Frank Sinatra and Liza Minnelli to Eric Clapton. It's also home to the most famous classical music festival in the world, the Henry Wood BBC Promenade Concerts, held every year from mid-July to mid-September. Box office open daily 9am to 9pm.

Sadler's Wells Theatre
Rosebery Avenue, EC1. ☎ **0171/713-6000.** Tube: Angel.

This is one of the busiest stages in London, and also one of the best. Host to top-visiting opera and dance companies from around the world, the theater offers great sight lines and terrific prices. Box office open Monday to Saturday 10:30am to 8pm.

St. John's Smith Square
Smith Square, SW1. ☎ **0171/222-1061.**

A slightly larger space than Wigmore Hall, it features many chamber groups. The BBC lunchtime concerts on Monday at 1pm are a bargain at £6 ($9.30).

South Bank Arts Centre
South Bank, SE1. Box office ☎ **0171/960-4242.** Discounted student standby seats sometimes available. Tube: Waterloo is closest, but the short walk over Hungerford rail bridge from Embankment Underground station is more scenic.

The South Bank Arts Centre, London's flagship performing arts complex, includes three well-designed, modern concert halls. **Royal Festival Hall** is the usual site for major orchestral performances. Smaller **Queen Elizabeth Hall** is known for its chamber-music concerts, and the intimate **Purcell Room** usually hosts advanced students and young performers making their professional debut. All three stages are lit almost every night of the year, and it's not all classical music: ballet, jazz, pop, and folk concerts are also staged here.

The foyer of the Royal Festival Hall is one of the city's hardest-working concert halls in and of itself. Regular, free, informal lunchtime music recitals are scheduled here, in front of the Festival Buffet café, daily from noon to 2pm. A Friday evening Commuter Jazz series is also held here during summer months only from 5:15 to 6:45pm. Box office open daily 10am to 10pm.

Wigmore Hall
36 Wigmore St., W1. ☎ **0171/935-2141.** Discounted student standby tickets sometimes available. Tube: Bond Street or Oxford Circus.

Considered by many to be the best auditorium in London for both intimacy and acoustics. Buy the cheapest seats, as it really doesn't matter where you sit. The Sunday Morning Coffee Concerts (all seats £7) are a great buy. Box office open Monday to Saturday 10am to 8:30pm; Sunday 45 minutes before performance.

3 The Club & Music Scene

CABARET/COMEDY

In addition to the clubs listed below, keep an eye out for performances at the **Canal Café Theatre,** the Bridge House, Delamere Terrace, W2 (☎ **0171/ 289-6054**); at the **Comedy Café,** 66 Rivington St., EC2 (☎ **0171/739-5706**), where there's no admission charge on Wednesday and Thursday nights; and at the **Comedy Spot,** Maiden Lane, WC2 (☎ **0171/379-5900**).

The Comedy Store

1 Oxendon St., SW1. ☎ **0142/691-4433.** Cover £8–10 ($12.40–$15.50). Tube: Piccadilly.

London's premier comedy club features top acts from Britain and the world. Performances Tuesday to Thursday and Sunday 8pm; Friday and Saturday 8pm and midnight.

Oranje Boom Boom

At De Hems Dutch Coffee Bar, Macclesfield Street, W1. ☎ **0181/437-2494.** Cover £4 ($6.20). Tube: Leicester Square.

This West End coffee shop is typical of the smaller venues where good, offbeat cabaret often lurks. Performances: usually Wednesday. Call the club for details.

ROCK/POP

Rock-and-roll may not have been invented in Britain, but in the 1960s the English fine-tuned a style that engulfed the world in waves of sound. London still boasts an excellent music scene, and several accessible, centrally located clubs stage up-and-coming acts almost nightly. Archaic drinking laws require most late-opening clubs to charge admission, which unfortunately often gets pricey.

Marquee

105–107 Charing Cross Rd., WC2. ☎ **0171/437-6603.** Cover £5–£18 ($6.20–$10.85). No credit cards. Tube: Tottenham Court Road or Leicester Square.

Since the 1950s, the Marquee has been considered one of the best centers of rock in the world. Groups like the Rolling Stones played here before achieving fame. Live bands perform daily from 7pm to midnight. Nonmembers are welcome—you just pay at the door. Well-known musicians frequent the place regularly on their nights off. Open Monday to Thursday and Sunday 7pm to midnight, Friday 7pm to 3am, Saturday 10:30pm to 3:30am. *Note:* The Marquee is relocating again as we go to press. Check *Time Out* for its new location.

Rock Garden

6–7 Covent Garden Plaza, WC2. ☎ **0171/240-3961.** Cover £8–£10 ($12.40–$15.50). Tube: Covent Garden.

The quality of music varies at this small basement club in Covent Garden. It's the club's policy to give new talent a stage. Dire Straits, the Police, and many others played here before they became famous. Triple and quadruple bills ensure a good variety. The place is usually filled with foreigners. Open Monday to Saturday 7:30pm to 3am, Sunday 7:30pm to midnight.

Wag

35 Wardour St., W1. ☎ **0171/437-5534.** Cover £5–£10 ($7.75–$15.50). No credit cards. Tube: Leicester Square or Piccadilly Circus.

The split-level Wag club is one of the more stylish live-music places in town. The downstairs stage usually attracts newly signed, cutting-edge rock bands, while dance disks spin upstairs. The door policy can be selective. Open Monday to Thursday 10pm to 3am, Friday and Saturday 10pm to 6am.

IN CAMDEN TOWN & KENTISH TOWN

Many of London's best music venues are in Camden Town and adjacent Kentish Town, just east of Regent's Park.

The Bull & Gate

389 Kentish Town Rd., NW5. ☎ **0171/485-5358.** Cover £3.50–£5 ($5.45–$7.75). No credit cards. Tube: Kentish Town.

Smaller, cheaper, and often better than its competitors, the Bull & Gate is the unofficial headquarters of London's pub rock scene. Independent and unknown rock bands are often served up back-to-back by the half dozen. It's open pub hours, with music Monday to Saturday 8 to 11pm.

Camden Palace

1A Camden Rd., NW1. ☎ **0171/387-0428.** Cover £5–£20 ($7.75–$31). AE, MC, V. Tube: Mornington Crescent or Camden Town.

From punk to funk. When the bands stop, the records spin, and feet keep moving to the beat. Open Monday to Thursday and Saturday 9pm to 2:30am, Friday 8pm to 2:30am.

FOLK

Cecil Sharpe House

2 Regent's Park Rd., NW1. ☎ **0171/485-2206.** Admission from £3–£5 ($4.65–$7.75). Tube: Camden Town.

CSH was the focal point of the folk revival in the 1960s and continues to treasure this music and to document and nurture it. Here, you'll find a whole range of traditional English music and dancing performed. Call to see what's happening.

JAZZ

You can get information on jazz concerts and events from **Jazz Services** (☎ 0171/405-0737) and the listings magazines. Another jazz organization worth contacting is the Jazz Umbrella, an organization of jazz musicians. For information, call **0171/729-0631.** Free jazz is usually offered every Sunday from 12:30 to 2:30pm on level 0 of the Barbican Centre, Silk Street, EC2 (☎ **0171/638-4141**); tube to Barbican or Moorgate. For fun why not attend the Sunday morning jazz brunch at the Victoria and Albert Museum, which runs from 11am to 5pm and has featured such greats as Django Reinhart. Cost is £8 ($12.40). For info, call **0171/581-2159.**

Club Bluenote

35 Coronet St., N1. ☎ **0171/729-2476.** Cover £3–£10 ($4.65–$15.50). Tube: Old Street.

This small club features alternative dance, funk, and soul. Latin and jazz on Sunday afternoons. Open Tuesday to Saturday 8pm to 2am, Sunday noon to midnight.

Brahms & Liszt

19 Russell St., WC2. ☎ **0171/240-3661.** Cover free until 9pm; £5 ($7.75) after. Tube: Covent Garden.

This wine bar presents live R&B nightly in its cellar. Local combos provide good background music to conversation. Bar prices are reasonable for a place within sight of Covent Garden Market. Open Monday to Saturday until 1am, Sunday until 10:30pm.

Jazz Cafe

5 Parkway, NW1. ☎ **0171/916-6060.** Cover £7–£15 ($10.85–$23.25) Tube: Camden Town.

The sounds are so great here that it's worth booking a table if you really want to hear anything and everything from rap to Latin jazz.

The 100 Club

100 Oxford St., W1. ☎ **0171/636-0933.** Cover £6–£10 ($9.30–$15.50); student discount available. Tube: Tottenham Court Road.

An austere underground club, the 100 usually hosts jazz nights on Monday, Wednesday, Friday, and Saturday. The stage is in the center of a smoky basement—looking just the way a jazz club is *supposed* to look. Open Monday and Wednesday 7:30pm to midnight, Tuesday and Saturday 7:30pm to 1am, Thursday 8pm to 1am, Friday 8:30pm to 3am.

Pizza Express

10 Dean St., W1. ☎ **0171/437-9595.** Cover £8–£12.50 ($12.40–$19.40), plus food. Tube: Tottenham Court Road.

One of the city's most popular jazz rooms finds an unlikely location in the basement of a chain restaurant. The house band shares the stage with visiting musicians. Open Monday to Saturday 8:30pm to 1am, Sunday 8pm to midnight.

✪ Ronnie Scott's

47 Frith St., W1. ☎ **0171/439-0747.** Cover £12–£14 ($18.60–$21.70) Mon–Sat; free Sun. Tube: Leicester Square.

Ronnie Scott's is the capital's best-known jazz room. Top names from around the world regularly grace this Soho stage, but fans be forewarned: The place is pricey. Call for events and show times. Open Monday to Saturday 8:30pm to 3am, Sunday 8 to 11pm.

Vortex

139–141 Stoke Newington Church St., N16. ☎ **0171/254-6516.** Cover £4 ($6.20). British Rail.

Some of the most original and talented jazz musicians in Britain and Europe perform in the jazz bar here.

DANCE CLUBS & DISCOS

The hippest Londoners go to "one-nighters," which are dance events held at established clubs. As the scene changes from one week to the next, it's impossible to make reliable recommendations, although the current trendsetters seem to be **The Hanover Grand,** 6 Hanover St. W1 (☎ **0171/499-7977**); **The Cross,** Goods Way Depot, N1 (☎ **0171/837-0828**); and **Iceni,** 11 White Horse St., W1 (☎ **0171/495-5333**). Check the weekly listings in *Time Out* for the latest crowd-pleasers. Meanwhile, the listings below have stood the test of time and survived the transformation from glitterati flash in the pans to long-term popular venues. Discount passes to dance clubs are sometimes available just inside the front door of Tower Records on Piccadilly Circus. Otherwise, expect to pay a heavy admission. *Note:* Cocktails for £4 ($6.20) are not uncommon.

The Hippodrome

Charing Cross Road, WC2. ☎ **0171/437-4311.** Cover £4–£6 ($6.20–$9.30); £10 ($15.50) after. Tube: Leicester Square.

Located near Leicester Square, the popular Hippodrome is London's big daddy of discos, with a great sound system and lights to match. Very touristy, fun, and packed on weekends. Open Monday to Saturday 9pm to 3:30am.

Limelight

136 Shaftesbury Ave., WC2. ☎ **0171/434-0572.** Cover £6 ($9.30) before 10pm, £13 ($20.15) thereafter. Tube: Leicester Square.

Although it's been open for several years, this large dance club, located inside a former church, has only recently realized its terrific potential. In addition to several dance floors and bars, there are plenty of nooks and crannies in which to "hide away." Open Monday through Saturday from 10:30pm to 3am.

Ministry of Sound

103 Gaunt St., SE1. ☎ **0171/378-6528.** Cover £12–£20 ($18.60–$31), reduced after 4am. Tube: Elephant & Castle.

Because it's removed from the city center, this club-of-the-moment is popular with the local sweat set and relatively devoid of tourists. It has a big bar and an even bigger sound system that blasts garage and house music to enthusiastic energetic crowds who fill the two dance floors or who relax in the cinema room. It's not cheap and the door policy is selective. Open only on Friday and Saturday nights from midnight to 9am.

Stringfellows

16–19 Upper St. Martin's Lane. ☎ **0171/240-5534.** Cover £8–£15 ($12.50–$24). Tube: Leicester Square.

Live music until 11:30 and then dancing to 3:30am on the club's famous glass floor. This is a members-only club, but you can usually join temporarily.

Subterrania

12 Acklam Rd., W10. ☎ **0181/960-4590.** Cover £8 ($12.40). Tube: Ladbroke Grove.

A mixed crowd dances to regular live shows and to London's best party vibes created by DJs. The stylish, minimalist decor attracts a lively 20-something crowd.

4 The Gay & Lesbian Scene

Old Compton Street in Soho is the equivalent of Christopher Street in New York City. In the clubs, gay nights are often one-nighters like the swish-and-glam bash "Bambina" held regularly on a Saturday night at the **Viper Room,** Bear Street, WC2 (☎ 0171/370-0148); or the fashion crowd's gathering, on Sundays, "Queer Nation" at the Gardening Club, 4 The Piazza, Covent Garden, WC2 (☎ 0171/497-3154). A similar lesbian event, "Kitty Lips," is held at **Mars,** 12 Sutton Row, W1 on Friday nights. To find out what's going on, pick up one of the gay newspapers that can be found in many if not all of the bars and venues listed below.

GAY at Busbys or at Astoria

157–165 Charing Cross Rd., WC2. ☎ **0171/734-6963.** Cover £3–£10 ($4.65–$15.50). Tube: Tottenham Court Road.

Loud music, colossal dance floor, and a trendy crowd makes GAY one of the best dance spots in the city. About 75% men, 25% women. Open Monday 10pm to 3am, Saturday 11pm to 4am.

The Box

Monmouth St., WC2. ☎ **0171/240-5828.** Tube: Leicester Square.

A small, comfortable and modern café-bar where people hang out during the day and gather for drinks in the evenings. Women's night is Sunday night. Food is available.

Brief Encounter
41 St. Martin's Lane, WC2. ☎ **0171/240-2221.** Tube: Leicester Square.

Everyone in the gay community seems to gather here. It becomes so crowded that it's hard to find elbow room in the bi-level bars. The crowd is varied—from leather and jeans to suits.

Coleherne
261 Old Brompton Rd., SW5 ☎ **0171/373-9859.** Tube: Earl's Court.

The leather bar. Crowded.

Compton's
53 Old Compton St. ☎ **0171/437-4445.** Tube: Piccadilly.

A lively, cruisey bar frequented by a young crowd. Plenty of shaved heads and leather jackets.

The Edge
11 Soho Square, W1. ☎ **0171/439-1313.** Tube: Tottenham Court Road.

A mixed gay/straight café/bar where you can obtain breakfast as well as hang out later in the day. A tri-level venue for the trendy and fashionable.

Freedom Cafe
60–66 Wardour St. ☎ **0171/734-0071.** Tube: Piccadilly.

A large, comfortable café and bar where people meet during the day over breakfast or lunch and coffee (salads, sandwiches, and pastries available, priced from £3 to £6.30). At night, the music gets hyped up and the place is jammed, although there's no dancing. You can even down a Long Island iced tea here. Downstairs theater space.

The Fridge
Town Hall Parade, Brixton Hill, SW2. ☎ **0171/326-5100.** Tube: Brixton.

Incorporating two bars and a restaurant, this club features different scenes nightly for different crowds. Some nights are dedicated to lesbians, other nights to gay males, and still others to myriad sexual orientations. Video, live performance, and go-go dancers add an extra dimension to the multiracial scene. The scene is so volatile that it would be wise to call ahead before making the 30-minute trek out to this spot. Take a cab.

Heaven
Villiers Street, WC2. ☎ **0171/839-3852.** Cover £5–£9 ($7.75–$13.95). Discounts before 11pm. Tube: Embankment or Charing Cross.

Hands-down, this is the most famous gay club in the city. A stage, where live bands sometime perform, overlooks a huge dance floor. The crowd varies (straights will find Thursdays their best night), but the sound system is always great. The club entrance is on a small street between Charing Cross and the Embankment Underground stations. Open Tuesday, Wednesday, Friday, and Saturday 10pm to 3am.

The King's Arms
23 Poland St., W1. ☎ **0171/734-5907.** Tube: Oxford Circus.

A busy gay men's pub on two levels, with good food and cheap double-measures in both bars.

Madam Jo Jo's
8 Brewer St., W1. ☎ **0171/734-2473.** Tube: Piccadilly Circus.

London's most popular transvestite showplace, right in the heart of the Soho sex club district. Revues are staged nightly at 12:15 and 1:15am. Every Monday this is also where Burt Bacharach and easy listening is making a "romo" comeback in the nineties. Open Monday to Saturday 10pm to 3am.

The Yard

57 Rupert St., W1. ☎ **0171/437-2652.** Tube: Piccadilly Circus.

A stylish spot that attracts an after-work crowd to its patio courtyard and upstairs bar.

5 The Pub Scene

There is nothing more British than a pub. The public house is exactly that, the British public's place to meet, exchange stories, tell jokes, and drink. Many people outside Britain have tried to build something that looks like a pub, but all fail to capture the unique flavor and atmosphere of the indigenous version. Even though they're listed here under evening entertainment, the Brits frequent them at lunch and in the evenings. At noon, they often repair to the pub for a glass of beer, or something similar, and a pub lunch. Later after work, they may stop in for an early evening drink before going home. (*Note:* Children under 14 are not allowed in pubs at all, and no one under 18 may legally drink alcohol.)

Beer is the main drink sold in pubs. Since January 1995, the law requires that alcohol be sold in metric measures: quarter-, half-, and liter-measures. The old imperial half-pints and pints have technically disappeared. The choice is usually between lager and bitter, and the locals more often than not opt for the latter. Expect to pay between £1.50 ($2.30) and £2 ($3.10) for a pint. Many pubs serve particularly good "real" ales, distinguishable at the bar by handpumps that must be "pulled" by the barkeep. Real ales are natural "live" beers, allowed to ferment in the cask. Unlike lagers, English ales are served at room temperature and may take some getting used to. For an unusual and tasty alternative to beer, try cider, a flavorful fermented apple juice that's so good you'll hardly notice the alcohol—until later.

As a rule, there is no table service in pubs; drinks and food are ordered at the bar. Tipping at a pub is unusual and should be reserved for exemplary service. A meal will cost anywhere from £3.50–£6 ($5.40–$9.30).

A recent change in the law allows pubs to stay open from 11am to 11pm Monday through Saturday, and from noon to 3pm and 7 to 10:30pm on Sunday. Not all pubs take advantage of this new freedom, however; some still close daily between 3pm and 7pm.

Carpeted floors, etched glass, and carved-wood bars are the hallmarks of most pubs. But each one looks different, and each has its particular flavor and clientele. Greater London's 5,000-plus pubs ensure that you never have to walk more than a couple of blocks to find one, and part of the enjoyment of "pubbing" is discovering a special one on your own. A few tried and true are listed below to help you on your way.

The Alma Tavern

41 Spelman St., E1. ☎ **0171/247-5604.**

A traditional East End "boozer," the Alma was opened in 1854 by Edward Tilney, a soldier who had just returned from the Crimean War. On the site of an old brewery, its back garden still sports a wellhead from which water for brewing was drawn. Steve Kane, the ultrafriendly owner, is a former actor who loves to talk about his establishment's, as well as his own, eventful past. Tell him I sent you, and he'll invite you to take a photo of yourself pulling an English pint behind his bar.

Cittie of Yorke

22–23 High Holborn, WC1. ☎ **0171/242-7670.** Tube: Holborn.

Walk through the narrow stone passageway into this pub, and you'll be standing in a soaring high-gabled room, which must contain the longest bar in England. Above can be seen huge vats that the original company used to dispense wine and liquors. Along one wall are private wood-carved cubicles, supposedly designed for lawyers to meet with their clients. Each features a *Vanity Fair* caricature. The pub dates from 1430 but has been rebuilt since.

De Hems

11 Macclesfield St., W1. ☎ **0171/437-2494.** Tube: Piccadilly or Leicester Square.

A Dutch outpost in the city. It's decorated in Dutch style and serves Dutch food and beers and even draught Dutch gin. Of course, English food and beer is available, too.

✪ The Dove

19 Upper Mall, W6. ☎ **0181/748-5405.** Tube: Ravenscourt.

A perfect riverside pub with a terrace for watching the Boat Race or just the river life. Along with what must be one of the smallest bars in the world, it has a series of comfortable oak-paneled rooms with copper tables and settle seating.

Ferret and Firkin

114 Lots Rd., SW10. ☎ **0171/352-6645.** Tube: Sloane Square, then bus no. 11 or 22 down King's Road.

David Bruce's Ferret and Firkin, in Chelsea, offers the best pub night out in London. The beer served here is brewed in the basement and really packs a punch. The best thing about this pub is the weekend entertainment—the Friday night piano player whose amplified instrument turns the place into a raucous sing-along party, and the Saturday night guitarist. You don't have to be under 30 to crowd in here, but perhaps only the younger revelers will know all the words. Nine other Firkin pubs are just as fun and flavorful. Unfortunately, most are difficult to reach.

The Flask

77 Highgate West Hill, N6. ☎ **0181/340-7260.** Tube: Archway.

Creaky floors, winding corridors, and plenty of tradition give this a definite village pub flavor. Frequented by Hogarth, who used the locals as subjects for his sketches of drunken revelry, and John Betjeman, who lived just up the road. Take the no. 271 or 143 bus from the tube station.

The French House

49 Dean St., W1. ☎ **0171/437-2799.** Tube: Tottenham Court Road.

Opened by a Belgian, it became the center of French life, especially during World War II when de Gaulle and his circle gathered here. Today, it still attracts a substantial number of French-speaking visitors.

✪ The George

77 Borough High St., SE1. ☎ **0171/407-2056.** Tube: London Bridge.

A real coaching inn. Although the George dates back to 1542—possibly earlier than that—the current building was constructed in 1676. Here in the galleried courtyard, it's believed Shakespeare's plays were performed, and today they still are during the summer. Dickens is also associated with the place.

The Jamaica Wine House
St. Michael's Alley, off Cornhill, EC3. ☎ **0171/626-9496.** Tube: Bank (Exit 5).

This is one of the oldest bars in the city, where Caribbean merchants met to make deals over coffee and rum. Today, investment bankers gather at the ground-floor bar or in the more cozy downstairs area to sip good wines, port, or beer.

The Grenadier
18 Wilton Row, SW1. ☎ **0171/235-3074.** Tube: Hyde Park Corner.

This mews pub is always crowded. It was an officers' mess in the Duke of Wellington's time, and the downstairs lounge originally housed the bar and skittles alley they used when they were on leave. It's filled with Wellington memorabilia.

The Lamb
94 Lamb's Conduit St., WC1. ☎ **0171/405-0713.** Tube: Oxford Circus.

A Victorian pub with decent food and an unmarred atmosphere. The etched and hinged glass screens that go all the way around the bar are called snob screens; they were installed so that customers didn't see the bartender. Apparently, they were the cat's pajamas at the turn of the century when such niceties really mattered.

Lamb & Flag
33 Rose St., WC2. ☎ **0171/497-9504.** Tube: Leicester Square.

The Lamb & Flag is an old timber-framed pub in a short cul-de-sac off Garrick Street in Covent Garden. The pub was dubbed the "Bucket of Blood" by the poet Dryden after he was almost beaten to death here (no doubt for being too witty at someone else's expense). The pub can be hard to find, but its great atmosphere and above-average food make the search well worth the effort.

Museum Tavern
49 Great Russell St., WC1. ☎ **0171/242-8987.** Tube: Holborn.

As you'd expect from its location opposite the British Museum, it's frequented by writers, publishers, and scholars using the library. Etched glass and oak provide Victorian atmosphere, but the pub dates further back to the early 18th century.

Prospect of Whitby
57 Wapping Wall, E1. ☎ **0171/481-1095.** Tube: Tower Hill

Named after a coal barge that operated between Yorkshire and London, this is an atmospheric riverside pub that offers a fine prospect of the river. Once frequented by smugglers and thieves and most of London, it dates back to 1520. Take a cab from the tube station.

The Punch Tavern
99 Fleet St., EC4. ☎ **0171/353-6658.** Tube: Blackfriars.

England's satirical magazine *Punch* was founded here by a group that included Charles Dickens. The tavern, one of the oldest in London, is also known for its Victorian gin palace interior—extraordinarily impressive. Today, the Punch is popular with local office workers. It serves simple pub grub and a variety of ales, bitters, and lagers. Next door to St. Bride's Church and within walking distance of St. Paul's Cathedral.

Salisbury
90 St. Martin's Lane, WC2. ☎ **0171/836-5863.** Tube: Leicester Square.

This popular Victorian pub has elaborately etched glass and a lincrusta ceiling. Radiant, it's lit by bronze art nouveau lamps with figures as bases.

Shepherd's Tavern

50 Hertford St., W1. ☎ **0171/499-3017.** Tube: Green Park.

Tucked away in a warren of streets off Park Lane, this early 18th-century pub has a warm and snug air. Among its more interesting features is the telephone booth, which is actually a sedan chair that once belonged to the Duke of Cumberland, son of George III. During World War II, it was a popular haunt for RAF pilots.

The Spaniard's Inn

Spaniard's Road, NW3, Hampstead. ☎ **0181/455-3276.** Tube: Hampsted.

A romantic Heath-side pub that has a lovely garden in summer and hearthside drinking in winter. Part of it dates back to 1585, and many a famous Brit has dallied here—from Keats and Shelley to Dickens and the highwayman Dick Turpin.

Star Tavern

6 Belgrave Mews West, SW1. ☎ **0171/235-3019.** Tube: Knightsbridge.

If your idea of a pub in winter is one that is warmed by a glowing fire, then this is the place to come, for it has two fires going. A Victorian atmosphere prevails.

Ye Olde Cheshire Cheese

Wine Office Court, 15 Fleet St., EC4. ☎ **0171/353-6170.** Tube: St. Paul's.

Open since 1667, this historical wooden pub is where Dr. Johnson took his tipple, and it's a sightseeing attraction in its own right. Ducking through the low doors will transport you back in time, as the wood benches and narrow courtyard entrance give it authentic period charm. Meals here are delicious and filling, but expensive.

Ye Olde Mitre

1 Ely Court, Ely Place off Hatton Garden, EC1. ☎ **0171/405-4751.** Tube: Chancery Lane.

This place is so well tucked away in a dingy little alley that first-time visitors often turn back halfway along the passageway, fearing they've gone the wrong way. It's understandable why Ye Old Mitre is often referred to as London's "best-kept secret." The pub's delightful snug Elizabethan interior has long been a favorite haunt of journalists, most working for the *Daily Mirror,* located across the road.

6 Wine Bars

Wine lovers will appreciate these welcome alternatives to pubs. Although not as ubiquitous as pubs, wine bars have become fairly common throughout London. Most have a good selection by both the glass and the bottle, and food is almost always served. Menus tend to have a continental flavor, with standards and prices that are higher than at most pubs. You don't have to eat, however, and a bottle of the house wine, usually costing £5 to £6 ($7.75 to $9.30), shared between two or three people, may come out cheaper than a visit to a pub. Most wine bars keep pub hours.

Brahms & Liszt

19 Russell St., WC2. ☎ **0171/240-3661.** Tube: Covent Garden.

The name is Cockney-rhyming slang for "pissed," which in British English means "drunk." Head downstairs for food, upstairs for rowdier times. The bar features live music nightly (see "The Club and Music Scene," above, for more information).

✪ The Cork and Bottle Wine Bar

44 Cranbourne St., WC2. ☎ **0171/734-7807** or 0171/734-6592. Tube: Leicester Square.

Located between Leicester Square and Charing Cross Road, this small basement bar is in the heart of the theater district and gets very crowded in the early evenings. It's cozy, the food is decent and reasonably priced, and there are about 20 wine selections available by the glass. Go after 8pm if you want a seat.

The Ebury Wine Bar

139 Ebury St., SW1. ☎ **0171/730-5447.** Tube: Victoria or Sloane Square.

The Ebury, a stone's throw from Victoria Station, is an appealing wine bar which is very popular at lunch with executives from nearby investment banks. The food is well prepared (priced from £8–£11—$12.40–$17.05). Every Sunday at lunch a traditional roast is served.

Olde Wine Shades

6 Martin Lane, Cannon St., EC4. ☎ **0171/626-6876.** Tube: Cannon St.

One of the oldest wine bars that's survived the many disasters that have struck the city. Dickens is rumored to have frequented the place. It still has a 19th-century air with its oil paintings and political cartoons.

Vats

51 Conduit St., WC1. ☎ **0171/242-8963.** Tube: Oxford Circus.

It looks very plain from the outside—just a few benches and tables and minimal decoration—but it's the wine selection and the prices that draw folks here. There are about 10 wines offered by the glass and a similar number of half- bottles available. The food ranges from £8–£13 ($12.40–$20.15).

10 Easy Excursions from London

Even if you're only staying a short time in London, try to make some time to get out of the city into the English countryside—"the green and pleasant land." Before you go, visit the **British Travel Centre, 12 Lower Regent St., W1 (no phone)**, just south of Piccadilly Circus, for information and advice. They will also book trains, buses, and tours for you.

For train journeys under 50 miles, the cheapest tickets are called "cheap day returns." Try to avoid day-trips on Friday, when fares increase to profit on the mass exodus of city-dwellers. If you're planning to do a lot of traveling by train in the southeast, then purchase BritRail's regional pass. The Southeast Pass will allow you to travel as far west as Exeter, as far south as Brighton and Eastbourne, as far north as Kings Lynn and Northampton and as far east as Canterbury. These flexipasses cost $69 adult, $24 child for three days out of eight, $89 adult and $24 child for four days out of eight and $119 and $24 for seven days out of fifteen. For information on specific trains, contact the British Travel Centre, **BritRail (☎ 0171/928-5100)**, or the departing station listed below.

National Express (☎ 0990/808080), the country's primary long-haul bus line, operates coaches to almost every corner of Britain. If you're planning to do a lot of touring, you may want to take advantage of their Tourist Trail Pass, which allows for unlimited travel within either 3, 5, 8, or 15 days, costing £49 ($75.95), £79 ($122.45), £119 ($184.45), and £179 ($277.45), respectively. National Express also offers discounts to seniors, families, and youths. Victoria Coach Station, located one block west of Victoria Rail Station, is the line's London hub.

Except for Stratford-upon-Avon and Bath, the excursions listed below are close enough to London to be visited in a day-trip from the capital, but each warrants a more thorough exploration; make an overnight visit if you have the time.

1 Windsor

21 miles W of London

Surrounded by gentle hills and lush valleys, this pretty riverside town—which was known to ancient Britons as Windlesore—is famous today for two things: a castle and a prep school.

GETTING THERE

By Train   BritRail trains depart from Paddington Station (☎ 0171/262-6767) and make the journey in about 30 minutes. Trains leave 13 times each day, and tickets cost £5.40 ($8.35) round-trip.

By Bus   Green Line buses (☎ 0181/668-7261) leave once an hour from London's Eccleston Bridge, behind Victoria Station. Day-return tickets cost £5.50 ($8.55) round-trip.

WHAT TO SEE & DO

✪ **Windsor Castle** (☎ 01753/868286) claims to be the largest inhabited castle in the world. For more than 900 years, English monarchs have made a home on this site. On a bend in the Thames, the castle is surrounded by 4,800 acres of lawn, woodlands, and lakes. A large fire at the end of 1992 devastated part of the castle, but it's still open to visitors. Until the completion of restoration work sometime in 1998, you won't be able to see all the rooms.

When the Royal Standard is not flying, the **State Apartments** are open to the public. Fabulous paintings, including works by Rubens and Rembrandt, adorn the walls, while elegant antique furnishings include Gibbons carvings and Gobelin tapestries. Call ahead to check if they're open.

The **Changing of the Guard** ceremony takes place May through August, Monday through Saturday at 11am; the rest of the year, it takes place every other day, excluding Sunday. To find out if the ceremony is taking place on the day of your visit, call the castle number and ask for extension 2235.

Queen Mary's Doll House is the most spectacular dollhouse you'll ever see. It was designed by Sir Edwin Lutyens and crafted by more than a thousand artisans over three years. It's built on a scale of 1:12 and everything in it actually works, from the miniature plumbing to a tiny electric iron. Even the bottles in the wine cellar contain vintage wine of its era.

When the queen is in residence, usually April, June, and December, the castle is closed. Otherwise it's open daily from 10am to 5pm March to October, and 10am to 4pm the rest of the year.

✪ **St. George's Chapel** (☎ 01753/865538), founded by King Edward IV in 1475 and completed in 1528 by Henry VIII, is one of the finest examples of late Gothic architecture in the nation. It's the resting place of ten sovereigns, including Henry VIII and his third wife, Jane Seymour. The chapel is named after the patron saint of the Most Noble Order of the Garter, Britain's highest Order of Chivalry. The chapel is usually open Monday through Saturday from 10:45am to 3:45pm. It's closed during services.

Exclusive **Eton College** (☎ 01753/671-0000) lies across a cast-iron footbridge. The prep school's students attend classes in collars and tails. Illustrious alumni include George Orwell and Aldous Huxley. Nineteen former prime ministers also call Eton their alma mater. The **Lower School** houses one of the oldest classrooms in the world, dating from 1443.

The school is open for visitors from Easter to the end of September daily from 2pm to 4:30pm. During summer holidays, hours are extended from 10:30am to 4:30pm.

2 Bath

110 miles W of London

Bath is an extraordinarily beautiful town, and one of the most popular excursions from London. The well-preserved remains of the original Roman baths are the town's primary tourist draw. They are perhaps the finest Roman structures in Britain.

ESSENTIALS
GETTING THERE

By Train   BritRail trains depart from London's Paddington Station (☎ **0171/262-6767**) every 90 minutes and make the trip in about 1¼ hours. Round-trip day return fares are £25.50 ($39.55); standard fare is $88 round-trip.

By Bus   National Express (☎ **0990/808080**) buses leave daily from London's Victoria Coach Station, and make the trip in about three hours. Special day return is £8.75, while a standard return is £21.50 ($33.30).

By Car   From London, take the M4 motorway to Exit 18.

ORIENTATION

Bath (pop. 83,000) is situated along the River Avon, which is traversed by two bridges: North Parade Bridge and Pulteney Bridge. Most of the city's main sights are crowded around the bridgeheads and the centrally located abbey. Both the bus and train stations are located at the end of Manvers Street, within easy walking distance to the city center.

VISITOR INFORMATION

Bath's Tourist Information Centre, the Colonnades Shopping Centre, Bath Street (☎ 01225/462831), opposite the Roman baths, will provide information and help you find accommodations at any one of a number of local bed-and-breakfasts. The center is open May through October, Monday through Saturday from 9:30am to 8pm, Sunday from 10am to 6pm; November through April, Monday through Saturday from 9:30am to 5pm, Sunday from 10am to 4pm.

WHAT TO SEE & DO

According to legend, Bath was founded by King Lear's father, Bladud, who was miraculously cured of leprosy after immersing himself in the town's legendary hot springs. In actuality, however, the warm waters of Bath have been a resort site since Roman times. Although it was founded in A.D. 75, Bath didn't become popular with the moderns until the beginning of the 18th century, when Queen Anne made it fashionable. It became the country's most fashionable spa, where the standards of society were set by Beau Nash. John Wood and his son transformed the city into a splendid example of Georgian town planning, building Queen Square, the Circus, and the Royal Crescent. Bath was heavily bombed by the Germans in 1942 and the Assembly Rooms were destroyed, but they have since been rebuilt.

The best way to see Bath is to take one of the free walking tours that leave daily, except Saturday, from outside the Pump Room.

Otherwise, begin your tour at the ✪ **Roman Baths and Museum** (☎ 01225/477000 ext. 2785). The baths were originally dedicated to Sulis, a local Celtic goddess who is closely identified with the Roman goddess Minerva. Hot mineral water still gurgles into large pools and, although you can no longer bathe here, you can sip the spring water from an adjacent drinking fountain.

The museum contains some stunning finds from local digs, including a bronze head of Minerva, and a small mountain of Roman-era pennies, tossed into the baths for good luck by superstitious ancients. It's open March through July and September through October, daily 9am to 6pm; August, daily 9am to 6pm and 8 to 10pm;

and November through February, Monday to Saturday 9:30am to 5pm, Sunday 10:30am to 5pm. Admission is £5 ($7.75) adults, £3 ($4.65) children.

The 18th-century **Pump Room,** which overlooks the baths, is a beautiful example of Georgian elegance. Created in 1786–95 by Thomas Baldwin and John Palmer, the architecturally stunning meetinghouse helped make Bath a fashionable luxury resort. It is still a major tourist attraction, as well as a civilized place for lunch or tea. Meals are usually accompanied by the classical music of the Pump Room Trio. It's open Monday to Saturday from 10am to noon, and again from 2:45 to 5pm. Admission is free.

Bath Abbey, located opposite the Pump Room, is the town's most magnificent church, dating from the 15th century. Restored in 1574 at the behest of Queen Elizabeth I, the abbey's many windows have earned it the nickname "Lantern of the West." It's open Monday through Saturday 9am to 5:30pm. Sunday hours vary, depending on services.

Royal Crescent House (☎ 01225/428126), is a painstakingly restored town house, made to look the way it may have late in the 18th century. Period furnishings, kitchen implements, and paintings give the house an air of lived-in authenticity. The house itself is located on one end of Bath's most elegant Georgian streets. Even if you don't want to visit the museum, be sure to take a stroll along this remarkable street. The house is open March through October, Tuesday through Saturday 10:30am to 4:30pm, November through mid-December, Tuesday through Saturday from 11am to 4pm; last admission is a half-hour before closing. Admission is £3.50 ($5.45) adults £2.50 ($3.90) seniors and children.

WHERE TO STAY

The Tourist Information Centre (see "Visitor Information," above) offers an exceptionally efficient accommodations booking service. Reservations for local hotels and bed-and-breakfasts—in all price ranges—are made with a 10% deposit and a £2.50 ($3.90) booking fee. The largest cluster of budget-priced B&Bs are located along Pulteney Road and Pulteney Gardens, just past the cricket grounds. Except during festival time, when hotels of all description are booked solid, you can usually get a room without prior reservations.

Leighton House
139 Wells Rd., Bath, Avon, BA2 3AL. ☎ **0225/314769.** Fax 01225/443079. 8 rms (all with bath). TV TEL. £45 ($69.75) single; £60–£70 ($86.80–$100.75) double. All rates include English breakfast. MC, V.

Proprietors David and Kathleen Slape offer terrific value in their big 1870s Victorian. All rooms have private baths, and there's a large comfortable lounge for guests. Hair dryers, tea/coffeemakers. A 10-minute walk from the town center, located on a bus route.

WHERE TO EAT

The Walrus and the Carpenter
28 Barton St. ☎ **0225/314864.** Reservations recommended. £8–£9.50 ($12.40–$14.70). MC, V. Mon–Sat noon–2pm; daily 6–11pm. CONTINENTAL.

Complete with checkered tablecloths and studied casualness, this budget bistro serves everything from steaks to salads. Daily vegetarian specials are available.

Crystal Palace
11 Abbey Green. ☎ **0225/423944.** Meals £2.50–£4.95 ($6.20–$12.40). V. Mon–Sat 11am–11pm, Sun noon–10:30pm. ENGLISH.

This large 18th-century pub/restaurant features traditional English fare, such as steak-and-mushroom pie and a variety of sandwiches. All is served up beneath wood-beamed ceilings. During winter, try to get a table beside the paneled fireplace. In summer, the best dining is al fresco, on the outdoor patio. The Crystal Palace is one of the few places in England where you can order Thomas Hardy Ale, a strong brew claiming the highest alcohol content of any beer in the world.

3 Cambridge

55 miles N of London

Cambridge competes with Oxford in everything. It loses in age—and usually in boat races—but it wins on charm. Unlike Oxford, which was a thriving center of car manufacture and other industry, Cambridge has a somnolent air, immediate captivating beauty, and a romance that can easily be felt on the banks of the Cam or standing on the Bridge of Sighs at St. John's College.

Settled by the Romans, who bridged the River Cam, the city did not begin to flourish until the 13th century, when the first college was founded here. Cambridge University now has 31 colleges. Year-round, the college grounds are open to the public. During the summer months when the schools are closed for vacation, the colleges are crowded with visitors.

ESSENTIALS

GETTING THERE

By Train   BritRail trains depart from London's Liverpool Street (☎ **0171/283-7171**) and King's Cross (☎ **0171/278-2477**) stations every 20 minutes and make the trek in about an hour. The day-return fare is £12.50 ($19.40). From Cambridge station, take the Cityrail link bus to Market Square, in the center of the city.

By Bus   National Express (☎ **0990/808080**) buses leave from London's Victoria Coach Station 13 times each day, take an hour and 50 minutes, and cost from £14.75 to £17.50 ($22.85 to $27.15) round-trip.

By Car   From London, take the M11 motorway to Exit 11.

ORIENTATION

Cambridge (pop. 103,000) has two main streets. Trumpington Road—which becomes Trumpington Street, King's Parade, Trinity Street, and finally St. John's Street—runs parallel to the River Cam. It's close to several of the city's colleges. Bridge Street, the city's main shopping street, starts at Magdalene Bridge; it becomes Sidney Street, St. Andrew's Street, and finally Regent Street.

INFORMATION

The **Tourist Information Centre,** Wheeler Street (☎ **01223/322640**), located behind Guildhall, offers transportation and sightseeing information, as well as maps and accommodations lists. The office is open November through March, Monday

Impressions

Cambridge is the least damaging place in England in which not to be found funny.

—Kingsley Amis, "No More Parades," *Encounter*, 1964

Cambridge

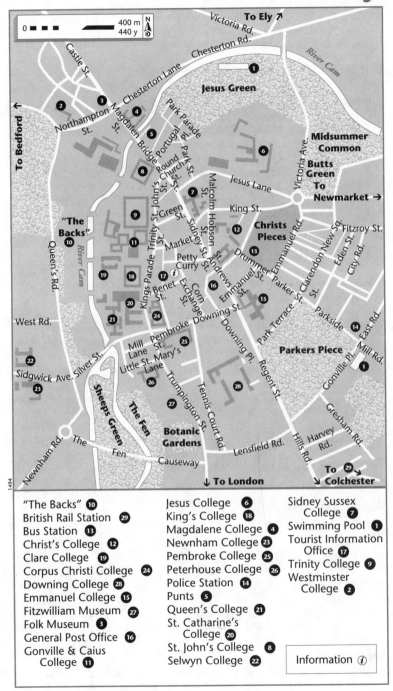

"The Backs" ⑩	Jesus College ⑥	Sidney Sussex College ⑦
British Rail Station ㉙	King's College ⑱	Swimming Pool ①
Bus Station ⑬	Magdalene College ④	Tourist Information Office ⑰
Christ's College ⑫	Newnham College ㉓	Trinity College ⑨
Clare College ⑲	Pembroke College ㉕	Westminster College ②
Corpus Christi College ㉔	Peterhouse College ㉖	
Downing College ㉘	Police Station ⑭	
Emmanuel College ⑮	Punts ⑤	
Fitzwilliam Museum ㉗	Queen's College ㉑	
Folk Museum ③	St. Catharine's College ⑳	
General Post Office ⑯	St. John's College ⑧	
Gonville & Caius College ⑪	Selwyn College ㉒	Information ⓘ

through Friday 9am to 5:30pm, Saturday 9am to 5pm; April through June and September through October, Monday through Friday 9am to 6pm, Saturday 9am to 5pm, Sunday 10:30am to 3:30pm.

WHAT TO SEE & DO

Even though you'll have to navigate your way through some dark cobblestone streets between stone buildings, the best way to see Cambridge is to do "the backs," a stroll along the riverside, behind the colleges.

✪ **King's College Chapel** (☎ 01223/331447) is a world-renowned Gothic masterpiece, and the town's most famous structure. Completed in the early 16th century, the chapel is one of the purest examples of early Renaissance architecture. Its fan-vaulted stone ceilings are complemented by magnificent windows, most of which were created by Flemish artisans between 1517 and 1531. A small exhibition hall features pictures and commentary on how and why the chapel was built. It's open during school term Monday through Saturday 9:30am to 3:30pm, Sunday 1:15 to 2:15pm. During vacation, it's open Monday through Saturday 9:30am to 4:30pm, Sunday 10am to 4:30pm. The chapel is closed December 26 through January 1, and occasionally without notice for recording sessions and rehearsals.

Trinity College (☎ 01223/338400) was founded by Henry VIII in 1546 and is the largest and wealthiest of Cambridge's colleges. The courtyard is particularly spacious. They say that the poet Byron used to bathe naked in its large fountain.

The college's particularly striking **Wren Library** was designed by Sir Christopher himself. It houses original works by famous former students. In addition to Byron, famous professors and alumni have included philosopher Bertrand Russell, poet John Dryden, author Andrew Marvell, and physicist Sir Isaac Newton.

Queens' College (☎ 01223/335511) is arguably the prettiest of all of Cambridge's colleges. Named for the wives of Henry IV and Edward IV, the college was founded in 1448. The Tudor courtyard is home to the half-timbered **President's Lodge,** which dates from the beginning of the 16th century.

"Punting," or pole-boating, on the River Cam is a Cambridge tradition. So is **Scudamore's Boatyards,** Granta Place (☎ 01223/359750). This boatyard by the Anchor Pub has been renting punts and rowboats since 1910. All boats rent for £8 ($12.40) per hour, and require a £30 ($46.50) refundable deposit. It's open during summer only, daily from 10am to 7pm.

WHERE TO STAY

Some of the city's best B&Bs are clustered along Chesterton Road, not far from the train station.

Ashley Hotel

74 Chesterton Rd., Cambridge, Cambridgeshire, CB4 1ER. ☎ **01223/350059.** 16 rms (14 with shower). TV. £28.50 ($44.20) single; £50.50 ($78.30) double. All rates include English breakfast. MC, V.

This good bed-and-breakfast is located close to the city center, between the River Cam and Jesus Green. Tea/coffeemakers and hair dryers in every room. If you want a single room, make reservations well in advance, as there are only two available.

Fairways

141 Cherryhinton Rd., Cambridge, Cambridgeshire, CB1 4BX. ☎ **01223/246063.** 14 rms (8 with bath). TV TEL. £24 ($37.20) single without bath, £30 ($46.50) with bath; £37 ($57.35) double without bath, £44 ($68.20) with bath. MC, V.

The rooms in this handsomely restored Victorian are cozy. Tea/coffeemakers. Hair dryers, ironing board, and iron will be provided on request. A lobby bar serves drinks. Located about 1.5 miles from the heart of the city.

Cambridge Youth Hostel

97 Tenison Rd., Cambridge, Cambridgeshire, CB1 2DN. ☎ **01223/354601.** Fax 01223/312780. 102 beds (none with bath). £10.50 ($16.30) per night with an IYHF card. Walk straight from the train station, and turn right onto Tenison Road.

Open year-round, this hostel is comfortable. It's conveniently located close to the train station. Guests can use kitchen and laundry facilities, the lounge with TV, and games room. There's also a licensed cafeteria where you can enjoy a three-course evening meal for only £4.15 ($6.45) and a small shop. If space permits, couples may share a room.

WHERE TO EAT

Hobbs Pavilion

Park Terrace. ☎ **01223/367480.** Reservations not accepted. £4.10–£8 ($7.75–$12.40). 2-course lunch £6.75 ($10.45); 3-course meal anytime £8.95 ($13.85). No credit cards. Tues–Sat noon–2:15pm and 7–9:45pm. Closed mid-Aug to mid-Sept. CREPES.

Located in a historic building, Hobbs is known for its imaginative crepes, more than 40 of them. They're stuffed with everything from vegetarian and hot chillied lamb to dijon chicken and black pudding, from banana, ginger, and cream to lemon, sugar, and butter. Soups, salads, and char-grilled meats and fish are also available. The ice cream is made here in flavors such as lavender and honey. No smoking is allowed.

The Anchor

Silver Street. ☎ **0223/353554.** £3.50–£4.50 ($5.40–$9.30). MC, V. Mon–Sat noon–11pm, Sun noon–3pm and 7–10:30pm. ENGLISH.

One of the city's most popular riverside pubs, the Anchor serves traditional English specialties at either of two bars. Traditional hand-pulled "real" ales are also available, along with the usual selection of lagers and bitters.

4 Oxford

57 miles NW of London

The spires of Oxford may be dreaming, but the rest of the city is hustle and bustle. In addition to being home to the world's oldest English-speaking university, Oxford is also an industrial city; its founding predates the school's by about two centuries. Wedged between the Thames and Cherwell Rivers, the city is blessed with dozens of parks and gardens and more than 600 buildings listed for their historical or architectural interest.

ESSENTIALS

GETTING THERE

By Train   BritRail trains depart from London's Paddington Station (☎ 0171/262-6767) and make the trip to Oxford in about an hour. Day-return tickets are £12.80 ($19.85).

By Bus   National Express (☎ 0990-808080) round-trip fares from Victoria Coach Station are £6 ($9.30) with day returns for under £3 ($4.65).

By Car   From London, take the M40 to the A40, to the A420 (or the A423, the scenic route via Windsor and Henley). Don't drive into the city center, however, as parking and traffic are horrific. Free **Park and Ride** car parks are located on the main approaches to the north, south, and west sides of the city. These are regularly served by buses that run into the heart of the city (there's a small charge).

ORIENTATION

Carfax, the city center, is surrounded by the colleges of Oxford, and intersected at right angles by Cornmarket Street, St. Aldate's Street, Queen Street, and High Street. Magdalen Bridge lies past the east end of High Street; the train and bus stations are located to the west of High Street.

INFORMATION

The **Oxford Information Centre,** St. Aldate's Chambers, St. Aldate's (☎ 01865/ 726871), can provide you with maps, brochures, and accommodations information. They also have a lot of information on local sights and attractions. Tours leave from the center at regular intervals during the day. The office is open May through September, Monday through Saturday 9:30am to 5pm, Sunday 10:30am to 1pm and 1:30pm to 4pm; October through April, Monday through Saturday 9:30am to 5pm (closed Sunday).

WHAT TO SEE & DO

Before setting out to see the city's sights, you might want to visit **The Oxford Story,** 6 Broad St. (☎ 01865/728822). Here you can learn about the history of Oxford and its university through a multimedia presentation. Visitors are transported Disney-style, on a moving coaster, through various tableaux, each depicting an important scene from the city's past. It's open April through October, daily 9:30am to 5pm; November through March, daily 10am to 4pm. Admission is £4.50 ($6.95) adults, £3.95 ($6.10) seniors, and £3.25 ($5.05) students.

Just 97 steps above Oxford, the top of Carfax Tower is one of the best places to look out over the colleges. Get a map of adjacent rooftops from the attendant at the bottom. It's open March through October only, Monday through Saturday 10am to 6pm, Sunday 2 to 6pm.

Although students were congregating here as early as the beginning of the 12th century, Oxford University wasn't founded until 1167, when Henry II ordered it built. Like many urban schools, Oxford has no central campus; its 35 colleges are scattered throughout the city.

Magdalen (pronounced "*Maud*-len") is one of the largest and most beautiful colleges in Oxford. The colorful flower-dotted grounds encompass one of the oldest botanic gardens in England. Begun in 1621, the garden originally grew plants for medicinal purposes.

In addition to a meadow, a deer park, and a river (spanned by the famous Magdalen Bridge), the college has a well-known perpendicular Bell Tower. Every year on May Day, the college choir assembles at the top of the tower to sing. The tower is open daily from 2 to 6:15pm.

Known colloquially as **The House,** the **College of Christ** features the largest courtyard, or "quad," of any college in Oxford. The intimidating stone walls of **Tom Quad** enclose **Tom Tower** which, in turn, houses the **Great Tom,** an immense 18,000-pound bell. Each evening at 9:05pm, the bell strikes 101 times, as it has since 1682.

Christ Church has England's smallest cathedral, dedicated to Oxford's patron saint, Frideswide. Parts of this church date from the 12th century, but its most

Oxford

To Woodstock & Stratford-upon-Avon

To Coventry

University Parks

To Station

To Abingdon, Reading, London

To London →
To Cowley
To Reading →

Deer Park

Merton Field

Botanic Garden

Christ Church Meadow

River Thames

River Cherwell

Path along River Cherwell

1495

All Souls College ❶
Ashmolean Museum ㉕
Balliol College ㉒
Brasenose College ⓴
Carfax Tower ⓰
Christ Church College ⑫
Corpus Christi College ⑪
Exeter College ㉑
Hertford College ❷
Jesus College ⑱
Keble College ㉘
Lincoln College ⑲

Magdalen College ❻
Manchester College ㉝
Mansfield College ㉛
Merton College ❽
Museum of Modern Art ⑮
New College ❸
Oriel College ⑩
Pembroke College ⑭
Queen's College ❹
Regent's Park College ㉖
Rhodes House ㉚
Sheldonian Theatre ㉞

Somerville College ㉗
St. Catherine's College ❺
St. Hilda's College ❼
St. John's College ㉔
St. Peter's College ⑰
Town Hall ㉟
Trinity College ㉓
University College ❾
University Museum ㉙
Wadham College ㉜
Worcester College ⑬

Information ⓘ

227

Impressions

*The world, surely, has not another place like Oxford: it is a despair to see
such a place and ever to leave it.*

—Nathaniel Hawthorne, *Notebooks*, 1856

distinguishing features, the vaulting over the choir and the Norman pillars, were
added over 300 years later. The cathedral is open in summer, Monday through Saturday 9:30am to 4:30pm, Sunday 1 to 4:30pm.

In addition to the colleges mentioned above, **Merton, New College, St. John's,
Trinity, Wadham,** and **Worcester** all have pretty grounds and gardens that are
definitely worth exploring.

The exciting **Museum of Modern Art** on Pembroke Street (☎ **01865/722733**)
is a well-planned counterpoint to Oxford's antiquity. It's a leading center for
contemporary visual arts. Exhibitions change regularly, and include sculpture, architecture, photography, video, and other media. Call for an exhibition schedule. It's
open Tuesday through Saturday 10am to 6pm (until 9pm Thursday), Sunday 2 to
6pm. Admission £2.50 ($3.85) adults, £1.50 ($2.30) seniors, children under 16 free.
It's free on Wednesday 10am to 1pm and Thursday 6 to 9pm.

Founded in 1683, the **Ashmolean Museum,** Beaumont Street (☎ **01865/
278000**), is England's oldest public museum. In addition to housing a terrific
archaeology collection—with Egyptian mummies and casts of Greek sculptures—the
galleries contain a Stradivarius violin, and works by da Vinci, Raphael, and Rembrandt. It's open Tuesday through Saturday 10am to 4pm, Sunday 2 to 4pm.

WHERE TO STAY

Accommodations in Oxford are limited, especially during the school term. The main
roads out of town are lined with affordable bed-and-breakfasts; these are fine if you
don't mind a healthy walk.

In addition to the listings below, the **Oxford Information Centre,** St. Aldate's
Chambers, St. Aldate's (☎ **01865/726871**) will book accommodations for a
£3 ($4.65) fee.

Adams Guest House

302 Banbury Rd., Summertown, Oxford, Oxfordshire, OX2 7ED. ☎ **01865/56118.** 6 rms
(none with bath; all with showers). £25 ($38.75) single; £40–£42 ($54.25–$57.35) twin. All rates
include breakfast. No credit cards.

Located in Summertown, 1.25 miles from Oxford, this is one of the best B&Bs
around. Rooms are comfortable and cozy. From this quiet neighborhood with a
number of restaurants, shops, and a laundry, a bus runs every few minutes to the city
center. It's opposite the Midland Bank.

Lonsdale Guest House

312 Banbury Rd., Summertown, Oxford, Oxfordshire, OX2 7ED. ☎ **01865/54872.** 9 rms
(7 with shower). TV. £26 ($37.20) single without shower; £42 ($65.10) double with shower.
All rates include English breakfast. No credit cards. Bus: 7, 7A.

About 10 minutes by bus from the city center, the Lonsdale has comfortably
furnished rooms. With down comforters and central heating, it's one of the nicest
B&Bs in town. Most rooms have a private shower. Tennis courts, a heated indoor
swimming pool, and a laundromat are all a two-minute walk away.

WHERE TO EAT

Munchy Munchy

6 Park End St. ☎ **01865/245710.** Lunch £5–£12 ($7.75–$18.60). Tues–Sat noon–2pm and 5:30–10pm. Closed three weeks in Aug and mid-Dec to mid-Jan. INDONESIAN/MALAYSIAN.

Lines form here on weekends for the city's best Southeast Asian food. Dishes change daily, according to the chef's mood and the availability of ingredients, but expect something creative and good.

5 Stratford-upon-Avon

92 miles NW of London

The Bard was born here. But even if Stratford-upon-Avon were not Shakespeare country, this beautiful and charming town would still be one of the most visited towns in Britain. Picture-perfect half-timbered houses are shaded by statuesque chestnut and poplar trees, while lazy willows hang over one of the world's most romantic rivers. In spring and summer, the town blooms with roses and honeysuckle clambers over every wall.

ESSENTIALS

GETTING THERE

By Train BritRail trains make the trip from London's Paddington Station (☎ 0171/262-6767) in about 90 minutes. Round-trip standard-class tickets cost from £25 to £35 ($38.75 to $54.25).

By Bus National Express (☎ 0990/808080) buses run every two hours or so. Departing from London's Victoria Coach Station, they make the trip in about 3.5 hours. Tickets cost from £13 to £15.50 ($20.15 to $24).

By Car From London, take the M40 motorway, then head north on A34.

ORIENTATION

Unchanged since the Middle Ages, Stratford's simple layout is an important component of its charm. Just three streets run parallel to the river, and three streets at right angles to it. Buses stop at the corner of Guild Street and Warwick Road.

INFORMATION

The Information Centre, Bridgefoot (☎ 01789/293127), offers tourist information, maps, and a helpful accommodations booking service. It's open April through October, Monday through Saturday 9am to 5:30pm, Sunday 2 to 5pm; November through March, Monday through Saturday from 9am to 5pm (closed Sunday).

A MONEY-SAVING TICKET

Collectively referred to as the "Shakespeare Properties," Stratford's five most important restored sites are administered by the Shakespeare Birthplace Trust. A money-saving ticket, good for admission to all five, can be purchased at any site for £7.50 ($11.65) adults, £3.50 ($5.40) for children under 15.

WHAT TO SEE & DO

Begin at the beginning, at **Shakespeare's Birthplace.** The famed playwright was born in this three-gabled, half-timbered house on St. George's Day (April 23) in 1564. In

Attending the Theatre

Founded in 1961 by Sir Peter Hall, the **Royal Shakespeare Company** is Stratford's repertory theater company. Not exclusively Shakespearean, the RSC produces classical theater of all periods, as well as contemporary plays. The troupe's primary playhouse is the **Royal Shakespeare Theatre,** located on the banks of the Avon and seating 1,500. During its season, which runs from early April to late January, about five different plays are staged. Opened by the RSC in 1986, the **Swan Theatre** was built in a neo-Elizabethan style, complete with gallery, and seats just 430. Here productions by post-Shakespearean playwrights are staged. The Swan also maintains a rotating schedule of about five plays each season, from early April to late January. The third theater, The Other Place, is modern and intimate and produces a range of dramas from classical tragedies like Euripides' *The Phoenician Women,* adaptations like *Lord of the Flies,* and rediscovered classics.

Making Advance Reservations   To obtain good seats, tickets should be purchased in advance from the theater box office, which starts taking reservations in early March. You can either call **01789/295623** (Mon–Sat 9am–8pm), fax to 01789/261974, or write with credit card details and an SAE with international postal coupon to Box Office, Royal Shakespeare Theatre, Stratford-upon-Avon, CV37 6BB (☎ **01789/295623**).

In the United States, tickets can also be purchased through **Keith Prowse,** 234 W. 44th St., New York, NY 10036 (☎ **212/398-1430** or 800/669-8687).

Getting Tickets on the Day of the Performance   You can sometimes get good matinee seats on the morning of a performance. Customer returns and standing-room tickets may also be available on the day of an evening performance. At the Royal Shakespeare Theatre, ticket prices range from £5–£42 ($7.75–$65.10). At the Swan Theatre, tickets range from £9–£28.50 ($13.95–$44.15). Discounted tickets for seniors are available for some performances at both the Royal Shakespeare Theatre and the Swan; prices are £10.50 ($16.30). Also at both theaters, standby tickets for students are sometimes available on the day of performance; prices range from £10 to £15 ($15.50–$23.25).

Backstage tours of the Royal Shakespeare Theatre are available, but must be booked two weeks in advance. They're usually scheduled Monday through Saturday at 1:30 and 5:30pm, and Sunday at 12:30, 2:15, 3:15, and 4:15pm. They're also offered after some evening performances. Tours cost £4 ($6.20) adults, £3 ($4.65) for students and seniors. Contact the box office for reservations.

addition to period furniture, the home supports a "life-and-times" exhibit of memorabilia. More than 660,000 annual visitors make their way through the narrow hallways and low doors of this charming home. Try to arrive before 11am, when the masses of day-trippers arrive. It's open April through October, Monday through Saturday 9am to 6pm, Sunday 2 to 5pm; November through March, Monday through Saturday 9am to 6pm, Sunday from 1:30 to 4:30pm.

Anne Hathaway's Cottage, pictured on tea trays, boxes of chocolates, and other souvenirs all around town, must be the prettiest cottage in England. Located one mile from Stratford in the hamlet of Shottery, the childhood home of the Bard's wife is surrounded by lush gardens and orchards. It's topped with a thatched roof. A large open fireplace and massive beamed ceilings have been preserved along with many original furnishings. If the weather is good, walk to the cottage from Stratford, across the meadow, along the marked pathway from Evesham Place. Or take the bus from Bridge Street. The cottage keeps the same opening hours as Shakespeare's birthplace, above.

Shakespeare's daughter Susanna lived in **Hall's Croft** with her well-to-do husband, Dr. John Hall. The exceptional Tudor home is traditionally furnished with oak dressers and tables. An exhibit illustrates Elizabethan medical practices. In back, the walled garden is worth visiting. The adjoining Hall's Croft Club serves morning coffee, lunch, and afternoon tea. It's open April through October, Monday through Saturday 9am to 6pm, Sunday 2 to 5pm; November through March, Monday through Saturday 9am to 6pm (closed Sunday).

New Place was the Bard's place of retirement. When he purchased it in his prosperity in 1597, it was one of Stratford's nicest homes. Unfortunately, only the foundation and gardens remain. **Nash House** is the 16th-century home next to New Place. Here Elizabeth Hall, one of Shakespeare's daughters, lived with her husband, Thomas Nash. These two homes are connected by **Knott Garden,** an Elizabethan green usually filled with visitors. The famous mulberry tree is from a cutting of a tree planted by Shakespeare, it's said. The site is open April through October, Monday through Saturday 9am to 6pm, Sunday 2 to 5pm; November through March, Monday through Saturday from 9am to 6pm (closed Sunday).

Located in Wilmcote, three miles from Stratford, **Mary Arden's House** is said to have been home to Shakespeare's mother. Today, this large Tudor farmstead contains traditional furniture and utensils. The adjacent barns house a farming museum. The neighboring **Glebe Farm** is a working country farm, using techniques from Shakespeare's day. Both are open April through October, Monday through Saturday 9am to 6pm, Sunday 2 to 5pm; November through March, Monday through Saturday 9am to 6pm (closed Sunday).

Shakespeare is buried in **Holy Trinity Church,** his local parish church. His grave is marked with a small plaque with the words, ". . . and cursed be he who moves my bones." It's open April through October, Monday to Saturday 8:30am to 6pm, Sunday noon to 5pm; November through March, Monday through Saturday 8:30am to 4pm, Sunday 2 to 5pm.

WHERE TO STAY

Although there are many bed-and-breakfasts available, during the summer it's wise to book ahead. **The Information Centre,** Bridgefoot, Stratford-upon-Avon, Warwickshire CV37 6W (☎ 01789/293127), can help you find accommodations on short notice.

The Hollies

16 Evesham Place, Stratford-upon-Avon, Warwickshire, CV37 6HT. ☎ **01789/266857.** 6 rms (3 with bath/shower). TV. £36 ($46.50) double without bath, £42 ($58.90) with bath. All rates include English breakfast. No credit cards.

Located in an old three-story schoolhouse, this spacious guesthouse offers comfortable rooms kept spotlessly clean by the resident mother-and-daughter proprietors. The sunny breakfast room is decorated with hand-cut crystal. Tea/coffeemakers.

Salamander Guest House

40 Grove Rd., Stratford-upon-Avon, Warwickshire, CV37 6PB. ☎ **01789/205728** (also fax). 7 rms (6 rms with shower/bath). £20 ($24.80) single without bath; £38–£42 ($58.90–$65.10) double with bath. All rates include English breakfast. No credit cards.

Fronting a wooded park, this homey guest house is efficiently run by Maurice and Ninon Croft. Home-cooked dinners are available for £8 ($12.40). A five-minute walk from the town center.

IYHF Youth Hostel

Hemmingford House, Wellesbourne Road, Alverton. Stratford-upon-Avon CV37 7RG.
☎ **01789/297093.** 150 beds. £12.60 ($19.55) per night with an IYHF card. MC, V. Closed
Jan–Feb.

> This busy hostel is two miles from the city center. The large 200-year-old building
> has 20 rooms. Guests have full use of kitchen facilities. It's closed from 10am to 1pm.
> With an 11:30pm curfew.

WHERE TO EAT

Black Swan

Southern Lane, Waterside, Stratford-upon-Avon CV37. ☎ **01789/297312.** £6–£13
($7.75–$18.60). MC, V. Mon–Sat 11:30am–4pm and 5:30–11pm, Sun noon–2pm. ENGLISH.

> Affectionately known as the Dirty Duck, this popular pub has been a regular
> hangout for local actors since the 18th century. Autographed photos of patrons,
> including Lord Olivier, adorn the walls. English specialties like braised kidneys are
> served, as well as steaks and the true specialty of the house, a honey roast duck.
> During cold weather, an open fire blazes. When it's nice out, you can take your drinks
> onto the terrace overlooking the river.

Index

The Kemwel Group, Inc.
106 Calvert Street
Harrison, NY 10528-3199

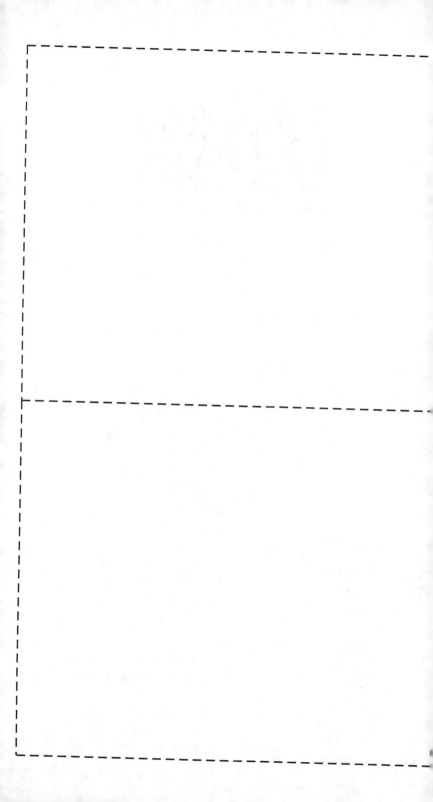

Established in 1975 the London Dungeon is set in huge dark vaults beneath London Bridge Station. Since its enlargement in 1993 and the subsequent addition of new and updated multi-media shows, it is now renowned, along with its sister attractions in York, for presentation of real history as a dynamic and entertaining experience. And, since April 1996, you can now experience the 'spirit' of Jack the Ripper as it returns to its old haunts. Of course the imagination plays tricks. But then so do we!

Normal Prices: Adult £7.95; Student £6.95; Child OAP £4.60

Offer: £2 OFF AN ADULT ADMISSION;
£1 OFF A CHILD/OAP ADMISSION

Expires December 31, 1997

WINNER
1992 + 1993
LONDON
FRINGE AWARDS

240 THE BROADWAY
WIMBLEDON
LONDON SW19 1SB

081 542 4258 (ADMIN)
081 542 7723 (FAX)
081 543 4888 (BOX OFFICE)

BUY ONE GET ONE FREE!

FOR EVERY FULL PRICE TICKET PURCHASED
FOR A MAIN HOUSE SHOW YOU GET ONE FREE.
THIS OFFER RUNS FROM OCTOBER 3rd 1996
TO AUGUST 16th 1997 INCLUSIVE.

28-34 Tooley Street, London SE1 2SZ Tel 0171 403 0606
Open every day except Christmas Day
from 10am to 4:30pm (last admission)

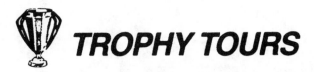

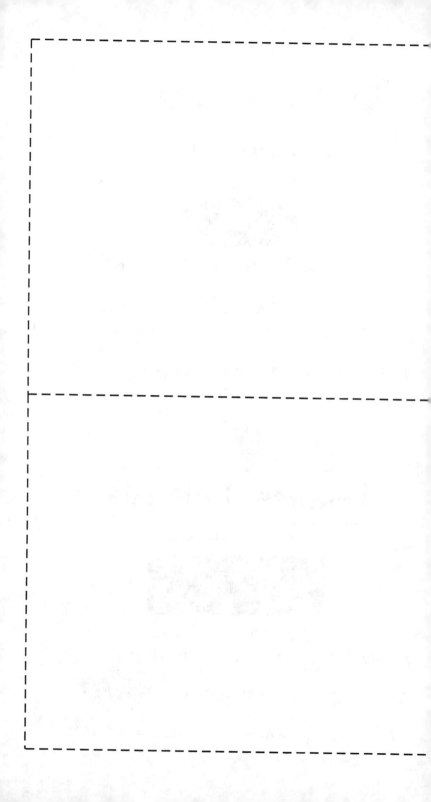

London Transport
Museum

Covent Garden Piazza
London WC2E 7BB
0171-836 8557

£1 Off Adult Admission
50p Off Concessions

Valid up to 4 in party

OPEN DAILY

Expires December 31, 1997

bfi on the South Bank

Museum of the Moving Image - Where film come to life

*The magical world of film and television comes to life before your very
eyes at the Museum of the Moving Image. See Chaplin's hat and cane,
meet Frankenstein's monster, fly like Superman, audition for a
Hollywood screen role, watch some of the hundreds of film
and TV clips and interact with the cast of actor-guides.*

£1 Off Adult Entry or 50p Off Child Entry
*(Not to be used in conjunction with any other offer or against the
Museum Family Ticket or to purchase gift vouchers. 1 voucher per person.)*

Call 0171 401 2636 for Information

Offer Valid until December 31, 1997.

MUSEUM
OF THE MOVING IMAGE
South Bank
Waterloo
London SE1 8XT

*The Museum is located on London's South Bank, a short walk
from Waterloo station and less than 10 minutes from
Covent Garden and Leicester Square.*

Open daily 10am-6pm. Last admission 5pm.
Allow 2 hours for a visit.

Closed December 24-26.

DISCOVERY WALKS

GUIDED WALKS OF LONDON
67 CHANCERY LANE
LONDON WC2A 1AF

**50p per person off
The Jack the Ripper & Ghost Walks**

Phone 0171.256.8973 to book

Expires December 31, 1997

Pollock's Toy Museum
1, Scala Street
London W1 P 1LT
Tel. 0171-63 3452

**Two Adults for the Price of One
Or
With One Full Paying Adult, One Child goes for Free**

Expires December 31, 1997

Pollock's Toy Museum

The museum was started in 1956 in a single attic room at
44 Monmouth Street, near Covent Garden, where Pollock's
toy theatres were also sold. As the enterprise flourished
other rooms were taken over for the museum, and the
ground floor became a toyshop.

By 1969 the collection had outgrown the Monmouth Street
premises and Pollock's Toy Museum moved to 1 Scala Street,
with a museum shop on the ground floor to contribute to its
support. The Museum was constituted an Educational
Charitable Trust (Reg. Charity No. 313622)

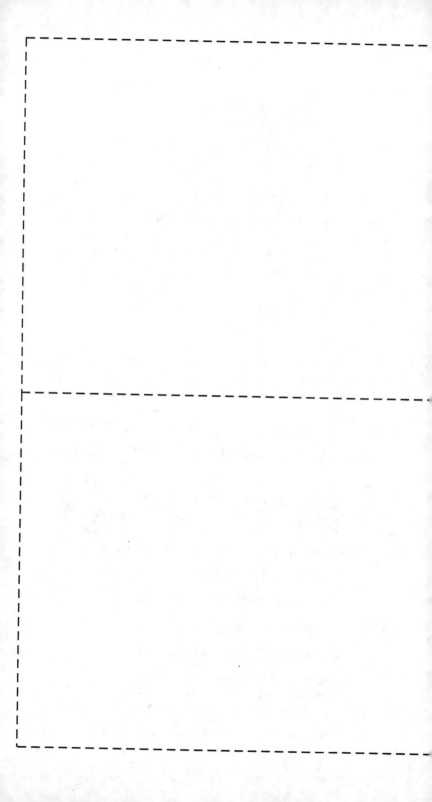

FROMMER'S FRUGAL TRAVELER'S GUIDES
(The grown-up guides to budget travel, offering dream vacations at down-to-earth prices)

Australia from $45 a Day

Berlin from $50 a Day

California from $60 a Day

Caribbean from $60 a Day

Costa Rica & Belize from $35 a Day

Eastern Europe from $30 a Day

England from $50 a Day

Europe from $50 a Day

Florida from $50 a Day

Greece from $45 a Day

Hawaii from $60 a Day

India from $40 a Day

Ireland from $45 a Day

Italy from $50 a Day

Israel from $45 a Day

London from $60 a Day

Mexico from $35 a Day

New York from $70 a Day

New Zealand from $45 a Day

Paris from $65 a Day

Washington, D.C. from $50 a Day

FROMMER'S PORTABLE GUIDES
(Pocket-size guides for travelers who want everything in a nutshell)

Charleston & Savannah

Las Vegas

New Orleans

San Francisco

FROMMER'S IRREVERENT GUIDES
(Wickedly honest guides for sophisticated travelers)

Amsterdam

Chicago

London

Manhattan

Miami

New Orleans

Paris

San Francisco

Santa Fe

U.S. Virgin Islands

Walt Disney World

Washington, D.C.

FROMMER'S AMERICA ON WHEELS
(Everything you need for a successful road trip, including full-color road maps and ratings for every hotel)

California & Nevada

Florida

Mid-Atlantic

Midwest & the Great Lakes

New England & New York

Northwest & Great Plains

South Central &Texas

Southeast

Southwest

FROMMER'S BY NIGHT GUIDES
(The series for those who know that life begins after dark)

Amsterdam

Chicago

Las Vegas

London

Los Angeles

Miami

New Orleans

New York

Paris

San Francisco